PLANTATION
CASTLES
on the ERNE

T0323200

PLANTATION CASTLES
on the ERNE

Bill Wilsdon

The
History
Press
Ireland

For Diane, Sophie, Vivien and Lois.
For your endless patience amongst the ruins and graveyards of Ireland.

First published 2010

The History Press
119 Lower Baggot Street
Dublin 2, Ireland
www.thehistorypress.ie

© Bill Wilsdon, 2010

The right of Bill Wilsdon to be identified as the Author
of this work has been asserted in accordance with the
Copyrights, Designs and Patents Act 1988.

All rights reserved. No part of this book may be reprinted
or reproduced or utilised in any form or by any electronic,
mechanical or other means, now known or hereafter invented,
including photocopying and recording, or in any information
storage or retrieval system, without the permission in writing
from the Publishers.
British Library Cataloguing in Publication Data.
A catalogue record for this book is available from the British Library.

ISBN 978 1 84588 980 7

Typesetting and origination by The History Press
Printed in Great Britain
Manufacturing managed by Jellyfish Print Solutions Ltd

CONTENTS

FOREWORD

Ulster is a land of immigrants. The very birth of Northern Ireland in the 1920s points to the fact that since the seventeenth century (and much before), this part of Ireland has attracted a sizeable migrant community from the rest of the British Isles, who have traditionally given their primary allegiance to the land of their origin rather than to Ireland. Ethnically composed of Welsh and English, and in particular Scots, and usually Protestant in faith, their arrival in north Ireland following the Plantation of Ulster in the 1610s was to create lasting tensions with the native Gaelic Irish (and predominantly Catholic) population. A little later in the same century, significant numbers of other peoples from northern Europe, displaced for religious reasons, also chose to settle in Ulster. Thus the non-native, non-Catholic inhabitants came to represent a myriad of Protestant sects and groups from across Europe, and eventually comprised the majority within the population. Although not all of the counties chosen for settlement in the plantation are today represented in Northern Ireland, the province's retention as an integral part of the United Kingdom is directly attributable to the commencement of the 1610 scheme and the subsequent events that involved it during the seventeenth century.

By contrast, the creation of the independent Republic of Ireland in 1922, incorporating over 80 per cent of the land surface of the island, including parts of Ulster and all of the other three Irish provinces, demonstrated the wish of the Irish to control their own destiny independently from Britain. After a fraught political relationship with the rest of the British Isles, which began in the twelfth century, Ireland fought a successful war of independence from Britain that resulted in the partitioning of the island. These circumstances, unsatisfactory to many inhabitants of the island, contributed to the conditions that later led to the long period of civil unrest in Northern Ireland at the end of the twentieth century. The complex effect of the current political arrangements on Ireland's inhabitants is amply demonstrated by the example of the meandering international border which now weaves its way through the lakes, bogs and hills of the River Erne catchment, to divide Northern Ireland from the Republic of Ireland.

This book, then, aims to cover those areas within the Erne catchment that were colonised in the Ulster Plantation scheme of 1610, and to account for the history of the castles built as a result of the conditions by which the new landlords were granted estates from the Crown. It therefore broadly covers the two counties of Fermanagh and

Cavan, as well as south Donegal and a small area of south Tyrone. Over one third of Monaghan also falls within the Erne's catchment area, but the county was not part of the 1610 scheme and therefore does not form part of this guide. Likewise, small areas of north Longford and SE Leitrim falling within the catchment area are not considered.

This area then defines the geographical limits of our story, as we seek to unravel the largely forgotten history of these castles of the Ulster Plantation. As this guidebook is being written, the island of Ireland is experiencing a huge influx of new settlers mainly from the eastern European countries of the recently enlarged European Union. Now, for the first time in many decades, the island is experiencing a growth in population encouraged by the stable political environment and a favourable economy. We are also witnessing, on a daily basis, the challenges and opportunities that this influx has created and the effects this has on the resident population, as all citizens compete for limited housing, employment, schools and health-care provision. This book will show that our present-day experiences have had their parallels in the past and confirm that the present circumstances are not unique in the history of the island. Perhaps an understanding of our past will allow us to create a positive future for all of us on our island.

To date, there has been no comprehensive survey of Plantation castles in the Erne basin and this is why I believe that a guidebook on them is now essential. On many occasions on holiday in this beautiful part of the country, I have come across the ruins of these castles but found little explanation for their existence. Several examples are in state care and lately some effort to inform the visitor about them has been provided, but only at the prime sites. Thus I felt it important to try and write a collective history of the castles found in the landscape and ascertain if there was a reason for their collective demise.

Castles in Ireland have, until recent years, been largely neglected. In part this was due to the association of many of the greatest ones with the supporters of the political connection with Britain. As a result, after partition in 1922, many castles in the Republic of Ireland were allowed to fall into decay without restorative works being undertaken to arrest the decline. Other, more iconic buildings received the limited available resources at the expense of the castle.

But thankfully that view has changed in recent times. Today, in both countries, castles are studied as a window to our shared socio-economic, cultural and political past. However, the treatment is still uneven, with the great medieval castles receiving the lion's share of attention. By contrast, the plantation structures, much smaller in scale and more domestic in form, are less dramatic and thus attract less interest. Yet these humbler structures were fundamental to the very survival of the settler community that arrived at the commencement of the plantation. I feel, therefore, that the time is now right to present this modest guide of castle sites so that we may take stock of those that remain and see if there is a better way to display this tangible part of our past.

Time has not been kind to the built structures of this region. North-central Ireland (which includes not just the Erne catchment but Longford, Leitrim and Sligo as well) appears as a land now devoid of substantial remains from any period. In his book *Castles of Ireland*, Brian de Breffny refers to only four castles in Fermanagh and none in Cavan. Other authors have followed this pattern too. Given the sparseness of survivals, particularly in Cavan, it might seem that these castles were not a success. Most were abandoned during the turmoil of 1641 or 1689 and though others survived longer, changing life-styles soon rendered them unfashionable homes. Often, fundamental rebuilding works changed them beyond recognition, masking their original features by adornment and façade. Today, after nearly 400 years, these structures are in need of some loving attention to arrest deterioration and allow their story to be told.

Twice in the space of fifty years during the seventeenth century, the future of the plantation was seriously challenged. In considering this period of history, it soon becomes apparent that if the series of fortified homes had not been built across Ulster in accordance with the articles of plantation, then its survival, together with that of the British population in the Erne basin and elsewhere, would now be in doubt. Except for the loughs, the Erne catchment contains no other natural defensive features. Therefore, if castles like Monea, Castlemervyn or Aghalane had not existed in 1641, then Rory Maguire could have overrun the town of Enniskillen in the way he was able to deal with Lisnaskea. Similarly the proximity to each other of Keelagh and Croaghan ensured that determined settlers could resist the efforts of the rebels, at least for a time, to remove them from the centre of Cavan.

Indeed, it could be argued that the disaster that befell the planters in 1641 would have been greatly mitigated if the obligations to build castles, as laid down in the original plantation conditions, had been more strictly observed by the settlers who received the land. But too often the conditions were avoided or ignored without punishment for default. In like fashion, many of the castles that survived the 1641 rebellion were to be used to great effect again as garrisons during the revolution of 1689. Crom never fell to the Jacobites, nor did Castle Caldwell or Portora. At this time, therefore, Enniskillen castle and town became a stony refuge for Williamite supporters from across north-central Ireland and their resistance to King James II assisted King William III to later restore the throne of Ireland with that of Britain.

However, the development of earthworks in that same war by Governor Hamilton, Colonel Wolseley and others, did point to a future landscape without castles. And, soon after the revolution concluded, and peace was restored to the country, undefended homes were erected at Dresternan, Hall Craig and Bellemont. Stable political conditions also heralded the tearing down of unnecessary bawn walls at Castle Caldwell and Necarne. The peace created by the so-called 'Glorious Revolution' of 1689 ultimately ensured that the castle as a living space would be consigned to the pages of history, just like the demise of the battleship or the longbow.

INTRODUCTION

WHAT IS A CASTLE?

The word 'castle' conjures up an image of high, stone, battlemented walls and towers, garrisoned by knights in armour and perhaps containing imprisoned maidens requiring rescue. In truth, the term 'castle' is best suited to the medieval period in history, when landowners, usually of noble birth, sought to fortify and protect their assets by constructing a stout and virtually impregnable (for the time) stone bastion. Indeed, in the period before gunpowder, the capture of a castle required the deployment of enormous resources by the attacker and often success was best achieved by starvation or by the treachery of the incumbent garrison.

Any dictionary definition would support this popular view of the castle as a fortified residence at which military considerations were paramount over all others. The buildings we recognise today as castles began in France, around the tenth century, as a response to the raids by the Norsemen of Scandinavia, later known to us as Normans. Most common were the wood and earthen 'motte and bailey' castles, which the Normans later copied when they came across to conquer England (and later Ireland) after the eleventh century. Later, they also built castles of stone, and early examples consisted of strong curtain walls, a gatehouse to protect the vulnerable entrance and a tall keep in the centre designed to act as a last refuge should an enemy manage to breach the walled perimeter.

In time, experience gained from observing Saracen fortifications during the Crusades in the Holy Land, saw the castle develop into the ultimate fighting structure, with the addition of moats, splayed arrow slits, polygonal towers, murder-holes, killing zones and the like. We are reminded of the great castles in Wales built by Edward I, such as Caernarvon, Harlech and Beaumauris. Closer to home, Carrickfergus, Roscommon and Ballymote represent the Irish expression of these developments. Castles, therefore, were not static elements in the landscape but were constantly evolving to stay one step ahead of the besieging force.

The end of the medieval castle was heralded at the far end of Europe in 1453, when the Turkish sultan Mehmet the Conquerer battered down the ancient walls of Constantinople and overthrew the last remnant of the Byzantine Empire. With the demise of this Christian city outpost, the era of secure defence behind tall stone walls and towers had passed, for gunpowder could now turn any fortification to rubble by a sustained artillery bombardment.

Initially, the significance of this change was slow to affect Ireland. Artillery was certainly known in Ireland from an early date, because King Richard II brought cannon, gunpowder and shot to Ireland on his visits in 1394 and 1399. The first recorded use of artillery in the siege of a castle occurred in 1488 at the MacGeoghan stronghold of Balrath in Westmeath. In March 1535, the Lord Deputy, Sir William Skeffington, attacked the castle of Maynooth, home of Garret Óg Fitzgerald, 9th Earl of Kildare. Kildare had created defensive earthworks protected by artillery, but Skeffington's guns proved more effective, and after five days of bombardment, Kildare surrendered his home. This defeat of Kildare, the most powerful of the Old English lords in Ireland, signalled the end of their traditional autonomy and confirmed the state's authority to extend its power throughout the island.

In a sense, this should have led to a rapid abandoning of the old places of safety, but other factors ensured the survival of castles well into the modern era. Despite the preeminence of artillery, it was an expensive commodity to produce (the jet fighter of its day) and it was difficult to transport across the muddy roads of Ireland. The great lords were worth the trouble to besiege but the smaller ones were too numerous to make a campaign with artillery so cost-effective. So, until artillery could be designed to be more portable, the big guns stayed in the arsenal in Dublin. Thus, the topography of Ireland conspired to allow the castle and fortified manor house a last hurrah, up to the middle of the seventeenth century and beyond.

CASTLE BUILDING IN THE ULSTER PLANTATION

The commencement of the Ulster Plantation in 1610 witnessed the last flurry of castle building in the British Isles, at a time when many other parts of Europe were already constructing defenceless manor houses. However, conditions in Ireland were still disturbed enough for defended buildings to be required and so small castles continued to be considered. Required to build fortified structures as part of the conditions of the land grants, Ulster Plantation landlords gave final expression to a building tradition of defence that was coming to an end after 600 years of use. In a building period lasting only a few years, at the beginning of the seventeenth century, the Ulster planters created a distinctive class of small castles, marking their twilight in the British Isles before the final shift to undefended house building as seen elsewhere.

Yet it is worth pointing out that though often referred to as such, strictly speaking these buildings were not 'castles' in the medieval sense of the word. These were fortified or defended manor houses occupied by a single family and their household, and have perhaps more in common with the wooden stockades and homesteads being erected in the New World at the same time. They were designed to be raid-proof only and were not expected to withstand a long siege, though several did. These castles were owner occupied and with only one or two exceptions they were not royal castles garrisoned with Crown troops. Thus, the end result was a smaller structure, less dominant in the landscape than the medieval fortress but nonetheless possessing defensible features, which allowed it to utilise firearms in a positive way.

THE CATCHMENT AREA OF THE RIVER ERNE

As every school child knows, Ireland, topographically, resembles a saucer, with the mountains concentrated near the coasts and the centre occupied by a low-lying plain. These central lowlands are in truth not flat but gently undulating, with low hills stretching across the whole width of the plain. Geologically, they are floored in the main by carboniferous limestone rocks stretching east to west from Dublin Bay to Galway Bay and north to south from Donegal Bay to Cork. These are in turn covered by a layer of glacial deposits, laid down at the end of the last Ice Age, which form 'drumlins', the distinctive, smooth-rounded hillocks so typical of SW Ulster and beyond. Creating a topography that has been described as a 'basket of eggs', these little hills form 'islands' of well-drained pasture and arable land, with the intervening hollows filled with bog and lakes, which impede the natural drainage.

Forming the NW part of this central lowland plain, the basin of the River Erne covers 4,340 square kilometres (1,736 square miles), making it the fourth largest river catchment in Ireland after the Shannon, Barrow and Bann. This catchment is almost equally shared by Northern Ireland and the Republic of Ireland, and covers most of counties Cavan and Fermanagh, as well as a large part of Monaghan and some small areas of Donegal, Leitrim, Longford and Tyrone. As a geographical region, the social and economic changes affecting both sides of the border here in modern times have been broadly similar. In general, north-central Ireland has traditionally been a difficult living environment and has witnessed continued demographic stagnation for at least a century and a half. This can best be demonstrated by comparing the fortunes of Fermanagh and Cavan, the two counties comprising the lion's share of the Erne's catchment area but located in different jurisdictions.

Located in the SW corner of Northern Ireland, Fermanagh comprises 1,876 square kilometres (724 square miles), 13.3 per cent of the total land area. However the population in the 2001 census for Northern Ireland returned only 57,527 persons in the county, equating to only 3.4 per cent of Northern Ireland's total. Similarly, Cavan, at 1,891 square kilometres (730 square miles), comprises 2.7 per cent of the land area of the Republic of Ireland, but with a population of around 60,000 (2003 estimate) this only represents 1.5 per cent of the burgeoning 3.92 million of the whole. Migration to the larger urban centres on the island or abroad has been a feature of life in both counties since the mid-nineteenth century. Thus, both counties are relatively sparsely populated and contain little manufacturing or industrial capacity, relying increasingly on tourism, particularly the amenities provided by the numerous loughs and rivers, for sustainable income.

THE RIVER ERNE

Beginning as a small stream on the southern slopes of Slieve Glah (320m) near Cross Keys, SE of Cavan town, in the Republic of Ireland, the Erne meanders SW to the many-faceted Lough Gowna on the border with Longford. From here, the river swings northwards to enter Lough Oughter, with its indented shoreline even more confusing than Gowna, before emerging as a river once more. Reaching Belturbet, the Erne, crossing now into Northern Ireland, swells into the broad expanse of sluggish water known as Upper Lough Erne. The little drumlins now form true islands in the 37.5 square kilometres (14.5 square miles) of the lough. Above Enniskillen, the lough narrows again as it passes the town but then opens out below Portora to form Lower Lough Erne, a broad expanse of 105 square kilometres (40.5 square miles), second only in size to Lough Neagh in the British Isles and half as large again as Loch Lomond. At Rosscor, the Erne becomes a river again and flows past Belleek. Just below Belleek, the Erne crosses again into the Republic of Ireland and enters Assaroe Lake, an artificial reservoir created to provide a supply of water to turn the hydro-electricity turbines. Tamed and harnessed by man, it now passes beyond the lake via the Cathaleen's Falls generating station. The river here is now heavily canalled as it passes Ballyshannon. The final widening estuarine stretch of 5 kilometres (3 miles) skirts tiny Inish Samer island, then meanders beside bare rounded hills to emerge through high dunes into the Atlantic Ocean at Donegal Bay.

The Erne has several important tributaries, including the Annalee, Finn, Colebrooke and Sillees, all measuring over 100 kilometres in length. Additionally, there are a number of other shorter, but equally important, feeder streams such as the Woodford, Tempo, Arney, Ballinamallard, Kesh and Termon. Flowing off the bare limestone uplands, some of these give rise to spate flows, particularly in winter. Together with all its tributaries, the Erne flows in a flat swampy basin with little relief, except to the west where Cuilcagh rises to 667m (2200ft). In total the river passes through 330 square kilometres (132 square miles) of open water on its journey to the sea. Regionally, the average annual rainfall is 1,161mm (46 inches) and falling as it does onto impermeable clay soils, there is an inevitable high run-off into river courses during heavy rainfall. There are extensive peat bogs to the east and west of Upper Lough Erne and to the north of Lower Lough Erne. Coupled with low natural relief, this topography has led to the traditional problem of flooding throughout the Erne's length.

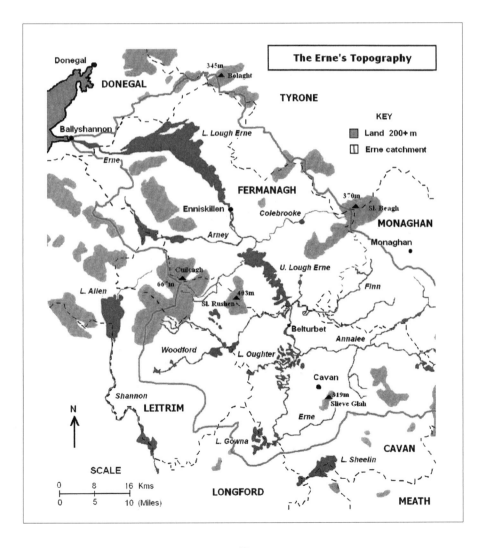

Where the upper River Erne flows beneath the R154 at Derrin, 3km NW of Kilnaleck, Co. Cavan, the altitude is only 80m (262ft). As the Erne enters Lough Oughter at Trinity Island, it is now 44.9m (147ft) above sea level. For the next 80km (50 miles) to the mouth of the final stretch of river above Rosscor Viaduct, the fall of the lake system is a mere 2.9m (9.5ft). It is only in the final 12km (7 miles) stretch from Rosscor to the sea, and particularly the 7km (4 miles) below Belleek, that the Erne becomes a mighty river, creating a 4kmph (2.5mph) current and providing the enormous flow necessary to turn the hydro-electric turbines at Cathaleen's Falls, just east of Ballyshannon. Over the period 1990-96, the estimated flow of the Erne at Ballyshannon, where it enters the sea, was 95.9 cubic metres per second.

Thus, the river is great for navigation but poor in its ability to drain off the high levels of rainfall that pour down onto the undulating landscape. Until the problem of drainage was addressed at the end of the nineteenth century, the former waterfalls at Belleek and the narrows at Enniskillen restricted the flow, causing the water to back up in times of prolonged rainfall and cause widespread flooding of the adjacent land. Describing the margins of Upper Lough Erne opposite Knockninny, Dean Henry writes of the problem in 1739, 'In the winter the scene is entirely changed. Lough Erne spreads over all up to the town of Lisnaskea and near to Maguires Bridge. These vast verdant flats become so many spacious bays, and the little hills that here and there are scattered through them are made islands.' Even today, locals will tell you that in the summer Lough Erne is in Fermanagh but in the winter Fermanagh is in Lough Erne!

It therefore came as no surprise when, in the late nineteenth century, the Lough Erne Drainage Board was established to create a uniform lake level for the whole basin by straightening and deepening some river channels. Additionally, the scheme saw the removal of the waterfalls at Belleek and their replacement with sluice gates to allow regulation of the lake levels between statutory limits. These tasks were undertaken between 1880 and 1891 and improved the flow of the Erne, reducing the water level by 1.8 to 2.4m (6 to 8ft), thereby benefiting local agriculture around the lough shores. Visiting the area soon after completion of the scheme, the writer W.F. Wakeman succinctly summed up the difficulties in his travel book *The Tourists' Picturesque Guide to Ireland*:

> The necessity for the drainage has long made itself painfully evident. The waters of Lough Erne along its entire length rise every year to a height of ten feet (three metres) over their summer level, submerging 17,400 acres (7,000 hectares) of land, and doing enormous mischief not only to the land covered but to the adjoining parts, by rendering them marshy and unproductive. The injury to the crops during excessive floods, is estimated at £40,000 to £57,000, affecting the counties of Fermanagh, Cavan and Monaghan.

The drainage scheme therefore brought some relief to the inhabitants around the lough shore (though it initially had a detrimental effect on sailing) but the limited works failed to create a permanent solution to the flooding of agricultural land, particularly on the eastern side of Upper Lough Erne. When Ireland was partitioned in 1922, the Erne catchment was bisected by the new international boundary, with both jurisdictions adopting a policy of minimal co-operation on almost all matters. However, a permanent solution to the problems of flooding became possible when a scheme to provide substantial electricity by harnessing the power of the Erne's flow was proposed in 1942 by the Irish Electricity Supply Board. This scheme proposed the creation of two hydro-electric power stations at Cathaleen's Falls near Ballyshannon and at Cliff near Belleek (both in the Republic of Ireland) to provide a combined output of 50 to 80MW of power.

From the outset, the scheme faced enormous political opposition from conservative elements in both the Belfast and Dublin parliaments. The Northern Ireland government were unwilling to provide any funds and were decidedly lukewarm to the idea of the Republic carrying out drainage works within Northern Ireland. At a time of strong anti-partitionist foreign policy in Dublin (the Republic of Ireland was with-drawing from the Commonwealth at the time), the scheme required careful diplomacy to achieve a successful outcome. Yet the potential benefits from the scheme were plainly evident and despite the public misgivings, the proposal lurched forward through various stages of approval. In Northern Ireland, the scheme had the private support of the Prime Minister, Basil Brooke (his constituency covered the Upper Lough Erne area), but he had to contend with cabinet colleagues who were unhappy at the Republic's power-generation company carrying out various civil engineering works within Northern Ireland and potentially controlling electricity supply to Fermanagh's inhabitants.

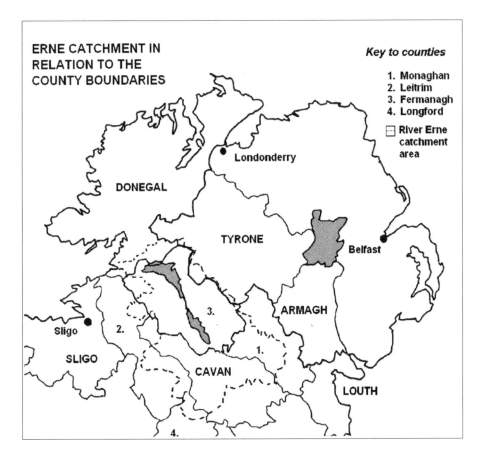

ERNE CATCHMENT IN RELATION TO THE COUNTY BOUNDARIES

Key to counties

1. Monaghan
2. Leitrim
3. Fermanagh
4. Longford

River Erne catchment area

Londonderry

DONEGAL

TYRONE

Belfast

Sligo

2.

3.

ARMAGH

SLIGO

1.

CAVAN

LOUTH

4.

Agreement was not finally reached until May 1950, when the Erne Drainage and Development Act was passed simultaneously in both parliaments, ensuring that water levels would be kept at statutorily agreed levels, and work began soon after. Cathaleen's Falls generating station was completed in April 1952 and Cliff in December 1954. All works were finally completed in 1957; fifteen years after the initial proposal had been raised. Nonetheless, the scheme has proved of enormous benefit to the communities around the loughs who had lived with the risk of flooding each winter and who could at last look forward to stable lough management. Although today local flooding remains a threat for some throughout a wet Irish winter, the scheme has proved its worth. Perhaps most of all, the Erne drainage scheme provided, during a long period of political non-co-operation, a glimpse of how everyone might benefit when mutual fears and prejudices are set aside.

THE SCOPE OF THIS GUIDE

The purpose of this guide is to describe the castles erected by the settlers and 'deserving' natives who arrived in the River Erne's catchment area after the establishment of the Ulster Plantation. As stated earlier, this area comprises almost all of Fermanagh and most of Cavan. In addition, a small area of south Tyrone and south Donegal lie within the catchment. These four counties were included within the scheme's original boundary and the castles built to the specifications of the lands granted to the beneficiaries are here considered.

A significant portion of western Monaghan also falls within the Erne's catchment. The county, however, was never formally planted, though it later acquired settlers due to its proximity to the Ulster scheme that surrounded it to the east, north and SW. So although it would become populated by a sizeable British community, no conditions for building castles were ever issued for the county and consequently there are no castles of this type. Two small areas of north and east Leitrim also fall within the catchment, as well as a tiny area of north Longford. Both these counties experienced their own plantation scheme a decade after Ulster. Neither scheme was particularly successful in attracting large numbers of new settlers, though Leitrim has some fine examples of fortified homes from this period.

HOW TO USE THE GUIDE

In order to use this guide effectively, it is best to obtain suitable maps that cover the area. The Ordnance Survey in both jurisdictions publish a set of four maps at a scale of 1:250,000 (1cm to 2.5km or 1 inch to 4 miles), which cover the whole island at a regional scale. Two maps, 'Ireland North' and 'Ireland East', cover the Erne catchment, allowing an appreciation of the surrounding topography and relief. However, for greater detail, it is necessary to use the 1:50,000 scale Discoverer Map Series (2cm to 1km or 1¼ inches to 1 mile) when attempting to locate castles and other features mentioned in the guide. The maps covering the Erne are sheet numbers 16, 17, 18, 26, 27, 28, 33, 34 and 35. (It should be noted that not all the sites listed are marked on these maps.) Copies can be purchased at tourist information centres or at any good newsagents.

With even greater detail, two maps entitled 'Fermanagh Lakeland' cover Upper and Lower Lough Erne at a scale of 1:25,000 (4cm to 1km or 2½ inches to a mile), which is also ideal for boat users. These maps give superb detail of sites near the lake edges and additionally show water depths, anchorages and safe passageways through the many channels. Many of the castle sites are near the lough side, and these maps are useful for navigating a route to them. Finally, many boat hire companies issue waterway maps of their own, which can also be utilised when formulating an outing plan.

Some of the sites are further away from a waterway and I have included brief details of local public transport. Though details given are correct at the time of publishing, it is recommended that the reader contact the provider prior to any planned trip. In Northern Ireland the public transport provider is Ulsterbus, with the local depot at Wellington Road, Enniskillen (Tel. 00 44 28 6632 2633). In the Republic of Ireland, public transport is provided by Bus Éireann, Farnham Street, Cavan (Tel. 00 353 49 4331353 or 00 353 49 4332533).

Each of the castle descriptions in the guide commences with a Discoverer Series sheet number and a six-figure grid reference. Of course the grid references are the same for both 1:50,000 and 1:25,000 maps. A short narrative follows, giving directions to the site, usually by road, but where appropriate by water as well. The guide continues by offering information on the history of the castle, including the personalities who were once inhabitants, followed by a description of the structure as it appears today. Though not essential, a compass can be useful as it allows orientation on each site.

Modern vehicle satellite navigation can also be very useful in orientating oneself between sites. The major drawback with using it is the paucity of rural road names. In this guide, the castle sites are usually identified using townland names and there is usually no road signage for these. Therefore, once close to the destination, local advice may need to be sought.

The history of each castle site cannot be properly understood without reference to the prevailing political circumstances of the time. I have therefore decided to include some introductory chapters which briefly explain the conditions in Ireland which led to the establishment of a plantation in six Ulster counties. I have included some detail of the conditions by which the 'undertakers' were allocated land and how this influenced the programme of castle building. In the concluding section, I have outlined the subsequent political events that affected Ireland, and particularly SW Ulster, during the rest of the century. Two events, the rebellion of 1641 and the constitutional crisis of 1689 known as the 'Glorious Revolution', profoundly shaped future relations between the various communities in Ulster and directly impacted on the ability of the castles to survive or perish. The settlement arrangements following each event are briefly explained, as is the final demise of the fortified home as a result of the improving political climate across Ireland after 1700.

For ease of reference, the castles have been grouped into three itineraries. These follow either a route around Lower Lough Erne, Upper Lough Erne or upstream to the Cavan sites. Of course it is possible to plan one's own itinerary to include any arrangement of sites. Many of the sites are now state managed and access is usually afforded at reasonable times. However, some sites remain in private ownership and the visitor should first gain approval from the relevant owner before examining them. Usually landowners are only too happy to allow you to see these places, so do ask. Remember, though, that these are ruined sites in the main, and great care must be exercised when inspecting them.

Good footwear is essential as many sites have uneven surfaces and may be overgrown. Also, disabled access is often limited but is usually better at state managed locations. Finally, it is worth pointing out that the usual countryside code rules. Leave no litter, take away only pictures and respect the monuments. Now go and enjoy the stories these largely forgotten stones have to tell!

1

THE PLANTATION OF ULSTER

In the sixteenth century, Ireland was to experience the gradual extension of English sovereignty across the entire island. This process, known to modern readers as the 'Tudor conquest', involved the reform of the island's traditional society, then a feudal patchwork of autonomous chiefdoms beyond the effective reach of government, into that of a modern centralised state. This modernisation of the social order fundamentally affected the traditional ability of the hitherto independent lords to, amongst other things, raise their private armies, choose their successors and control their chief vassals. In addition, English Common Law and the reformed faith of northern Europe replaced the ancient Gaelic Irish Brehon law and Roman Catholicism.

Historically, the northern province of Ulster had been least influenced by the Crown's modernisation policy, then being progressed from the capital in Dublin. Any change to the existing status quo, therefore, was likely to meet the greatest resistance from the current trio of senior Ulster lords, namely Hugh O'Neill, Earl of Tyrone, Hugh Roe O'Donnell, Earl of Tyrconnell (modern Donegal), and Hugh Maguire of Fermanagh. By the 1590s, this increasing centralisation had caused each lord in turn to rebel against the government, which they believed was intent on completing the programme of social change, with or without their consent.

O'Neill, as the senior figure of the trio, led the subsequent guerrilla war which was to see many successes against the Crown, notably at Yellow Ford in August 1598 and in the Curlew Mountains in August 1599. The war gradually extended across the length and breadth of Ireland and ultimate success for O'Neill appeared possible with the arrival of 4,000 Spanish troops at Kinsale, near Cork, in late 1601. After much delay he moved down from Ulster with his army to effect a junction with the Spaniards and to destroy the army of Lord Deputy Mountjoy, at that time laying siege to Kinsale. But the subsequent battle at dawn on Christmas Eve 1601, which lasted little more than an hour, saw O'Neill's army smashed and his hopes of continued independence reduced to dust. The Spanish soon surrendered to Mountjoy and O'Neill retreated once again to the boggy fastnesses of Ulster, where he continued his guerrilla war against the Crown. But he was now hemmed in between the Lord Deputy's army approaching from the south and another led by Sir Henry Docwra, which had landed on the north coast at Derry with the support of Niall Garbh O'Donnell, a rival claimant to the O'Donnell leadership in Tyrconnell. Ulster became ravaged by a scorched-earth policy, which brought widespread hunger to O'Neill's territory.

Despite his deteriorating military situation, O'Neill was able to secure a conditional surrender to the Crown at Mellifont in 1603. He was granted extraordinarily favourable terms which allowed him to remain (contrary to Gaelic law) as the absolute ruler of the remainder of his lordship and that of the O'Cahans, chieftains of County Coleraine. In return, he was to surrender only 300 acres for each of the new Crown castles to be established at Charlemont and Mountjoy, near his Dungannon home.

Why had the Crown granted such lenient terms to a man who had ravaged Ireland for nine years? There were many reasons, but chief amongst them had been the death of Elizabeth I just prior to O'Neill's surrender. This fact was apparently kept from him during negotiations, when the vacant crown was offered to James VI of Scotland, who now presided over the three kingdoms as James I of England, Scotland and Ireland. James had long been suspected of aiding the rebel earl in the late war, and there was a fear that O'Neill could negotiate further concessions from this Scottish king. Anxious to broker a deal, the government agreed terms. The war had already cost the exchequer £2,000,000.

However, the deal angered the representatives of the government in Dublin, who watched the policy of appeasement to O'Neill and the decommissioning of the army to a mere 900 infantry by 1606. Yet despite the government's friendly overtures, O'Neill remained defiant and unreformed and began to foment a new rebellion from at least 1605. As before, he went about rebuilding his power base amongst the Irish nobles, but this time also amongst the Catholic Old English lords who had stood aloof from involvement in his earlier rebellion.

But his plotting came to an abrupt end when he believed that a spy had informed the Crown of his plans to once again obtain Spanish assistance. Thus, on 4 September 1607, occurred the event ever since known as the Flight of the Earls, when the former rebels O'Neill, O'Donnell, Cuconnaught Maguire (successor of Hugh) and a retinue totalling ninety-nine persons set sail from Rathmullan, in Donegal, for the continent. The flight of these major figures of Ulster's aristocracy left a huge political vacuum and cast doubt on the efficacy of the previous kid-glove policy.

But worse was to follow. In April 1608, Sir Cahir O'Doherty rebelled in Inishowen, County Donegal, and attacked the garrisons at Derry, Doe castle and Culmore fort. Sir Niall Garbh O'Donnell of Donegal and Sir Donal O'Cahan of Coleraine covertly supported his cause, which at its height involved no more that 800 fighting men, not all of whom were adequately armed. All three of these chieftains had initially supported the government during the late rebellion but were now dissatisfied with the estates awarded to them by the Crown as a reward for their loyalty. The rebellion was, however, confined to the north-west of the province. O'Doherty was killed at Kilmacrenan in July, promptly ending the rebellion. For their covert support of O'Doherty, both Niall Garbh O'Donnell and Donal O'Cahan would receive capital punishment.

This time the government, which had previously followed a policy of appeasement, was thoroughly alarmed at the possibility of another expensive rebellion in Ulster.

Moreover, it viewed O'Doherty's rebellion as merely a prelude to the return of O'Neill with Spanish assistance from the continent. It called for a radical departure from the existing policy and a new approach to the difficult province of Ulster. The Flight of the Earls and the rebellion of O'Doherty had resulted in the forfeiture of extensive estates across Ulster to the Crown. The government decided to pay for the cost of the suppression of the rebellion and of the secured governance of the province, by the sale of the confiscated lands of the rebels. The King and his advisors took control of these estates and sought advice on how best to proceed with an extensive plantation of loyal British settlers in Ulster.

LORD DEPUTY CHICHESTER

Arthur Chichester, the youngest son of a Devon landowner, was no stranger to Ulster. Made Governor of Carrickfergus, he had witnessed the death of his brother John during O'Neill's rebellion. He had assisted Deputy Mountjoy's campaign with a thrust across the waters of Lough Neagh in a fleet of locally constructed boats and earned a reputation for brutality by his wholesale slaughter of men, women and children.

Born in 1563, Chichester had had a chequered career up to this point. He had commanded a ship against the Spanish armada, accompanied Sir Francis Drake on his last voyage and service as a soldier on the continent. As a reward for his Irish services, Chichester was appointed Lord Deputy in February 1605 (a position he would hold for eleven years) and immediately began a policy of heavy fines and imprisonment for failure to attend the Anglican Church. He had the Book of Common Prayer translated into Gaelic and transplanted the troublesome Graham clan from the Scottish border to Roscommon. He was first made aware of the King's determination to create a plantation in Ulster via a letter sent to him almost immediately after the Flight of the Earls, which expressed the view that the land would be granted to a mixture of British and loyal Irish subjects. In the years ahead, Chichester would become one of the leading architects in the creation of what became known as the Plantation of Ulster.

Initially, Chichester had his own ideas regarding the future settlement of the escheated estates. He favoured the idea of a limited plantation in the confiscated lands of the former rebels and believed that the 'servitors' (soldiers who had given good service in the late war) should receive the lion's share, with Scottish and English 'undertakers' (settlers migrating from both countries) taking up the remainder. Deserving native Irish should then receive extensive re-grants totalling one half of all land in each county.

With the Flight of the Earls in 1607, six whole counties in Ulster were now available for redistribution; namely Donegal, Coleraine (later reconfigured as Londonderry), Armagh, Tyrone, Cavan and Fermanagh. Of the other Ulster counties, Down and Antrim were being privately settled, with lowland Scots brought in by Sir James Hamilton and Sir Hugh Montgomery. In Monaghan, land ownership had been settled in the 1590s with the break-up of the MacMahon lordship and the creation of a native freeholder class (Monaghan would be revised in the early years of the next century). But the confiscation of the six counties provided the King with an opportunity to create a much more comprehensive plantation model than that envisaged by his Lord Deputy.

At the outset, Chichester argued that the proportion set aside for native Irish in the plantation scheme was insufficient and would store up future grievances that would 'kindle a new fire in those parts at one time or another if they be not well looked to or provided for in some reasonable measure'. Ultimately, James ignored his advice and in the end the Irish received less than a quarter of all the land, sometimes even less than this in some counties. The scheme was introduced in Cavan first, as the proportion of land to the Irish there was greatest. Chichester failed to win his argument with the King regarding the Ulster Plantation but his model would be revived in subsequent schemes. His championing of the servitors bore fruit, with a series of minor plantations in Leitrim, Longford and elsewhere later in the century, in which he set aside only the proportions he had favoured in Ulster.

SIR JOHN DAVIES

Sir John Davies was a Wiltshire man, although born in Wales in 1569. He first arrived in Ireland in November 1603 as Solicitor General. A brilliant lawyer, he also possessed a violent temper, which once caused him to break a cudgel across the skull of a fellow barrister at the table in the Hall of the Middle Temple. This incident caused his disbarment and only the penning of a poem verbalising his penance allowed his return.

In addition to law, Davies was a scholar, poet and writer of historical records, which allows us to know more about him than many of his more famous contemporaries. He wrote *Discovery of the True Causes Why Ireland Was Never Entirely Subdued*, which brought him to the attention of government and allowed him to develop ideas of plantation which differed from his contemporary Chichester. He travelled widely around Ireland, often ignoring its infamous damp climate by preferring to sleep under canvas.

Davies argued that there should be a full-scale colonisation of Ulster, with the undertakers playing the prominent role. The undertakers should be men of economic substance who would only be granted the land if they agreed to a set of conditions which obliged them to build villages and churches, erect castles, settle British colonists on their land and provide them with arms. The servitors and deserving natives would receive their reward of land too, but without the compulsory obligations outlined above. James favoured this more radical model of plantation for Ulster as he had taken a personal interest and was perhaps more convinced of the ultimate success of Davies's model over that of Chichester.

Davies would become an important landlord in the Ulster Plantation (the only civilian awarded land as a servitor in Ulster), being granted the 1,500-acre estate of Moyeghvane in Clanawley, Fermanagh in 1611. Nothing of his building work survives there but in another grant (the 2,000-acre estate of Gavelagh in west Tyrone), two of his castles still survive at Castlederg and at Castle Curlews, near Drumquin. On his death in 1626, his estate passed by his daughter Lucy into the family of the Earl of Huntingdon.

THE CONCEPT OF PLANTATION

But what exactly did the concept of plantation mean to the early Jacobeans? Actually, the idea of a colony of persons being installed in a foreign place was nothing new to them, as settlements of new colonists had been underway in many places since the latter half of the previous century. It is therefore worthwhile, at this point, to briefly explain the rationale and explore the experiences of contemporaneous settlements in the virgin territory of the eastern American coast.

Until the sixteenth century, territorial acquisition meant the military conquest by a neighbouring power and the installation of a new set of political overlords. The territory, together with its people, was then absorbed into this new, greater kingdom. There was usually a corresponding movement of persons accompanying their master into the new territory. However, the discovery of the New World and the vast areas this opened up to conquest, was to change the dynamic of this relationship. With religious zeal, the nations of Europe in the sixteenth century were to carve out empires for themselves in the Americas, Africa, the Caribbean and the Far East, but their relationships with the indigenous populations of these lands were quite different to that of earlier times.

'Plantation' came to mean the introduction of pioneering colonists together with the laws, customs and values of their homeland into the designated area, in order to civilise and educate. The plan did not envisage merely the co-existence of separate peoples but the replacement of the indigenous culture with that of the colonists. This idea was best suited to virgin territory where there were few local inhabitants, such as eastern North America. And given the technological differences between the protagonists there, the colonisation of Virginia, and later Massachusetts, was more easily achievable.

In Ulster, the conditions found in the New World and elsewhere were not present, and the plantation had to take place within the context of an already occupied territory. Thus the settlement conditions applied to Ulster and their expected outcomes could never be the same as in other schemes.

COLONISATION IN THE NEW WORLD

Plantations were not a new phenomenon to Elizabethan or Jacobean Britain. Throughout the late sixteenth century, English adventurers were busy exploring the eastern seaboard of North America with a view to exploiting its rich and untapped natural resources. Initially, these were private commercial ventures, often fronted by well-known figures of the day, but funded by English speculators.

In the 1570s, Martin Frobisher explored the northern waters looking for the fabled 'North-west Passage' to China and the Far East, which would avoid having to evade the Spanish galleons that controlled the waters further south. He was unsuccessful (as no viable route exists) but his adventures inspired others. In 1583, a voyage by Sir Humphrey Gilbert explored the coast of Newfoundland, but his ship was lost on the return journey.

The first serious attempt at establishing a colony in North America was undertaken by Walter Raleigh. In July 1584, an expedition explored the area of Roanoke Island (off modern North Carolina) and Raleigh arrived in June of the following year in a fleet of seven ships with 108 colonists, all men. But conditions proved difficult and in June 1586, Francis Drake removed the survivors of this colony back to England. Undeterred, in 1587, Raleigh again sent out colonists from England to Roanoke Island to establish the city of 'Raleigh'. This time the 150-strong colony included women and children as well as men. By 1590 though, this venture had failed. In the meantime, Raleigh and others continued to explore the region, collecting plant samples and making tentative contact with the native inhabitants.

With the death of Elizabeth I in 1603, James I and VI ascended the throne of the British Isles and the pace of development immediately quickened. In June 1606, James granted a charter to a group of London entrepreneurs known as the 'Virginia Company'. This company was to establish an English colony in the Chesapeake area, find gold and a trade route to the East. In December, 105 settlers (all men or boys) sailed from London, arriving in the James River on 14 May 1607 and landing on Jamestown Island (in modern Virginia). Amongst these colonists was the famous Captain John Smith of *Pocahontas* fame. The site was chosen for its deep-water anchorage, but it proved a poor choice for the health of the colonists. The surrounding swampland brought disease and the colony was under constant attack from the native Algonquians. Famine always threatened and the colonists steadily succumbed to one cause or another.

Smith described the efforts to fortify their new settlement, which they completed within a month, 'The fifteenth of June we had built and finished our Fort, which was triangle wise, having three Bulwarkes, at every corner, like a halfe Moone, and foure or five pieces of Artillerie mounted in them.'

On 2 January 1608 a first resupply of sixty new settlers arrived from England. They found only thirty-eight survivors from the first winter. Hopes rose with this timely arrival but were soon dashed, when only five days later, an accidental fire destroyed most of the town. The inhabitants lost most of their clothing and had to endure a bitter winter. Later that year, a second resupply of colonists, which included two women, arrived from England.

In the summer they rebuilt and refortified their settlement, again described by John Smith:

> Jamestowne being burnt, we rebuilt it and three forts more, besides the Church and Store-house, we had about fortie or fiftie severall houses to keepe us warme and dry, invironed with a palizado of fourteen or fifteen feet … we had three Bulwarkes, four and twenty peeces of ordnance of Culvering, Demiculvering, sacar and falcon and most well mounted upon convenient platforms…

The hardship of the colonists continued. When the colony was again visited in May 1610, a mere sixty had survived the 'starving time' of the previous winter. The settlement was then briefly abandoned but later reoccupied under the instruction of Lord De La Warr. Despite the seemingly endless difficulties of the early years, the first tobacco crop was grown, harvested and transported to England to be sold there in 1614. There was now a steady rise in population, as the settlements began to expand beyond the original site. A supply of 'young maids to make wives for so many of the former Tenants' arrived in 1619.

Despite these positive developments, relations with the native Indian population had always been strained. In March 1622, without warning, and following the killing of one of their number by the colonists, the Indians attacked the settlements killing 350 settlers.

But the timely warning of an Indian child named Chanco saved Jamestown and the survivors retaliated by poisoning 200 Indians during subsequent negotiations. As a result of these incidents, King James revoked the Virginia Company's charter in May 1624 and Jamestown became a Crown colony. A second massacre of settlers occurred twenty years later and resulted in the first Indian reservation being created near present-day Richmond, Virginia, for the native Indian survivors.

By this time, other colonists (most famously the puritans on the *Mayflower* at Massachusetts) had arrived on the eastern seaboard of America and were slowly establishing settlements, cutting down forests, growing crops and exploring the endless fastnesses of the interior. Though Jamestown would be abandoned in 1698 for the nearby Williamsburg, the idea of colonisation was now firmly established and the tide of emigration continued throughout the century and ever since.

The idea of a Plantation in Ulster, therefore, took place at a time when these English adventurers and speculators had already accumulated a great knowledge of the early difficulties. Many of the challenges and opportunities that had been experienced by the early Virginian settlers would be repeated in the Ulster scheme.

SCOTTISH PLANTATION EXPERIENCES

The Scots themselves were no strangers to the idea of plantation in their own land in the sixteenth century. Keen to exert control over the western isles, James VI of Scotland agreed to a scheme of plantation in 1597, paid for by the Duke of Lennox and others, with the aim of bringing 'civilitie and polecie' to the 'most barbarous Isle of Lewis' and to develop the resources for the public's benefit and that of the King. In the autumn of 1599, 500 to 600 settlers arrived on the island to begin the process of settlement. But many died in that first winter from the harsh conditions and the remainder were massacred three years later by the local inhabitants. A renewed scheme on the island in 1605 also failed.

In 1605, James, now also king of England and Ireland, granted Kintyre to the Earl of Argyll. Kintyre was the territory of the troublesome MacDonald clan and this grant aimed to curb their power in the western isles. Despite MacDonald resistance to the scheme, Argyll brought in some tenants. In 1607 he successfully petitioned for the rent of the grant to be waived for five years in order for him to establish the burgh town of Campbeltown. However, after 1617 the scheme was unable to progress as planned, as Argyll had exiled himself and been proclaimed a traitor.

The Scottish schemes were therefore unsuccessful in establishing the long-term settlements necessary to show a profit. Contemporary commentators believed that the Scots were able organisers but lacked the necessary finances to carry them over the difficult, first few years before a profit could be shown. The Plantation of Ulster would change all that. Scots and English were to embark on a joint venture with the Dublin administration bearing responsibility for the plantation's security.

The Plantation of Ulster thus coincides almost exactly with the initial settlement period at Jamestown in modern Virginia and there are many parallels between the developments of both schemes, separated as they were by the width of an ocean.

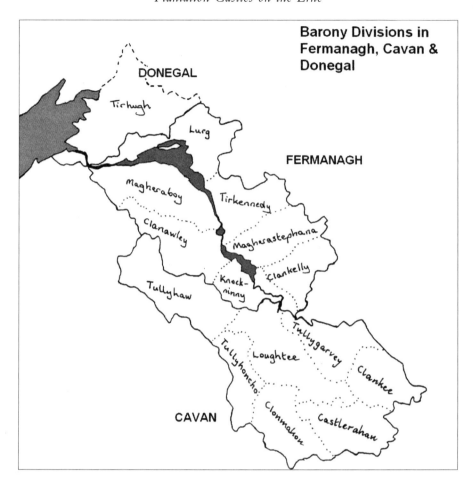

THE CONDITIONS FOR A PLANTATION IN ULSTER

Exactly why had so much land in Ulster become available for plantation? The reasons for the confiscation of estates by the Crown from their previous owners were complex and differed across Ulster. But the net result was that the King inherited a huge swathe of land with which to plan a permanent solution to the troublesome province.

With the Flight of the Earls from Lough Swilly on 3 September 1607, their vast possessions across Ulster were immediately escheated to the Crown. This land included all the non-Church lands of County Tyrone, Armagh (except Orier barony), Donegal (except Inishowen barony) and about half of Fermanagh, representing the personal territory of the exiled lords. However, other lands not directly involved with the Earls' flight were soon to become included in the area to be planted.

In Fermanagh, the land had been in the ownership of Sir Hugh Maguire, son-in-law of Hugh O'Neill, the exiled Earl of Tyrone. In 1595, Sir Hugh had been in open rebellion against Queen Elizabeth and his estates were re-granted to his cousin Conor Roe Maguire, who was allied to the Crown. Hugh died during the rebellion and with the end of hostilities, the Fermanagh lands were then equally divided between Conor Roe and his cousin Cuconnaght, half-brother of the deceased Hugh and therefore heir to the whole of the estates. However, Cuconnaght was unhappy with this lesser allocation and was to accompany the Earls into exile in 1607. Conor Roe was therefore left with his half, representing three full baronies. But Lord Deputy Chichester considered this far too generous in the overall scheme of the Plantation and Conor Roe was persuaded to surrender his lands and receive only one barony, Magherastephana, in exchange. As events transpired, he was not even to receive this in full, as some of it was withheld to provide estates for additional undertakers.

In Cavan, Sir John O'Reilly had been involved in the surrender and re-grant scheme of the late sixteenth century. In 1595, he joined the Earl of Tyrone's rebellion and was therefore proclaimed a traitor and his estates forfeited to the Crown. He died soon after and his escheated estates were granted to his son Mulmorie (married to a niece of the Duke of Ormonde), who was an ally of the Crown. But Mulmorie was killed with Bagenal at the battle of Yellow Ford in 1598 and his son, also Mulmorie, a minor, was expected to inherit. Despite his aristocratic connections, this Mulmorie was persuaded to accept confiscation of his inheritance in return for a 'proportion' like other claimants.

Elsewhere in Ulster, the lands of former allies of the Crown were also confiscated and placed within the scheme of the Plantation. In Donegal, the territory of Sir Cahir O'Doherty in Inishowen became forfeit following his abortive uprising in 1608. Likewise, the property of Niall Garbh O'Donnell around Lifford became forfeit when he was suspected of secretly supporting O'Doherty. Both of these leaders had been effective thorns in the flesh of their kinsmen in the recently concluded O'Neill wars, but had become disillusioned with their former allies when they failed to secure the lands promised to them. As with the servitors, loyal native Irish princes were unhappy that James had simply re-granted former rebel chieftains to their lands without also rewarding them.

In some cases, though, loyalty to the Crown was eventually rewarded. The territory of Tiranny had been controlled by Henry Óg O'Neill. Henry was killed on the English side during O'Doherty's rebellion in 1608. His lands were initially placed within the plantation scheme but were eventually re-granted to his family.

THE LAND SURVEY

The way was therefore clear for King James to instruct Lord Deputy Chichester to tour the escheated lands, now covering a total of six counties. These were Londonderry (an amalgamation of the old Coleraine county with the barony of Loughinsholin), Tyrone (minus Loughinsholin), Donegal, Armagh, Fermanagh and Cavan. In the summer of 1608, Chichester set out from Dublin to survey this territory. At this time no plan of the form and scale of this Plantation had been agreed. However, in Chichester's mind was the experience of other recent failed plantations in Ireland and he was determined to ensure that the same fate would not befall his plan for Ulster. Remarkably, this survey was completed by 2 September, less than nine weeks later.

The Munster Plantation and its near destruction were still memories in the recent past. In Munster, the opportunity to create a plantation had arisen with the conclusion of the Earl of Desmond's rebellion and the acquisition of large tracts of land by the Crown in that province. In 1586, extensive grants of land in Kerry, Limerick, Cork and Tipperary were parcelled out to influential Elizabethan gentlemen, including Sir Walter Raleigh, who were obliged to plant them with sufficient colonists from England in a manner similar to the schemes underway in Virginia.

However, the Munster grants created large estates, between 6,000 and 24,000 acres each, and it soon became clear that these were too great to manage efficiently. Insufficient colonists were initially persuaded to take up the offer of lands and the whole scheme was almost swept away by the O'Neill rebellion only ten years later. Nonetheless, the settlement survived and was to see prosperous times in the following century.

Armed with all this knowledge, Chichester was determined that the conditions in Ulster would be more attractive in order to persuade sufficient colonists to the province.

THE PLANTATION PLAN TAKES SHAPE

King James I would prove to be the greatest proponent of plantation and throughout his reign he remained its implacable ally. However, writing to Lord Deputy Chichester in October 1604, he voiced his concerns with the enormous cost of the recently concluded war with O'Neill and was keen to entertain ideas for the reduction of future spending, 'Bethink you some course howe the north may yeld some composition towards the maintenance of some of those Garrisons'.

As the areas of escheated land became available throughout 1608, the idea of creating a strong colony of British settlers in Ulster to defend it from future unrest began to take shape. In addition, the granting of land with conditions provided a ready revenue for the King. Initially, Chichester had floated the idea of placing some British settlers amongst the Irish at key points within the province. This was seen as more cost-effective than maintaining a permanent garrison in Ulster. In effect, this would have resulted in merely a change of landlord from Irish to British, without widespread colonisation. The idea of a substantial plantation only took root after land became available with the Flight of the Earls in 1607 and the later confiscations in Coleraine, Donegal and Cavan.

But by now other men were indicating opinions on the form the scheme might ultimately take. The Attorney General of Ireland, Sir John Davies, voiced his concerns at restricting the settlement to a limited area and warned that the settlers would become overwhelmed 'as weeds overgrow the good corn' if they did not outnumber the Irish from the beginning. During the winter of 1608, the scheme was refined and an approved prospectus agreed with the King. 'A Projecte for the Devision and Plantacion of the Escheated Landes in 6 Severall Counties' was published in January 1609.

James saw the strategic, economic and religious logic for the creation of an Ulster settled with English and lowland Scots. For the first time, this troublesome province lay between the united twin polities of Scotland and England. By creating a British colony in Ulster, James immediately offset the huge expense of maintaining a standing army to overawe the restless population and in fact initiated circumstances whereby the Crown would receive an income from the escheated territories. Writing to Chichester in December 1612, with the plantation well under way, he summed up the grand vision

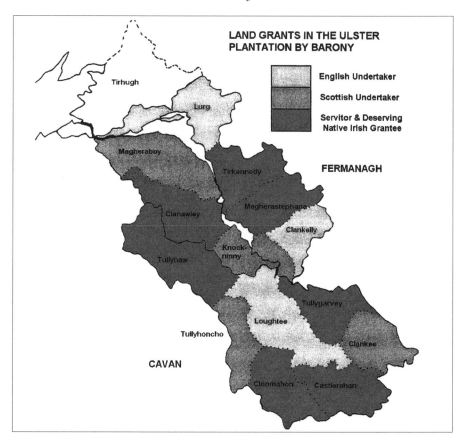

LAND GRANTS IN THE ULSTER
PLANTATION BY BARONY

English Undertaker

Scottish Undertaker

Servitor & Deserving
Native Irish Grantee

of his scheme, 'the settling of religion, the introducing civility, order and government amongst a barbarous and unsubdued people, to be acts of piety and glory and worthy always of a Christian prince to endeavour'.

In March 1609, the conditions under which the plantation lands would be granted were published. This document, entitled 'Collection of Such Orders and Conditions as are to be Observed by the Undertakers upon the Distribution and Plantation of the Escheated Lands in Ulster', laid out in some detail the arrangements deemed necessary to make the scheme work.

Lands were to be granted in one of three estate sizes called 'proportions'. The greatest proportion was to contain 2,000 English acres (800 hectares), the middle proportion was to contain 1,500 acres (600 hectares) and the least proportion to contain 1,000 acres (400 hectares). It was recognised that the land in each of these proportions may have to be scattered and the scheme allowed estates 'to contain such or so many parcels as shall make up'. In addition to the grant of arable land, each proportion was to be allowed 'such quantity of bog and wood as the country shall conveniently afford', thereby ensuring that the marginal land would be exploited as well.

The grants were to be offered to three classes of persons defined as undertakers, servitors and 'mere' (Latin: undiluted or pure) or native Irish. The undertaker class was to consist of English or lowland Scottish gentlemen who were only permitted to tenant their estates with fellow countrymen. The servitor class consisted of persons who had loyally served the Crown and they were able to take English, lowland Scots or 'mere' Irish as their tenants. Finally, deserving, loyal, native Irish were to be permitted to bid for proportions and tenant them with native Irish.

English and Scottish undertakers were assigned to particular baronies, termed 'precincts' within the conditions. Servitors and native Irish were to be assigned to the remaining precincts. It was not possible to lay claim to any particular proportion. Those interested in taking up the scheme were only able to indicate the county of their choice. The allocation of individual proportions in each county was to be done by lottery.

Articles relating to each of the three classes of grantee were then defined. The undertakers, who were to be the chief group, were to agree the following conditions for their grants:

1. Rent of land was to be at the rate of 6s 8d for sixty acres.
2. Rent on land would be waived for the first two (later increased to four) years to allow the estate to be built up.
3. Land was to be held 'in common socage' i.e. services would be owed by the tenant to his lord in relation to ploughing, hedging and manuring.
4. Estates were to be granted 'in fee farm' to them and their heirs.

Within two years (also increased to four) each undertaker was to erect a fortified dwelling along the following lines: each 2,000-acre estate was required to 'build thereupon a castle, with a strong court or bawne about it'; each 1,500-acre estate was required to 'build a stone or brick house thereupon with a strong court or bawne about it'; and the owner of a 1,000-acre estate was required to 'make thereupon a strong court or bawne at least'.

In addition to this, all undertakers were ordered to 'draw their tenants to build houses for themselves and their families near the principal castle, house or bawne for their mutual defence or strength'. This was to ensure that villages would become established and tenants were not thinly dispersed across the estate lands, making themselves vulnerable to attack. Tenants were also to be allowed free wood from the estate for a period of two (later four) years.

Each estate, depending on its size, was expected to have a specified number of armed men available as a kind of militia. The largest estates were expected to provide twenty-four men capable of carrying arms, the middle proportions to supply eighteen men, and the small proportions to supply twelve men. Each estate was to muster and review this militia twice a year. The Scots and English were expected to take the Oath of Supremacy, which renounced the spiritual supremacy of the Pope and thereby excluded Catholics. Furthermore, undertakers were forbidden to sell land back to the Irish.

It was expected that sufficient English and Scottish tenants would be resident in the first two years. Land was to be offered to the tenants in a number of ways to encourage them to remain. One third of the land on each estate was to be offered as fee farm, one third was to be offered in leases of up to forty years, with the remaining third in the possession of the undertaker. In order to ensure that the undertaker did not neglect his estate, it was also written in that he or his principal agent must be resident on the estate for the first five years. Finally, each undertaker had the power to create tenures, erect manors within the estate and to hold a Court Baron (a kind of petty sessions for land matters) twice a year.

Servitors were granted the same conditions pertaining to their estates as undertakers, with a few notable exceptions. They were permitted to recruit Irish tenants on their estates but were charged 10s per sixty acres, half as much again as the undertakers. The Irish tenants were further handicapped by being charged 13s 4d per sixty acres, twice the rent of the undertakers' holdings. In addition, they were forbidden to till the land in traditional fashion.

Chichester, the Englishman who had spent years in conflict with the islesmen in NE Ulster, was privately dismayed at the idea of the Scots being actively canvassed to take up the opportunities in the scheme. But his sovereign, James I, was also a Scotsman, and he was committed to the idea of Scots benefiting from such an enormous enterprise. Chichester was therefore obliged to attempt a damage-limitation exercise by ensuring that Scots and English would be intermingled, preventing the development of future powerful self-interest.

THE LAND GRANTS

County Fermanagh

In County Fermanagh, the available land was located in six 'precincts' that corresponded with existing barony divisions. These were the full baronies of Magheraboy, Clanawley, Knockninny, Lurg and Clankelly, and the half baronies of Coole and Tirkennedy. Magherastephana the seventh barony of Fermanagh, was already assigned to Conor Roe Maguire. The precincts of Lurg and Clankelly were assigned to English undertakers, Magheraboy and Knockninny were assigned to Scots, and Clanawley and Tirkennedy being set aside for servitors and native Irish.

Each 'precinct' contained a number of individual proportions totalling twenty-six for the county. These proportions, which were hereafter to represent the individual estates, were composed as follows:

Sixteen proportions of 1,000 acres
Six proportions of 1,500 acres
Four proportions of 2,000 acres

In addition to these grants were specific donations. The Church received 3,147 acres as 'Termon' land for the bishop (i.e. land for the personal use of the bishop). Another 1,228 acres were given to Trinity College Dublin and a further 625 acres for the creation of a free school for the education of the planters' children (later called Royal School Portora). Finally, a total of 937 acres were set aside for the establishment of three new towns. These were to be situated at Lisgool, Castleskagh and midway between Lisgool and Ballyshannon.

County Cavan

In Cavan, the county was divided into seven 'precincts' that comprised a total of thirty-two proportions that made up the following estates:

Twenty proportions of 1,000 acres

Seven proportions of 1,500 acres

Five proportions of 2,000 acres.

These proportions were spread across seven precincts or baronies. One of these, Loughtee, was assigned to English undertakers, whilst two, Tullyhoncho and Clankee were assigned to Scots. The remaining four precincts, Tullyhaw, Castlerahin, Clonmahon and Tulloghgarvy were assigned to servitors and native Irish. Again, a number of additional grants were awarded to institutions. The Church received 3,500 acres whilst 750 acres were set aside for the creation of three new towns to be located at Belturbet, Cavan and Virginia. Another 144 acres was for the planned military garrisons at Clough Oughter and Cavan castles, and a further 346 acres for a free school.

DISTRIBUTION OF THE GRANTS IN FERMANAGH AND CAVAN

County Fermanagh

	Barony	Allocation
English Undertakers	Clankelly	5,000 acres
	Lurg & Coolemakernan	9,000 acres
Total		14,000 acres

	Barony	Allocation
Scots Undertakers	Knockninny	9,000 acres
	Magheraboy	9,000 acres
Total		18,000 acres

	Barony	Allocation
Servitors	Clanawley	2,246 acres
	Coole & Tirkennedy	4,848 acres
Total		7,094 acres

	Barony	Allocation
Native Irish	Clanawley	6,408 acres
	Coole & Tirkennedy	4,240 acres
Total		10,648 acres

(Excludes Magherastephana grants to Maguire)

Corporate towns: 937 acres

Trinity College: 1,228 acres

Free school: 625 acres

Church: 3,147 acres

Total: 5,937 acres

County Cavan

	Barony	Allocation
English Undertakers	Loughtee	11,760 acres

	Barony	Allocation
Scots Undertakers	Tullyhoncho	6,000 acres
	Clankee	5,000 acres
Total		11,000 acres

	Barony	Allocation
Servitors	Tullyhaw	5,600 acres
	Clonmahone	4,500 acres
	Castlerahan	3,900 acres
	Tullygarvey	4,250 acres
Total		18,250 acres

	Barony	Allocation
Native Irish	Tullygarvey	6,012 acres
	Tullyhaw	5,050 acres
	Clonmahone	3,737 acres
	Castlerahan	6,550 acres
Total		21,349 acres

Corporate towns: 750 acres
Church: 3,500 acres
Cavan & Clough Oughter castles: 144 acres
Free school: 346 acres
Monastery lands: 500 acres
Incumbent glebes: 2,500 acres
Total: 7,740 acres

Summary

Scots Undertakers: 29,000 acres (23 per cent)
English Undertakers: 25,760 acres (21 per cent)
Servitors: 25,344 acres (20 per cent)
Native Irish: 31,997 acres (25 per cent)
Others: 13,677 acres (11 per cent)
Total: 125,778 acres

2

A TYPICAL PLANTATION CASTLE

BACKGROUND

At this point it is worth pausing to look at the castles of the undertakers in greater detail. Despite the inference of the above title, there was no typical Plantation castle plan to which undertakers could refer for guidance, as they attempted to fulfil the conditions by which they had received their grant of land. The successful British patentees came from two very different jurisdictions, namely Scotland and England, and it is no surprise, therefore, that they brought knowledge and experience peculiar to their respective homelands, which they then applied to the articles of their plantation grant. The native Irish grantees too had their own distinctive building traditions and the resulting plantation architecture was therefore a hybrid of styles that forms a distinct building period in this part of Ireland.

In building their homes, the undertakers were guided by the terms of the original articles of plantation. However, the articles did not specify any particular size or style of castle to be erected and it was left to the individual undertaker to decide what they might erect. As a result, these castles or defended homes varied greatly in their designs.

Every undertaker was expected to provide a defensible structure. As previously stated, the obligation depended on the size of the grant. Each grantee of a 2,000-acre estate was expected to 'build thereupon a castle, with a strong court or bawn about it'. The owner of a 1,500-acre estate was to 'build a stone or brick house thereupon with a strong court or bawne about it'. Finally, the 1,000-acre estate was to 'make thereupon a strong court or bawn about it'.

The word 'bawn', which is used in the articles as a particular condition of a grant, is from the Gaelic 'bódhśn', a composite word from 'bó' (meaning oxen) and 'dśn' (meaning fort). The Oxford English Dictionary defines it as 'a fortified enclosure, enceinte or circumvallation, the fortified court or outwork of a castle'. The term was commonly used by documentary sources from at least the mid-sixteenth century and its meaning has not changed. Obviously, then, grantees were expected to be occupying a land where some defence from rural unrest was a necessity.

The conditions defining the erection of a fortified home were imprecise in practice and allowed the patentee the freedom to more or less erect a structure of their choice. Brick construction was rare, but stone was usually available in large quantities within easy reach of planned castle sites. By the previous definition, the bawn did not have to be constructed of stone or brick, and in many estates granted to the native Irish was made of sods. Finally, it will be seen that the bawn of a 1,000-acre estate could contain a timber house. In practice, then, the type of castle that was created varied from undertaker to undertaker.

CASTLE-BUILDING TRADITION IN ENGLAND, IRELAND AND SCOTLAND

Creating a comfortable home that could be defended in times of trouble was a way of life familiar to the Scots and Irish patentees who were charged with carrying out their plantation obligations. By contrast, the English were now, by and large, without a tradition of building defended homes, as their country had not been a battleground since the Wars of the Roses in the later fifteenth century. The migration of many English gentlemen and their retainers to Ulster at the beginning of the seventeenth century would thus require a revision of usual building practices in order to fulfil the strict requirements of the plantation conditions.

However, in Ireland and Scotland the tradition of fortified domestic building was long established and would continue well into the seventeenth century. In Scotland, tower houses had been built since at least the 1380s, originally consisting of a simple rectangular-plan structure with accommodation arranged vertically. The ground floor was often stone vaulted with small windows to prevent unauthorised entry and to act as a cool storeroom. In addition, the vault protected the rooms above should the main entrance be forced and a fire started in the store. Above on the first floor was the main living space with a fireplace and larger windows. Private chambers were located in the upper floors. Later tower house examples incorporated turrets and returns, which allowed the occupier lateral movement between rooms without reducing the essential defensive qualities of the tower house design.

In Ireland, the tower house building tradition began around the mid-fifteenth century and continued for the next 200 years, with the greatest number being constructed in the sixteenth century. Here, the simple rectangle, similar to the earlier Scottish models, prevailed throughout the period, although occasionally more complex tower house designs were also built.

In England, there was no corresponding tower-house building period except along the northern marches between Scotland and the northern counties of Cumberland and Northumberland. Here, the unsettled nature of border life prompted a response that was similar in intent, if different in detail, from the Celtic towers. The 'bastle' and 'barmkin' were variations of the defended mansion idea which lasted into the early seventeenth century until the kingdoms were securely united under a single monarch. A 'bastle' was a strongly built stone farmhouse where the small landowner lived above a barrel-vaulted ground floor used to securely stable his livestock from a raid by local cattle-rustlers known as the 'Border reivers'. The 'barmkin' was a defensive stone enclosure built around a tower house, which again provided a safe pound for livestock in the event of these raids.

Elsewhere in England, the more settled nature of the growing power of the Tudor monarchs ensured that the need for castles became unnecessary. The centralisation of power begun by Henry Tudor after his victory on Bosworth Field in 1485 was continued throughout the sixteenth century. Coupled with this was the growing importance of military ordnance, which could easily batter down the finest of masonry. The result was the development of the undefended or only lightly defended country houses of the later Tudor and early Jacobean period, with the emphasis on living space. Numerous gables, large window lights and bay windows were the common features of house building at this time.

The English, Scots and Irish were thus to approach the matter of security versus comfort from opposite perspectives. The English were to adapt their undefended home tradition by adding security features to their domestic arrangements. By contrast, the Scots and Irish would try and make their castles in Ulster as modern and comfortable as befitted any Jacobean gentleman.

THE 'TYPICAL' CASTLE OR FORTIFIED MANOR HOUSE

Despite the earlier comments regarding the vagueness of the terms surrounding the Plantation obligations, Pynnar's survey results for Fermanagh and Cavan in 1619 indicate a pattern of castle building, which has some common features. There were few restrictions on the undertakers with regard to the shape and size of their building, but in general they erected a home that acknowledged something of their provenance. All patentees were obliged to build at least a strong bawn around their homes. In practice, this often resulted in a stone enclosure measuring around 18m by 18m (60 by 60ft) being erected, with the gated entrance, 2m (6ft) wide, in the centre of one of these walls. Several of these gated entrances had a date stone placed above the doorway. The best preserved one today is at Castle Archdale, though it is recorded that the coat of arms of the Bishop of Clogher was carved above the doorway of Portora. There are two small date stones of uncertain purpose above a house at Gortindarragh, near Rosslea, which may well prove to be one of the oldest inhabited houses in the county.

The bawn walls were around 4m (13ft) high, sufficient to deter any intruders who came without a ladder. In the event of a disturbance, this space provided the planter with a reasonably sized, protected enclosure. Sometimes the bawn walls were thick enough to support a continuous wall walk for sentry duty. However, other bawn walls were much narrower and a wooden platform was built against the inside to provide the necessary walkway. In both cases, the walls were crenulated to provide protection to the defender in the event of any assault. However, in many instances there was no wall walk as it was deemed unnecessary. As stated, the bawn entrance was usually in the centre of one of the bawn walls. Passing through the gateway, one normally entered a yard area, which held the various functions of a working demesne farm and could be used in an emergency as a secure pound for precious livestock.

Many bawns appear to have been built without any additional protection in the form of corner turrets called 'flankers' (such as Corratrasna). Pynnar indicates that almost half the castles he visited were without flankers. Examples of these survive, from the grand, Y-shaped design of Tullykelter, to the simple, loopholed residence of a lesser tenant as seen at Doohat.

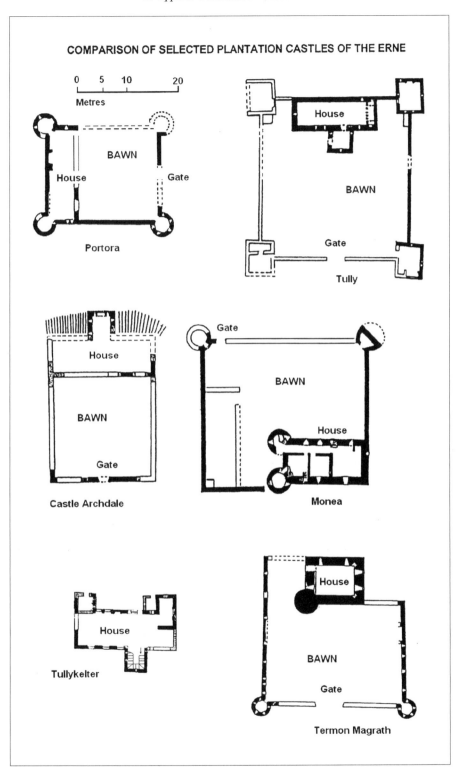

COMPARISON OF SELECTED PLANTATION CASTLES OF THE ERNE

However, the preferred bawn design was to construct two (Termon Magrath), or less commonly three or four projecting flankers at the corners of the bawn walls (Portora, Castle Archdale). Entered at ground level from inside the bawn, flankers could be either square or circular in plan, but their purpose was always the same, to provide defensive fire, via loopholes, along the base of vulnerable outer bawn walls. Any would-be attacker who had reached the base of the bawn walls and was preparing to scale them would be an easy target for a defender firing out at them from one of the flanker loopholes. Indeed, the defence of the bawn was in many cases to be carried out by defenders occupying the flankers alone rather than defending behind the parapet wall of the bawn.

Some flankers were large enough to provide additional accommodation for members of an undertaker's household (Tully). These flankers were then provided with a fireplace, flue and a window, opening towards the bawn interior.

In the case of those bawns with two flankers, the most economic and efficient use was to place them at diametrically opposite corners, forming a 'Z-plan' arrangement. This meant that all four external faces of the bawn could still be adequately defended by flanking fire. However, this arrangement was liable to interfere with the manor house sited at the rear of the bawn, and on occasion the two flankers are located along the front wall of the bawn to at least provide full protection to the vulnerable entrance, such as at Aghalane and Monea.

In some cases all four corners of the bawn were provided with flankers. At Tully, these flankers are detached from the manor house, which takes up only part of the length of the rear wall. However, at Portora the manor house stretched along the entire rear bawn wall and so the two rear flankers are incorporated into the main house plan, providing extra accommodation in addition to their defensive role.

Bawns with three flankers are more rare but can still be viewed (Castle Archdale). In this design, two flankers were located at the front of the bawn to provide protection to the main entrance and defensive fire along three walls. A flanker that projected rearwards from the line of the manor house protected the vulnerable rear bawn wall. In addition to being provided with loopholes for defence, this projection allowed the occupant space to incorporate a grand staircase accessing the upper storeys of the house.

The design of the loophole in the flanker wall was a matter of personal taste. Loopholes were created by making a large opening in the inner face of the wall and then narrowing (known as splaying) to a small aperture on the outside. This allowed the defender to lean into the wall and take aim without presenting himself to danger from retaliatory fire. Sometimes the external shape was a small circle (Monea) but teardrop-shaped loops were common as well (Castle Archdale, Aghalane)

The main living accommodation, regularly referred to as the castle, was usually located against the rear bawn wall and often running its full length. This was a stone-built manor house for the planter and his family. This house, with a centrally located doorway (there is no rear door), was entered from the enclosed bawn and was usually of two or three (occasionally four) storeys with large windows opening into the bawn. By contrast, only small apertures or loopholes were allowed on walls that faced outside the bawn. The Irish commonly continued the tradition of the tower house for their main residence, as occurred at Termon Magrath. For added protection, the castle roof was covered with slate or tile rather than thatch or shingle.

In other areas of the plantation, houses were sited in a detached position in the middle of the bawn. This allowed freedom from the restriction of window size and the owner could erect a residence to resemble the manor houses of the settled parts of England. However, this arrangement often compromised the efficient use of the limited space within the bawn. These detached houses are therefore rare and there are no extant examples known in the Erne valley.

The building of the castle or manor house often indicates the provenance of the builder. The Scots tended to build a stone vault on the ground floor, much in the style of the tower houses. This allowed a store/kitchen on the ground floor, with only small windows required. The main living accommodation was on the first floor, with sleeping accommodation provided in the attic rooms above. All rooms would have been provided with a fireplace. Monea, Tully and Castle Balfour were originally built with a stone-vaulted ground floor.

Irish, Scots and English were all prepared to separate the kitchen from the living quarters. In many castles, a large fireplace both heated and served as the place where food was cooked. However, in some castles, a separate oven was constructed into the thickness of a gable wall, thus separating the two domestic functions. Oven design was very much at the discretion of the owner. At Castlemervyn the oven was brick lined and semicircular in plan, while that at Termon Magrath was square and built of stone into the thick corner wall of the basement.

Once again with defence in mind, the Scots tended to prefer the tradition of a stone spiral staircase contained within a corbelled turret, as seen at Castle Balfour, or contained within the thickness of an exterior wall as at Monea. The English preferred an open wooden staircase design that was more contemporary and grander than the restricted spiral arrangement. Examples of this occur at Castle Archdale and possibly Portora. But a Scottish planter could display a compromise and construct both, as seen at Tully. Some builders constructed only one stair, while others preferred a second, which could be used by house staff. Finally, as already mentioned, stairs were sometimes located in a square projection at the rear of a castle that could double as a flanker with the addition of loopholes (Castle Archdale, Tullykelter). Internal subdivision of the floor area was often timber rather than stone, which allowed for thinner walls and thus more space.

Diagnostic building features of the English and Scots have already been alluded to. It only remains to point out some superficial design characteristics peculiar to both groups. English patentees were familiar with the current Jacobean rage for high-gabled elevations and bay windows, and incorporated these into their plantation designs. The Scots castles typically incorporate crow-stepped gables, corbelled turrets and spiral stairs.

But such features were not necessarily confined to one ethnic group. Despite being the home of a Scottish undertaker and displaying many diagnostic Scottish features, Castle Balfour incorporates a bay window in the ground-floor plan. At Enniskillen, Cole's 'Watergate' tower incorporates a pair of perfect, corbelled Scottish bartizans. Likewise, at Tully castle, the corbelled-out spiral stair in a re-entrant angle at first-floor level has been given a smooth finish and may indicate that Irish tradesmen carried out this work. Thus, undertakers from all traditions were aware of contemporary fashion and were prepared to incorporate features that took their fancy.

Finally, it is worth examining the various castles to determine if there was an expected building size proportionate to the size of the estate. By examining the remaining ruins, it would appear that the new landlords generally expected to live in a home of 470 to 650 sq m (5,000 to 7,000 sq ft) as would befit their new-found status (Termon, Archdale, Monea). Additionally, however, the original size of the estate proportion does not seem to be significant in determining the size of the castle built as its manor house. For example, even a large proportion like Tully could have a much smaller dwelling of 400 sq m (4,200 sq ft), which was still considered suitable for the needs of the lord. Perhaps we need to be cautious here, as the flankers at Tully may have provided the additional accommodation space for house staff, thereby reducing the dimensions of the main dwelling.

GROWTH OF THE ULSTER PLANTATION

The vast majority of the estates were granted to their respective new owners during the summer months of 1610, with a small number receiving their lands during 1611 and 1612. Sir John Dunbar did not take possession of his small proportion of Drumcrow, near Derrygonnelly, until January 1615, but by then most of the other grantees had been in possession for quite some time.

However, despite the favourable terms by which the land was granted to the various undertakers, it soon became obvious that many assignees were not carrying out the various conditions that accompanied their grant. Even as early as the autumn of 1610, Chichester was concerned that the scheme of plantation would not be performed in the manner laid down. Writing to the Earl of Northampton in October he disclosed his misgivings with regard to those who had been assigned the grants:

> ...considering the greatness and difficulty of the work, and the conditions and qualities of the parties that have undertaken ... these are not the men who must perform the business, for to displant the natives, who are a warlike people, out of the greatest part of six whole counties, is not a work for private men who seek a present profit.

James continued to take a special interest in the scheme and was to insist that the undertakers carry out the full conditions of their grants. During his reign (1603-25) he established six Commissions of Enquiry to report on progress. By contrast, his son Charles I (1625-49) never carried out any surveys, though he was frequently interested in raising revenue by penalising individual defaulters.

As James became increasingly frustrated, the extent and completion time of each inquiry grew. Each was carried out by a respected government official of the day, as follows:

Sir George Carew, 1611, 21 days
Sir Josias Bodley, 1613, 79 days
Sir Josias Bodley, 1614, no trace left of survey
Sir Josiah Bodley, 1616, no trace left of survey
Nicholas Pynnar, 1618/19, 119 days
Perrott & Annesley, 1622, Cavan & Fermanagh only, 9 weeks

The survival of several of these reports does allow us a unique insight into the development of a major royal scheme of plantation as seen through the eyes of early Jacobean bureaucrats.

The first Commissioner, Sir George Carew, a former soldier and government official with thirty years experience in Ireland, visited Ulster in the autumn of 1611, barely a year after the scheme had begun. His report relied on the information supplied by county sheriffs and governors and his tight schedule did not permit him to visit Cavan. Nonetheless, his report confirmed the patchy nature of development; some planters were well on their way to completing their conditions and others had not even appointed a land agent. The arrival late in the year of many of the undertakers delayed the planting of crops and many suffered a hungry winter. However, given the tight timescale for the completion of the grant conditions, it showed that at least the scheme was underway.

As a result of Carew's report, the undertakers were spurred into action, and with more favourable economic conditions in Ulster, the scheme advanced during 1612 and 1613. James instructed Sir Josias Bodley, recently appointed director general of fortifications in Ireland, to carry out a further review that summer. This time Bodley visited the individual proportions to observe progress for himself. Again, progress was reported as mixed, with improvement overall since Carew's survey.

From the time of the 1613 survey, the plantation experienced a period of sustained growth. By now, the first few difficult years were past and land was beginning to show some profit from agriculture. Immigration, especially from Scotland, increased. James was still keen to see the scheme succeed and he now threatened forfeiture of grants from those undertakers who had not fulfilled their conditions, 'Seize into our hands, the lands of any man, whatsoever, without respect of personnes, whether he be a British Undertaker, Servitor or Native that shalbe found defective in performing any of the articles of the Plantation.'

Bodley was instructed to carry out two more Commissions of Enquiry, but the results of these have been lost. In 1618, Captain Nicholas Pynnar, a servitor in Ulster since 1600, was instructed by the Lord Deputy to make yet another report. His mandate was to confirm that:

1. Castles and bawns had been constructed in accordance with the conditions of the grant.
2. Requisite numbers of British families had been established on the estates.
3. Suitable tenancies had been offered to these families.
4. Sufficient arms were available within the estate.
5. Tenants had been established in villages for mutual defence and safety.
6. Irish tenants were tilling the land in the English manner.

Pynnar carried out his inspection of the entire escheated counties in a four-month period between 1 December 1618 and 28 March 1619, allowing time for greater detail. His report describes the buildings constructed, lists numbers for the various tenants groups, gives totals of families and armed men, and occasionally indicates how many had taken the Oath of Supremacy. In summary, he acknowledged the construction of 108 castles and bawns and the settlement of 36,000 settlers, creating a potential muster of 8,000 men capable of bearing arms.

In Cavan and Fermanagh it was noted that many of the original patentees had sold their estates and new men had come forward to take their place. Often the new owners were neighbouring landlords who had developed their own estate and saw the potential for economies of scale in enlargement. Pynnar's survey also showed that whereas the English undertakers had carried out more of the building conditions, the Scots were better at encouraging tenants onto their estates.

By 1619, Scottish immigration had peaked and the plantation experienced a period of decline that lasted for the whole of the following decade. New plantation schemes were underway in Longford and King's Counties in 1619 and in Leitrim in 1622, though on a much smaller scale than in Ulster, thus diluting the pool of available resources. Many undertakers also blamed the threat of forfeiture for the decline and so they petitioned the King for new patents, relaxing some of the conditions in return for more rent. In addition, they requested that Irish conforming to English religion and custom be allowed to reside on the estates. While the government examined the proposals, James ordered another survey to be carried out.

This, the sixth survey of its kind, involved twenty-one persons of which seven were to work in the field, obtaining the necessary information. These seven were split into teams of two or three men to cover specific counties. Cavan and Fermanagh were to be surveyed by Sir Francis Annesley and Sir James Perrott. Annesley was one of the secretaries of state in Ireland and Perrott had been an English parliamentarian. This time the commissioners were charged with not only accruing facts but passing judgement on individuals and making recommendations. Perrott and Annesley toured the two counties and took some care to cross-reference statements regarding families and tenants. Their report confirmed that the plantation population had stagnated since Pynnar's previous report. They also noted that eight of the original Scottish estates in these two counties had now passed to Englishmen.

Absentee landlords were also a problem. Tenants of Sir Archibald Acheson in Cavan and Sir John Hume in Fermanagh, both often absent from their estates, complained that the Irish were given leases in preference to British settlers. Furthermore, leases were often short and discouraged tenants from improving the land.

The final report was completed and forwarded to the King for scrutiny. It was scathing in its condemnation of undertakers who had failed to carry out the conditions of their grants. But the commissioners did recommend the undertakers' proposals with regard to conforming Irish tenants and forfeiture of estates. Despite this, the King appeared more aggrieved by the defaulters than by the report of positive progress. He lamented, 'wee see, how muche our goodnesse and bounty, hath bene abused; our Intentions, and directions eluded; and many things doone that must be reformed'.

A second undertakers' petition was presented and in February 1625, the King acceded to the idea of Irish tenants and removal of the forfeiture clause. James died later that year and it was not until 1629, during the reign of his son Charles I, that new patents were issued.

A muster roll of tenants capable of bearing arms survives from 1630 and it gives an insight into the provenance of the first British settlers in Ulster. In Fermanagh, the most frequently occurring surnames are Johnston, Armstrong, Elliott and Beatty, all Scottish names commonly found near the English border. Names common to the SW of Scotland, Montgomery, Cunningham and Crawford, appear less frequently.

By the early 1630s, conditions were again favourable for the influx of new settlers. From the documentary evidence available, many of the new arrivals were Scots arriving from west-coast ports such as Irvine and Portpatrick. The causes of this new wave of immigration to Ulster are complex. Economic conditions in Scotland had deteriorated through high rents and poor harvests. By the 1620s and 30s, emigration to Nova Scotia was also an option, but the more established circumstances pertaining to the Ulster Plantation must have seemed more favourable to restless tenants. Others have claimed that the deteriorating religious situation in Scotland, where Archbishop Laud was endeavouring to impose episcopacy, caused many to leave. It must be pointed out, though, that this policy applied equally to all three kingdoms and therefore no great advantage would have accrued by a move to Ulster.

Whatever the reasons, the population within the plantation counties continued to rise throughout the decade. There was now genuine competition for leases and landlords were increasingly able to grant terms to British rather than Irish tenants. After thirty years, the plantation had taken root in the Ulster countryside and its undoubted success ensured that a new political entity, the British Protestant settler, had been created in Ireland. From this point on in Irish history, the interests of these peoples could not be dismissed in the wider political issues of Ireland and beyond.

THREE DECADES OF PLANTATION

By 1640, Ireland had experienced three decades of relative peace and the Ulster Plantation was well on its way to transforming the landscape into a modern and thriving market economy. Thousands of new colonists had arrived from Britain, bringing with them new skills in farming and mining, and were building new villages, castles, churches, mills and the like. But already storm clouds were gathering which would shatter the peace and eventually plunge Ireland into twelve years of political and ethnic turmoil. The role of the small castles and fortified homes of the Erne basin, established by the conditions of the plantation grants, would prove critical to the survival of the colonists scattered across the countryside in the opening phases of the civil disorder about to unfold.

FATE OF THE CASTLES IN THE SEVENTEENTH CENTURY

It is not the aim of this introduction to cover in detail the remainder of the seventeenth-century history of this part of Ulster. That task has been carried out many times before and to a greater depth than could be achieved by this author. However, the fate of the plantation castles was intimately wrapped up in events later in the century and their ultimate demise stems from this period of history. It is therefore necessary to briefly outline the main political events affecting Ulster and Ireland generally and then to show the effect these events had on the local scene in the Erne basin.

Without doubt, the two major events of the century are the 1641 rebellion and the 'Glorious Revolution' of 1689. No understanding of Ulster's present condition can be made without returning to these major historical episodes. As events unfolded, the role played by the plantation castles established earlier in the century proved crucial to the survival of the British influence in Ulster.

CAUSES OF THE 1641 REBELLION

The causes of the rebellion have been argued by historians for decades and in many ways the debate continues. What is now clearer is that the plantation itself, though still much resented after thirty years, was not itself the immediate cause. Events on the larger British and European stages were more important in the outbreak of the rising.

By the late 1630s, the three kingdoms of England, Scotland and Ireland, ruled over by Charles I, were each opposing the King's will in different ways. Despite a chronic shortage of revenue to fund his foreign policy schemes, Charles had consistently refused to call an English parliament to raise tax, as this would have exposed him to its increasingly Puritan membership demanding radical constitutional reforms in return for revenue. Internally, his demands for Episcopal conformity were also causing difficulties with his Scots and Ulster subjects. In 1637, the King had attempted to overrule Scottish opposition by introducing a prayer book in Scotland similar to that of the Church of England, an act that had provoked riots in Edinburgh. In February 1639, the Scots countered by drafting and signing a national covenant that rejected any move from Presbyterianism, thus defying the King's wishes.

Across the North Channel in Ulster, there was considerable sympathy amongst the settler community for the actions of the Scots. Therefore, in January 1639, as a measure to overawe the Ulster Scots and frighten the covenanters in Scotland, the Irish Lord Deputy Thomas Wentworth devised an oath whereby Ulster Scots would be compelled to disassociate themselves from the treasonable activities of their fellow countrymen in Scotland. Many signed what was dubbed the 'black oath' under duress, but others refused and fled to join the ranks of the covenanters in Scotland. However, on 18 June 1639, Charles signed the 'Peace of Berwick' with the Scottish covenanters. By this agreement, both armies were disbanded and Charles agreed to summon a general assembly and parliament in Scotland. No longer relevant, administration of the black oath in Ulster collapsed.

Few expected the peace treaty to last for long. Each side spent the next few months consolidating their forces. In 1640, Thomas Wentworth raised a mainly Catholic Irish army of 9,000 men, paid for by the Irish parliament, and marched it north into Ulster. He planned to use it first to intimidate the Ulster settlers and then pass across the North Channel to assist the King's planned invasion of Scotland. But in August, before Charles had time to act, an army raised by the Scots covenanters captured Newcastle and Wentworth's army remained across the North Channel in Ulster. For a second time the King was forced to negotiate with the Scots on unfavourable terms, a cessation being signed at Ripon on 17 October 1640.

The Irish watched nervously as Wentworth's army was disbanded in May 1641 and noted the success of the Scots in forcing redress from the King by their occupation of Newcastle. They watched as Protestant discontent with Wentworth's policies, across all the three kingdoms, now combined to bring about his overthrow and execution in the same month. In the interim, two Lord Justices, Sir William Borlase and Sir John Parsons, replaced him in Dublin.

Never viewed as an ally of the Catholic interest in Ireland, Wentworth's passing was not mourned there. During his time in Ireland, Wentworth had continued to examine the ancient land claims of the native Irish and Old English lords and had prepared for further plantations in Connacht. But would his demise and the corresponding weakening of the Crown's power in Ireland assist or hinder Catholic interests? Irish Catholics now had a choice. They could either wait to see how events unfolded across the three kingdoms or they could act directly now, as the Scots had done, to maximise their own position and await an opportunity to negotiate a favourable outcome with regard to matters of faith and inheritance. In the event, they chose the latter course and changed the politics of Ireland forever.

PLANNING FOR A REBELLION

In May 1641, native Irish leaders met in Dublin and proposed to initiate a plan of rebellion that would paralyse the government of Ireland and force the King to consider their long-standing grievances. The plan was simple; an armed faction would overwhelm the Dublin garrison and secure its vast arsenal of gunpowder and weapons. Simultaneously, across Ulster, Irish chieftains would seize the local strong points and castles of the settlers by force and overthrow the local administration. Chief amongst the conspirators were Sir Phelim O'Neill of Tyrone, Lord Conor Maguire of Enniskillen (only twenty-six years old) and Hugh Óg MacMahon of Armagh. They settled on October 1641 as the date for the rising.

However, the plan to capture Dublin castle and secure its arsenal was betrayed to the Lord Justices only hours before it was due to commence. The informant was an Owen O'Connolly, servant to Sir John Clotworthy and the foster brother of one of the chief conspirators, Hugh Óg MacMahon. Curiously, MacMahon had taken O'Connolly into his confidence even though he was married to an Englishwoman and had become a Presbyterian, perhaps indicating that the motives for the rebellion were in fact more ethnically than religiously inspired. The citizens of Dublin were thus hastily mustered in a show of strength deterring the rebels from attacking the city. By morning, MacMahon and Maguire were captured and a vital target in the planned uprising had been stymied.

Unaware of the disaster in Dublin, native leaders in Ulster continued to carry out the plan of seizure. Led by Sir Phelim O'Neill, hoping to emulate the success of the Scots the previous year, the rebels prepared to take possession of most of the province in a lightning coup.

FROM THE OUTBREAK OF THE REBELLION
TO THE 1643 CESSATION

On Saturday 23 October 1641, the colonists throughout Ulster suddenly found themselves the victims of a province-wide coup, which overwhelmed the established order and threatened to destroy the very fabric of the thirty-year-old plantation. The traditional view of the outbreak is best summed up by the following contemporary extract:

The suddennesse of our surprisall, and the nature of it, was so unexpected that the inhabitants could scarcely believe themselves prisoners, though in their chaines, and the Irish servant which overnight was undressing his master in duty, the next morning was stripping master and mistris with a too officious tyranny.

Here in the twinkling of an eye, the corporations, townes and villages proclaimed their scituations farre off by their fire and smoak; here you might see hundreds of men, women, children, of all conditions and estates that have lived in most plentifull and secure habitations, exposed to the rocke for shelter, to the heavens for cloathing, so that many hundreds in a few dayes starved upon the mountaines...

These words, written in 1642 by Colonel Audley Mervyn of Trillick castle, resident just across the Fermanagh border in south Tyrone, sum up the suddenness of the coup engineered by the rebels on that fateful Harvest Saturday. In an instant, all of Deputy Chichester's careful plans, conceived to thwart just the kind of unrest that now spilled out across Ulster, were almost completely swept away. Mervyn's shock at the ease with which the rebels had overthrown the plantation was all the more bitter when he considered that his sister Deborah of Crevenish castle in Fermanagh had married Rory Maguire, chief architect of the local uprising in Fermanagh. Mervyn had reason to see this as a gross betrayal of the trust bestowed by his settler neighbours on Maguire, who was accepted as part of their society.

However, it is clear that the Dublin authorities were already well aware of a planned rebellion but were unable to confirm the actual date for which it was planned. Captain William Cole had written from Enniskillen to the Lord Justices on 11 October, warning them that he had received reports from two Irish informants of suspicious movements by the Gaelic chieftains, notably Lord Conor Maguire. Three others, named as Tirlagh Óge McHugh, Cuconnaght MacShane Maguire and Oghie O'Hosey, had been appointed as captains, supposedly to raise troops for transfer to Spain, but Cole describes them as 'these three men so named to be captains are broken men in their estates and fortunes'.

Clearly Cole smelled a rat and was not going to be caught unprepared. The information, though worrying for government, was too vague to warrant action, and he was instructed to increase his surveillance. By Thursday 21 October, he had precise information regarding the commencement of the rebellion and sent this to the Lord Justices. His letter of warning to Dublin was intercepted at Lough Ramor, but other letters written to nearby lords were received and allowed time for defensive preparations to be carried out. Indeed, the outraged Mervyn had also been informed of the intention of Catholics to rebel by none other than his brother-in-law Rory Maguire, who had requested that Mervyn represent their position in London to King Charles. Mervyn had declined the request but used the information to warn his neighbours and despatch his family safely to Londonderry.

That said, it is clear that the scale and extent of the rebellion on 23 October 1641 caught the British off balance. All across the Erne valley, as across most parts of Ulster and beyond, the planters were surprised in their homes by bands of insurgents who seized their goods and livestock, robbed and stripped their owners and ordered them to leave their property or face the awful consequences. Despite assurances given by the leaders of the rebellion that persons would not be harmed, as law and order suddenly broke down, it proved impossible to guarantee a cool head at every eviction or robbery and inevitably atrocities were committed. By sundown on 23 October, countless assaults, robberies, evictions, murders and even massacres had already been carried out. From the following January, depositions of these events were taken from the survivors. Today in Trinity College Dublin, there are deposited thirty-two volumes that contain these sworn statements from the victims. And they make grim reading.

THE DEPOSITIONS

Arthur Champion, sub-sheriff of Monaghan, was attacked and killed at the gate of his castle at Shannock, near Rosslea, by a band of rebels numbering over 100. This band also killed a further six persons, all men, and reportedly killed a further twenty-four Englishmen who were Champion's tenants. They then forced their way into the castle and burned it.

Likewise, Anne Blennerhassett of Castle Hassett (later Castle Caldwell) near Belleek, testified that her husband and family had been forcibly deprived of their estates worth £1,850 and imprisoned for seven weeks at Rory Maguire's house. Her husband was taken to Ballyshannon castle where he was later shot, and she spent a further eighteen months in captivity before she and her children were released to make their way to Dublin by ship.

Both of these examples involved the targeting of important local figures in the civic governance of the province, and their quick removal would have created the necessary power vacuum required for the success of the rebellion. But the attacks did not stop there and with the breakdown of law and order the rebellion became widespread, as the rebels soon began to target all settlers.

Ellen Adams of Waterdrum, near Lisnaskea, deposed that on 24 October her husband was relieved of his cattle, corn and goods to the value of £200. Later that night, the rebels, led by Rory and Donough Maguire, returned and murdered her husband Thomas Adams, as well as John Adams, Joseph and William Berry and Sarah Brent, who was pregnant. Sarah Brent's death was particularly brutal; she was first stripped naked, 'and then running a skean [a dagger] into her body ripping her up'. Ellen Adams and her daughter were also brutally attacked and mutilated but survived the ordeal.

At Callowhill, on the opposite shore of Upper Lough Erne, Charles Shorter testified that he had been robbed of goods worth £103 and that 'the said rebels stripped this deponent, his wife, and three small children of all their clothes; and one of his daughters, when he was flying for his life, was left behind, who was afterwards, he credibly believed, murdered'.

In County Cavan, James Hickman, a yeoman of Tinakeertagh, was robbed of lands and goods worth £43 and removed from his home, which was then occupied by the rebels who went on to strip his wife and father-in-law. Thomas Loisanie of Markane deposed that he had been robbed and stripped by local Irish. Three days later, as Thomas, his father Charles and three other English settlers were heading for Dublin, they were attacked by a large group of local Irish rebels 'who then and there murdered them most woefully with swords and skeans, calling them "English dogs!" and telling them that they should go no further to carry news to England. And this deponent hath his arms almost cut asunder by them'.

Until the rebellion broke out, relations between the Scots and native Irish were believed to be good. Colonel Mervyn later reported to the House of Commons that:

> ...in the infancy of the Rebellion the rebels made open proclamations, upon pain of death, that no Scotchman should be stirred in body, goods or lands, and that they should to this purpose write over the lyntels of their doors, that they were Scotchmen, and so destruction might pass over their families...

Mervyn does not name his sources and the reference is clearly biblical and must be treated with caution. However, it does encapsulate the climate of fear and rumour that must have gripped those settler communities during that first uncertain winter.

THE FIRST WINTER

Nonetheless the Ulster rebels led by Sir Phelim O'Neill were, at the outset, highly successful. On the first day, 23 October, they captured most of counties Tyrone, Armagh and Monaghan, including the garrisons at Charlemenit and Mountjoy. By the end of the month, large swathes of the Erne valley (including Belturbet) were under their control, with only isolated garrisons holding out at Ballyshannon, Enniskillen and Killeshandra. By mid-November, the rebels held sway over most of Ulster. On 15 November Lurgan fell and a siege of Drogheda begun. But an assault on Lisburn by Sir Phelim O'Neill on 28 November failed to capture the town. Strabane castle surrendered in December and in the early spring of 1642, Dundalk was captured. But after this there were few victories for the rebels.

RESISTANCE AND A SECOND WAVE OF MURDERS

As time passed the settlers began to consolidate their own positions. The Erne valley, Londonderry and east Ulster still held out, with troops raised and paid for by their local landlords. In east Ulster they were led by Lord Conway and Sir George Rawdon. Obtaining a trickle of supplies and weapons through the ports of Carrickfergus and Belfast they built up their defences and in November 1641, successfully repulsed an attempt by Sir Phelim O'Neill to capture Lisburn.

Royal commissions for the raising of four regiments of infantry and three troops of horse, collectively known as the Laggan army, were issued in November to protect the settlers' interests in western Ulster. The four infantry regiments were led by Sir Robert and Sir William Stewart, veterans of the continental wars, Sir Ralph Gore of Donegal and Sir William Cole of Enniskillen. Gore's regiment was raised amongst the settlers of southern Donegal, while Cole recruited amongst those of Fermanagh and its environs. The Laggan army, named after the fertile area of land that lay between the Rivers Foyle and Swilly, acted as the main base for the troops, but the Erne valley, Tyrone and Donegal were included within the sphere of operations. The army additionally included several more independent infantry companies commanded by the mayor and governor of Londonderry and several more companies at Coleraine, held by Captain Thomas Phillips.

Initially defensively deployed in a reactive mode, the Laggan army ensured that the rebels failed to capture any more settlements. In December 1641 they successfully raised the siege of the isolated garrison at Augher castle held by Sir Audley Mervyn. In March 1642, they relieved the garrison and refugees at Sir Ralph Gore's castle at Donegal. Withdrawing them back to Londonderry through the Barnesmore Gap, the army was ambushed by Sir Phelim O'Neill who had set a well-prepared trap. However, the better armed and trained Laggan army decisively defeated their ambushers and returned successfully to base.

The earlier incidents of murder were localised, if ferocious in scale, and generally involved robbery and theft rather than killing, but later episodes were more sanguine. Particularly in the following weeks and months, when it slowly became clear to the rebels that ultimate victory was unlikely, attitudes to the treatment of opponents changed. As settler resistance to the rebellion in the Erne valley began to gather, notably around Enniskillen under the leadership of Sir William Cole and at Killeshandra under the command of Sir James Craig, more concerted efforts to find a permanent solution to the settler population were undertaken by the rebels.

On 30 January 1642, William Gibbs of Belturbet, a butcher by trade, witnessed the rebels take 'about thirty-four British Protestants, men, women, and children, and drowned them in the river at Belturbet' and then hanged two others. A rope was then put around Gibbs's neck but he was saved by the timely intervention of an old Irish acquaintance, which prevented the murder taking place. Gibbs named the perpetrators as members of the O'Mulpatrick sept and another witness from the town, William Smith, corroborated this. Smith stated that fifty-eight Protestants were drowned at the bridge and those who tried to swim to shore were shot or piked by the O'Mulpatricks. He further added that the local rebel leader Philip MacHugh O'Reilly, who was not present at the drowning, was highly displeased with the murders and publicly stated his disapproval.

Likewise the murder of over eighty villagers taking refuge at Tully castle, by the shore of Lower Lough Erne, on Christmas day 1641, indicated a more ferocious stage in the war against the plantation. In this raid by Rory Maguire, more settlers were killed at nearby Monea and at Lisgoole, upstream from Enniskillen. But the success of the rebels was not complete and as time passed during that first awful winter, it became clear that the chief objective of the rebels to destroy the plantation across the province would not be achieved without a very bloody fight. The planters were not going to surrender their investment without a deadly struggle for control.

Throughout the winter of 1641/42, the rebels continued with diminishing results to expel the remaining colonists from their strongholds on the Erne, particularly around Enniskillen and Killeshandra. The rising was debated at Westminster and money was voted to send troops to Ireland. The King appointed the Earl of Ormond as commander of the King's army and troops were duly raised. Meanwhile the Ulster insurgents, frustrated by their lack of success in Ulster, now turned their attention to Dundalk and Ardee, which they captured at the end of October 1641. They then began a siege of Drogheda but, lacking sufficient siege equipment, were unable to take the town and they began a general investment. A relieving force of government troops from Dublin was defeated at Julianstown on 29 November 1641, providing the rebels with large quantities of arms and ammunition. These would soon be used to effect against the surviving colonist outposts in Cavan and Fermanagh.

ESTIMATES OF THE LOSSES

In the mid-1630s, the population of the British settlement in Ulster has been estimated as 34,000 and it would have been greater than this by the time of the rebellion of 1641. The numbers of persons actually killed during the early stages of the rebellion has remained one of the great areas of contention by serious academics ever since. Indeed, some have argued that wholesale murders never took place at all and are an invention of the dark forces of British misrule. Such a state of denial has not been helpful to the debate and today should be viewed in the same manner in which we regard those who deny the Holocaust.

In his book *The Irish Rebellion*, written in 1646, Sir John Temple estimated that 154,000 were murdered. Clearly this total is a gross exaggeration of the truth but agreement on an acceptable figure of deaths has not been reached. Scholarly interpretation of the murders committed in County Armagh (Ulster's smallest county) has returned a minimum figure of 527 deaths, which, if multiplied by nine for the Ulster counties (and ignoring the British settlements in Leitrim, Sligo and elsewhere) would give a total of around 4,500 persons. This is a much smaller figure than that given by Temple but should be put in the context of its time. The recent Troubles in Northern Ireland began in the late 1960s and lasted for thirty years, during which time around 3,500 people were killed in a population of around 1.5 million. Committed on a much smaller settler population over a much shorter space of time (generally under six months) the scale of the 1641 deaths can be fully appreciated.

Most historians have refuted the claim that the rebellion was planned to commit the wholesale massacre of Protestants. But there is no doubt that there were many atrocities committed by rebels, usually as a result of lack of discipline, religious fanaticism or private vengeance. In many cases, the leaders of the uprising took great efforts to restrain their followers from this type of outrage. However, many mass murders were committed as the colonists were forced off their land and ordered to make their way to the nearest government garrison. All over Ulster the same picture emerged. From Belturbet to Bloody Bridge, from Tully to Loughgall, large numbers of British Protestant settlers were despatched in all manner of ways. There were several notable interventions by local Catholics, such as the provisioning of the beleaguered villagers at Ballintoy in north Antrim by a local priest and the provisioning of Coleraine by the Catholic Earl of Antrim.

Inevitably, as they gathered strength during the winter, the settlers meted out vicious reprisals. Following the killing of a number of Protestants at Clough castle in north Antrim, upwards of thirty Catholics were killed at Islandmagee in the south of the county. At Manorhamilton, Frederick Hamilton gained notoriety for his wholesale hangings of rebels. Invariably, anyone caught in rebellion would suffer the maximum penalty of the law. Fear and hatred were now often dictating the actions of formerly rational men.

ARRIVAL OF THE SCOTS ARMY TO THE CESSATION OF 1643

On 15 April 1642, the first troops of the Scottish army arrived in Ulster. Lieutenant General Robert Monro, a veteran soldier from the Thirty Years' War which was still devastating Europe, landed at Carrickfergus with 2,500 men and promptly set about restoring the control of the province. Picking up British settler reinforcements, he marched south and swiftly captured Newry and Dundalk, executing sixty prisoners at Newry and hanging more at Loughbrickland, eventually linking up with the royal army near Drogheda. Murders carried out as acts of reprisal were commonplace as Monro's victorious army progressed through the countryside. In May the Laggan army recaptured Dungannon, helped raise the siege at Coleraine and in June destroyed 2,000 rebels in Glenmaquin, near Raphoe, in Donegal. By August, 10,000 Scottish troops had arrived in Ulster and the way seemed clear to completely remove the rebels from Ulster.

In the Erne valley, these developments allowed the British settler forces under Cole to open lines of communication with Londonderry and Belfast. Despite the loss of Sir William Craig and Sir Claude Hamilton's garrisons at Killeshandra in June, the positions around Enniskillen were consolidated, as the Gaelic Ulster army was restricted to the south Ulster/north Leinster area, too far away to carry out any sudden attack.

But now new political and military developments in Ireland began to emerge. The original rebellion had attracted only Gaelic Irish leaders to its cause. However, the Anglo-Norman aristocracy in Ireland, known as the Old English, were increasingly alarmed at the progress of events as the retaliatory tactics of the government and settler armies no longer discriminated between them and other Catholic factions in Ireland. Fearful that an anti-Catholic backlash might target their interests as well, this group was now in a quandary – should they remain aloof and await events or enter the conflict? Thus in May 1642, leaders of the Gaelic Irish and Old English factions met at Kilkenny and agreed to form a Catholic Confederation to jointly co-ordinate their interests. Despite strains in the relationship, the Confederation provided the Catholics of Ireland with a unique political structure to lobby on the continent for diplomatic and material support.

In addition, the return to Ireland of two veteran soldiers of the Thirty Years' War provided the flagging rebel military campaigns with a much-needed shot in the arm. On the brink of suing for terms with Ormond, the sudden arrival of Owen Roe O'Neill at Doe castle, Donegal in July with a boatload of military supplies and 100 experienced officers allowed the rebel leadership to continue their insurrection. O'Neill was promptly given command of all the Confederation's Irish forces in Ulster, with Sir Phelim stepping down to become Lord President of the Council of Ulster. Meanwhile, Colonel Thomas Preston, a member of the Old English Gormanstown family, returned from Europe to take command of the Confederation's Leinster army.

Clearly the return of O'Neill was, for Sir William Cole and the settlers along the Erne, the bigger threat. Despite being able to call on the assistance of the Laggan army in an emergency, Cole was now wary of this growing threat on his southern and eastern flank. Initially though, O'Neill was focused on reorganising his poorly trained troops and imposing a military discipline amongst them and was thus not interested in committing them in open battle with the superior Laggan army, Monro's Scots or the Royal forces under Ormond. For a year he ventured into central Ulster only to make cattle raids and provide his hard-pressed army with supplies.

In June 1643, O'Neill's well-laid plans were almost completely destroyed when Sir Robert Stewart's 3,000-strong Laggan force moved to intercept his foraging army west of Clones, County Monaghan. Passing through Enniskillen, Stewart had picked up reinforcements before continuing SE to cut off O'Neill's escape route to Connacht.

Forced to turn and fight, on 13 June 1643, O'Neill's 1,500 troops were overwhelmed and routed. He lost 150 men (many of them the experienced officers he had brought from Europe the previous year) and hundreds of much-needed arms. This victory enhanced the reputation of the Laggan army and seemed to confirm the view that an Irish army could never withstand a British one in a pitched battle.

Momentarily, the Ulster settlers stood supreme, with the possibility of finally eradicating the rebel threat from the whole province. But once again, the political situation overtook the purely military one, as King Charles, anxious to enlist the Royal army in Ireland for his own cause, now intervened to bring hostilities to an end. On 15 September 1643, the Earl of Ormond, acting on behalf of King Charles's interests in Ireland, agreed to a ceasefire with the Confederation. Though the King had not yet agreed a response to the stated grievances of the Confederates, Clanrickarde's army in Connacht, Lord Inchiquin's settler army in Munster and Ormond's royal forces in Leinster accepted the ceasefire.

But the Ulster armies remained defiant. Monro's Scots army was replenished from Scotland and sensing that the King was sacrificing their interests for his own, refused to accept it. Likewise, the Laggan army, undecided in its loyalty to king or parliament in the Civil War, were aware that the Confederation could now concentrate its forces and permanently remove the settlers from Ulster and so they too remained on guard. Having so recently achieved superiority over their enemy, it seemed poor judgement to allow that to be frittered away.

FROM THE CESSATION TO THE SECOND CIVIL WAR

CONTINUING WAR IN ULSTER

The changed political situation immediately opened up divisions within the Ulster settler populations, between those who supported the King and those who wished for a parliamentarian victory in the Civil War now raging in England. In general, the Laggan army officers were pro-Royalist but were forced to accede to the Scots army's view which sided with parliament. As a direct response, on 25 September 1643, the English parliament agreed to the 'Solemn League and Covenant', promising to adopt Presbyterianism into Church government in England thereby ensuring Scottish support in the war against Charles. By April 1644, most of the Ulster British, both Scots and English, had accepted the Solemn League and Covenant, drawing Scottish troops in to the Civil War on the side of parliament. For outposts that operated within a largely hostile hinterland, such as Enniskillen, the signing up to the Covenant was essential to ensure continuing supplies from Scotland.

The Presbyterian ministers charged with answering queries and administering the oath travelled around the country throughout the spring of 1644. Beginning with the Scots army in the east of the province, they proceeded to Londonderry and administered the oath to the Laggan regiments of the Stewarts and Mervyn. Word reached them that the Enniskillen garrison also wished to take the oath and even threatened to abandon the town if their desire was not granted. Cole sympathised with the parliamentary cause but initially declined to take the oath (though he later acceded along with General Robert Stewart).

The cessation also had a favourable effect for King Charles, who was now able to draw off Protestant troops from the Royalist Protestant Irish garrison to assist him in his war with parliament. By January 1644, Ormond had, by reducing the garrisons in Ireland to a dangerous level, supplied his king with over 6,000 troops. In addition, Monro was forced to return 3,500 troops from his army to Scotland to resist the threat created by the Scottish Earl of Montrose's victorious Royalist army. Furthermore, 1,200 Ulster Catholic troops had gone to Scotland with the Earl of Antrim in November 1643 to assist Montrose's Scottish Royalist army. Thus, all the armies in Ireland found themselves weakened by political events outside their control. Though both sides in the English Civil War were boosted by these developments in Ireland, the local situation in Ulster prevented the total dilution of troops from the province.

As feared by Monro, the Confederation now concentrated its forces to drive the settlers out of Ulster. In spring 1644, the two armies of O'Neill and Preston, with the Earl of Castlehaven in overall command, began assembling in north Leinster. Recognising the growing danger, Monro reacted first by moving his army into southern Ulster on a twenty-day campaign in June. Before Castlehaven was ready to contest his passage, he had managed to march through Cavan to burn Kells, County Meath and, feigning towards Dublin, returned to his base in Ulster. On their way, the Scots army defeated 1,000 Irish at Finnea, where the celebrated rebel leader Myles 'the Slasher' O'Reilly was reportedly killed.

Castlehaven responded in July by marching his two armies north into Armagh. His combined strength now numbered 11,000 men. Despite being outnumbered, Monro reacted by bringing his army to face Castlehaven. Joined by the Laggan army, Monro's army swelled to around 10,000 men. A seven-week stand-off took place at Charlemont, with neither side prepared to attack the other. Eventually in late September, Castlehaven, with his supplies running out, blinked first and withdrew his armies into south Ulster/ north Leinster for the winter. Ulster was thus saved. Reflecting on the failure of his campaign, Castlehaven commented gloomily, 'Thus ended the Ulster expedition, like to be so fatal to the Confederate Catholics of Ireland.'

In July 1644, the Earl of Inchiquin in Munster switched sides to join parliament. Preston was therefore obliged to keep troops close to Kilkenny. The following March, the Confederates began a major operation in Munster to destroy Inchiquin's army. They succeeded in capturing Duncannon, but a siege of Youghal was lifted in September, and both sides soon after withdrew into winter quarters. For Ulster, the campaigning in the far south allowed them a respite from direct military operations.

In 1645, another 1,500 Scots troops were withdrawn to Scotland leaving only 5,000 men, widely spread across northeast Ulster. Meanwhile, in July that year, the Laggan army assisted Sir Charles Coote's parliamentarian army against Clanrickarde's Royalist army, culminating in the capture of Sligo. However, the Laggan troops were never keen to campaign far from home and they returned soon after.

Captain Dillon, writing to Clanrickarde of the town's loss, claimed that the 'Scots' had lost 500 men in the assault, including a lieutenant colonel and several other officers. The Irish garrison had been beaten back to a large house in the town, where they had repulsed an assault. Following a parley, the garrison survivors had then been promised quarter but 'after cominge into the street, were disarmed, stript, and mostly murthered'. This had become a war without pity.

On 17 October 1645 a Confederate army of 2,000 infantry and 300 cavalry surrounded Sligo. Though a force of the Laggan army was already marching to their relief and had reached Bundoran, the Sligo garrison sallied out to attack their besiegers. Led by Captains Cole and Coote, the cavalry charged and routed the enemy, assisted by Lieutenant Colonel Saunderson's infantry and more cavalry under the command of Sir Francis Hamilton. They killed around 200 of the rebels including their leader, the Archbishop of Tuam, in addition to capturing a quantity of horses, munitions and provisions for the loss of, 'but 1 man and 6 hurt ... And our men, with the Lagan army, have since entered the barony of Tereragh and taken 13 castles, in which our men have good quarters for this winter about the said castles, which keep this country under contribution'. Clearly the securing of castle accommodation was crucial to the comfort of an army constantly under threat of attack from an enemy beyond their walls.

The following month, Sir Charles Coote ordered Sir William Cole to bring his troops to Sligo. Already encamped on Boa Island, Cole had his troop of cavalry move to Ballyshannon where he picked up two companies of infantry quartered in the vicinity. When they had advanced as far as Bundrowse, on 26 November, they received news that behind them Rory Maguire had crossed to Boa Island with a force of 500 men and as Cole reported later, 'with two of our own boats by the treachery of one Bryan O'Harran and other protected persons', who began to burn and plunder the families of the soldiers who had recently departed. Maguire took captive the small number of soldiers left at the camp and preceded to evacuate the island with his booty.

The Laggan cavalry, with some of the infantry mounted behind them under the command of Captain John Folliot, left Bundrowse and galloped north around Boa via Termon Magrath castle, arriving at Kesh, where they were able to follow the trail of Maguire's retiring column. In the early hours of 27 November they vigorously attacked Maguire's army at Irvinestown and put them to flight, recovering their lost victuals and releasing their colleagues. They soon learned that the main army of 2,000 infantry and 200 foot were encamped at Ballinamallard. However, this large force withdrew across Slieve Beagh into Monaghan without further incident.

These actions around north Fermanagh and beyond reflect the nature of the constant war of attrition that flared up from time to time. Though Cole was able to thwart the rebel intentions with ease, any failure on his part could have jeopardised the survival of the settler enclave around Enniskillen.

O'NEILL'S VICTORY AT BENBURB

On the political front, however, negotiations between Ormond and the Confederates following the cessation had continued apace. The King was willing to grant political and economic concessions to the Confederates but remained unwilling to accede to full toleration of Catholicism. But defeat at Naseby in June 1645 made Charles desperate and he sent the Catholic Earl of Glamorgan to negotiate a treaty openly allowing Catholic worship. A premature revelation of the deal in January 1646 forced Charles to disavow it to his supporters in England. Ormond reopened his own negotiations but these became meaningless in May when the King surrendered to the Scots.

In the spring of 1646, Hugh O'Neill's army was on the march again. Now properly armed and provisioned from the war chest of the recently arrived Papal Nuncio Rinuccini, the army had spent seven weeks training on the slopes of Galdanagh hill in Cavan. Now totalling 5,000 infantry and 400 cavalry, it headed north through Ulster to Charlemont. As in 1644, Monro gathered his army, 3,500 Scots and a further 2,000 British settlers and confronted O'Neill at Benburb. This time Monro decided to attack. On 5 June 1646 his tired troops failed to dislodge O'Neill's army from behind their entrenchments. Late in the afternoon, O'Neill counter-attacked and routed the Scots. At least 1,800 Scots and 1,000 British settlers were killed, with vast quantities of arms and ammunition left behind by the fleeing army.

Momentarily, O'Neill stood supreme in Ulster, with only the Laggan army left to defend the Protestant interest. But at this pivotal moment he opted to return his victorious army to quarters. There was still hope for the Confederate cause. By now it was obvious that with the King removed from the picture, the Confederates would soon have to withstand the full might of the English parliamentary army. Once again it was decided to launch both Preston's Leinster army and O'Neill's Ulster one to capture Dublin. But despite reaching the capital's outskirts by October, personal rivalry between the two generals ensured that Dublin was not attacked and each withdrew into winter quarters. For the Confederates, this failure would ultimately prove fatal, for the following June, 1647, Ormond handed the city over to the parliamentarians and left Ireland.

Now parliament assisted the Laggan army by providing much-needed supplies of food and munitions. They also insisted on Sir Charles Coote becoming commander of all western Ulster forces in preference to the Stewarts who were Royalist sympathisers. In addition, fresh troops were sent to garrison Dublin under a new commander, Michael Jones. By August, Jones felt strong enough to campaign in Leinster. Preston decided for once to face this threat and placed his army in good defensive positions on Dungan's Hill near Trim. On 8 August, Jones attacked and shattered Preston's army, causing his six regiments of foot to disintegrate. He now cleared the Confederate garrisons of central and northern Leinster.

In Munster, Lord Inchiquin destroyed the Confederate army of Lord Taaffe at the battle of Knocknanuss on 13 November 1647 and overran many Confederate garrisons. In the space of barely three months, two of the provincial Confederate armies in Ireland were thus destroyed. Only Clanrickarde and O'Neill remained in the field. During this time O'Neill campaigned in Connacht and failed to assist the other Confederate armies.

A SECOND CIVIL WAR

Despite these military reverses, once again the political situation in England influenced events in Ireland. The argument between parliament and the New Model Army regarding the ultimate fate of King Charles resulted in a second civil war. Always a lukewarm parliamentarian, on 20 May 1648 Inchiquin again changed sides and agreed a ceasefire with the Confederation. But disagreement within the Supreme Council between Old English and Irish over the acceptance of this ceasefire fatally divided the Confederation. O'Neill then marched his Ulster army away to fight independently of the Confederation.

The Scots and their Ulster settler supporters were unwilling to see Charles put on trial and many entered the second civil war on the Royalist side. In Dublin, Jones was thus isolated and survived only because the Confederates were also divided. But with the defeat of the Scottish army at Preston on 17 August 1648, the Ulster Scots, now under the command of George Monro, son of Robert, were disarmed by the parliamentarian troops of George Monck. In western Ulster, Coote seized the Laggan army leaders in a coup, replacing them with his own trusted lieutenants. Sir Robert Stewart and Audley Mervyn were sent as prisoners to London and units unwilling to support Coote were forcibly disbanded.

Coote trusted few of the Laggan officers but Sir William Cole was an exception. He wrote to Cole asking him to arrest his pro-Royalist subordinates. However, Cole knew that his rank and file might oppose this and he wrote back that he could only do it if Coote sent some of his own troops to assist. This was duly done and parliamentarian garrisons were then placed in Londonderry, Sligo and Enniskillen. Forced to accept these changes of fortune, the British settlers bided their time. Ulster was now nominally under parliamentary control.

In October 1648 in Leinster, the armies of Taaffe and Inchiquin co-operated to remove garrisons loyal to O'Neill. This was now a brutal civil war amongst former allies. In mid-December, while Sir Charles Coote seized towns and cattle in SW Ulster from the Confederates, Rory Maguire was sent by O'Neill to take Jamestown and Drumrusk, County Leitrim, from Clanrickarde's Confederate army. Though successful, Maguire was killed along with several officers and upwards of 500 men.

Meanwhile, the Earl of Ormond had returned from exile and was trying to broker a new peace deal with the Confederates. Rumours that he was close to agreeing religious concessions caused a mutiny amongst Inchiquin's Protestant army, fearful of the loss of their privilege in Munster. Though order was restored, deep suspicions remained. But the decision of the English parliament to put the King on trial in January 1649 convinced the Confederates that they must drop the demand of full religious liberty. Likewise too, the Royalists amongst the settlers were appalled that the King should be executed. Thus in March, the Laggan soldiers in Enniskillen mutinied against Cole, freed the previously imprisoned officers and declared for Ormond. A grateful Ormond, writing to their new leaders, responded by congratulating the 'successful attempt made by you to free yourselves from any dependency upon the bloody rebels that have murdered our king'.

Charles was duly tried and beheaded in January 1649. In the same month, what became known as the Ormond Peace was signed between the Confederation and Inchiquin. Toleration of Catholic practice was accepted, as was a simple oath of allegiance and a promise that they would not be economically threatened. In return Ormond became Lord General of a nominally united Royalist force in support of the monarch-elect, the young Prince Charles. It included the fragmented Ulster Laggan army and Monro's Scots, in addition to the armies of Clanrickarde in Connacht, Preston in Leinster and of Inchiquin and Taaffe in Munster. In total it numbered 15,000 infantry and 3,000 cavalry but was well dispersed across the island. Incredibly, O'Neill remained aloof from this arrangement. Negotiations with O'Neill were fruitless, as he demanded the return of ancestral Ulster lands to former Gaelic owners. Ormond could never accept such a demand as it threatened the entire land settlement of the plantation and would have alienated every Protestant in Ireland.

The parliamentary position in Ireland remained precarious in 1649. Jones held Dublin but Coote and Monck were hemmed in at Londonderry and Dundalk. By late July, Monck had surrendered Dundalk leaving only Coote's army at large in Ulster. In late March, a siege of Londonderry began with the reconstituted regiments of the Laggan army under Colonel Humphrey Galbraith. Coote was pinned inside with 2,000 men. In May, Sir Robert Stewart and Colonel Mervyn escaped captivity in London and arrived to take charge of the siege. The besiegers lacked suitable ordnance to batter the walls of the city and settled down to starving them out. Some supplies arrived via the river, but when this was blocked in mid-July it seemed only a matter of time before Coote would be forced to capitulate. (A garrison loyal to Coote under William Cole held Enniskillen but was too weak to assist.)

More Royalists arrived under the command of George Monro but they consisted of Catholic Irish and Highland Scots and so his presence was not welcomed. An assault against the city on 28 July was beaten off with loss, as settler now fought settler. Later, Presbyterian leaders from Belfast came to discourage further action due to the presence of the Catholics, stating that the besiegers were 'preferring the King before religion'.

The effect of this was to weaken the besiegers' resolve and many now left to aid Charles's cause elsewhere in Britain. In mid-August 1649, Owen Roe O'Neill stunned the besiegers when he brought his army of 4,000 infantry and 300 cavalry to western Ulster to assist Coote and raise a twenty-week siege. Together they were able to outnumber their besiegers and they swiftly overran the Laggan army entrenchments, causing Sir Robert Stewart to withdraw into north Connacht. George Monro withdrew his polyglot army to Belfast. O'Neill entered Londonderry in triumph, if momentarily.

Though this was a major setback, further south Ormond had already sustained a greater blow. Accepting the need to take Dublin in order to prevent an imminent parliamentarian army arriving in Ireland, he moved his own army to Rathmines, south of the capital. Here, on 2 August 1649, Jones had sallied out with the full garrison and scattered Ormond's troops, ensuring that later that month Cromwell would be able to land the New Model Army unmolested in Dublin.

CROMWELL'S ARRIVAL TO THE END OF THE WAR

Oliver Cromwell had been appointed as the Lord Lieutenant of Ireland by the English parliament in March 1649 and made military commander in anticipation of his mission in Ireland. He arrived in Ireland at Dublin on 15 August 1649, in a fleet of thirty-five ships carrying 8,000 infantry and 4,000 cavalry of the victorious New Model Army. In addition, for the first time in Ireland, he also brought a substantial train of artillery, capable of reducing any fortress in the land. Before he returned to England in May 1650, his presence had transformed the military situation in Ireland forever and ensured for him a lasting reputation.

His first target was the Royalist garrison at Drogheda, with its garrison of 3,000 men under the command of the respected English Catholic Sir Arthur Aston. Arriving before its defences on 3 September, he immediately began battering the walls with his artillery. When a sizeable breach had been created he ordered a general assault on 11 September. His famous instruction for no quarter to be given ensured the complete destruction of the garrison, including Aston, who was beaten to death with his own wooden leg.

Cromwell next turned south, capturing Wexford on 11 and New Ross on 19 October. Before he did so, he ordered Colonel Robert Venables north into Ulster to secure the remaining Royalist strongholds. Venables swiftly captured Carlingford, Newry, Lisburn and Belfast, securing a vast array of guns and ammunition at each. Clearly the resolve of many of the British settlers was to find an accommodation with Cromwell rather than fight for a Royalist coalition, which was becoming increasingly Catholic. Further mutinies in Cork and Kinsale amongst Inchiquin's Protestant Munster forces brought these towns under parliamentarian control too.

In early November, Coote moved against Coleraine from his base at Londonderry. The garrison in the town was betrayed by the inhabitants and massacred by Coote, who went on to join forces with Venables and mop up the remaining small garrisons. Now only Carrickfergus remained in Royalist hands in east Ulster. George Monro desperately moved his remaining forces to block its investment. Venables promptly moved south and destroyed Monro's force as it crossed a river near Lisburn. The remnants surrendered and Monro fled to Enniskillen.

By now the Royalist cause was all but extinguished in Ulster. On 20 October, Owen Roe O'Neill had finally gained the concessions he had wished from an increasingly desperate Ormond and he placed his Gaelic Irish army, resting in Finnea, Westmeath, at the Lord Deputy's disposal. But O'Neill had become seriously ill and did not live to see his army adopt its new role, for he died on 6 November 1649 and was buried in the Franciscan abbey at Cavan. On 18 March 1650, the officers of the army were invited to a meeting in Belturbet to elect a new commander. George Monro was also invited and sent his representative Humphrey Galbraith to canvass for the Earl of Antrim. However, the officers elected a compromise figure in the military novice Heber MacMahon, Catholic Bishop of Clogher. Monro could not commit his forces to following a Catholic prelate and later the following month he surrendered Enniskillen, the last British Royalist garrison in Ulster, to Sir Charles Coote for £500 and a pass to Scotland. Coote now garrisoned Enniskillen with his own men, consisting of part of Colonel Hunk's foot regiment and 200 horse of Colonel Richard Coote's regiment.

In May 1650, MacMahon moved the Gaelic Ulster army, numbering 4,000 infantry and 300 cavalry, north to Loughgall in Armagh. From there he moved swiftly north, capturing Dungiven and Ballycastle (Aghanloo). Though all the evidence was contrary, he had hoped to raise the British settlers again but they failed to respond and he turned west and entered Donegal at Lifford, brushing aside an attack by Sir Charles Coote.

Coote retired to Londonderry and, once reinforced with the 1,000-strong regiment of Colonel Fenwick, he set out to intercept MacMahon. On 21 June, he found the Irish drawn up on a hillside at Scarriffhollis near Letterkenny, in a strong position. MacMahon's officers begged him to remain on the defensive but he scorned their advice and moved his army to lower ground. In the ensuing battle, the Irish were comprehensively defeated and MacMahon fled to Fermanagh where he was captured by the Enniskillen garrison, tried and hanged at the Sconce, beside the castle. The only remaining Gaelic field army in Ulster had been destroyed. The last important Irish garrison in Ulster at Charlemont surrendered on 14 August.

Elsewhere in south Ulster, resistance to the parliamentary army was now directed through guerrilla tactics, which slowed down the inevitable Royalist defeat. In early 1651, parliamentarian forces launched a punitive expedition into the last Royalist strongholds east of the river Shannon. The fort at Finnea was stormed and Cavan wasted. Later that summer, Ireton began his campaign to breach the defensive line of the Shannon. Though the capture of Limerick was achieved by 27 October 1651, the final Royalist stronghold of Galway was not surrendered until 12 May 1652.

Guerrilla bands continued to harass the parliamentarian forces in Ulster and elsewhere but their purpose was now meaningless. The last band of rebels, under the command of Colonel Philip O'Reilly, surrendered at Clough Oughter on 27 April 1653, finally bringing twelve years of devastating war to an end.

THE CROMWELLIAN LAND SETTLEMENT

It had been established practice for the government to confiscate the lands of rebellious subjects to help pay for their ultimate defeat. In the 1580s, the Earl of Desmond and his supporters had lost nearly 600,000 acres through forfeiture, of which around 200,000 was later planted with new English Protestant landowners.

In March 1642, the English parliament had tried to raise £1,000,000 (the estimated cost of suppressing the rebellion) through the Adventurers' Act, whereby speculators (known as adventurers) loaned money for a share of a future 2,500,000-acre share out of confiscated land. Only around one third of the target was raised and by 1652 the cost had soared to include the huge arrears of the New Model Army's troops, present in Ireland since August 1649.

In order to pay these debts, the government passed the Act of Settlement, which established which persons would be punished for their involvement in the rebellion and the manner in which they should pay. In addition, the principle of distributing the confiscated lands between the adventurers and the soldiers was agreed. The Act witnessed around 3,000 Catholic landowners losing their estates, with their subsequent transplantation to Connacht or Clare. However, there was much delay in the final distribution to the adventurers and soldiers, with many selling their debentures and moving on. Eventually around 7,000 soldiers remained in Ireland to take up their land options.

The Cromwellian land settlement saw the greatest redistribution of land ever, with 11,000,000 of a total of 20,000,000 acres being affected. Though the Act referred to those persons who had sided with the King against parliament, in reality this support was mostly Catholic and these persons were therefore most affected. The result was that Catholics in Ireland, whether Old English or Gaelic, saw their share of land ownership fall from 59 per cent in 1641 to only 22 per cent by 1660. In Fermanagh 15 per cent and in Cavan 43 per cent of the total land area was confiscated. The net winners were the Protestant families and landlords who had been established in Ireland before the date of the rebellion.

THE RESTORATION

When the monarchy was restored in 1660 with the coronation of Charles II, many Catholic Royalists believed that they would have their former lands returned to them and be able to worship with some degree of toleration. The King was sympathetic to their plight but was unable to fully respond, as his return had only been made possible by the Commonwealth army who insisted that he maintain the Cromwellian settlement.

In 1663, he passed an Act of Settlement which allowed what were termed 'innocent' Catholics to return to their land and which compensated the Cromwellian settlers with other land of equal value. However, there was not sufficient land to carry out these wishes in full and Charles was forced to pass a second Act whereby Cromwellian settlers were to give up one third of their estates in order that Catholics could receive some compensation.

This satisfied neither party, as the Cromwellians were loathe to surrender what they had been granted and the Catholics found it increasingly difficult to recover their former lands. Writing years later, Jonathan Swift commented in a succinct if rather jaundiced tone:

> …the Catholics of Ireland … lost their estates for fighting in defence of their king. Those who cut the father's head [Charles I], forced the son to fly for his life, and overturned the whole ancient frame of government … obtained grants of the estates the Catholics lost in defence of the ancient constitution, and thus they gained by their rebellion what the Catholics lost by their loyalty.

Likewise, the Catholic Church was not to be restored to its former status. Though many, like the Duke of Ormond, were prepared to accept an oath of obedience from Catholics, in practice the Catholic Church could not agree to allow the state rather than the Pope supremacy in spiritual matters. Thus the Catholic faith was often tolerated in practice but did not receive official support. Despite these setbacks, the economy progressed through the twenty-five years of relative peace. Dublin became the second city of the British Empire and the population of Ireland rose to around two million. Despite restrictions placed on Irish beef by the Westminster parliament, Irish wool and butter flourished in new English and continental markets.

Charles died in 1685 and was succeeded by his Catholic brother James II. Protestants in Ireland were obviously anxious about their land settlements and viewed James's accession with some suspicion. James, however, appeared to calm fears when he appointed his Protestant brother-in-law Lord Clarendon as Lord Lieutenant, who promptly announced no change to any settlement issues.

But in 1687, Richard Talbot, a leading Irish Catholic and confidante of James, was made Earl of Tyrconnell and commander of the Irish army. He immediately began to dismiss Protestant officers and replace them with Catholics. Catholics were appointed to the Privy Council and as judges. When Clarendon was recalled to England, Talbot replaced him, thus controlling two of the most important appointments in Ireland. Talbot was the first Catholic viceroy for over 100 years. It was soon clear that a new land settlement would result which would penalise Protestants and favour Catholics. The only uncertainty was in the final arrangements.

4

WILLIAMITE WARS IN ULSTER

THE CONSTITUTIONAL CRISIS

By the late 1680s, political events on the British and European theatres were once more to thrust the Erne into the forefront of constitutional affairs. On 6 February 1685, James II ascended the throne of Britain, the first Roman Catholic monarch for over a century. That year also saw the revocation of the Edict of Nantes by the French king Louis XIV, which ended political toleration of Huguenot Protestants within the kingdom and saw them emigrate to sympathetic Protestant states throughout Europe including Britain and Ireland.

James's openly practiced Catholicism caused uneasiness in England, which immediately set in motion a challenge to his authority. In June 1685, James Scott, the Duke of Monmouth, landed in SW England from Holland to claim the throne. Monmouth was the eldest illegitimate son of Charles II and even claimed that his mother had secretly married his father, thus legitimising his claim. Though several thousand flocked to his standard, poor leadership ensured he remained confined to the West Country. Pursued by a dogged royal army, Monmouth carried out a bewildering series of marches and counter-marches. He eventually attempted a stunning victory with a surprise night attack on 6 July across a bog to the royal encampment at Sedgemoor, east of Bridgwater. The attack failed miserably and Monmouth was quickly captured and executed. A series of punitive prisoner courts martial were undertaken by Judge Jeffries, earning them the epithet of 'bloody assizes'. But James had successfully defended this first challenge to his throne.

Nevertheless, James recognised the potential for further dissent. In order to consolidate his hold on power, he instructed three Irish infantry regiments and one of dragoons to take up residence in England. The move proved extremely unpopular with his English subjects, who viewed it as an affront to their own army. There were several well-publicised clashes between the Irish troops and the civilian population. Though there were serious concerns about James's reign, people comforted themselves in the knowledge that James's daughter Mary, the Protestant wife of the Dutch prince William of Orange, would one day succeed him.

However, in Ireland, his plans to advance the Catholic cause seemed more assured. In February 1687 he appointed the Catholic peer Richard Talbot, Duke of Tyrconnell, as his Lord Deputy. Talbot immediately began to appoint Catholics to positions of judge and councillor at the expense of Protestant candidates. The Old English Catholics of Ireland now sensed their moment had arrived and lobbied Talbot for a resolution to the Cromwellian land settlement. In spring 1688, he forwarded proposals to James that allowed the Cromwellian settlers to remain in possession of half of their holdings while the remaining half would be returned to the former proprietors. James accepted these proposals and gave notice for a parliament to be called later in the year to carry out these wishes.

But events in Britain were to overtake James's plans for Ireland. His new wife, Mary of Modena, had become pregnant and gave birth to a son, which now assured a Catholic succession. The young prince, also named James, was born on 10 June 1688 and before the end of July, William of Orange had been invited to invade England by a group of discontented political and religious figures known to history as 'the immortal seven'. William was the leading Protestant figure in Europe and as he was married to James's Protestant daughter Mary, he was viewed as a worthy adversary of the French king Louis XIV, who appeared bent on securing control over much of Europe. With the support of Spain, Pope Innocent XI and many minor German princes behind him, William assembled over fifty warships and 200 merchant vessels to transport his invading army of 15,000 men to England.

THE 'GLORIOUS REVOLUTION' IN BRITAIN

On 5 November 1688, this fleet landed unopposed at Torbay, on the SW coast of England, and disembarked within two days. On 9 November, William entered Exeter. Meanwhile, James set out from London with the army but as he advanced west, support for him began to haemorrhage away and at Salisbury he lost his nerve and returned to the capital. James then attempted to cobble together a new alliance, but as William approached London unrest within the kingdom grew worse. Dithering throughout the gathering winter as William advanced on his capital, James eventually fled his kingdom forever on 23 December.

The kingdom was now without a king. A convention of lords and commoners was assembled who declared that James's action amounted to abdication. The crown was therefore offered jointly to William of Orange and his wife Mary, who were formally proclaimed sovereigns on 13 February 1689. In English history, the end of James II's reign in 1688 and the accession of his daughter Mary and her husband William the following year are known as the 'Glorious Revolution', because of the bloodless nature of the coup orchestrated by the prominent aristocrats and financiers of the City of London.

But England was only one part of the story. In the rest of the kingdom, the transfer of power was much more sanguinary. In Scotland, 'Bonnie' Dundee raised a Highland Scots army for James and ambushed General MacKay's Williamite army in the pass of Killiecrankie, thirty miles NW of Perth on 27 July 1689. MacKay's army was badly mauled and few were able to continue on to their destination of Stirling. But in this moment of victory, the resistance to William was stillborn as Dundee fell on the battlefield and the Jacobite resistance in Scotland melted in the face of sterner opposition. In Ireland too, the change of sovereign was to cause political upheaval and trigger a three-year civil war, during which the island was to see the arrival of continental armies and the extension of the European conflict between William of Orange and the French king Louis XIV to Irish soil.

REACTION IN ULSTER

But the story has moved on and it is necessary to return to the situation in Ulster at the end of 1688 and follow the parallel local events that unfolded there. The constitutional crisis growing apace in England was certainly known about and was being eagerly followed. Ireland had a mainly Catholic population so there was great sympathy for the cause of James. But in Ulster, the population also included a substantial Protestant community who feared that their political and economic future would be jeopardised by a Catholic succession.

While these matters were unfolding, an anonymous letter appeared in the town of Comber in County Down. This letter was found lying in the street and marked, 'To my Lord, this deliver with haste and care', addressed to Lord Mount-Alexander and dated 3 December 1688. It was a letter which appeared authentic and its warning was as chilling as that delivered to Lord Monteagle on the eve of the famous parliamentary gunpowder plot, eighty years previously. It read:

> Good my Lord, I have written to you to let you know that all our Irishmen throughout Ireland is sworn that on the ninth day of this month they are to fall on to kill and murder man, wife and child, and I desire Lordship to take care of yourself and all others that are judged by our men to be heads, for whosoever can kill any of you, they are to have a captain's place; so my desire to your honour is to look to yourself and give other noblemen warning, and so not out either night or day without a good guard with you, and let no Irishman come near you, whatsoever he be; so this is all from him who was your father's friend, and is your friend, and will be, though I dare not be known as yet for fear of my life...

The letter was immediately copied and sent post haste to all the major towns in the province.

On 7 December, a copy arrived at Londonderry and Enniskillen. At Londonderry the letter coincided with the imminent arrival of the Earl of Antrim's Catholic regiment to garrison the city and it therefore appeared to confirm the fear of a repeat of the massacres of 1641. A vigorous debate occurred amongst the citizenry, with many, supported by the Presbyterian minister Revd James Gordon, wanting admittance of the troops to be refused. But the Anglican bishop Dr Hopkins urged restraint and pointed out the treasonable nature of any such act being carried out. Thus, as the Catholic troops approached to within fifty metres of the city walls, the argument was decided by thirteen young apprentices who slammed shut the gates of the city and refused to negotiate with the bishop's party. This act would ultimately lead to the invasion of the city by James's army, culminating in the historic 105-day siege.

Meanwhile, at Enniskillen, 9 December passed without incident. Then two days later a letter arrived from Dublin instructing the town to prepare quarters for two companies of soldiers belonging to Colonel Newcomen's regiment, now marching towards them. As at Londonderry only a few days before, the meaning of the Comber letter was discussed. It was known that Newcomen's soldiers were mostly Catholic and some argued that perhaps the only inaccuracy of the letter was in the date of the proposed massacre. Many inhabitants felt uneasy, with some urging direct action to be taken to prevent their entry to the town. Three citizens, William Browning, Robert Clark and William MacCarmick (later joined by James Ewart and Allen Cathcart) ,resolved to refuse admittance to the soldiers and began to canvass support for their position. In addition, they arranged for the construction of a drawbridge at the east end of the town.

However there was by no means a consensus for such action amongst the citizens of Enniskillen since, if carried out, it would be viewed as illegal and severely punished. Amongst others, the town's magistrates, led by Captain James Corry of Castlecoole, were opposed to these confrontational acts. On 12 December, a letter arrived indicating that the soldiers under Captains Nugent and Shurloe had now arrived at Clones on their journey to Enniskillen. This letter created greater alarm but Corry and a majority of the citizens were for admitting the soldiers when they arrived.

Unperturbed, MacCarmick went out to Monea castle, the home of Gustavus Hamilton, a major landlord in the county, to consult with him. Hamilton agreed to lend his support and together they made their way to Enniskillen. On the way in, they were given a letter that showed the town's continuing irresolution. At Enniskillen, the issue was again vigorously debated and this time Hamilton's influence resulted in a decision to resist. The drawbridge was then completed and Catholics living in the town were expelled. Protestants from the surrounding district were invited to come in and give their support to the growing mood of resistance.

On 15 December, the citizens of Enniskillen elected Gustavus Hamilton as governor of their town and instructed Allen Cathcart and William MacCarmick to travel to Londonderry to state their case and also obtain arms and ammunition. Hamilton was not present at this meeting but gladly assented to their wishes. He was evidently engaged in moving his family from Monea to Enniskillen castle, as the owner, Sir Michael Cole, was absent in England at the time. Hamilton next organised the armed men of the town into two infantry companies under the command of Allen and Malcolm Cathcart. The latter was made up of Presbyterians and Revd Robert Kelso, minister of the town's Presbyterian congregation, gave them much support.

THE FIRST ACT OF REBELLION

On 16 December came news that Newcomen's infantry were at Lisbellaw, four miles away. As it was a Sunday many of the leading citizens were at worship, but they immediately retired and gathered their troops, which mustered 200 foot and 150 cavalry. Though poorly armed, they set forth along the road to confront the army. Their plan was to persuade the Irish troops to retire but resist them should they refuse.

However, the proposition was never delivered. At the sight of these grimly determined citizens, the approaching troops fled to Maguiresbridge and thence to Cavan to await orders. Their officers, Shurloe and Nugent, had been dining at Captain Corry's house at Castlecoole and they too were forced to flee. Corry was outraged at this show of defiance and felt it a direct snub to his policy of compromise. Two days later he attempted to arrest William Browning at the head of a party of horse on a charge of treason. But following their success with the royal troops, Corry had underestimated the growing determination of the townspeople to continue their resistance. Instead, the citizens warned Corry that on the contrary he would be detained if he obstructed their designs. Taking the hint he withdrew to his estate.

GROWING RESISTANCE IN ULSTER

Meanwhile, Cathcart and MacCarmick had reached Londonderry to find that the city, since the show of defiance to Antrim's troops, had since negotiated with Lord Mountjoy for the quartering of two companies of his regiment within the city. Mountjoy's troops were Protestants and were led by the Scottish Anglican Colonel Robert Lundy. Nonetheless, the Enniskillen men were well received. Returning via Newtownstewart, they met Lord Mountjoy who was returning the rest of the regiment to Dublin. They delivered a letter to him outlining their reasons for earlier refusing admittance to the town of Newcomen's troops. (At this time their actions had been carried out purely for reasons of self-protection and had not resulted in the citizens of Enniskillen declaring for William of Orange.) Mountjoy listened but urged them to accept the protection of their King, James II, but Cathcart prophetically replied, 'if all that we hear be true, his Majesty will find it hard enough to protect himself'. From these sentiments it seems that word of James's growing constitutional difficulty in England was already known in Ireland.

Mountjoy promised to go to Enniskillen within a few days to resolve the situation, but on arrival in Dublin he was sent on a foreign mission and never made the engagement. Throughout the winter, Enniskillen was in constant touch with other centres of resistance in Ulster. Lord Kingston held Sligo, Lord Mount-Alexander led the Association of North-East Ulster (Armagh, Down and Antrim Protestants) and Lundy held Londonderry. Elsewhere throughout the rural areas, individual lords continued to support those in the main centres. From that point on, those who supported James were known as Jacobites and those who followed William were termed Williamites.

On 16 January 1689, Allen Cathcart and Hugh Hamilton were sent to England to request arms and ammunition from Prince William. It was known that James had fled the kingdom but the status of the Crown was still uncertain. In the interim, further recruitment of soldiers continued apace. At the end of the month, the citizens of Enniskillen elected Gustavus Hamilton Colonel of Foot, and Thomas Lloyd of Croaghan in Roscommon, Lieutenant Colonel. A request via the NE Ulster association to have Gerald Irvine of Necarne and James Corry made colonels of regiments at Enniskillen was politely but firmly refused. Irvine continued to prevaricate by accepting a commission in the Earl of Granard's Jacobite regiment. Arriving at Cavan with supplies and ready to begin recruiting, Irvine was promptly captured by Daniel French and Henry Williams from Belturbet. Sent to Enniskillen, he argued that he had taken the position to secure the arms for Enniskillen. His reputation was now in doubt and though he later raised a troop of horse for Schomberg and died that winter at the camp at Dundalk, history has not been kind to this irresolute lord. It must be remembered, in defence of Irvine and Corry, that they owed their position to the administration of James II and until the issue of the crown was resolved, the actions of the Inniskilliners were treasonable. But the flood of history allows us only one chance to decide our fate, and as both men chose the wrong course of action, they were drowned in its tide.

On 11 March, news came that James's defection had been deemed an act of abdication and William of Orange and his wife Mary were to be offered the joint crown. William and Mary were proclaimed joint sovereigns at Enniskillen, but events on the island were now taking a fast course. From Dublin, Lieutenant-General Richard Hamilton had gathered together an army and had set forth to rid Ireland, once and for all, of the troublesome Ulster Protestant menace and bring the whole island under the control of King James.

ARRIVAL OF KING JAMES IN IRELAND

James landed in Ireland at Kinsale, near Cork, on 12 March 1689. With him were the French Lieutenant General Conrad van Rosen and a group of French, Scottish, English and Irish officers. Moving to Cork to meet Tyrconnell, he reached Dublin on 24 March and was greeted by the population 'as if he had been an angel from heaven'. Unwisely, James was advised to proceed to Londonderry, where the famous siege had recently commenced and where, he was informed, his arrival would ensure the swift surrender of the garrison. He left Dublin and arrived before Londonderry on 18 April. But his supporters had seriously misjudged the mood of that city's inhabitants. Fired upon by the cannon of the citizen soldiery within the city, he was forced to withdraw to Dublin.

On 7 May, James called a parliament in Dublin. Though they were not excluded, only six Protestants attended, as many refused to send a representative from the disaffected boroughs in Ulster. The majority of those attending were Old English lords whose primary concern was the restoration of their former lands. James agreed to a Declaratory Act, which ensured the English parliament could not pass legislation for Ireland, but he did not repeal Poyning's Law, which would have restored full self-governance for Ireland. In addition, he reluctantly repealed the Act of Settlement whereby lands would now be restored to their pre-1641 owners. Similarly, he cancelled the Londonderry Plantation but he did not restore these lands to the O'Cahans nor to the other lords who had previously owned it.

James also passed an Act of Attainder, naming several thousand (mainly Protestant) citizens who were now in rebellion against him, who would, as a consequence, risk losing their estates. In addition, Catholics were once again permitted to pay tithes to their own clergy. But James resisted the call to re-establish the Catholic Church to its former position in Ireland, granting only 'liberty of conscience', which effectively made all denominations equally valid. Parliament was finally prorogued on 18 July.

It had been a difficult process for James and he has been viewed in Ireland as a reluctant reformer. But clearly he was in a difficult position, as he had not yet re-established his power. His actions in Ireland were designed to reward his Irish supporters without alarming his English and Scottish ones, many of whom were Protestants themselves. But in early spring, his army appeared on the cusp of a complete victory in Ireland that would serve as a convenient stepping stone for a victorious return to Britain.

THE SIEGE OF DERRY

In 1689 the Catholic cause in Ireland had the greater authority, for the Old English and Gaelic lords were supporting the rightful king and could expect their reward if James prevailed. In addition, Louis XIV, then sovereign of Europe's most powerful state, supported James. Thus James's Irish supporters did not delay in beginning their assault on the troublesome Williamites.

The first move to restore Tyrconnell's authority occurred in Munster. General Justin MacCarthy arrived before Bandon, which the plantation Protestants had only recently declared for King William and ejected Catholics from the town. He negotiated the Williamites' surrender before dismantling the town walls. He then proceeded to subdue the rest of the province. Clearly this time there would be no centre of Protestant resistance in Munster as had occurred in 1641. Richard Hamilton then gathered his army together and moved north to subdue Ulster.

On 12 March, Hamilton routed the forces of the Williamite North-East Ulster Association at the 'Break of Dromore', and by 27 March lay before the Williamite-held town of Coleraine, commanded by another Gustavus Hamilton. Despite an initial repulse in front of its poorly constructed walls, his army forced a crossing of the River Bann further south at Portglenone. Realising that they would soon be encircled, the Coleraine garrison together with its citizens fled west to swell the surge of refugees fleeing inside the walls of Londonderry. Richard Hamilton pursued and on 13 April his army laid opposite the city, separated by another mighty river, the Foyle. Unperturbed, he marched upstream, and on 15 April forced the fords of the River Finn and marched along the west bank of the Foyle to Londonderry. So began on 18 April the longest and most famous siege in British history; one that was to last for 105 days.

ACTION ALONG THE ERNE

Meanwhile, along the Erne valley, things had also changed. To cover Richard Hamilton's advance into eastern Ulster in mid-March, Viscount Galmoy, Piers Butler, had been sent simultaneously NW from Dublin into the Erne valley, to secure the army's left flank. This brought Lord Galmoy's notorious dragoons into Cavan town, where they seized Captain Dixie, son of the Dean of Kilmore, Lieutenant Charleton and eight or ten troopers. Panic gripped the Protestant community of the county and they decided to abandon their vulnerable position in Cavan and take up the offer of protection from Lundy at Londonderry. The vestry records of the Church of Ireland parish in Clones, just across the border in County Monaghan, records, '1688 March the 19th day of this month, the last of the Protestant inhabitants deserted the town and parish of Clowneis, the Irish possessing themselves of that part of the country'. It appeared that the traditional topographical barrier to Ulster presented by the Erne's loughs and rivers might be surrendered without a fight.

On 20 March, in atrocious weather, this column of Cavan refugees arrived at Enniskillen. Here they were offered the opportunity to join the resistance with the Inniskilliners (as the polyglot defenders of the town were termed). Most refused and three days later they set off for Londonderry. However, Governor Hamilton had wisely refused to harbour extra civilians in Enniskillen unless their husbands were prepared to stay and help defend them. As a result, many others stayed on and the garrison benefited from the addition of three or four foot companies and as many troops of cavalry.

Their addition came none too soon. As the weary column of Cavan refugees set out for Londonderry, news arrived that Galmoy's troops were at Lisnaskea, twelve miles away. He forwarded a demand to Enniskillen for their surrender and presumably believed that the town would accede. But the Inniskilliners had resolved to fight, and on 23 March, Governor Hamilton mustered their forces in anticipation of an attack by the Jacobite army, said to be at Lisnaskea. However, the assault never came and word soon arrived that Galmoy had returned to Crom castle on the Upper Erne and placed its owner Abraham Creighton under siege.

Galmoy had no siege artillery, but he came up with the cunning idea of creating two mock cannon from tin and making threatening movements in front of the castle. However his plans were thwarted when an incautious gunner experimented with one of the 'cannon' to see how good it was, and blew it up. Unperturbed, Creighton held on, making use of long-barrelled fowling pieces to disrupt attempts by Galmoy to approach the castle. Meanwhile, Governor Hamilton had collected 200 of his best troops, sending some overland and others via boats to Creighton's assistance. Despite attempts to stop them, the waterborne relief column reached the castle and together with the garrison sallied out and scattered Galmoy's troops, killing thirty of them and causing their retreat to Belturbet.

While at Belturbet, Galmoy carried out an act that was to galvanise the Inniskilliners and to convince them of his perfidy. Creighton held a Captain Bryan Maguire as a prisoner at Crom and Galmoy requested his release in exchange for Dixie and Charlton, whom he had previously captured at Cavan. Creighton agreed and released Maguire but Galmoy promptly court martialled the two officers on a charge of levying war against King James II. Both were condemned to death, but to save themselves Galmoy offered them the chance to renounce their Protestant faith. Both refused and they were summarily hanged and their heads struck off and kicked around the street by the dragoons. Later the heads were nailed to the market house. For Captain Bryan Maguire, whose freedom had been honoured by Creighton, this ghastly crime was too much and he resigned his commission and took no further part in the war.

Meanwhile, on 25 March, news came of the arrival in Lough Foyle of arms and ammunition brought by Captain James Hamilton. But Colonel Lundy, now Governor of Londonderry, released to the Inniskilliners only five barrels of powder and sixty musket barrels without any stock. Apart from those captured in combat, these were the last weapons delivered to Enniskillen before the timely intervention of General Kirke in July.

In mid-April, Lord Kingston at Sligo had been ordered by Lundy at Londonderry to retire and take up positions near the Foyle crossings to prevent Richard Hamilton's Jacobite army from crossing near Strabane. But the message arrived too late and Kingston arrived to observe Hamilton's army across the river and moving inexorably towards Londonderry. Instead he retired back through the Barnesmore Gap in Donegal and fortified Ballyshannon and Donegal. The remainder of his force, consisting of six infantry companies and two troops of horse, he ordered to Enniskillen. He then seized a French ship in Killybegs harbour and proceeded to Scotland to report the dire situation to the new King.

Henceforth, from Crom to Ballyshannon, the course of the River Erne, together with the two great loughs between, was to become the frontline between Williamite and Jacobite forces. The 'Inniskilliners', as the Enniskillen troops were now termed, unlike the garrison at Londonderry, were never willing to endure a miserable existence behind formal siege lines. In fairness, the main concentration of Jacobite arms was directed at reducing the only city left to William III's supporters. Nonetheless, there were always sizeable concentrations of Jacobite forces around the Erne loughs which threatened Enniskillen with encirclement. However, the town benefited from its central location, which prevented the Jacobites from effective joint actions. In the end, the failure of these separate Jacobite armies to co-operate in joint actions ensured that the Inniskilliners could deal with each threat separately.

'LITTLE CROMWELL'

The arrival of Kingston's troops seems to have spurred the Enniskillen garrison into offensive action. During late April the Jacobites began establishing posts nearer to Enniskillen in order to strangle their movements and overawe them. On 24 April, at the head of a flying column, Colonel Thomas Lloyd, a landowner from Croaghan in County Roscommon, surprised a Jacobite unit, which was hoping to set up a garrison at Trillick. They quickly dispersed but left provisions and cattle, which were brought in to Enniskillen. Four days later another Jacobite garrison was being established at Augher and again Lloyd set off to intercept them. However, they fled before his arrival and he burnt down the castle before setting off over the hills into Monaghan and returning home on 2 May with much plunder.

Only two days later, Captain Ffolliet reported that his garrison was under siege at Ballyshannon by a Jacobite army led by Patrick Sarsfield. Lloyd collected horse and foot and set off to assist. At Belleek on 8 May, Sarsfield's army, positioned behind a bog with only a narrow track across, blocked their path to Ballyshannon. Nonetheless, Lloyd managed to outflank them and the Jacobites fled, hotly pursued by the victorious Inniskilliners. Nearly 200 cavalry were slain, but the bulk of the infantry escaped through a bog. Sixty more men were captured on Inis Samer Island in the mouth of the Erne at Ballyshannon. Two small cannon, horses and weapons were also brought back to Enniskillen.

At the end of May, Lloyd collected 1,500 foot and horse and set out on his most audacious raid to date. Picking up some more volunteers at Crom, he crossed Wattlebridge and captured two Jacobite outposts at Redhills and Bellanacargy castle, before raiding as far as Kells, only thirty miles from Dublin. When he returned, he brought 3,000 cattle, 2,000 sheep and 500 horses, as well as meal for the animals. For these exploits Lloyd has been rightly commended as 'little Cromwell'.

MIXED FORTUNES

On 3 June, two troops stationed at Castle Mervyn near Trillick captured 160 horses belonging to Jacobite cavalry that had been allowed to graze unguarded at Fireagh, outside Omagh. This encouraged Governor Hamilton to attempt a relief of the beleaguered garrison of Londonderry. For an unknown reason, the Governor decided to lead the 1,500 troops and two cannon and instead left Lloyd in charge at Enniskillen. Almost immediately, the scheme ran into difficulty. They reached Trillick, where the Jacobites retreated into Mervyn's castle. Hamilton called on them to surrender but they refused. News then arrived of the approach of a large Jacobite contingent on its way to Londonderry. Hamilton cautiously concluded that it was unwise to proceed with so many enemies between him and his destination and the scheme was wisely abandoned.

LLOYD'S RAID TO BELTURBET

The timely return of Hamilton thwarted Jacobite plans to occupy Enniskillen in his absence. Nevertheless, news arrived from Crom castle to warn that a Jacobite force under Brigadier Sutherland had fortified Belturbet and left a force of 200 foot and 80 dragoons under Colonel Scot. Lloyd immediately set forth with a large contingent and reached Belturbet on 19 June. The Jacobites had fortified the churchyard, but Lloyd's men secured adjoining buildings overlooking their positions and poured in heavy fire. After two hours, Scot surrendered and the prisoners, together with two barrels of powder, 700 muskets and fifty horses were taken back to Enniskillen. Such haemorrhaging of the Jacobite cause in the Erne basin could be ill afforded and so matters were soon stepped up to deal decisively with the thorny Inniskilliners.

Meanwhile, on 3 July, word came from the frigate *Bonaventure*, laying in Killybegs harbour, that General Kirke was aware of their predicament and had promised military supplies. Lloyd and a few others were sent on board to return to General Kirke's camp at Inch in Lough Swilly to report their need more thoroughly and in particular to receive commissions and the services of some experienced officers.

BATTLE OF KILMACORMICK

While Lloyd was thus engaged, the Duke of Berwick, James II's illegitimate son, arrived before Enniskillen with a large force on 13 July. The Inniskilliners, under MacCarmick, went out to meet them at Kilmacormick, just beyond the town, but were roundly defeated, with fifty killed and a further twenty captured. Berwick, however, did not follow up his attack on the town, probably because he had no artillery and because the town was now protected by a battery on the hill to the east, today known as Forthill. This fort had been constructed between May and June by Majors Hart and Rider and formed the main defence for the eastern approach to the town.

BATTLE OF NEWTOWNBUTLER

General Kirke then sent several experienced officers to Enniskillen, most notable of whom was Colonel William Wolseley. In addition he supplied twenty barrels of powder, 600 dragoon firelocks and 1,000 infantry muskets, together with eight small cannon – a most formidable arsenal. Lloyd set sail from Inch on 24 July and arrived at Ballyshannon two days later. The next day they went to Belleek and then on to Enniskillen by boat, where they arrived the following day. News had arrived that Justin MacCarthy was on the move in the upper Erne area moving towards Enniskillen.

On his arrival, Wolseley was immediately given overall command at Enniskillen. His first task was to relieve Crom castle, which was under siege for a second and more deadly time, for this time Justin MacCarthy, Jacobite general, had artillery and was battering the walls. On the evening of 30 July, Wolseley sent Lieutenant Colonel Berry on ahead with a mixed force of eight horse troops, three foot companies and two dragoons to fortify Lisnaskea castle and promised to bring up the main army from Enniskillen. Berry advanced and found the castle too ruined to garrison and so spent the night in the open.

The following morning, he was informed that a large force of Jacobites was moving towards him from Crom. Falling back outside Lisnaskea, he ambushed them and forced them to flee, killing 200 and capturing another 30. Berry pursued them, but when he became aware that the main Jacobite army under MacCarthy had now raised the siege at Crom and were on the move, he awaited the arrival of Wolseley with the main Inniskilling force.

A conflict now looked inevitable, but Wolseley felt compelled to solicit the opinion of these citizen soldiers. The officers and men unanimously agreed to advance towards MacCarthy's awaiting army. Wolseley had with him sixteen troops of horse, three troops of dragoons and twenty-one companies of foot, totalling over 2,000 men. Opposing him, MacCarthy had over 6,000 men and some cannon. Initially, MacCarthy skilfully contested each narrow point of the road by volleys of musketry from his advance guard before retiring to the next point. Then, a mile beyond Newtownbutler, Wolseley came upon MacCarthy's main position. Here the Jacobites had placed their army behind a bog with the cannon commanding the narrow path through it, with the infantry on the side of the hill and the cavalry behind.

Wolseley ordered his infantry forward to cross the bog on either side of the road, covered by the cavalry. Despite a heavy fire from the Jacobite cannon and infantry, the Inniskilliners crossed the bog and engaged the infantry in heavy hand-to-hand combat. The Inniskilling horse now charged up the road to engage the enemy cavalry on the hill, but whether from receiving a confused order or whether gripped by fear, the Jacobite cavalry left the field. The Jacobite infantry were now surrounded and began to disintegrate. Many took to their heels and attempted to flee, but unfamiliar with the countryside, they found themselves trapped by the waters of Upper Lough Erne. In the subsequent pursuit, hundreds were killed or drowned. MacCarthy was captured and brought back to Enniskillen but later escaped and found his way to Europe.

For the loss of trifling numbers of their own men, the Inniskilliners had removed any direct threat to their town and won a resounding victory over the Jacobites. Wolseley returned to Enniskillen but ordered part of Colonel Tiffin's regiment to occupy Ballyshannon. Sarsfield's army, encamped at the River Drowes, struck camp and retired to Sligo.

ARRIVAL OF THE WILLIAMITE ARMY IN ULSTER

On 4 August, Wolseley informed General Kirke that he had given orders to Sir Albert Conyngham to raise a regiment of Dragoons, consisting of twelve troops, from amongst the horsemen of the Inniskilling army. This was to become the famous Inniskilling Dragoon Guards, who later won fame at Waterloo and Balaclava. Zachariah Tiffin had already received his commission on 20 June from Kirke to become colonel of a regiment of foot from the Inniskilling forces. This regiment would later become the 27th Foot or Royal Inniskilling Fusiliers, who would earn undying fame when holding the crucial crossroads of La Haye Sainte against the French attack at Waterloo.

On 13 August 1689, Count Schomberg landed a large Williamite army at Bangor, which proceeded to capture Carrickfergus and marched south, clearing east Ulster, before arriving at Dundalk in early September. Schomberg judged himself too weak to continue further south and spent the next few months facing the main Jacobite army encamped in north Leinster.

RAID AND COUNTER RAID

Despite the change in the military balance of power, the fighting in the Erne basin was far from over. In late August 1689, Patrick Sarsfield abandoned Sligo; Conyngham promptly occupied it with three troops of his dragoons, two of horse and five foot companies. On 10 September, Colonel Lloyd arrived in Sligo to take command, bringing the remainder of Conyngham's Dragoons, together with six companies of Hamilton's foot and three troops of horse. Never one to rest on his laurels, Lloyd planned a raid deep into the enemy-held territory of north Connacht.

Moving by night via Coloney and the Curlew Mountains, he set out on 19 September towards Boyle on a lightning raid. The following daybreak, his men surprised a small Jacobite outpost at Ballinafad, but his presence in the area was now known. Colonel O'Kelly, the Jacobite commander at Boyle, sallied out with his garrison of 850 men and attacked Lloyd as he approached the town. But again Lloyd was victorious and the Williamites went on to take Jamestown and Drumsna House in County Leitrim.

These bold moves threatened to open a back door into Jacobite-held Connacht and south Ulster. Recognising the danger, Sarsfield reorganised his troops and counter-attacked on 15 October, recapturing Jamestown and forcing the garrison in Boyle to promptly evacuate. On the sixteenth, Sarsfield reached the outskirts of Sligo, held by Lloyd, who brought the garrison out to meet him. For once, 'little Cromwell' was roundly defeated and retreated into the town. Colonel Russell then arrived alone from Ballyshannon and both judged Sarsfield's army to be too strong. Leaving a small garrison in the town's Green Fort, the main army retired to Ballyshannon. Sarsfield promptly invested the town and attacked the garrison, forcing its surrender on 21 October. Though defeated, the garrison was permitted to march to Ballyshannon still possessing their weapons and colours.

In mid-November, Schomberg ordered his army into winter quarters and the Inniskilliners took up lodgings in Clones, Ballyshannon, Enniskillen, and further afield. On 4 December, Wolseley, with a mixed party of Inniskilling horse and dragoons, occupied Belturbet in a night move that brought the town again under Williamite control as an outpost. With the exception of Charlemont fort in Armagh, most of Ulster had now been cleared of Jacobite troops. But in the SW of the province, the threat of enemy raids was still very much in the minds of the Inniskilling forces. For a second successive winter, the Erne basin was to form the frontline between the wintering troops of both sides with Cavan and north Leitrim, forming a kind of no-man's-land between them. Both sides used the winter months to prepare for the year ahead.

THE BATTLE OF THE BOYNE

In February 1690, Colonel Wolseley was at Belturbet when he learned of a concentration of Jacobite forces under the Duke of Berwick at Cavan. He quickly marched a mixed force of foot and cavalry across the Annalee River at Ballyhaise and arrived before Cavan. A fierce fight ensued but presently Berwick was forced to retreat through the town to prepared fortifications. The pursuing Inniskilliners then began looting, and when Berwick rallied and returned to the attack, Wolseley set fire to the town to force out the pillagers. For a second time Berwick was unsuccessful and Wolseley was eventually able to return safely to base. The following month, another Inniskilling raid to Cavan resulted in the rest of the town being fired, but the Jacobites remained unmoved in their fortifications. This time the Inniskilling army was assisted by Danish troops employed under contract to William III.

With the approach of spring, rising military activity levels heralded that a final decision regarding the throne of Britain was imminent. On 6 April, Wolseley captured Killeshandra, again making use of the Danes. On 12 May he marched from Belturbet with a mixed force of 1,200 men and laid siege to Bellanacargy Castle After a fierce battle, the garrison of 200 men surrendered under generous terms. Meanwhile, Schomberg had finally captured Charlemont fort in Armagh, thus removing the last Jacobite garrison in Ulster.

The following month, William III landed at Carrickfergus with a substantial army and, marching south, linked up with Schomberg. On 22 June, he reviewed his army, now numbering around 36,000 troops, at Loughbrickland. This was very much a polyglot European army. Apart from the local Ulster troops there were Danes, Dutch,

French, Scots and English. On 1 July, William forced the crossing of the River Boyne and defeated James's army in a battle that still resonates down through the island's history to the present. James fled to Dublin and later to France, leaving Tyrconnell in command in Ireland.

In late July, William ordered part of his army, under General Douglas, to force the River Shannon crossing at Athlone. When this failed, Douglas returned to join the main Williamite army, which had begun to advance against Limerick. In early August, William's army began an ultimately unsuccessful siege at Limerick and with the summer weather already deteriorating he ordered the troops into winter quarters. Before returning to England, he ordered the newly arrived Duke of Marlborough (of later Blenheim fame) to lay siege and capture the main ports of Munster. Marlborough duly obliged, capturing Cork and Kinsale by early October, thus reducing the threat of another French landing in the rear of the Williamite army.

Again, the Erne basin was the frontline between the opposing forces. Like a great arm hinged on the mouth of the river Erne, the Williamites had managed to liberate a great swathe of Ireland, clearing most of Leinster and Munster and causing the Jacobites to retire behind the line of the River Shannon. The only land route into this heartland was through the traditional crossing points between Ulster and Connacht at Ballyshannon and Enniskillen. But equally it was possible for the Jacobites to break out through these points to ravage deep into Ulster. Thus the winter of 1690/91 was still fraught with danger for the watchful Inniskilling army.

FROM THE BATTLE OF AUGHRIM
TO THE SURRENDER AT LIMERICK

The Inniskilling regiments appear to have wintered that year around Enniskillen and Belturbet. The continued breakdown of order in Ireland as a result of the war had now caused the countryside to be full of a lawless banditry known as 'rapparrees'. In April, a force of 200 foot and 100 dragoons under Colonel Tiffin left Ballyshannon and swept towards Sligo in an operation to clear them out. Tiffin's search-and-destroy mission reportedly 'killed 40 rapparrees, took 60 prisoners and brought off a good prey'.

In June, the Inniskillings were ordered to join the new Williamite commander Ginkel at Rathcondra, where the army was assembling for the forthcoming campaign. Ginkel's main objective was to breach the line of the Shannon, and he began a siege at Athlone on 19 June. Despite stubborn resistance from the Jacobites, now led by the French general Marquis St Ruth, he managed to get his troops across by 30 June and St Ruth ordered a withdrawal to the village of Aughrim, thirty miles east of Galway. Here, on Sunday 12 July 1691, was fought the bloodiest battle in Irish history. Upwards of 45,000 men were engaged and by the end of the day as many as 6,000 lay dead, but the Jacobite field army in Ireland had been decisively and finally defeated.

The remnants of the Jacobite army retreated once again to Limerick but this time Ginkel could assault them from the Connacht side as well. Galway surrendered on 21 July and the Siege of Limerick began. On 3 October, after a week of negotiations, the Jacobites signed the Treaty of Limerick. Patrick Sarsfield and 14,000 soldiers were given liberty and transport to exile to the continent, where they continued to fight for the French. The three-year war was finally over but the repercussions were only just beginning. The result was the final large transfer of land from those remaining Catholic landowners to Protestant worthies, a process which also heralded the beginning of a century of peace in Ireland.

The parishioners of Clones returned to their town in April 1692. On 15 April that year, the vestry book recorded:

> ...the parson of the parish, Mr William Smith, returning to the parish from whence he was forced with all his Protestant parishioners, the 19th of March 1688 [1689], finding the roof, glass and seats of the church all destroyed, calling a vestry to be held upon the 3rd day of May following.

For the previous three years, the Erne countryside had formed the frontline for constitutional upheavals. Many of its buildings had suffered destruction and were in a grave state of disrepair. But despite the devastation, the castles and defended homes of the area had satisfactorily performed their function and had again acted as islands of refuge in the turmoil. But it was also clear that the new order that had been created by the political changes would result in home building becoming less defensive and more domestic in nature.

5

THE END OF THE CASTLE AND THE FLOWERING OF DOMESTIC ARCHITECTURE

UNFORTIFIED BUILDINGS IN SEVENTEENTH-CENTURY ULSTER

Throughout Ireland, new castles and fortified homes were built right up until the middle of the seventeenth century but in ever-decreasing numbers. Already throughout the century, newer purely domestic-style houses were being erected which sought to imitate the latest British and continental designs. The conflict between constructing for comfort or defence was only finally won by the former at the end of the 1689 revolution. The stability created by the victory of William of Orange over his father-in-law James II ensured that the need for fortified living space was no longer necessary. Ireland was soon to enter a century of peace, the longest period of stability that the island has ever experienced.

Though rare, substantial undefended houses of the gentry had been erected even in the seventeenth century. In the 1660s, Sir William Tichbourne erected a two-storey, seven-bay house at Beaulieu, near Drogheda, County Louth, which had no defensive features, save a tall hedge which surrounded the building until the 1800s. Closer to home, in Ulster, Richhill Castle was built in the 1660s and is reputedly the oldest undefended house surviving in the province. Built by the Richardson family in the style of a Dutch-gabled manor house, the floor plan has symmetrical projecting wings and a rear stair projection, thus showing some similarities to the manor houses at Castle Archdale and Tullykelter. But, unlike them, Richhill has no loopholes or other defensive features to repel attackers. Likewise, Waringstown House, County Down, was built in 1667 by William Waring without any defensive arrangements.

Back in the Erne valley, there is scant evidence of any remaining unfortified domestic architecture of the seventeenth century, though a few structures claim this distinction. One such place is the little cottage at Bolusty, near Belleek, traditionally associated with the Morrow family. Believed to date from the 1690s, it is set back 600m from the main Enniskillen to Belleek road, in a fold of the hillside, nestling below the steep limestone cliffs of Lough Navar and almost invisible to the passer by. The storey-and-a-half cottage measures 14.1m by 6.9m (47 by 23ft) with walls 0.6m thick and is constructed of well-cut local stone, rendered over with rough cement. There are central doors located in both long walls, with the front entered via a porch. The main living room has a centrally located large stone-cut fireplace and there is a smaller second fireplace in the next room. A narrow wooden stairway located off a rear passageway (reminiscent of

Gardenhill) leads up to a bedroom lit by two skylights, with two further bedrooms located at each side, lit by a gable window. Orientated north–south, the cottage displays no defensible features at all, though perhaps the windows could be shuttered.

Nearby at Rosscor, close to the viaduct, a long, thatched single-storey cottage, reputedly from the seventeenth century, survived to be photographed at the start of the twentieth, but extensive rebuilding mid-century has resulted in a two-storey house and no visible remains of the former building. Similarly, a house at Curragh, near Carrybridge, associated since the Plantation with the Boardman family (who still inhabit the house), was rebuilt in the 1940s and only a single thick wall remains of the original structure. Another contemporary example is at Curragh, on the shores of Upper Lough Erne near the modern Share Centre, Lisnaskea. Set well back from the road but close to the lough shore, Curragh is a two-storey, three-bay house with additions, built originally in the 1690s, though it looks of the following century. It has thick rubble stone walls with limestone dressings but no defensive features.

All of these sites in the Erne present problems with accurate dating and should be treated cautiously. Suffice to say that seventeenth-century buildings were severely ravaged by continuous campaigning across the Erne in both wars and hence we have few examples that have survived to our time.

THE EIGHTEENTH-CENTURY UNFORTIFIED HOUSE

However it was the ending of hostilities, as reflected in the 1691 Treaty of Limerick and the establishment of the 'Protestant nation' in Ireland, which gradually allowed the idea of a truly undefended home to take its place in the landscape. But first the emphasis was to restore the buildings damaged by the late war and indeed there are few remains of any architecture before the end of Queen Anne's reign (1701-14). It is probable that the economic conditions in the country had not improved sufficiently to see the creation of many new houses.

As the century progressed, however, Ireland entered into a period of stability. From the perspective of our own times, as we emerge from a long period of civil disorder, the century of peace that followed the cessation accord at Limerick in 1691 is difficult for us to fully appreciate. As confidence in the new political order in Ireland grew throughout the eighteenth century, the landscape began to become populated by houses that copied the most contemporary European designs. Around forty years after the end of the Williamite war, conditions appear to have become favourable enough to permit a period of extensive house construction right along the Erne.

The Erne has several very fine examples of this trend, which have survived to the present day. First among them is the Georgian manor house of Little Hall Craig, built in 1721 by Robert Weir, who chose to place it directly in front of his old Plantation home. The new house, of three storeys and three bays (though recent restoration work has revealed it to have been originally five-bay), is rendered and has no apparent defensive features at all. A datestone of 1721 is located low down on the east gable. Two long windows shedding light into the hall behind, making the entrance quite undefended, frame the narrow door case. The door case is surmounted with a scrolled marble pediment with an inscription identifying Weir as the builder.

This house is reputed to be the oldest inhabited building remaining in Fermanagh and it is hard to dissent from that view. On entering the front hall, the visitor has to pass through another door to the staircase enclosure. This is not an overtly defensive feature, but prevents the visitor from having immediate access to all rooms and floors of the house. The front of the house faces south across a long view of the hills, but Weir chose to build his house on the slope rather than on the summit, perhaps with anonymity in mind. By the early years of the eighteenth century, Ireland was in a subdued state but it was still wise to remain discreet in the landscape. Even today, one is only able to catch a glimpse of the house through the trees from the nearby road.

On a much grander scale, Thomas Coote of Cootehill, County Cavan, Lord Justice of the King's Bench in Ireland, had built for him the Palladian villa later known as Bellamont Forest in 1730. This perfect example, inspired by the Italian models of Villa Rotunda and Villa Pisani, to the design of Sir Edward Lovett Pearce, was built in brick rather than stone. Of two storeys over a basement and incorporating a superb pedimented Doric portico, ornate plasterwork cornices and ceilings, the building represents the growing optimism and aspirations of Ireland's gentry to leave behind the restrictive defensive designs of the previous century and adopt the European neo-classical model of comfortable living.

Likewise at nearby Ballyhaise, Colonel Brockhill Newburgh employed the German-born architect Richard Cassels (who also built Powerscourt and Russborough) to design a seven-bay, two-storey house with basement in 1733. Built of locally fired brick with ashlar dressings, the house has a central entrance with pedimented front containing pilasters in Greek architectural style. Both basement and ground floor are brick vaulted and contain the original ceiling plasterwork. The saloon is one of the earliest-surviving oval rooms in the British Isles and features a curved chimney piece and doors. A wing was later added to the house in the 1800s and original hand-painted wallpaper from the 1830s still adorns the walls. Clearly the continuing political stability allowed house design to flourish along the Erne without thought of defence.

Other building examples of a greater and lesser scale survive along the Erne. On a slightly smaller scale, the Dundas family erected a modest country house at Teevan, Farrancassidy, near Belleek, in 1731, without defensive features. Of two storeys and seven bays, it was still thatched in the early years of the twentieth century but is now tiled. Near Derrylin on Upper Lough Erne, the Winslow family built a modest two-storey house in 1740 without defence, called Dresternan House. A few miles away, the Cole family finally abandoned their draughty castle at Enniskillen to build Florencecourt in the 1730s. In Cavan, Moynehall was abandoned for a new house nearby, which probably robbed us of any survival of the seventeenth-century Farnham castle for the adjacent grand Georgian mansion.

Thus, all of these great ascendancy mansions rested undisturbed for over a hundred years after the Treaty of Limerick. When the United Irish rebellion broke out in 1798 there were sporadic attacks on country estates, but in the main property was not deliberately or systematically targeted, and unlike the destruction of the previous century, these examples of Irish architecture survive to the present. So despite their lowly status in the pantheon of contemporary style or taste, the modest castles and defended homes of the settlers ensured the survival of the Plantation populations in Ulster and across

Ireland right up to the present – surely a testament to the Plantation planners all those years ago who insisted on the creation of defended homes and bawns as a condition of the original granting of estates in Ulster.

WERE PLANTATION CASTLES A SUCCESS OR FAILURE?

It only remains to ponder the importance of the Plantation castles and to assess their performance against the role for which they were originally conceived, as well as their subsequent impact on events during the seventeenth century. Can we, 400 years later, assess their influence on the survival of the Ulster Plantation? The seventeenth century was very much a time of great political upheaval in Ireland, which consequently affected the economic and civil stability within the country, resulting in enormous destruction to the built landscape. In making our assessment, certain aspects of the original Ulster Plantation need to be considered.

It has long been acknowledged that the original plantation plan was not carried out in full by the grantees and subsequent government commissions reinforced this picture of incompleteness. Bodley, Pynnar, Perrott and Annesley, though pointing out individual successes, painted a picture of failure by grantees to carry out all the instructions to the full. By association, other aspects of the plantation, particularly the settlement arrangements, have been deemed equally unsuccessful.

But is this really true? The commissioners were civil servants and such is the way with public auditors. Pointing up shortcomings and emphasising areas needing improvement in this seventeenth-century government scheme was surely as expected of them as it is in our own time. To make a fully informed judgement we need to understand and appreciate the role of the castles during the calamitous century that followed their construction. For it was during this time that the very future of the plantation settlement itself was put in doubt on two occasions. What role did castles play in ultimate survival?

The scheme of conditions was published in January 1609, at a time when the province was recovering from a prolonged period of disorder and was still threatened by a return of these conditions. It was only in the wake of the Flight of the Earls and the O'Doherty rebellion that order returned to the province. During the early 1610s, as settlers arrived and stability returned, the necessity to construct defensive buildings began to recede and other projects besides castles competed for the limited resources of the landlords, as they strove to develop their estates. That said, many landlords did build castles according to the conditions of their grant and in some cases they exceeded the minimum requirements.

It must also be pointed out that the written conditions expected the landlord to build a modest, family-occupied building which would be proof against local raids where attackers had the use of only small arms. The model for the castle was the Scottish tower house and the bastle of the borders. In the end, the plantation castles were to be subjected to a much more protracted and damaging type of warfare than the original planners had envisaged. It is no wonder then that many castles were casualties in the wars that resulted later in the century and so did not survive to the present time.

Of those castles actually constructed across the Erne's catchment area, their individual stories reflect the complexity of the political landscape of the seventeenth century.

Generally speaking, those castles that were not initially captured by the rebels in the 1641 rebellion served as bastions for the planters and would be similarly employed in the later Williamite wars. Equally, the failure to resist the rebels, as evidenced across the upper lough area, led to an almost complete eradication after 1641. Thus, today there are few remnants of plantation architecture anywhere across the whole of Cavan. Unlike the Lower Lough Erne area, Cavan provided no sustainable centre of resistance and thus the plantation there was more fundamentally affected by the rebellion. By contrast, the enclave centred on Enniskillen, including the castles at Monea, Termon, Castle Caldwell, Crom and Castle Balfour, ensured a stable base from which to rebuild once hostilities had ceased. The midlands of Ireland, including Cavan, were more heavily campaigned over during the twelve years of conflict and later in the war Cromwell's army destroyed captured fortresses to prevent their reoccupation. The removal of the British settler population was therefore more complete in Cavan and consequently the resettlement after 1653 abandoned the plantation principles for a pattern of nucleated clusters throughout the county. It was, after all, the cluster of castles at Killeshandra in 1641 that had provided the only real zone of resistance to the rebels.

During the later revolutionary war of the late 1680s, the example of Enniskillen in 1641 meant that it was chosen once again as the natural focus for planned resistance. By contrast, the experience of that earlier war in Cavan caused the settlers there to evacuate *en masse* for Enniskillen and Londonderry. Though initially points of resistance were established, Lord Galmoy's swift occupation of the Upper Erne in March 1689 showed the vulnerability of an area which had few natural obstacles favouring a defence.

Cavan thus became a frontier county and many of its buildings were destroyed in subsequent campaigning and raids by both sides. By contrast, Enniskillen remained undamaged as it was never captured, and the line of the Erne from Crom to Ballyshannon became the *de facto* frontline of the war in 1689. As a result, Fermanagh and the Lower Lough Erne area generally contain several plantation castle survivals that are in good order.

One of the chief reasons for the continued use of the castle in Ireland was the rareness of mobile artillery. In practice, castles were only captured by starvation or deception. It was really only with the appearance of the artillery train of the New Model Army after 1649 that castles began to become vulnerable structures. Oliver Cromwell has been cited as the cause of destruction of most Ireland's castles, although he only remained in Ireland for a period of nine months. However, the employment of artillery by his generals on the Confederate and Royalist garrisons after 1649 must have caused the same alarm as the first tanks that rumbled across seemingly impregnable trench lines at the Somme in 1916.

Beyond the primary function of resisting localised raids that used only small arms, the plantation castle struggled to survive. It is no surprise, therefore, to observe the native Irish, towards the end of the war, resort to the forests and crannogs rather than resist behind the stone walls of fortresses. Only at Clough Oughter castle on the Upper Erne was this rule excepted. The final surrender by Philip O'Reilly took place there on the island castle in 1653, where it was too much bother for the Cromwellians to haul heavy ordnance through the mire of the upper reaches of the Erne catchment to reduce it to rubble.

In conclusion, the castles generally served the purpose for which they were constructed. Despite two serious challenges to the very continuance of the plantation during the century, the castles assisted in the survival of the settler populations across the Erne catchment area and provided the necessary springboard for the further absorption of additional arrivals in the following years. At the beginning of the twenty-first century, as the island experiences the arrival of a new wave of immigration, let us hope that the assimilation of these settlers will be much less difficult.

FINAL THOUGHT

Although the events of the seventeenth century are now somewhat distant, many outside commentators have noted that the effects of those times are yet all too evident in Ulster society on a day-to-day basis. Let us therefore consider the words of George Storey, an officer in the army of King William III, who observed the return of native Jacobite Ulstermen in 1691 following their earlier exile to Munster during the war. Understandably, this return was a risky business for them as there was neither a guarantee of regaining their abandoned possessions nor any security retaliation from the settlers, but as Storey commented, 'the reason of this is plain, for there is so great an antipathy between the Ulster Irish and those in other parts of the kingdom, as nothing can be more, and the feuds amongst them greater than between either and their injured Protestant neighbour'. Surely this points out the obvious to those who inhabit as neighbours the same small space on this part of the island.

6

SOME PLANTATION CASTLES ON THE ERNE

Above left: Castle Archdale.   *Above centre*: Castle Caldwell.   *Above right*: Corratrasna.

Above left: Castle Mervyn.

Above centre: Crom.

Above right: Monea.

Far left: Necarne.

Left: Ballymagauran.

Above left: Termon Magrath.   *Above right*: Gardenhill.

Above left: Crevenish.   *Above right*: Tully.

Above left: Enniskillen.   *Above centre*: Portora.   *Above right*: Castle Balfour.

EXAMPLES OF CORBELLING

Above left: Monea – the SE bartizan corbelling incorporating a loophole above.
Above right: Monea's finely constructed bartizans.

Above left: Tully – corbelling as interpreted by Irish masons.
Above centre: Enniskillen – Watergate corbelling.
Above right: Castle Balfour – corbelling on third floor bartizan.

EXAMPLES OF LOOPHOLES

Above left: Monea – exterior profile of loophole. *Above centre*: Monea – interior view of loophole.
Above right: Monea – exterior profile of another loophole.

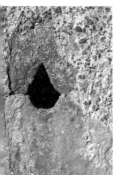   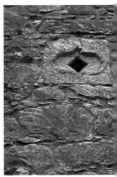

Above left: Castle Archdale – loophole exterior view.
Above centre left: Castle Archdale - internal view of loophole construction.
Above centre right: Crom – arch-headed loophole within irregular pentagon frame.
Above right: Crom – diamond-shaped loophole in decorated surround.

  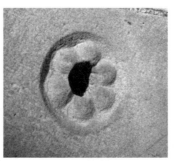 

Above left: Aghalane – comma-shaped loophole.
Above centre left: Aghalane – internal view of the same loophole.
Above centre right: Castle Balfour – decorated loophole.
Above right: Castle Balfour – double shaft for loophole at castle entrance.

EXAMPLES OF WINDOW AND OVEN FEATURES

Far left: Castle Archdale – windows in rear return.

Left: Termon Magrath – upper window in tower house.

Above left: Aghalane – bawn window with sockets for iron bars.
Above centre: Termon Magrath – squared stone oven built into corner.
Above right: Castle Mervyn – brick-lined oven built into gable corner.

SOME OTHER CASTLE FEATURES

Far left: Castle Archdale – bawn entrance.

Left: Termon Magrath – base batter, machicolation and finely detailed windows.

Below left: Termon Magrath – roof parapet corbels and rain spouts.

Below right: Castle Balfour – corbelled detail on upper wall.

7

LOWER LOUGH ERNE CIRCUIT

ENNISKILLEN
OS SHEET 17, GR 231442

Enniskillen town is an island site and the castle is located at the edge of the lough on the west end of the island. It can be reached by walking west from the town centre, known as 'The Diamond', for about 350m. The castle is signposted. There is a small entrance fee for the castle grounds and museum. Opening times are posted outside.

For those arriving by boat, there are numerous berthing facilities around Enniskillen town centre. A short stroll of a few minutes takes the visitor to the castle.

History

The site of Enniskillen castle has had a long and eventful history, stretching back long before the plantation. It is in fact the oldest castle in the Erne basin still in use, though now serving as the town's museum and as a regimental museum for the Royal Inniskilling Fusiliers, one of the oldest regiments in the British army.

A castle at Enniskillen belonging to the chief branch of the Maguire clan is mentioned in the ancient Annals of Ulster in 1439. Some parts of this castle remain beneath the later construction. The castle was the centre for several power struggles between the Maguires and their neighbours during the sixteenth century.

During the rebellion of Hugh O'Neill, at the end of the sixteenth century, the castle played an important role. By the 1590s, the Maguire clan were led by Hugh Maguire, who was the first to open hostilities with the government. But Hugh was defeated by government forces under Sir Henry Bagenal at the ford of Belleek in October 1593 (ironically, Bagenal was being assisted by Hugh O'Neill, who had yet to rebel) and Enniskillen castle became a prime target. Bagenal ordered a force of 300 men including Hugh Maguire's kinsman and anglophile rival, Connor Roe, to invest the castle.

Captain John Dowdall finally captured the castle for the Crown in February 1594 after a nine-day siege. Using a prisoner to act as a guide, he placed over 100 of his own soldiers in a boat protected from missiles, with a framework of hurdles covered with hides. The boat was floated against the castle wall where the troops, under this protective cover, set to work with pickaxes and bars. They managed to create a breach, and rushing into the castle they threatened to blow it up, at which point the garrison of thirty-six men and many women and children surrendered. Dowdall left a garrison of thirty men in the castle under the command of James Eccarsall as constable and then withdrew.

Maguire was to have his revenge the following year. Assisted by Hugh Roe O'Donnell, he invested the castle with an army of 3,500 men and brought its garrison close to starvation. A relief column commanded by Sir Henry Duke and Sir Edward Herbert, consisting of forty-six cavalry and 600 infantry with a train carrying supplies, was assembled and set out to relieve the beleaguered garrison. Leaving O'Donnell to occupy the garrison's attention, Maguire took 1,000 men, of whom many were Scottish mercenaries known as 'Galloglass', a few miles south to intercept the approaching relief column.

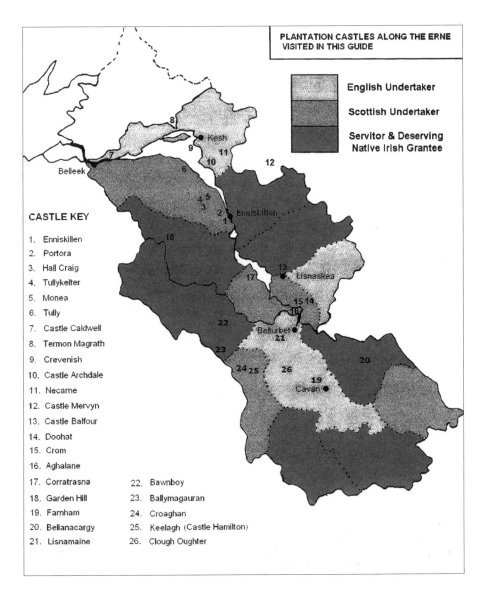

PLANTATION CASTLES ALONG THE ERNE VISITED IN THIS GUIDE

English Undertaker

Scottish Undertaker

Servitor & Deserving Native Irish Grantee

CASTLE KEY

1. Enniskillen
2. Portora
3. Hall Craig
4. Tullykelter
5. Monea
6. Tully
7. Castle Caldwell
8. Termon Magrath
9. Crevenish
10. Castle Archdale
11. Necarne
12. Castle Mervyn
13. Castle Balfour
14. Doohat
15. Crom
16. Aghalane
17. Corratrasna
18. Garden Hill
19. Farnham
20. Bellanacargy
21. Lisnamaine
22. Bawnboy
23. Ballymagauran
24. Croaghan
25. Keelagh (Castle Hamilton)
26. Clough Oughter

On 7 August 1594, as the column made its way across a shallow ford on the River Arney at Drumlane, just south of the modern-day hamlet of Bellanaleck, Maguire ambushed them, inflicting many injuries and scattering the supplies into the river. From that time, the site has been known in Gaelic as 'Bel atha na in Briosgadh' or Bellanaleck, which translated means 'Mouth of the Ford of the Biscuits' and has thus given its name to the nearby settlement, which is located on the main Belturbet road five miles south of Enniskillen.

Another relief column guarded by a greater force was immediately assembled and set out on 18 August, arriving unmolested at Enniskillen at the end of the month. The garrison welcomed this timely arrival as they had been driven to eat dogs, cats, horseflesh and salt-hides. One observer in the column noted, 'the castle had but one horse left alive, which the day after was to be slaughtered'. A new garrison was put into the castle and left six months' supplies.

However, the deteriorating military situation ensured that the government were unable to send a relief column when it next became due. By May 1595, the garrison, starved again to desperation, negotiated surrender on promise of quarter being given. These terms were not honoured and the entire garrison was killed.

A picture of Maguire's castle made during Dowdall's assault in 1594 shows a four-storey keep surrounded by an asymmetric bawn with water on all sides. Part of this keep survives in the battered ground storey of the present castle, but the four storeys were later reduced to three and the windows were enlarged. When the war concluded in 1603, the castle reverted to the Crown.

William Cole, a soldier originally from Slade in Devonshire, was appointed as captain of the King's longboats and barges at Ballyshannon and on Lough Erne in 1607, and later, as Governor or Constable of Enniskillen castle in 1609. Cole was highly regarded by his masters and was to play a crucial role in the development of the new town of Enniskillen, which was to be built on the island.

William Cole was a professional soldier who had previously served in the Low Countries and had arrived in Ireland in 1601, serving under Sir George Carew, Lord President of Munster. In June 1611, as part of the plantation settlement, the castle and two-thirds of the island were assigned to William Cole for a period of twenty-one years. He was obliged to rebuild the castle and in addition was later awarded the other third of the island to 'builde a towne thereon, wherein must be planted twenty English families, and whereon must be builded a church, a cemetery, a market-house, and a gaol'. In the next few years most of these conditions were successfully achieved and in recognition of this, in 1623, he became the outright owner of the entire island.

In 1611, Cole also received a grant of the 1,500-acre manor of Cornagrade and the following year purchased the manor of Drumskeagh. To fulfil his obligations, he built a bawn with two flankers at Cornagrade (now completely erased) and a castle at Portora, which he leased out for a time to James Spottiswood, Bishop of Clogher. Cole had clearly become one of the most important and successful of the new settlers.

However Cole's chief residence, once it was completed, was the castle at Enniskillen. Reporting in 1611, Carew comments on the work in progress:

…there is a fair strong wall, newly erected, of lime and stone, 26 feet [8m] high, with flankers, a parapet and a walk on the top of the wall, built by Captain William Colle constable thereof, towards which he had £200 sterling from the King. A fair house begun upon the foundations of the old castle, with other convenient houses for store and munition, which, besides the laying out of the captain's own money, will draw on some increase of charge to the King. The bawn is ditched about with a fair large ditch, and the river on one side, with a good drawbridge. The King has three good boats ready to attend all services. A large piece of ground adjoins the fort, with a good timber house, after the English fashion, built by the captain, in which he and his family dwell.

It was long believed that the so-called 'Watergate' overlooking the lough was the work of Maguire in the late sixteenth century, as it seemed to appear in the drawing depicting the capture of the castle by Dowdall in 1594. However, the work is undoubtedly Scottish in character and must belong to the rebuilding carried out by Cole at this time.

The town of Enniskillen was granted borough status in 1613 and continued to develop under the watchful eye of the constable even after an accidental fire in 1618 damaged many properties. In the muster roll of 1630, a total of fifty-three men were available in Enniskillen for military service if called upon, which indicates a population of around 180 persons in total, similar to the population of Belturbet.

Cole was knighted in 1617 and was later MP for the county in 1634 and 1639. But it was as guardian of the plantation in Fermanagh that Sir William Cole achieved his greatest fame. Tradition records that Cole and other notable settlers were invited by Rory Maguire to a banquet at his castle at Crevenish. During the meal, Cole was informed by one of Maguire's servants of his master's intention to detain his guests as prisoners and Cole immediately had his horse made ready and departed before the trap could be sprung. Despite this story, it is clear from written evidence that he was aware of suspicious behaviour long before this and was sending information to the authorities in Dublin. When the rebellion broke out in October 1641, he maintained an active defence in the neighbourhood of Enniskillen, which ensured that the rebels were never able to take the town. As a result, Enniskillen became an island of refuge for many displaced settlers during these troubled times.

In 1640, Cole had travelled to the court of Charles I to complain about the activities of the then Lord Deputy William Strafford. During the long period of political unrest in the 1640s, Cole remained a Parliamentarian sympathiser and initiated a mutiny by arresting several pro-Royalist officers in the Enniskillen garrison. In 1645, he led a column which intercepted a raiding party of Ulster Irish at Irvinestown and routed them, reclaiming their booty in the process.

Sir William Cole died in 1653, having lived for almost eighty years. As his elder son Michael had predeceased him, he was succeeded by Michael's young son, also called Sir Michael Cole. This Sir Michael married his cousin Elizabeth in 1671 but did not enjoy good health. In 1664, he was appointed the castle's constable by Charles II but at the time of the 'Glorious Revolution', he moved to England and the castle was taken over by Gustavus Hamilton of Monea. Hamilton was elected Governor of Enniskillen and it was from this castle that he conducted the successful Williamite defence of the town and district during 1689. Just like fifty years earlier, the town held out and was not ever seriously threatened by the forces loyal to King James II.

There is no remaining evidence to show that Hamilton added any additional accommodation to the castle site, but it seems certain he would have been active here as it was the principal barracks for the horse and foot regiments which were raised in the town. At the conclusion of hostilities, Sir Michael Cole returned to Enniskillen castle and took an active lead in restoring the town after the disastrous fire of 1705. He later preferred to live in the family's other castle at Portora, as the castle's previous usage as a barracks had made the place less attractive. Additionally, Cole may have wanted the privacy of the out-of-town location.

Sir Michael died in 1710 and was succeeded by his son Sir John Cole. Born in 1680, Sir John was married to Florence Bourchier Wrey of Cornwall and it was he who began the erection of Florencecourt in honour of his wife. However, she died in 1718 and it is clear that the house was not complete when he died in 1726. Sir John was succeeded by his son, also called John, who was MP for Enniskillen in 1729. This John was connected with the Irish Parliamentary Speaker William Conolly, who had his home in nearby Ballyshannon. At this time, the German-born architect Richard Cassels (or Castles) was building Castle Hume for Sir Gustavus Hume, a few miles away on the lough shore, and it has been suggested that he may have designed Florencecourt as well. Meanwhile, John had been raised to the peerage as Baron Mountflorence in 1760. When he died in 1767, John was succeeded by his son William Willoughby, who was later created Viscount Enniskillen in 1776 and an Earl in 1789. It was he who finally finished the mansion at Florencecourt in 1771.

Thus Enniskillen castle was presumably not in regular use throughout much of the eighteenth century, for in 1762 John Wesley declared that the town had no castle. However, during the Napoleonic period, there was a belief that the French might invade Ireland. This led to a rash of barrack building and Enniskillen benefited from this. An infantry barracks was established at the castle and enlarged to accommodate increased troop numbers. Presumably at this time the ditches around the castle were filled in to provide more space. A stone fort was also erected at the old redoubt on the west side of the town. This site had previously been fortified during the 1689 siege. It later became a hospital.

Throughout the nineteenth century, the castle was enlarged with blocks being built against the perimeter walls. The site was enhanced by the erection of another barracks at the bottom of Queen Street, currently used as a police station. Other features remain in the vicinity of the castle, which indicate that Enniskillen was a garrison. Halfway down Queen Street is a row of stone-built shops that were formerly known as 'the She-Barracks', as they were built to accommodate the wives of the garrison. Also visible at the junction of Queen Street and Anne Street are two neatly carved bollards on opposite sides of the road, each preserving an iron hook on the side facing the road. This once held an iron chain, which was placed across the street during the nightly curfew.

The site was used by the military up until the 1950s when it passed into state ownership. Today, the castle has become the county museum and the home of the regimental museum of the Enniskillen Fusiliers who date back to the revolution of 1688. This latter museum contains some fascinating items, including a flag carried at the Battle of the Boyne in 1690 and several Victoria Cross medals won by members of the regiment.

Castle Tour

Though billed today on its noticeboard as a 'Maguire castle', in truth this site represents the remains of Cole's seventeenth-century plantation castle together with the accumulation of 250 years of barrack building one would normally associate with a garrison town. The former Maguire castle now survives only in the lower courses of the later plantation-period rebuilding of the keep. However, there is much to interest the visitor on a tour of this complex of sleeping quarters, workshops and storerooms.

This site has been in constant use for nearly 600 years and it is therefore no surprise to learn that there have been great changes over time. Today the castle appears as a polygonal enclosure of an acre or so, enclosed by a stone wall of various periods of construction, with the keep in the centre. The main features remaining from the plantation period are the central keep and the watergate, together with some lower courses of the western perimeter wall, which also date from the period. Although the castle is well worth a visit, it can be best appreciated from outside, especially when viewed from across the water.

Today the castle grounds are entered through a pair of modern gates on the east side of the perimeter wall. Passing the Fermanagh County Museum shop and audio-visual presentation building on the left, the building straight ahead is the keep, now located in the middle of the parade ground. This keep, measuring 13m by 19m (41 by 63ft), is the rebuilding of the original Maguire tower house, carried out by Cole at the beginning of the seventeenth century. The lower part of the strongly battered base, together with two stone vaults on the ground floor within, are all that remain of the fifteenth-century Maguire stronghold. Cole rebuilt the rest of the keep using the original ground plan and lowered it in height from four to three storeys.

Built of squared rubble blocks, the entrance to the keep is in the west wall. The large Georgian windows with sandstone dressings were inserted in another refurbishment of the 1790s. The slate roof has a double pitch. Today, the keep acts as the regimental museum of the Inniskilling Fusiliers. Uniquely, for any town in the British Isles, Enniskillen raised two regiments for the British army, the Inniskilling Fusiliers and the Inniskilling Dragoons, both of which had their origins in the disturbed times of the Williamite wars.

South of the keep is the feature known as the watergate, the most distinctive and problematic building of the plantation period. Located in the perimeter wall overlooking Lough Erne, the watergate is the remains of a tower built between 1615 and 1620 by Sir William Cole, soon after he became constable of the castle. Carew's description of the 1611 alterations at Enniskillen does not appear to describe this tower, so it is generally believed that this work was carried out a little later. Measuring approximately 8m by 4m internally with walls 0.9m thick, only the outer walls, strongly battered, remain complete. The interior ground level is 1.5m to 2m above the external ground level, which falls away to the lough.

Built of rubble with ashlar dressing and partly harled, it is three storeys in height, with two cylindrical corner turrets, or bartizans, neatly corbelled out on five courses from first-floor level. The turrets still retain their conical stone caps and two rows of rectangular windows at first and second floor level. Access to the turrets was probably through doors from the tower at first-floor level, now blocked. The uppermost part of the turrets would have provided reasonably weatherproof lookouts to the west and along the river. Between the turrets, the wall top still retains its stepped merlons and a dog-tooth string course similar to that at Castle Balfour. On the ground floor are two splayed windows measuring 0.3m wide by 0.45m deep. Due to the slope of the ground, these windows are about 3m above external ground level.

It was once believed that the long vertical slits near the top of the wall indicated the position of arms for lifting a drawbridge and that the site of the entrance below this had been later blocked up, thus providing the name watergate. This is now accepted to be wrong; the name may refer to the feature called the 'watergatte' that existed at this point in the 1594 map prior to the erection of the current structure, which then retained the same name. Moreover, there is a well against the perimeter wall on the inside, some 3m deep and 0.9m in diameter, which provided the garrison with a secure water supply and again the tower's name may allude to this feature. Whatever the reason, the watergate was not a means of access to the river.

From the NW corner of the watergate, the castle perimeter wall traces a broad curve as it follows the lough shore. There are at least two distinct building periods visible in the external coursework, the lower denoting the early curtain wall attributed to Cole. Built on top of this are the bays of the finely constructed arcaded barrack buildings dating from the 1790s. Together with the renovations carried out on the keep, these works cost £7,000.

The rest of the buildings within the boundary post-date the plantation but indicate the continuing importance of Enniskillen as a garrison town. Moving in a clockwise direction, against the north perimeter, are the barrack buildings of 1825 costing £3,000, built along the line of the earlier moat. To the east is another barracks and coach house erected after 1835. Flanking the modern entrance are the married quarters. Beyond the modern museum building in the SE corner is the former magazine. Finally, located between the magazine and the watergate is the barrack store.

There is one last conundrum. Flying from a pole on the watergate is the red cross of St George. This flag was the English national flag until 1606, when the Scottish cross of St Andrew was added to signify the unifying of the two states under the crown of James I and VI. In the 1690s, according to tradition, Tiffin's regiment, later known as the Inniskilling Fusiliers, fought under this flag. William III then conferred the honour of flying the flag of St George from a twin-towered castle on their regimental badges and colours.

The museum building provides two short local histories and regularly houses a variety of exhibitions. In addition, the Inniskilling Fusilier Museum houses one of the finest collections of militaria to be found anywhere, including those Victoria Crosses (Britain's highest award for bravery) earned during the First World War. Also on display in the drill ground are several cannon, including a captured 0.21m German mortar from the First World War. In 2007, the Boer War memorial to the Inniskilling Fusiliers was relocated from Gaol Square at the east end of town to its new home outside the castle grounds and can now be inspected there.

Before leaving the castle behind, the visitor must view the magnificent watergate from the water's edge outside, as only then can the graceful architecture of Cole's castle be truly appreciated. In conclusion, therefore, as a surviving example of plantation military architecture still in use, the castle and its museums are a must on any itinerary of works.

PORTORA
OS SHEET 17 OR 18, GR 222454

The ruins of Portora castle are on the edge of Enniskillen. From the centre of the town take the A46 signposted for Belleek. Passing the grand pillared entrance to Portora Royal School on the right, proceed a further 500m and turn right down a narrow lane, signposted for the castle, between iron gates. Drive to the end of the lane where there is a small car parking area. Portora castle will be visible on the right.

The nearest anchorage for a boat is at 'The Round O' quay on the west side of town. From here it is about 1km along the edge of the lough beside Portora Royal School, to the castle.

History

The manor of Drumskeagh in Magheraboy precinct, a small proportion of 1,000 acres, was originally granted to Jerome or Jeremy Lindsay in September 1612. The following month William Cole, the warden of Enniskillen castle, bought the estate and set about building a castle at Portora. Pynnar visited the site in 1619 and described the works, 'Upon this proportion is a Bawne with Lime and Stone, 68ft square and 13ft high with Four Flankers and a stone House or Castle 3 stories high strongly wrought. He hath an excellent windmill.'

Perrott and Annesley also visited the site during their tour of 1622 and described Portora in greater detail:

> …a strong bawn of stone and lime, 60 feet square and 14 feet high, with four strong flank-ers. Within the bawn there is a castle or strong house of stone and lime builded the fill breadth of the bawn, three stories high, with many good rooms in the said castle and two of the flankers, which are builded with equal height with the house and slated. The other two flankers are but two stories high and thatched as yet. Within the bawn there are two cagework English-like houses, three stories high, 48 feet long apiece, for houses of office. The Lord Bishop of Clogher hath a lease of 21 years of the said castle and bawn … wherein his Lordship intendeth to reside with his family.

The Bishop of Clogher referred to was none other than James Spottiswood, who became involved in a dispute with Lord Balfour over an attempt to purloin land grants originally given to the new Royal School (later to become sited here at Portora and still a fully functioning grammar school). One account states that the initials 'J.S.' were once located on a stone above the entrance to the castle, together with the arms of the See of Clogher.

It is clear, therefore, that William Cole did not build this castle as his principal home and he instead resided in the nearby castle at Enniskillen. A third account of the castle was made at an inquisition during the reign of Charles I. It described Portora as follows:

> Sir William Cole erected upon the tate called Lurgaveigh, alias Learganaffeagh, alias Portdorie [Portora], one fort and bawn, of lyme and stone containing 60 foot square every way and 10 foot in height with two flankers of lyme and stone, each containing 16 foot in height; and hath likewise erected, adjoining thereto, one castle or capital messauge, of lyme

and stone, containing 66 foot in length, 23 in breadth and 30 foot in height, with two flankers of lyme and stone, containing 30 foot in height and 10 foot wide. There is also planted
upon and within the said proportion 22 English-like houses, and therein now dwelling and
inhabiting 22 British tenants with their families.

During the rebellion of 1641 the castle remained in the hands of the settlers and was
an important outpost of the Enniskillen garrison, protecting the ancient ford. Likewise,
Portora acted as an outpost of Governor Hamilton's defence of Enniskillen during the
Williamite wars in 1688 and 1689. One source states that the ford here was protected at
that time by upwards of 100 tenants collected from the surrounding estate.

Cole's descendants were to live in Portora castle again for a brief period while their
new residence at Florencecourt was being constructed in the 1720s. After this time it
would appear that the castle was allowed to fall into ruin. In 1859 some idle schoolboys
from the nearby Royal School damaged the castle with homemade explosives! The
castle suffered further damage during the storms of 1894. In September 1912, Edward
Carson held a Unionist rally in the adjacent field here prior to the signing of the Ulster
Covenant.

In the 1950s, during the building of a barrage below the castle to control the flow of
water between Upper and Lower Lough Erne, some restorative work was done at the
castle, and some further repairs were carried out in 1997.

Castle Tour

The castle we see today at Portora lock is essentially that described by Pynnar, Perrott and
Annesley in the seventeenth century. The Queen's University archaeologist Martyn Jope
surveyed the castle in 1958 prior to its recent renovation and there are some differences
between the restoration work carried out by the then Environment and Heritage Service
in 1997 and the sketch he created. It can also be somewhat confusing when attempting to
differentiate between the original structures and the subsequent restoration works.

Portora castle is located above the edge of the lough at the western end of a long
drumlin ridge. Portora Royal School is situated at the other end of this ridge, which
gently slopes down to the castle entrance. The castle therefore appears to be poorly
sited, as it is partially overlooked by the higher ground to the east. However, the primary
consideration was the control of the ford across the Erne at Portora, which additionally
allowed access to the lough, and this outweighed the other considerations.

Like many other plantation castles, Portora follows the practice of placing the manor
house along the northern side of the bawn. However, the ground on the NE falls
steeply to the river crossing and so the castle has beeen forced to re-orientate itself by
45 degrees anticlockwise. For the purposes of clarity in providing a description of the
castle, it will be assumed that the entrance to the bawn is on the south wall with the
manor house occupying the north side.

The castle then consists of a manor house in a bawn with four flankers. The original
entrance to the castle was probably in the middle of south bawn wall. The exact site
cannot now be determined as the wall here is mainly ruined, though it was probably where the recent concrete path has been located. To the right, a part of the bawn
wall has been rebuilt to a height of approximately 1.8m. Sadly nothing remains of the

armorial arms of Bishop Spottiswood that formerly existed above the entrance, but presumably it would have resembled the plaque still extant at Castle Archdale.

A low wall has been constructed for safety reasons on the foundations of the east bawn wall, as the ground outside falls steeply to the lough. The west bawn wall, 0.9m thick and constructed of carboniferous limestone rubble, remains to a height of about 2.6m (9ft) above the present internal ground level. The bawn courtyard is roughly rectangular in shape, measuring 18.3m (60ft) wide in front of the manor house, and narrowing to 16.1m (53ft) wide along the south bawn wall. From the entrance, the bawn measures 15.6m (51ft) to the front wall of the manor house. Today the courtyard is surfaced with small stones which may resemble its original seventeenth-century condition. Extensive disturbance of the bawn's interior surface has removed any trace of the timber-framed houses described by Perrot and Annesley.

Circular flankers measuring 2.75m (9ft) in diameter internally are provided at the SE and SW corners of the bawn. The SW flanker was the more important, as anyone entering the castle had to pass close to it. It was therefore essential that this flanker had sufficient loopholes to protect the bawn entrance. It was described originally as being equivalent to 5m in height and the present ruins, which exist to around 3.3m in height, would support this view. The flanker was accessed directly from the bawn, though the ruined entrance does not allow certainty with regard to the original door width. The 0.8m-thick walls are rebated 2.1m above the current interior level to carry the joists for the floor above.

Recent restoration work has created five loopholes at ground-floor level (though Jope's plan showed only four), providing the defender with a range of defensive and offensive options. The best-preserved loop is in the middle of the five. Internally it measures 0.5m by 0.5m, at a height of 0.9m from the ground. Flat lintels progressively step down the roof of the loop through the thickness of the wall until it measures only 0.15m by 0.05m wide on the external face of the wall.

The SE flanker was probably identical to its neighbour, but it has been destroyed by the construction of the waterway lock directly below and only a fragment of its circular perimeter remains. Jope's plan in the mid-twentieth century identified part of a loop at ground-floor level facing west towards the entrance, but unfortunately this can no longer be seen. The defensive strength offered by the two flankers probably rendered unnecessary the use of a wall walk (for which there is no evidence) along the bawn walls.

Internally, the manor house measures 18.3m (60ft) wide by 5.1m (16.5ft) deep, with the walls 0.9m (3ft) thick. The house is of two and a half storeys and extends across the full length of the bawn's north side. The north wall and both gables of the house, together with their attached NE and NW flankers, still survive to a height of approximately 6m (20ft). However, the south wall facing into the bawn has been reduced to foundation level and the exact site of the entrance cannot now be traced with any certainty, although it was probably in the centre of the front elevation.

The ground floor of the manor house has been interpreted as comprising three rooms separated by stone walls, each roughly similar in size, but with different functions. If this theory is correct, then the central room comprised an entrance hallway and staircase. There is a window in the north wall directly opposite the entrance, at a between-floors level, which would have lit the otherwise dark hallway. To the right of this window there are three sockets for joists at a height of 2.7m (9ft) above the present ground level.

The room to the east of this, here postulated as the hall, measures 6.8m by 5.1m (22ft by 16.5ft). It contains a reconstructed grand fireplace and was probably lit by a large window facing into the bawn courtyard. There is also a small splayed lancet window on the east gable measuring 0.5m by 0.1m externally. A doorway led into the NE flanker and the rebate for the frame can still be traced in the masonry.

The ground-floor room to the west of the entrance may have contained a fireplace in the thickness of the north wall, but appears less grand. This room may have been used as a kitchen and there is a curious feature that could be interpreted as a sluice for waste. The room was probably lit by a window in the south wall and there is also a lancet window or loophole in the west wall identical to that in the room described above. Similarly, access to the NW flanker was by a doorway accessed directly from this room.

The family members probably used the first-floor rooms accessed from the central stair as private apartments. The first-floor room to the east contains a fireplace on the east gable and above this the wall narrows into what appears to be another flue on the floor above. There are no gable windows here, so windows facing into the bawn on the south side must have lighted the rooms on the first floor. The attic floor above would have contained the sleeping accommodation and again would have been lit by dormers facing into the bawn. All the floors and internal walls in the house were presumably constructed of timber.

The two attached flankers formed an integral part of the house and were entered via doorways at each floor level. The NE flanker, measuring internally 3m (10ft) in diameter, is the better preserved and contains four loopholes in the ground floor. The wall is rebated at a height of 2.7m (9ft) to carry the joists for the floor above. Three ample windows light the first floor and there are sockets above these for the joists of the attic-floor level. The NW flanker, of similar size, is much more ruined but still contains a window on the first floor similar to that in the NE flanker and one must presume that the arrangement of loopholes and windows was identical in both. The roof line is now mostly missing, but the 1997 repair work discovered fragments of tiles indicating that the roof was tiled rather than slated.

Looking out from the north wall of the bawn, poised above the passing boats beneath, there are picturesque views along this stretch of the river in both directions. Thus, in addition to its defensive qualities, the more aesthetic reasons for William Cole building his castle at this important crossing point can easily be appreciated.

MONEA
OS SHEET 17, GR 164493

From Enniskillen take the A46 Belleek road for 3km (2 miles) and then turn off left onto the B81 Derrygonnelly road for a further 7km (4 miles) to Monea. Turn right at Devenish parish church and the remainder of the route is signposted. There is a small car-parking area near the castle. There is no nearby water access to Monea so visitors will need to use the bus service from Enniskillen to Derrygonnelly (Service 59) which has a frequent daily weekday schedule. The following two sites are also within easy reach of each other and could be visited simultaneously.

History

The middle proportion of Dirrynefogher in Magheraboy precinct was originally granted to Robert Hamilton in August 1610. However, the estate passed into the hands of his son Malcolm Hamilton, rector of Devenish and chancellor of Down, in 1612. Hamilton quickly set about building a residence for himself on his newly acquired land, but the terms of the original grant were still not fulfilled by 1618, when Pynnar visited the estate:

> Sir Robert Hamilton was the first Patentee. Malcolm Hamilton has one thousand five hundred acres, called Derrinefogher. Upon this proportion there is a strong castle of Lime and Stone, being fifty four feet long, and twenty feet broad; but hath no Bawne unto it, nor any defence for the succouring or relieving his Tenants.

Malcolm Hamilton had established three freeholders on the estate and a further nine tenants holding various leases from 20 to 180 acres.

The missing bawn was however built by 1631, when it would appear that the estate was forfeited to the Crown for further non-compliance with the original terms of the grant. The estate was regranted to James Hamilton, Viscount Clandeboye in December of that year. As Clandeboye was a relative anyway, this would appear to have been a family arrangement to maintain the land in Hamilton's possession.

In 1623, Malcolm Hamilton became the Archbishop of Cashel, succeeding Myler Magrath (see Termon Magrath Castle). He now had a large family of five sons and three daughters. Three of these five Hamilton brothers served in the Swedish army – Hugh, Alexander and Lewis or Ludavick. Lewis was later created Baron Hamilton de Deserf (a Swedish title) in June 1654, and married a Swedish girl, Anna Catharina, daughter of Lars Grubbe, Lord of Ry Nabben. Lewis and Anna had two sons, Gustavus and Malcolm and a daughter whose name is unknown.

When Archbishop Malcolm Hamilton died in 1628, his estate passed initially to his fourth son, also called Malcolm. However, this Malcolm soon died without male issue and Archbishop Hamilton's youngest son Lewis inherited the estate. Lewis and Anna and their three children embarked on a journey back to Ireland in 1662 to lay claim to the Castletown estate but Lewis died on the voyage. Anna, a widow at thirty-one with three small children, took his body back to Sweden for burial before setting off again for Castletown, where she took up residence at Monea castle.

The Widow Hamilton must have been something of an exotic commodity in the midst of this often-dreary landscape and she was not long to remain alone on her estate. She married a further three times and outlived each husband. Her second husband was Richard Dunbar of Derrygonnelly, but he died in January 1667. Her next choice was widower Captain William Shore. It would seem that Shore died before 1677, as Anna was by then the wife of James Somerville of nearby Tullykelter castle. Somerville died in 1688 but Anna was still alive in 1705.

Lewis Hamilton was succeeded by his son Gustavus Hamilton, the most famous and influential member of the family. With a Swedish mother and probably named after the famous Swedish general Gustavus Adolphus, this Gustavus was to become Governor of Enniskillen in 1688 and it was his actions which ensured the town's undying fame in the revolution which was to engulf the British Isles for the next three years.

He married twice, though the identity of the first woman is now unknown. The marriage produced only one child, William. Gustavus then married Margaret, daughter of Edward Cooper Esq. – a union which produced five more children. One of the major landowners in the county, he was a magistrate for County Fermanagh. He was also a cornet in a troop of horse raised by his uncle Lord Clanawley, until James II disbanded many of the Protestant-officered regiments.

By 1688, he was considered to be one of the most important personalities in the area and his approval was crucial in the events subsequently unfolding in the politics of Ireland. As the political climate deteriorated during that winter, he was approached in mid-December by William MacCarmick and other members of the resistance party and Gustavus vowed his support for their cause.

Elected Governor of Enniskillen, he immediately raised a company of foot and a troop of horse from amongst his tenants at his own expense. In addition, he raised money to build the defences at Forthill. During the following months he was the commander of forces in Enniskillen, though much of the actual leadership in the field was devolved to Colonel Thomas Lloyd, the celebrated 'little Cromwell'. Hamilton was not a great general, as shown both by his handling of the Omagh expedition in June 1689 and his failure to support MacCarmick at the battle of Kilmacormick in July. However as Governor, his primary responsibility was the security of Enniskillen and its citizens. He was therefore unwilling to rashly deploy the army lest it should result in the loss of the town, a huge blow to the wider Williamite cause.

Later in July 1689, his negotiations with General Kirke at Donegal delivered him the necessary arms and experienced officers necessary to destroy the large Jacobite army at the battle of Newtownbutler. From that time, the security of Enniskillen was never in any doubt and it is therefore as an organiser and administrator that Hamilton should be best remembered.

His regiment quartered in Belturbet during the winter of 1689 and he accompanied it to the Battle of the Boyne in July 1690. However he was not to enjoy the fruits of the ultimate Williamite victory in Ireland. Gustavus Hamilton died around 1691, with the estate heavily in debt as a result of his activities during the revolution. In 1697, his widow Margaret petitioned the Irish House of Commons for compensation. Her plea stated:

> …that her said husband was one of the first who took up arms for preservation of the Protestant interest in this Kingdom, and being chosen Governor of Inniskillen, borrowed and laid out several sums of money for fortifying the Town and buying arms, for which he gave bond and judgement, and that now his estate is actually extended for the same; and praying that this House will take into consideration her husband's services, and the miserable condition of her and her five children.

The Commons voted Mrs Hamilton £600 but it is not clear if this money was actually ever paid. Clearly, by the rules of inheritance at that time, William Hamilton was not obliged to allow his stepmother to remain on the estate, and the petition to the Commons was intended to ensure a measure of financial security for the widow and her young family.

William Hamilton, eldest son and heir of Gustavus, does not appear to have had any great interest in the estate. He was said to have married a woman of inferior social standing, and in 1704 he sold the estate to Robert King and Hugh Montgomery for £295 in cash. Soon after, William joined the army and died at an unknown date. It was a sad end to a family that had such made such an impact on the history of the area.

Castle Tour

The approach to Monea castle is along a superb avenue of beech trees. Turning sharply to the left the ruins suddenly come into view and they are certainly worth the visit, for undoubtedly Malcolm Hamilton erected the finest castle in the whole Erne basin, here in this now rather bleak bog. Before leaving it is essential that one take in a full circuit of the castle grounds, as the stunning vistas of these ruins from all angles reward the patient observer. In addition, one can locate the stone-lined spring well, located south of the castle towards the crannog, which provided a much-needed source of fresh water for its inhabitants.

Monea is constructed of a hard local limestone finished off with sandstone detailing and the whole gives a favourable impression outlined against the greenery of its surroundings. The whole castle sits upon a low rocky knoll that outcrops only on the south, above the nearby lough containing a crannog. The bawn walls are today ruined to near foundation level (except on the west), but a quick tour of the perimeter will confirm the clever use of the available topography. The site is entered via the north bawn wall through the foundations for the ruined gateway only 1.8m (6ft) wide. This entrance would have undoubtedly been defended by a loophole in the adjacent NW flanker, sadly now ruined to a low level.

Passing through the entrance one stands within the bawn perimeter, approximately 32m by 23m (105ft by 90ft), with the castle dwelling situated along the SE side. The bawn wall is best preserved on the west side, which is almost a metre (3ft) thick and contains two flankers on the NW and NE corners to protect the vulnerable northern approach. The west wall and NW flanker also indicate that the interior level was infilled to create a level surface here, 1.5m (5ft) above the external level, and the SW corner is buttressed perhaps to provide a stronger footing in the boggy ground. Originally the wall would have been about 3m (10ft) high. Located against the west wall are the lower courses of a later sub-rectangular building some 20m by 6m (65ft by 18ft) internally. As the floor level is below that in the rest of the bawn, this building must have had a domestic function such as a byre or stable. There are no visible signs of any other buildings within the bawn walls.

The bawn has two circular flankers, of which the NW one is better preserved. Due to the falling ground level externally, entrance to this flanker from the bawn led down to a basement used as a dovecote. Undoubtedly the flanker was at least another storey higher, but no vestige remains. We can deduce that it contained loopholes to protect the north and west bawn walls. There is no evidence of a fireplace and the flanker appears on the small side to have been used as living accommodation.

The NE flanker is a curious semicircle shape today but that is likely the result of a later rebuilding. The stump of a tree located immediately outside the wall may have been planted inside the original circular flanker to create a romantic ruin at a time when the need for such defence had receded. No other features remain, and again we must infer the location of loopholes covering the north and east walls.

The castle itself is a rectangular tower house, 14.4m by 5.9m internally (48ft by 20ft) as described by Pynnar, and three storeys high plus an attic level. It is elongated east–west, with two symmetrical, circular towers located at the NW and SW corners and two corbelled bartizans high up on the NE and SE corners. Unusually, the castle is located on the south side of the bawn.

The castle's only entrance is via a doorway in the NW tower, commanded by a loophole at ground level in the opposite tower and by two drop holes above, in the arch spanning the gap between the two turrets, at second-floor level. These towers, with walls over a metre thick, are both corbelled out at attic level into square cap houses with crow-stepped gables, so much a feature of Scottish tower-house building of the period. It is this front elevation of Monea that is so striking, making the castle instantly recognisable amongst the plantation structures of the Erne.

Entering via the doorway we encounter the interior of the NW tower. This tower, internally measuring 2.7m (9ft) in diameter, contains the base of a spiral stair that gave access to all the floors above. Curiously, this stair is sinistral (as it rises it turns to the left) rather than the more common dextral spiral. At the foot of the stair there is a splayed loophole providing flanking fire along the north wall of the house. Two more loops can be spotted at intervening levels above, each providing additional flanking fire along the north wall. Long narrow windows light the stair at intervals.

To the left of the NW tower entrance, the house is entered through an arched doorway. Straight ahead is a long, narrow passage, 1.4m (5ft) wide, which runs along the north side of the castle wall for about half its length, terminating at another doorway. This passage was lit by two narrow splayed slits in the north wall, measuring 0.7m by 0.13m externally, with dressed sandstone surrounds. At the end of the passage, a narrow, spiral stair gave servants access to the chambers above without needing to use the main stair.

On the south side of the passage there are two chambers. The first room is really a lobby, as it is poorly lit and led to two different levels in the SW tower. Due to the falling ground surface outside, the SW tower actually has five levels. The lower ground floor is reached down a stone stair of eight steps and contains a splayed loophole that provided flanking fire along the base of the south wall of the house. A single narrow, splayed window, almost at the exterior ground level, lighted this room. The roof of this circular room, 2.8m in diameter, is stone vaulted.

From the lobby, another narrow stone stair straight ahead led up through the wall thickness to the first-floor level of the SW tower. This room contains two splayed loopholes. One loop protects the south wall of the castle while the other covers the castle entrance in the NW tower. The loop covering the entrance is a perfect circle, 7.5cm (3 inches) wide, created by drilling through a single stone block.

The second ground-floor chamber off the passage is square in plan and lit by a single narrow slit similar to the others on this floor. Returning now to the passage the kitchen is reached through the entrance at the far end. It is the full width of the castle and would have contained a fireplace and oven against the east gable, all now removed. It was lit by narrow splayed slits in the north and south walls. On the outside of this wall, at ground level, is what appears to be a waste or latrine chute, leading down through the wall thickness from above.

Originally, all of the ground-floor rooms were stone vaulted and traces of the footings for the arches can be seen in each. The narrow windows combined with the vaulting provided fireproofing for the ground-floor accommodation from both accidental and deliberate ignition. Finally, the whole floor was flagged in local stone.

Due to the removal of the stone vault at some time in the past, access to the upper floors is no longer possible. It is therefore difficult to accurately interpret the layout. Above first-floor level, all the floors were wooden in both the main house and in the SW tower. There is no sign of joist holes and the joists may have rested on the ledge created by successively narrowing the walls at each level. The first floor was probably used as the main living area for the family. Above, on the second floor, was the sleeping accommodation. Both floors were probably subdivided into several chambers by partition stud walls. The main fireplace on each floor was on the east gable but there are additional smaller ones on the west and north walls. As these floors were less vulnerable to hostile attack, they are amply lit by large windows on the north, south and west walls.

Access to the upper levels of the SW tower was via doorways leading from each floor. The square corbelled tops of both towers contain a small fireplace and are lit by windows. The two bartizans at either end of the east gable were similarly accessed from the house, but only that on the SE has substantial remains. It contains two circular loopholes on the underside of the corbelling, which provided defensive fire along the east and south walls. Though incomplete, the opposite bartizan probably provided a similar defence. Beyond this function, the purpose of the bartizans is unclear, as they have limited space as private chambers.

The obvious defensive capabilities of Monea can now be fully appreciated. Each of the towers and bartizans was amply provided with loopholes at all levels, which provided the defender with various fire options should the house come under attack. Coupled with the fireproof design of the ground floor, and the additional protection around the entrance to the house, Monea successfully combined defence with comfortable living for a seventeenth-century landlord.

HALL CRAIG (MONAGHAN)
OS SHEET 17, GR 158473

From Enniskillen, proceed along the B81 signposted for Derrygonnelly. Passing through the hamlet of Springfield, proceed a further 1.5km (one mile) to a minor crossroads. Turn left at the crossroads, up a steep and narrow road. About 500m along this road, Hall Craig is located down a lane on the right. The bus from Enniskillen to Derrygonnelly passes close to this site. Boat users should also avail of this means of transport.

History
The castle in Monaghan townland was associated with the family of Weir, originally from Craig Hall, near Edinburgh. Robert Weir was a descendant of Baltredus de Vere, a native of Flanders who settled in Scotland in 1165. The family name gradually changed to Weir and the family held substantial estates in their native Scotland.

Robert Weir fell out of favour with the Duke of Hamilton, English Viceroy for the newly crowned James I, and, selling up his family estates in Scotland, he travelled to Ireland in 1610 with family members including two brothers. In 1613, he married a sister of Sir David Lindsay and joined Malcolm Hamilton in the purchase of two thirds of Derrinfogher estate in the barony of Magheraboy from Hamilton's brother Robert, the first plantation patentee, for £530. As undertaker, he was expected to plant an orchard, build a corn-mill and a tuck-mill and to develop the land.

The estate consisted of 384 acres (150 hectares), including the townlands of Dromore, Drumarraw, Tullymargy, Magherageeragh, Fartagh, Drombiggin, Drumlish, Drumaville and Monaghan. Today these townlands can be identified as a cluster just west of the hamlet of Springfield. Robert Weir lived initially at Monea and also at a fortified house at Tullymargy, a little south of Monea and east of Tullykelter. He also built a fortified home for himself here on the hill of Monaghan, a short distance south of Tullymargy.

After twenty years in possession of his estate, Robert Weir died in 1633. He was succeeded by his son John, who continued to reside at Monaghan with his widowed mother and his other siblings. What befell the castle in the 1641 rebellion is unknown, though the fate of the Weir family is recorded. As at Killeshandra, the clustering of a number of fortified settler homes in the local area would have made this a less attractive target to any but the largest of marauding rebel bands. Despite this, John Weir, his widowed mother, brother Alexander (a boy of only eleven years) and sister Jane, joined around fifty other settlers who took refuge at Lisgoole abbey, a few miles south of Enniskillen.

The exact reason for abandoning their home to take up residence at Lisgoole is unknown. The fact that the abbey was supposedly sacred ground may have induced the settlers to believe that they would be safe there. Around the middle of December 1641, a large body of rebels besieged Lisgoole abbey. John realised that the settlers' position at Lisgoole was untenable, as they were not sufficiently well armed or provisioned to withstand an assault. He therefore accepted terms to surrender the abbey and deliver up all arms in return for safe conduct to Enniskillen. But having carried out their part of the agreement, the settlers were seized by the rebels and systematically murdered. The Weir family were only saved by the timely intervention of an influential Maguire – possibly Rory Maguire. He immediately took them under his protection and sent them to Enniskillen by boat. When the rebellion later developed into a more complex struggle for democracy during the 1640s, the Weirs returned to Monaghan.

Although all of the settlers had resisted the attempt by the rebels to overthrow the plantation, they were divided between loyalty to parliament or to the King. Enniskillen was, for the most part, a Parliamentarian garrison, commanded by Sir William Cole. When Charles I was beheaded in 1649, the garrison was persuaded to support his son Charles II as successor. Alexander Weir had Royalist sympathies and he joined the Scots army, which marched south to secure Charles on the throne. However, in September 1651 the Royalists were soundly thrashed at Worcester and Charles was forced to flee. Alexander Weir spent some time in Scotland before returning once again to Monaghan.

The 1659 census return for Fermanagh records that an 'Alexander Weire, gent' lived at 'Ferlagh' (modern Fertagh), while a 'Robert Weire, gent' lived at Monaghan and at Magherynagiran (modern Magheranageeragh). This Robert is presumably a brother or other family relation. Only four people are recorded as residing in Monaghan, four at

Magherynagiran and five at Ferlagh, of which a total of nine were designated as English. Clearly the Weirs survived the rebellion and were still in residence here. Alexander Weir later married Sarah Goodwin and they had a son Robert, who was born in 1676 and later succeeded his father.

At only fourteen years old, Robert enrolled in his father Alexander's horse troop at Boyle, probably employed as a cornet or drummer. The Dublin parliament of 1689 attainted Alexander Weir and a 'Robert Wear' (probably Alexander's kin and not his young son). After the Jacobite defeat at Newtownbutler in July 1689, Alexander signed a loyal address from the Enniskillen garrison to William III and Queen Mary.

Meanwhile, the young Robert saw service during the Williamite wars and was present at the Boyne, Athlone, Aughrim and Limerick. He lost his left arm at the Boyne and was evidently so seriously wounded that he was overlooked for a vacant commission in the troop. Recovering from this trauma at home, Robert later returned to his regiment the following spring. In 1694, following the break-up of his own regiment, he went to England with the intention of crossing to Flanders and offering his services there. An officer in the regiment of Colonel Bellasis's Regiment of Foot, who accommodated him over the winter, befriended him and both went across to Flanders the following spring. Robert eventually served a further three years there. However, during his absence from Ireland, his father Alexander died and another family member tried to seize the Weir estates from Robert. He was therefore obliged to regain his inheritance on his return to Fermanagh.

In 1699, Robert married Anne Carleton, daughter of Captain Christopher Carleton of Tullymargy castle. The castle at Monaghan was accidentally burned in February 1713 and the family lost all their possessions, managing to escape dressed only in their nightshirts. They were forced to live for a time with Captain Carleton at Tullymargy. Robert planned the erection of a new manor house on the slope below the old castle but it was not until 1721 that this country house, first known as Little Hall Craig, was ready for occupation. By reversing the remaining words, Robert chose the name to resemble that of the former family estates in Scotland. Eventually the word 'little' was dropped from the house's title and it was known simply as Hall Craig.

It is likely that Robert Weir used the masonry from the original fortified house to build his new residence and the location of the old structure is no longer certain. Weirs continued to occupy Hall Craig for almost two centuries and eight generations. Finally, in 1896, with the death of Thomas Weir, fifth son of John and Caroline Weir, Hall Craig and the surviving estate was abandoned and it was later sold off to a family named Scott. The house has since been sold again and recently underwent much-needed refurbishment, which will secure its future for succeeding generations.

Castle Tour

The white, three-storey country house, known as Little Hall Craig, was built by the Weir family, below the summit of the hill in Monaghan townland in 1721. About 50m behind this house and closer to the top of the hill are some stone-built outhouses, the largest of which may contain the remnants of the original castle built by Robert Weir.

The main shed, now used to accommodate livestock, measures approximately 9m by 6m (30ft by 20ft) internally. This structure contains at least four loophole windows along the north wall. Two of these are now blocked up, but the remaining two are approximately

0.8m by 0.8m (30 by 30 inches) internally, at a height of 0.9m above the internal floor level. Both splay to a narrow window measuring 0.75m by 0.1m externally (30 by 4 inches). Both retain their flat masonry lintels and sills. The walls are 0.6m thick. Outside, the ground level has now risen by over half a metre but this may be due to more recent infill.

The shed shows at least two different phases of building work. On the east wall, the lower courses are of undressed irregular field stones, with better dressed and mortared blocks above. Additionally, the shed entrance at the eastern end of the south wall has a well-dressed east jamb constructed of well-cut limestone blocks, though the west jamb is now gone. Just to the west of this is a masonry buttress which appears not to be original and may have been constructed later to support a sagging wall.

If a castle was originally constructed here, one would expect that the stones would be reused in the later house of 1721. Well-cut limestone blocks would have been sought after and it is unlikely that the builders of Little Hall Craig could have ignored them. Therefore, the shed doorway and the better-constructed upper courses of the east wall were probably built much later. However, the lower courses and the loophole windows do appear more promising and are surely worth a fuller inspection to determine if they are indeed the last remaining vestiges of the plantation castle erected by Robert Weir in the early seventeenth century.

On balance, this site would have been attractive to a plantation undertaker wishing to build his family home. The loopholes, as previously described, are located along the north wall facing out towards the hilltop. If this was a small manor house with attached bawn or outhouses, such as Doohat or Gardenhill, one would expect only loopholes along the vulnerable north side of the building. The shed's current dimensions are not large for a prosperous tenant like Weir, but there are no fixed rules regarding this and it may have been sufficient. One nagging flaw is the absence of evidence for a fireplace. Perhaps the later alterations completely removed this from the visible structure.

Taken in the round, Hall Craig needs to be included as a plantation castle site. There are few enough examples of homes belonging to the tenant class, below that of the main undertakers. Further examination here may discover the ruins of the original castle structure hidden amongst the later outhouse buildings.

TULLYKELTER
OS SHEET 26,155483

Travel along the B81 Enniskillen–Derrygonnelly road. At Monea, take the road left beside a roadside shop, signposted 'Boho 5 miles', with a brown fishing sign for Carran Lough. After 400m, a minor road to the left leads up a steep hill. The castle ruins are behind an empty cottage on the right at the top of the hill. Access is through a farmyard gate. Boat users must again avail of the Enniskillen to Derrygonnelly bus service. The site is in private ownership and requires permission to enter.

History
Tullykelter formed part of the original lands of Dirrynafogher, a middle proportion estate centred on Monea, which was granted to the Hamilton family. James Somerville of Cambusnethan, Ayrshire, obtained a grant of Tullykelter, Drumscollop and Carran

from Malcolm Hamilton, the proprietor of Derrynafogher, in March 1615. Pynnar records that in 1618 Hamilton had three freeholders on his estate, of which one was James Somerville, who occupied sixty acres of land. Somerville immediately began to erect a house for himself at Tullykelter. It included several defensive features designed to make it less vulnerable to attack. It is surprising to note, therefore, that in the muster rolls of 1630 for Devenish parish, he is recorded as possessing only a sword.

Somerville was married to Elizabeth, daughter of Thomas Hamilton of Brimhill, and had at least three children who survived into adulthood – James, the eldest son, Thomas and Jean. The family were thus resident in the castle at the outbreak of the 1641 rebellion. Tullykelter's role in the defence of the plantation settlement is unknown. The proximity of other castles at Monea, Hall Craig, Derrygonnelly and Tully, would have encouraged Somerville and the other owners to stay and resist rather than abandon everything for the relative security of Enniskillen. However, younger family members would have been removed to safer locations in town leaving the castles occupied by an armed garrison.

This did not prevent Captain Rory Maguire from appearing at Monea on Christmas Eve 1641, where he burned down the parish church, killing eight people, before setting off for Tully. Maguire does not appear to have captured Tullykelter at this time. He would not have had the means to conduct a long siege and in any case his main objective was the castle at Tully. The Somerville family are described as resident at Tullykelter immediately after the rebellion so we can deduce that it never suffered destruction.

James Somerville died in 1642 and was succeeded by his son James. The castle appears to have quickly settled down again following the end of the war. James was able to consolidate the family lands and obtain further grants from Alexander Weir of Craig Hall. He was four times churchwarden of Devenish church, and High Sheriff of Fermanagh in 1680. In 1678 he became a JP and his name is listed in two loyal addresses to King Charles from the JPs, freeholders and gentlemen of Fermanagh, dated 1682 and 1683. By 1677, he had married Anna Catherina, widow of Baron Ludavick Hamilton of Monea, and they had one daughter, Sydney. James died before 1688, leaving Anna and Sydney resident at Tullykelter.

As with many other plantation families in Fermanagh, the growing constitutional crisis of the late 1680s saw the Widow Somerville side with the Williamite faction and the name of Anna Catherina appears among the list of those attainted by King James's patriot parliament of 1689. This inclusion caused Anna to flee the kingdom and it is unclear what happened to Tullykelter at this time.

Sydney Somerville married Colonel John Caulfield of Tullydowy, County Tyrone, a son of Lord Charlemont. Caulfield served in Spain and Ireland and was a lieutenant colonel in Abraham Crichton's Regiment of Foot in 1698. He certainly resided at Tullykelter and he had at least two children by Sydney. A daughter (whose name has been lost) married Colonel Thomas Cuffe and resided for a time in Galway. Caulfield died in 1705 and Sydney died in Dublin in 1725, so Colonel Cuffe's family may have been the next occupants at Tullykelter.

The last known occupant of the castle was the Colonel's grandson Revd Francis Cuffe, born in 1715, who was curate of Inishmacsaint from 1747 to 1757. After this time the castle was abandoned and allowed to fall into disrepair. Since then the castle has been reused and adopted for many domestic roles, explaining its present ruined state.

Castle Tour

The ruins today are a mixture of the original plantation structure and modern additions. Tullykelter is in a much dilapidated and overgrown state, forming part of a pen for cattle, and the ground here is rather muddy. However, there is still much to appreciate by a closer inspection. The house has a much more domestic appearance than many other examples, but contains the protective measures necessary in a defended home.

Thus, unlike the plantation estate castles in the area, Tullykelter was constructed as a fortified residence without a bawn. As a principal tenant and not a landlord, there were, of course, no obligations on James Somerville to provide one. The building consists of a rectangular, two-storey house, built of harled rubble blocks, with two corner projections on the front (east) elevation and a third projection on the rear (west) wall, which contained the stair. Little of the castle remains above first-floor level, though modern walling has tended to follow the initial shape of the house.

The original doorway of the house is in the east wall, approached from the farmyard between the two projecting wings. It can be now appreciated that the purpose of the two wings was to act like flankers, providing protection to the doorway between. The NE projection was later adapted into a store, but it still contains a pistol loop on the south wall. Likewise there is a loophole in the north wall of the SE projection. (Again, a shed built later against the wall means that this loop is only visible from inside the ruins.) An unwelcome visitor approaching the doorway would have been vulnerable to a pistol shot from either of these two loops.

The doorway is at the south end of the east wall and although much ruined, contains an ornately carved roll-moulding and door rebate on the south jamb, which is to full height. The adjoining wall contains a drawbar socket, which could be pulled across the door to strengthen it. Unfortunately, the north jamb wall has been lost down to foundation level.

Passing inside the main part of the house, the internal space measuring 18m by 6m is undivided and may indicate that the original internal partitioning was of timber. The south gable has been rebuilt at some time and is heavily overgrown with ivy. Likewise, the north gable is heavily vegetated but looks original. It does not appear to have had any windows at ground-floor level. There are three ground-floor windows, 1.1m wide, along the east wall, together with the flue for a fireplace between. The windows show splayed ingoings and would have contained wooden frames. The wall here does not rise above 3m and therefore it is not possible to discern any additional features from the floor above.

Similarly, the west wall contains three ground-floor windows, 1.2m wide by 1.8m high, to the north of the stair projection, with perhaps two more windows, now lost, to the south. The wall here survives almost to full height and it is clear that the first floor had windows located directly above those below. This arrangement would have allowed all these rooms to be pleasantly well lit.

The rear projection, located in the southern half of the west wall, contained the wooden stairs, which ascended directly opposite the main entrance door. The sockets for the half-landing are still visible, 1m above ground level, and this stair was lit by a window in the west side at half-storey height. There are also a series of four brick-lined loops in the projection at ground-floor level; two face north and one each face south and west, which help to protect the approaches to the castle's vulnerable west wall. These loops are smaller than usual, measuring only 0.4m by 0.3m internally, tapering externally to only 0.1m, and were evidently only for the use of handguns.

The castle to the south of the stair projection is much altered, although the general shape can be appreciated, as the modern walls here follow the original structure. As stated earlier, the wall here would allow for two windows, similar to those on the north side of the stair projection. If this was so, then it is tempting to postulate that the ground floor consisted of a long hallway extending from the entrance to the stair, with two main rooms off this to north and south. Presumably the two projections functioned as small, separate chambers off these main rooms. Additionally, one might expect another fireplace along the south gable but unfortunately this cannot be confirmed due to the later alterations.

There is currently no access to the interior of the NE projection, as it is being used as a store. However, the SE projection can be inspected and its east wall has a window at ground-floor level and a similar one on the floor above. This arrangement probably existed in the more ruined NE projection as well. One can also view the loophole covering the doorway mentioned previously, as well as another unusual loop in the south wall. This wall contains a partly brick-lined recess from which a loop penetrates the wall at an unusually oblique angle, giving some protection to the otherwise undefended south gable here. The shaft created for the loop is 1.5m long, opening externally to only about 0.15m at chest height, and was probably best served using a musket rather than a handgun.

The castle is therefore an interesting mixture of domestic and defensive features. Clearly the builder wished to live in a modern family home with numerous large windows to allow the maximum amount of light to brighten the interior. However, he was also aware of the unsettled nature of the surrounding countryside and the need to provide some protection for this vulnerable design. The compromise finally settled upon appears to have been successful, for the castle survived the turbulent seventeenth century and continued in use as a home at least into the middle of the next. Tullykelter is worth a visit to appreciate the domestic Jacobean designs flourishing along the Erne at this time.

TULLY
OS SHEET 17, GR 126566

Tully castle is situated just off the A46, midway between Enniskillen and Belleek on the SW shore of Lower Lough Erne. A signposted lane leads one down a narrow roadway to the site, which has good car parking. There are good landing places for boats in Sand Bay, directly below the castle.

History

Situated on the top of a hill overlooking Lower Lough Erne, Tully castle had a short but eventful life. For centuries after its abandonment it slowly decayed, until the 1980s when it was restored by the state. A nearby building has now been converted into a small museum and interpretive centre. There is normally a small entrance fee for the castle.

The area on the SW side of Lower Lough Erne forms the precinct of Magheraboy, which was allocated to Scottish undertakers in the plantation. Three sons of Patrick Hume of Manderstown, Berwickshire in Scotland, Alexander, John and George, were to have a crucial impact on the early development of this part of the kingdom. Sir John Hume, Patrick's fourth son, received the 2,000-acre estate of Ardgorte in July 1610. This great proportion stretched from Rosscorr to Inishmacsaint and included the upland areas of Magho and Blackslee. Sir John's elder brother Alexander received the adjacent small proportion of 1,000 acres known as Drumcose in April 1611.

Writing in 1611, Sir George Carew reported unfavourably on both estates. In Drumcose, Alexander had taken possession but done nothing. Likewise, of Ardgorte he wrote, 'Sir John Home [Hume], Knight, 2,000 acres; has taken possession, returned into Scotland, nothing done nor any agent present.'

However it was soon after this that the work necessary to fulfil the terms of the grant was begun on both estates. Pynnar reported on the progress of the manor of Carrynoe (as Ardgorte is now named, because the castle was situated there):

> Upon this Proportion there is a Bawne of Lime and Stone 100 feet square and 14 feet high, having four Flankers for the Defence. There is also a fair strong Castle, 50 feet long and 21 feet broad. He hath made a Village near unto the Bawne, in which is dwelling 24 Families.

The land had been distributed amongst these tenants in parcels of between 2 and 240 acres. A total of 1,274 acres had thus been divided between freeholders and lessees and these were capable of providing thirty men at arms. Hume was clearly intent on fulfilling his obligations! He was also one of only a minority of landlords who were always resident on their estates.

In addition to his interest in Carrynoe, Sir John had acquired by purchase in July 1615 the middle proportion of Moyglasse, consisting of 1,500 acres, from William Fowler. Fowler had been the original grantee of this estate, which stretched from Springfield to Lough Erne, in May 1611, but Carew reported later that year, 'William Fuller ... taken possession, returned to Scotland, nothing done.' Sir John had therefore less time to develop his lately acquired interest and Pynnar reports the progress on the estate as follows, 'Upon this Proportion there is nothing built. I find planted on the land, of British Families a good number of Men; but they have no estates but by Promise from one year to another.'

Fifteen families were able to muster thirty men and Pynnar had not seen any Irish families living on the land. As Hume consolidated his holdings, it is probable that no castle or bawn was ever built on this part of his enlarged estate. Pynnar also reported on the state of affairs at Drumcose, where Alexander had in the meantime sold his interest there to his younger brother George and returned to Scotland:

> Upon this Proportion there is a Bawne of 80 feet square, of Lime and Stone, 12 feet high. There is no House in it. I found but very few to appear before me, for the Undertaker was out of the country, but the land was well planted with Brittish Families and good store of Tillage; and not any Irish Family that I could learn of.

Only three leases had been agreed at this time and the remainder of the tenants were living on an annual basis until such time as terms could be agreed. Despite this, five years later Malcolm Hamilton of Monea testified that George had now fulfilled all the obligations of the grant. Sir John Hume bought this estate from George in June 1626, enlarging his total interest in Magheraboy to 4,500 acres and making him the greatest landowner in Fermanagh. His holdings now stretched along the whole length of Lough Erne, from Belleek to Enniskillen. As if to confirm his single interest in his plantation lands, he sold his family estate in north Berwickshire in 1633 and the following year became MP for the county of Fermanagh.

Sir John's wife Margaret died in 1612 but had produced three sons, Alexander, George and Patrick. When Sir John died in September 1639, he was succeeded by his second son, now Sir George (the eldest, Alexander, had died some years previously). Sir George, made a baronet in later years, was married to Mary and they had at least five children. However their life at Tully castle was soon to be thrown into turmoil.

Soon after the beginning of the rebellion of 1641, the inhabitants of the area sought protection at their lord's door, and Tully became a refuge for the local population. On Christmas Eve 1641, Captain Rory Maguire and 800 rebels appeared before the walls of the castle and demanded its surrender. Sir George was absent at the time, and the castle was held by his wife Lady Hume and two young sons, Patrick and Alexander, together with John Greene who was probably in the Hume household. Relating the events under oath to a Commission of Enquiry in April 1654, Patrick Hume, then a captain, described the subsequent negotiations which took place on nearby Tully hill:

> …it was agreed upon by the said Lady Hume, John Greene, Esq., Examinant and the rest of all the men, women and children who were there with them in that Castle should have quarter for their lives and all their goods with free liberty and safe conduct to go either to Monea or to Iniskillen, at their choice, provided the said castle and arms in the same should be yielded and rendered up into the hands of the said Rowry Magwire, all which was granted and promised yea upon Oathes, and confirmed by Writ by the said Rowry unto them. And thereupon the said Rowry did enter into the castle the day and year beforesaid and received the arms that were there. And afterwards, the same day, the said rebels having stript the said protestants of all their clothes (except the said Lady Hume), they imprisoned them in the vault or cellar of the said Castle, where they kept them with a strong guard on them all ye night. And the then next day morning, being the Lord's Day, and the 25th of December, 1641, they took the said Lady Hume, Alexander Hume, John Greer [Greene], this examinant, with their wives and children, from amongst the rest of the said prisoners forth of the said Castle, and placed them in the barn of one John Goodfellow, at Tully aforesaid, with[in a] stones cast from the Castle, putting them in hopes that they would convey them to the Castle of Monea upon horses which they had provided for them; but as for the rest that were left there behind them in the Castle at Tully, the said rebels told those in the barn that they should go on foot after them to Monea aforesaid.
>
> But immediately after, upon the said 25th day of December, 1641, at Tully Castle, within and about the Bawne and Vault of the same, in the said County of ffermanagh, the said Rebells did most cruelly, bloudily, and barbarously murther and kill the said protestants to the number of fifteen men and three score women and children of thereabouts…

Hume was then able to go on and name some of the men killed that day, including Thomas and Francis Trotter, Alexander Chirmfild, Alexander Bell, George Chirmside, Robert Black, James Barry, Thomas and James Anderson. He concluded:

> The Actors of which massacre and murthers this examinant saith for the most parte are since that tyme dead or slaine, as he heard; and as for such of them that surviveth them, this examinant remembers not their names; and this examinant further saith that after the said Rebells did plunder and pillage the goods that were within that Castle, they did burn the said Castle the day and yeere beforesaid.

Although Hume's deposition does not mention it directly, it would appear that Lady Hume's party arrived safely at Monea, probably under escort from Rory Maguire. However, Maguire cannot easily be excused for the horror that took place during his absence from Tully. Following the burning by Maguire's troops, the castle was rendered unfit for habitation and it was probably the barbaric events of Christmas Day 1641 that ensured that the Hume family would never again occupy it. This was the end of Tully castle, but it was not the end of the Humes' connection with Fermanagh. The family moved closer to Enniskillen and settled at Castle Hume, erecting a new home near the lakeshore.

Sir George Hume died in Edinburgh in 1662 and was succeeded by his eldest son, Sir John, then 2nd Baronet of Castle Hume. Sir John was married to Sydney Hamilton, daughter of James Hamilton of Manorhamilton in Leitrim and they had ten children. Sydney died in 1688 and at this time Sir John, who was by then of advanced years and conscious of the gathering constitutional storm, removed the younger members of the family to the safety of England. Nevertheless, his house at Castle Hume was described as being fortified by him in the interest of Prince William of Orange, later William III.

Sir John was attainted by the patriot parliament of 1689, together with his brother Revd George Hume, rector of Inishmacsaint, and James, his eldest son and heir. With Alexander Weir of nearby Monaghan, James went on to raise a troop of horse that saw active service during the war. As well as this, Sir John's second son, also named John, who had previously studied at Trinity College in Dublin, joined the expedition of Colonel Kirke to raise the Siege of Derry. However, on the passage across the Irish Sea, he took ill and died of fever.

James was also to die young, and so when Sir John died in 1695, the title of 3rd Baronet of Castle Hume passed to the third son, Sir Gustavus Hume. Gustavus married Lady Alice Moore, daughter of the Earl of Drogheda, and they had six children. During his lifetime he rebuilt Castle Hume at the cost of £30,000, using the services of a young little-known German architect called Richard Cassels, who later went on to design Powerscourt House in Wicklow and Leinster House in Dublin. Gustavus was High Sheriff of Fermanagh in 1701, Provost of Enniskillen in 1711 and MP for the county in 1713, 1715 and 1727. When he died in 1731 he was succeeded by his daughter Mary, who had married Nicholas Loftus, MP for Fethard. Loftus was created Earl of Ely in 1766 and when their son Nicholas died without issue, the estates passed to an uncle in the Ely family. Thus, the Hume family interest with their former holdings in Fermanagh ceased from this moment.

Castle Hume did not survive for long, for it was dismantled in 1806 and a new residence known as Ely Lodge was built on nearby Gully Island, which was joined to the mainland by a bridge. This house was itself dismantled in 1870 and replaced by the present structure. This last house was bought by the fifth Duke of Westminster in 1948 and has remained in his ownership to this day. Part of the estate has recently been developed as a golf course.

Castle Tour

Tully is one of the best-preserved and documented castles of the plantation era and is definitely worth a visit. It had a brief life of only thirty years before it was destroyed and as a result it preserves only features of early-seventeenth-century design without the overlay of later alteration or addition. As well as this, the castle displays an interesting mixture of Scottish and Irish features in its construction. Although of a definite Scottish design, like Monea or Castle Balfour, there are features of this construction which would indicate that Irish masons actually carried out the building work.

Tully castle is beautifully located on a peninsula jutting into Lough Erne. The approach from the main road presents wonderful views of the castle and the lake beyond. Walking from the car park, Tully castle is approached up a narrow path from the little visitor centre. It is sited just off the summit of a low hill, and within easy access of the lough. Within the castle site the ground slopes down towards the SW corner.

The bawn is nearly square in shape and at 28.5m (94ft) square is larger than the norm, with rectangular flankers on each of the four corners. The entrance was in the middle of the south wall but this, together with the west wall, has been reduced to foundation level only. The original bawn wall is best preserved on the east side, where it reaches 3m in height and retains its coping course. At only 0.6m thick though, it was unable to sustain a wall walk. Excavation has shown that cobbled pavements ran around the internal bawn perimeter, indicating that there were no buildings adjoining the walls.

There were originally four rectangular flankers, but only those on the SE and NE have been substantially preserved. These flankers were approximately 5.5m by 3.7m (18ft by 12ft) internally and each had a fireplace, which would indicate that they provided living accommodation, perhaps for staff in the castle household. Both flankers had additional accommodation on the first floor, probably reached by means of an internal ladder.

The SE flanker was entered via a doorway from the bawn and has a loophole in the north wall, which allowed defensive fire to be aimed along the full length of the east bawn wall. The loop measures 0.5m by 0.5m (20 by 20 inches) internally but the external stones have been removed. Another narrow window in the east wall of the flanker allowed fire to be directed at any intruder in the adjoining field, in addition to providing some light to the interior. It measures 0.75m by 0.6m (30 by 24 inches) internally but is splayed to only 0.75m by 0.2m (30 by 8 inches) on the external face. In addition, there is a window in the north gable at first-floor level and what has been interpreted as part of a doorjamb, which presumably led out to a partial wall walk on the east bawn wall.

The NE flanker contains loopholes on all four walls, measuring 0.5m by 0.5m (20 by 20 inches) internally but tapering to only 0.3m by 0.15m (12 by 6 inches) externally. These provided a mixture of offensive and defensive fire options for the garrison should the castle come under attack. Once again, an upper storey created additional living space.

The NW and SW flankers are destroyed down to foundation level but it is likely that only the former had a similar function to those on the opposite side of the bawn. The SW flanker is more problematical. The natural slope of the bawn is towards this corner and it would therefore have made an unsanitary apartment. Moreover, the room was divided internally by a stone wall, which suggests it was used as a stable.

Excavation within the bawn during restoration in the 1980s did not uncover any buildings normally associated with a working estate. Although the exact function of the area within the bawn cannot now be confirmed, it is tempting to postulate that a formal garden, similar to the one now on site, was used by Lady Hume to grow herbs for culinary and medicinal use. A leaflet on the possible types of plants grown can be obtained from the visitor centre.

The main residence was located roughly midway along the north wall of the bawn. It was T-shaped in plan, three storeys high and consisting of a main block approximately 16m by 6.5m (52ft by 21ft) externally, with a wing projecting southwards into the bawn, measuring 5m by 4m (16ft by 13ft). This projection contained the main entrance and the stairway to the upper rooms of the building. The entrance door here has a stone lintel with a relieving arch above.

Passing through the main entrance doorway, one enters the hallway where a modern iron staircase now occupies the space of the original wooden stair, which would have led to the upper floors of the main block. Three narrow splayed loopholes on the south, west and east walls light the interior. Additionally, there is a window high up on the west wall near the entrance that would have added more light. A socket and rebate for a wooden drawbar can be seen inside the door frame. Each of the loops appears to have a small shelf above it, upon which it would have been useful to rest a powder flask and shot.

From the entrance hallway an arched doorway to the left led into a vaulted storage area. Curiously, there is a socket and drawbar located on the inside of the frame, which would have allowed this room to have been secured. Several small splayed apertures in the south and west walls lit this internal space but only one (for obvious security reasons) penetrates the north wall. In the middle of the west end there is a slop hole for waste products. At the east end there is a fireplace occupying the full width of the house and containing ovens on both sides, indicating that this area was used as the castle kitchen. Finally, there is a square hole in the stone-vault roof that has been interpreted as a 'murder hole' but, given its location, may have served more mundanely as an early form of 'dumb waiter'. Was it also possible to descend through the hole to secure the kitchen door with the drawbar?

Special mention must be made of the vaulted stone arch, which forms the fireproof ceiling for the floors above. This semicircular barrel vault, 2.4m high in the centre, appears to have been constructed by Irish masons, as the marks of wicker used to support the arch during construction can clearly be seen on the underside of the mortar. This type of construction was well known in Ireland during the late medieval period and it would appear that the masons have made use of this traditional method to complete their task. Though of Irish construction, the need for a stone-vaulted ceiling above the ground floor was also a feature of Scottish defensive building at this period.

Proceeding up the stairs one enters the main accommodation of the castle. The floor area is divided into two rooms separated by a stone partition wall. The larger room on the west, probably the main living room, measures 10m by 5m (33ft by 16ft) and is amply lit by two splayed, flat-arched windows in the south wall, facing into the bawn. There is a recess between these windows measuring 2.2m high by 1.2m wide. Two windows were also provided on the north wall of the room, which was the most vulnerable direction for the house as it faced out of the bawn, but was probably deemed safe enough at this height from the ground. A large fireplace was located on the west gable. Interestingly, a wide window to the left of the fireplace was blocked up at some time and pierced only by a small circular loophole measuring just 7.5cm (4 inches), which has been suggested as part of the defensive precautions taken in 1641. If so, then it is surprising that no attempt was made to block up the windows on the north wall, which represented a greater threat to the castle's security.

The smaller apartment on the first floor, to the east, probably used as a private drawing room, measures 5m by 4m (13ft by 16ft) and has a fireplace located on the NE corner. It is lit by two ample-sized windows in the south and east walls. Running along the full length of the north wall, at a height of 3m, can be seen a line of twenty-two sockets in the wall (some also reflected on the south wall) into which the joists for the wooden floor above were placed.

There was also a small first-floor room in the south wing, lit by small lintelled apertures in the south, west and east walls. The four sockets for the floor joists can still be seen in the walls. The east wall curves internally here, suggesting that the room was accessed via a spiral stair.

Access to the second floor was via a stone stair within a turret, supported on a squinch at the SE re-entrant angle, between the main house and the wing. Ordinarily one would have expected this turret to be neatly corbelled, but it is in fact smooth rendered on the exterior, suggesting again that Irish masons unfamiliar with Scottish practices carried out the work. The stair led first to the small room in the south wing and then to the main accommodation on this level.

As in the floor below, the room in the wing contains three windows on the south, west and east walls. These finely dressed windows are lintelled, with the one on the south wall containing two lights. There is a well-cut sandstone fireplace on the south wall with the flue intact to chimney level. The sockets for the floor joists can also be traced in the walls.

The spiral stair also led to the bedrooms of the main part of the house at second-floor level. These rooms were lit by three dormer windows on the south side and by windows in the east and west gables. The lintelled window in the east gable is grooved for the addition of glass, with a socket behind the glass for a wrought iron bar. The two bartizans located on the NE and NW corners of the house appear to have been entered via doorways from the bedrooms at second-floor level. Part of the doorjamb of one of these can be seen in the NE corner. These turrets, which are corbelled out over the line of the castle, would probably have had loopholes in them giving additional protection on the vulnerable north side of the castle, but must have been rather cramped. Once again, the construction shows evidence of Irish masons at work. Unlike the perfect corbelled turrets at Monea or Castle Balfour, these turrets have smooth rubble masonry.

Of all the castles in the Erne basin, a visit to Tully provides a unique snapshot in time of a defended home located in a marcher area of the plantation at the outset of the 1641 rebellion. The site fairly reeks of its place in history and the events which overtook it at Christmas 1641. Tully must therefore feature in any tour of plantation castles along the Erne.

CASTLE CALDWELL
OS SHEET 17. GR 017605

From Belleek take the A47 towards Kesh for 5km (3 miles). Signposted on the right is Castle Caldwell Forest Park. Follow the signs to the car park. The ruins of Castle Caldwell are reached by a footpath through the trees. There is a good berth for cruisers directly below the castle.

History

The complex ruined site of Castle Caldwell today reflects its long period of continuous occupation over three centuries. Surrounded by trees and occupying the summit of a low gentle hill, and with its northern walls resting on a low cliff, there is easy access to the exterior of the castle. Unfortunately it is difficult to inspect the interior at close hand, due to the dangerous condition of the surviving masonry, making interpretation of this complex site a difficult task.

Sir Edward Blennerhassett, a native of Pockthorpe in Norfolk, was granted the 1,500-acre estate of Bannaghmore in Lurg precinct on 3 July 1610, and he promptly set about erecting a fortified residence for himself and his large family at Castle Caldwell (originally named Hassett's Fort), as required under the conditions of the grant. There are several contemporary descriptions of the castle constructed here during the plantation. These are useful given the accretion of additional extensions in later years, which now make the site difficult to interpret. In the 1611 Carew survey, commissioner Gatisfeth described the castle already under construction, 'They have made one English house, with three rooms beneath, a chimney and an oven, with a loft, and part of the house is already thatched; some boards are already sawed for the loft and about fifteen trees felled and squared.'

Visiting the area in 1618, Captain Nicholas Pynnar described the castle and the adjacent village of Belleek thus:

> …upon this proportion there is a strong bawn of lime and stone, being 80 feet long and 60
> feet broad and a stone house 3 storeys high, all furnished himself and family dwelling in it.
> He hath also built a village near unto the bawn, consisting of 9 houses of good cagework.

But later, in August 1622, Perrott and Annesley visited the estate and reported that the house inside the bawn had not been completed, though they did confirm that the other houses had been erected and also the existence of a functioning water mill. In addition, the bawn was described as having two flankers.

Finally, an inquisition in 1629 described Hassett's Fort as having a bawn wall of 316ft in circumference and measuring 14ft high (4m). The bawn contained a house 67ft by 26ft (20.5m x 8m) and was 27ft (8.2m) high. All of these descriptions broadly conform to the same dimensions and describe a substantial defensive residence for the landlord and his family.

In addition to these lands, Sir Edward also became co-owner, with his brother Thomas, of the 1,000-acre estate of Tollimakein, an area rich in timber, which had originally been granted to John Thurston. Thomas Blennerhassett had already been granted a 1,500-acre estate around Kesh, so the family were now the pre-eminent landowners in north Fermanagh.

Despite these encouraging pictures, Sir Edward's chief difficulty at Hassett's Fort was achieving his required quota of British tenants to settle on the estate. In a 1618 muster of British tenants, it was noted that the estate could provide twelve men, but could only arm them with three muskets and four calivers as no swords, pikes or halberds were available. The following year, Pynnar stated that a total of twenty-two British families had been settled, mustering forty men, but Blennerhassett commonly leased land to Irish tenants who were prepared to pay premium rates for land. As a result of this, a large number of native Irish were to remain on the land regardless of the precise terms of the grant.

Sir Edward died in 1618 and was succeeded on the estate by his son Francis, who had acted as estate manager since the family's arrival in Fermanagh. Francis erected the parish church at Rossbeg, near the present entrance to Castle Caldwell forest (another of the conditions of the original grant), but evidently it was still incomplete when the rebellion began in 1641. The evidence for the events that took place at this time is recorded in the deposition of Anne Blennerhassett, wife of Francis, in July 1643.

The castle was seized by Captain Rory Maguire in December 1641 and Francis, his wife Anne and five children were robbed of all their livestock, money and clothing and incarcerated at Ballyshannon castle. Whilst at Ballyshannon, Francis was killed by the rebels. Anne Blennerhassett and her family were then forced to endure a year and a half of arrest before being allowed to board a ship with other captives and sail to Dublin, where she later told her story to the Royal Commission established to hear the plight of the displaced settlers.

The Blennerhassett family returned to Hassett's Fort at the end of the war. An 'Edward Bleurhassett Esq.' was living at Belleek and a 'Philip Bleurhassett gent' at Druminillar at the time of the 1659 census. The estate passed through various members of the family before being sold off by Augustus Blennerhassett to James Caldwell in 1670, thus ending the family's connection with the county. The new owner, James Caldwell, born in 1630, was a rising commercial figure in the restoration period. The family were originally from Straiton in Ayrshire and appear to have come across to Fermanagh at the beginning of the plantation. James became involved in various land purchases around the Erne area, accumulating an estate totalling 1,300 acres in Clanawley in 1661, including land at Crilly near Belturbet, before finally settling on the Blennerhassett estate (which he later renamed Castle Caldwell) in about 1670. With his growing wealth came increasing influence in the affairs of the county. He was High Sheriff of Fermanagh in 1664 and again in 1677, becoming a Baronet in 1683. He married Catherine Campbell, by whom he had four sons and four daughters.

He was described by a contemporary as, 'a man of lifty [*sic*] principles, lover of sciences, and a great lavisher among nobility; he was a portly able man in person, a skillful head-piece in law suits, a terror to his adversaries, a tower of defence for his adherents'. These virtues were soon to be tested to the full. During the crisis regarding the royal succession, he sided with the Williamite faction who were determined to ensure a Protestant would succeed the Catholic King James. As a result of his opposition to King James's authority in Ireland, the Patriot Parliament attainted Sir James and his sons Charles and Hugh in 1689. Undeterred, he raised a regiment of foot for himself and two troops of horse for his two sons from amongst his tenants to support the Protestant cause and used the strategic location of his estate to blockade any attempt by King

James's army to force the Erne crossings between Castle Caldwell and Ballyshannon. On several occasions his daughter Elizabeth even travelled to Dublin to obtain much-needed powder and shot. Another son, Henry, was imprisoned for fourteen months in Dublin during this crisis.

In late March 1689, Sligo was abandoned by the Williamites under Lord Kingston, who was then ordered by Governor Lundy of Londonderry to fall back to the line of the lower River Erne. As a result of this, the various fords across the river were fortified and to prevent its use by the enemy, part of Belleek's stone bridge was pulled down. Castle Caldwell was now in the front line.

Hugh Caldwell was ordered to Donegal town with his troop of horse and three infantry companies to strengthen its garrison. The town was soon invested by an army of 2,000 men under the command of the Duke of Berwick, who demanded its surrender. When this failed, Berwick offered inducements, but the Williamites were not to be influenced. An assault on the garrison was beaten off and when a relief force of 700 men under Sir James approached from Ballyshannon, Berwick fired the town and withdrew, leaving around 100 dead.

On 2 May 1689, 3,000 poorly trained troops under Colonel Patrick Sarsfield approached the Erne crossings from Sligo and began to cannonade Ballyshannon from the south side of the river. On 10 May another relief force was assembled at Enniskillen consisting of four troops of horse and twelve companies of foot under Colonel Thomas Lloyd, which marched around the south shore of Lough Erne and arrived opposite Castle Caldwell. Sir James then reinforced this army with 400 of his own regiment and some of Ffolliot's Ballyshannon defenders, which he sent across the river on boats, the horses being later swum across.

Sarsfield now disengaged from his activities around Ballyshannon and drew up his army on a low ridge facing east, with his left flank on the River Erne and his right flank protected by a broad bog. His front was only approachable along a narrow track that crossed a small stream with a broken bridge. Here Sarsfield awaited the arrival of Lloyd's army.

Lloyd ordered the cutting of faggots to use as footing for the cavalry as they crossed the bog but a local man informed him of a path through it. Lloyd's cavalry was then able to make their way through the bog and outflank Sarsfield's troops. Concluding that their position was untenable, the Jacobite army began to disintegrate as units fled along the road to Sligo. Over 100 were killed and more taken prisoner, including sixty who had taken refuge on Inis Saimer island, off the mouth of Ballyshannon harbour. The pursuit continued as far as Bunduff, with Lloyd's victorious army capturing two small cannon, forty horses and all the Jacobite baggage.

Following this victory, Sir James visited Major General Kirk's army at Inch, County Donegal on June 24 1689, to obtain arms and ammunition for his depleted arsenal. Sir James was concerned at the lack of movement of Kirk's army to relieve the besieged and starving city of Londonderry. He was further alarmed at the fraternisation that occurred regularly between Kirk's officers and the Jacobite army besiegers, and made his concerns known. Finally, on 20 July, Kirk granted Sir James his requests, offering 8 cannons and 1,600 muskets together with sufficient ammunition. In addition to this, Sir James received a commission from King William confirming him as colonel of the regiment that he had raised from his own tenants.

However, there were to be conditions attached to his appointment. Regular officers chosen by Kirk were to accompany Sir James on his return to Castle Caldwell and assume key commands in the regiment, including Colonel Wolseley and Major Tiffin. This was done at the expense of the amateur gentlemen soldiers who had served alongside Caldwell during the previous actions.

This group returned to Castle Caldwell on 28 July 1689 to be informed of the threat by Lord Mountcashel's Jacobite army to Crom castle at the far end of Upper Lough Erne. The Governor of Enniskillen, Gustavus Hamilton, was urgently assembling a relief force and requested the services of Sir James. Responding immediately to this call he set off, together with his new officers and his regiment, for Enniskillen. Sir James accompanied six companies of his regiment on its journey towards Crom but he was ordered back to Enniskillen by Governor Hamilton to defend it from a possible attack from Sarsfield's Jacobite army, which was advancing from Sligo. He was therefore not present at the battle of Newtownbutler on 31 July, when his newly equipped and officered regiment took part in the Williamite army's complete destruction of Mountcashel's force.

When the Duke of Schomberg landed in Bangor bay in August, Sir James accompanied his troops to Schomberg's camp and was involved in the Duke's activities around Dundalk. With the normal seasonal lull in fighting, he invited some of Colonel Tiffin's regiment to winter on his land, but was later to regret this as the troops were to cause damage on the estate. At this point Sir James withdrew from his prominent role in the Williamite cause, but the reasons for this may have been domestic. His wife Catherine had died in 1689 and on 23 July the following year he married again, this time in London to Susanna Becke.

Castle Caldwell was then able to settle down to a more sedate lifestyle. Sir James was to pursue several claims for damage to his estate sustained during the war and was to receive some compensation. He remained critical of General Kirk's inactivity at Londonderry in 1689, but this was later rendered fruitless as Kirk was killed at Athlone in July 1691, when he was beheaded by a cannonball. Sir James died in 1717 having had a long and eventful life.

His son Henry, who had been imprisoned in Dublin during the revolution, succeeded Sir James at Castle Caldwell. Sir Henry appears to have had a poor relationship with his father and was at one time in danger of being passed over for his own son John Caldwell. When Henry died in 1726, Sir John inherited the estate.

A staunch Protestant, Sir John was, however, a reasonable landlord. An interesting story is recorded of him during the Penal era of the early eighteenth century, when it was unlawful in Ireland to carry out Catholic Mass. Returning home on a wet and windy day, he chanced across a Franciscan priest under a hedge practising Mass with his congregation. Though the law was clear enough on the offence, Sir John cleared his cattle from a nearby barn and permitted the priest to carry out his duties under cover from the elements and in a place where he would not be disturbed. In due course this favour was returned in a most unlikely manner. Sir John's son Hume Caldwell was in Austrian military service and living in Prague. As the result of an accidental fire at his lodgings, he lost all his possessions and was being financially pursued by his landlord for the cost of the damages. Aware of his family background, the local Irish Franciscan monks paid his debts and ensured he did not endure hardship over the incident.

When he died, his son and successor James Caldwell paid Sir John a fitting tribute, 'There was no man living, in my opinion, who had a livelier faith in the merits of our Saviour or a greater degree of honesty, charity and compassion.' This second Sir James Caldwell would be a man as accomplished as his great-grandfather of the same name.

In the 1740s, Britain found itself allied with Austria in a war against the French, Spanish and Prussians, later known as the War of Austrian Succession. James Caldwell served with distinction in the Austrian army in northern Italy and as a result was created Count of Milan in the Holy Roman Empire by the Empress Maria Therese. In addition, she presented Sir James with a precious ring taken off her own finger. This was lavish recognition of his service as he was, with the famous Duke of Marlborough, the only foreign Protestant to receive such an award.

Returning to Ireland, he took up residence at Castle Caldwell and devoted his life to the improvement of his estate. He renovated the house and built two large walled gardens with fish ponds and a mock temple, costing £16,000. In addition he planted four orchards, totalling over 2,000 fruit trees, mainly apple but also pear and figs. He wrote many pamphlets on topics such as improving the land and the social condition of its tenants, encouraging the use of new strains of grass, and the growth of winter fodder. For his endeavours he was made a Fellow of the Royal Society in 1753. However his lifelong ambition to be raised to the peerage as a reward for his public service would prove ultimately unsuccessful.

In addition, Sir James became well known for lavish entertainment and hospitality at Castle Caldwell, and the travel writer Arthur Young was certainly charmed and impressed by a visit made in August 1776, which he described in his diary:

Nothing can be more beautiful than the approach to Castle Caldwell; The promontories of thick wood, which shoot into Loch Earne, under the shade of a great ridge of mountains, have the finest effect imaginable … take my leave of Castle Caldwell, and with colours flying and band playing, go on board his six-oared barge for Inniskilling [Enniskillen]; the heavens were favourable, and a clear sky and bright sun, gave me the beauties of the lake in all its splendour.

However the merrymaking on the lake was sometimes taken too far, with tragic consequences. In 1770, a local fiddler called Denis McCabe was drowned in Lough Erne whilst returning to the castle by open boat. A memorial in the shape of a stone fiddle still stands at the entrance to the estate and records the event thus, 'To the memory of Dennis McCabe, fiddler, who fell out of the St Patrick's barge, belonging to Sir James Caldwell, Bart, and Count of Milan, and was drowned'. A rhyming obituary wryly concludes:

Beware ye fidlers of ye fidler's fate
Nor tempt ye deep least ye repent too late:
Ye ever have been deemed to water foes.
Then shun ye lake till it with whisky flows;
On firm land only exercise your skill,
There you may play and safely drink your fill

Sir James died in 1784 and was succeeded by his son Sir John. On his return to the estate John began a programme of rebuilding at Castle Caldwell. Writing in the 1790s, he described the work in progress, 'Part of the old house to the south was so shattered and its walls in so ruinous a state that I was obliged to pull it down and a new and commodious building is now rising from its ruins.' John added a new east wing, which housed his collection of curiosities in a museum on the ground floor, with six rooms above. In addition, the house was given the Gothicised external appearance still visible today.

John married Harriett Meynall in 1789. They had two daughters, Frances Arabella and Louisa Georgina. Harriett died in 1795 leaving John to raise the two girls alone. When he died in 1830, he was buried in Castle Caldwell churchyard. His two daughters were co-heiresses and the estate passed into the Bloomfield family as a result of Frances's marriage to Major John Bloomfield in 1817.

The Bloomfields were active in launching various commercial schemes in the area during the course of the nineteenth century, including the world famous Belleek Pottery, which still survives today. But other schemes were less successful and debts began to mount. As a result of this, Major John's son Benjamin Meynall Bloomfield sold the accumulated treasures of two centuries when he auctioned off the estate in 1876. At this time the estate still measured 1,367 hectares (3,418 acres). The castle and estate went rapidly into decline, but the government bought the land in 1913, making it one of the UK's oldest state-owned forests.

Today the Forest Service of Northern Ireland manages the 200 hectares (500 acres) of this forest, planted in the main with coniferous trees. Thus the view today is perhaps not very different to that first seen by Sir Edward Blennerhassett almost 400 years ago, when he first set eyes on the wooded peninsula upon which he decided to build his new home.

Castle Tour

Walking through the narrow forested path from the car park, the ruined splendour of Castle Caldwell comes suddenly into view. Today the castle is in such a perilous state and so completely overgrown that a close inspection is not recommended. In any case, the accumulations of 300 years' occupation on the site make difficult the task of deciphering the ruins. However, part of the castle described by Pynnar may well yet survive within the crumbling masonry.

In 1854, the traveller J.B. Doyle in his book *Tour of Ulster* described the castle in its twilight years, 'The house is situated upon a long and very narrow peninsula which runs out into the lake, and is thickly planted with noble forest trees, which quite enshroud the ancient and gloomy mansion.' One hundred and fifty years later, that picture of Castle Caldwell still holds true, for the trees have enclosed the site and the remaining structure is almost invisible beneath a layer of ivy. Despite this handicap, an inspection of the ground plan can uncover something of the original structure amongst all the accretions.

Sited on the edge of a low limestone cliff, with access to Lough Erne beyond, the castle was well positioned to provide both defence and comfort for its occupants. To make any sense of the jumble of cross-walls and collapsed structures, the castle must first be divided into two large parts. The larger, western portion encloses a space measuring

20.8m by 27.2m (68ft by 89ft) and is two and three storeys high. This gives the length of the perimeter as 96m or 314ft, remarkably close to the description of the castle in the inquisition of 1629.

The current entrance to the castle is in the middle of the west wall, which was in later years Gothicised by the addition of pointed arched windows and two curved projecting walls which terminated in mock flankers. The approach to Castle Caldwell would therefore have presented any visitor arriving through the woods with a very dramatic entrance.

However, the castle still has more to reveal. The north side of the above rectangle encloses a space 20.8m by 8.1m (68ft by 26.5ft) and is constructed of walls that are a metre thick. Again, these dimensions are very similar to the castle described by both the 1629 inquisition and by Pynnar, who is a little less precise in his figures. Seen externally from the north, the building appears as a two-storey, six-bay manor house. The windows of the first floor are not exactly in alignment with those below, but there is evidence of later brickwork being used to infill voids, so perhaps the windows we see today are alterations from the original plan. A closer inspection of this is difficult, as the building retains a coat of coarse render.

The north elevation of this castle is also similar to that at Crevenish, where the surviving manor-house walls would indicate a similar plan size of 22.1m by 6m (72.5ft by 19.5ft). Related members of the Blennerhassett family commissioned both of these castles and Crevenish had been built by 1619, so it possible that the same architect, masons and joiners were employed to complete Castle Caldwell's manor house.

The internal walls of the manor house are of stone and subdivide it into four rooms, but all the roofing and flooring above has collapsed and it is impossible to know what the layout there might have been. A large brick fireplace survives on the ground floor south wall and beside it is a brick-lined semicircular oven, measuring 0.9m (3ft) in diameter and 0.5m (18 inches) high. Immediately east of this room is a passageway 1.1m (3.5ft) wide, which leads down to a chamber below the front lawn of the house, measuring about 4m by 3m (13ft by 10ft). This chamber is brick vaulted and has an additional chamber opening off on each side, reminding us of the description of 'three rooms beneath'. This central chamber in turn led out through a doorway to a lower ledge above the lake. Access to the lake would have been essential for the castle dweller and this underground route would have allowed both Blennerhassett and Caldwell egress to a waiting boat.

In addition to the outer walls of the manor house, part of the west wall and a small section of the SE corner have walls measuring 1m thick. In contrast, all the other walls are narrower, measuring around 0.6m, and these walls must surely represent the later alteration and refurbishment work which took place during later centuries. One would then have expected the bawn entrance to be opposite the manor house in the middle of the south wall rather than the west, as it appears today, but later rebuilding here has destroyed any trace of this. The two flankers could have been positioned at the SW and SE corners of the bawn. However, the later phases of rebuilding, which included the removal of the south part of the castle, make any interpretation difficult and there is no evidence of any of this above ground level.

Having considered the western part of these ruins, one should now turn one's attention to the eastern extension. The eastern portion of the castle is much smaller and is surely the six-room extension built by John Caldwell in the late eighteenth century.

This part of the building measures approximately 20m by 15m (66ft by 50ft) and is two storeys high. The large room that comprises the full length of the eastern extension must surely be the 'museum' which housed his fine collection of artefacts.

In conclusion, therefore, it is worth considering the suitability of the site as the centre of a manor. Defensively, it would have made good sense to build the house on the north side of the bawn area, near the edge of the low limestone cliff. The house had an ideal aspect facing into the bawn but in addition was able to benefit from its position perched above the lough. This may explain why the house could have windows on the ground floor along the vulnerable external north wall.

Beyond the main castle there are other interesting features that indicate the accretion of several hundred years of occupancy. At some time in the past, the area between the north side of the castle and the lough was enclosed by walls. Steps from a basement allowed the occupier to descend to a boat shed hewn out of the limestone cliff below. A small berth for a boat can still be seen at the edge of the lough. This may of course explain how Rory Maguire was able to seize the house without difficulty in 1641.

On the south side of the castle is an open area which may well have been originally lawned or landscaped. The remains of James Caldwell's gardens can still be seen to the SW of the castle. Beyond the entrance gate in the high stone perimeter wall is a large water-filled depression, which is the remnant of one of the two fish ponds. Further east, near the end of the peninsula, his temple is still visible.

Today the peninsula on which Castle Caldwell is situated is one of the most picturesque and tranquil parts of the lough. There are pleasant walks laid out by the Forestry Service, past the castle and beyond, along the shore to the temple. The location is well worth a visit.

TERMON MAGRATH
OS SHEET 17, GR 096653

From the centre of Pettigo village, take the R232 Donegal road for 1.5km before turning left at a minor crossroads signposted for Aughnahoo Art Studios. Passing under an old railway bridge, the castle ruin is situated at the end of the lane in a field about 1km further on. There are moorings at Lackboy on Boa Island. The low road bridges at each end of the island prevent many craft from approaching any closer to the castle. Surprisingly, the ruins are not indicated on the 1:50,000 OS map.

History
The lands around the modern village of Pettigo in Tirhugh barony were formerly 'termon' or church lands associated with the nearby St Patrick's Purgatory on Lough Derg and had been traditionally maintained by the Magrath family as herenagh. When this area of south Donegal was being assessed for inclusion in the plantation, a dispute arose over its ownership between the Archbishop of Cashel, Myler Magrath and Montgomery, the Bishop of Derry, Raphoe and Clogher.

Montgomery claimed that King James had granted him these lands as part of his bishopric of Clogher and produced evidence to prove this. However, the argument was settled in favour of Magrath, who was able to produce a document showing that Queen

Elizabeth had previously granted him these lands in part payment of his renunciation of Catholicism and his conversion to the Anglican faith. Unlike many other grants, King James was unable to set this claim aside and the lands were re-granted to James Magrath, the Archbishop's fifth son, in December 1610.

This estate was substantial and included the famous site of St Patrick's Purgatory on Lough Derg itself. Unlike other grants, the boundaries here were defined by referring to geographical features such as rivers, bogs and hills. Magrath was also licensed to hold a weekly market on a Saturday and a fair on 16 and 17 July each year. Finally, he was also permitted to divide his possessions into individual 1,000-acre estates and was obliged to build a 'capital house' within seven years.

The site chosen by James Magrath for his chief residence was at Aughnahoo, on a tongue of land between the Termon and Waterfoot Rivers, overlooking Lough Erne. In 1611, Carew reported the castle under construction thus, 'hath begun a prittie castle at termon Magragh w'ch he entends speedily to finish, haveing his materials ready at the place wher he meanes to buyld a bawne and finish the castle'.

Pynnar was not required to visit this estate in his survey of 1618/19, but it is certain that the castle was completed at an early date. Aerial photography has shown that a village became established immediately to the north of the bawn walls, with the main street bisected by a road running from the castle entrance.

James Magrath was evidently still in possession of Termon Magrath in 1632 when Bishop Spottiswood visited Lough Derg to dismantle the buildings associated with St Patrick's Purgatory on Station Island. James subsequently lost the estate to Bishop John Leslie in return for a lease arrangement whereby he paid a small rent.

The Magraths were seemingly not involved in the scheme to overthrow the plantation in 1641. A 'Terence Mac-gragh' was mentioned by Sir Charles Coote as one of those Royalists who surrendered Enniskillen to him in April 1650. (This may be the eldest son of the former Archbishop.) The castle was evidently assaulted by Cromwellian troops, reputedly led by Colonel Henry Ireton, in their campaign of 1650. Artillery was brought up and used to destroy the north side of the castle, causing it to collapse. This action may also account for the scarce remains of the north bawn wall. The castle was then abandoned and never subsequently repaired, though 'Tarmon McGragh Castle and Towne' are marked on the mid-1650s Down survey map of the parish of Carn.

This story cannot be concluded without a final mention of the former Archbishop of Cashel. Myler Magrath had begun his career as a Franciscan friar and was appointed Bishop of Down by Pope Pius V. However, he then renounced his Catholic faith and in September 1570 Queen Elizabeth appointed him Anglican Bishop of Clogher. Visiting him in 1617, Father Mooney (a Franciscan) reported that:

> Magrath is still alive, extremely old and bedridden; cursed by the Protestants for wasting the revenues and manors of the ancient see of Cashel, and derided by the Catholics who are well acquainted with his drunken habits. Nevertheless … there is some reason to hope that he will return to the Church; and, if I be not misinformed, he would now already exchange the Rock of Cashel for that of the Capitoline, where he spent his youth.

He died in 1622.

Castle Tour

Termon Magrath sits in a flat field used for rough grazing, with the Woodford River 100m away to the west, and is best approached from its eastern side. The substantial castle ruins consist of a five-storey tower house situated on the south side of a large bawn. The bawn, built of roughly coursed stone and mortar, is L-shaped, measuring 27m by 27m (90ft by 90ft) with the east and west walls substantively preserved. The bawn has two projecting circular flankers on the NE and NW corners, but the intervening north wall, which contained the entrance, has disappeared. (Traces of a roadway are visible running north from the middle of this wall.) There are some indications of a ditch along the exterior on the east side. The bawn walls, a metre thick, are still preserved up to 4m high, especially along the east side, and contain loopholes at regular intervals. The south walls that connected the bawn to the tower house at its NE and SW corners are only represented by foundations.

The NE flanker is entered through a dressed limestone door frame only 0.65m wide, which still retains the socket for a drawbar behind both jambs. Entering through the low doorway, the ground floor contains five spayed loopholes providing both defensive and offensive fire options in a 270-degree arc. Sited at shoulder level, the loopholes measure 0.4m wide by 0.3m high internally, tapering to only 0.05m by 0.05m (2 by 2 inches) on the external wall. The loops were created by simply leaving a gap between the bawn wall stones on the outer surface, consequently making them difficult to spot from the outside. The whole appearance here is of a well-engineered fighting position.

The joist holes for the floor above can be seen in the wall 2.2m up. Access to this level must have been by an internal ladder. The first floor contains three loopholes like those below. Above this floor the wall narrows, perhaps to carry joists on a scarcement for a further floor level. However, the wall is very much incomplete and as easy access to this level is not possible, this remains only a hypothesis.

The NW flanker is similar to its neighbour but in a more ruined condition. Rubble from the upper walls has filled the space so the true ground level cannot be determined. The entrance is via a dooway comprising two dressed limestone jambs and a lintel block. Once again there are five loopholes on the ground floor and three on the first floor. There is no evidence for a wall walk but this was probably unnecessary, as the bawn walls contain several loopholes that could be used to defend the castle.

The tower house, measuring 11m by 9m externally, is situated in the middle of the south side of the bawn and consists of a five-storey rectangular block with a projecting circular stair tower of 2.8m internal diameter on the NE side. The ground floor is battered, perhaps due to the soft nature of the site, resulting in massive walls almost 2m (6.5ft) thick. The entrance was on the east side, well protected by a gun loop from the floor above. The pointed-arch doorway is comprised of two matching carved limestone blocks. Additional security at the entrance door was provided by an external hinged grill, which could be secured from within the castle by a chain that passed through a hole in the door jamb. There is also a machicoulis at roof level over the doorway, providing more protection.

Inside the tower house there is much rubble and loose masonry, and inspection of the site here requires great caution. The wooden floors have completely disappeared and with the north wall forcibly demolished 350 years ago, the structural safety of the building must be in question. Two sides of the tower house, the south and west, faced out of the bawn and so natural lighting was provided at ground-floor level here by means of narrow horizontal slots measuring 0.46m by 0.18m (18 by 7 inches). The sockets for iron bars are preserved and the interior sills are sloped to enable greater light to enter the interior. Ovens are preserved in the walls on the NW and SW corners. Given the gloomy ambience of this chamber it must have been used as the castle kitchen and for storage.

Access from the front door probably led to a lobby or hallway, with a doorway in a wooden partition wall to the kitchen beyond. To the right, there must have been a wooden stair up to the NE tower, as the stone spiral stair in the NE tower only begins above this level. A single dressed limestone jamb survives at the base of the tower, which may have led to first-floor level. The stair tower, rising anticlockwise, is well provided with narrow lights and loopholes as it rises to successive floor levels. A lintelled doorway at each floor gave access from the stair.

The first-floor chamber was well provided with light. There are three generously sized windows on the south wall, two on the west and one on the east. The huge fireplace is long gone but was probably in the middle of the south wall, thus suggesting that this floor comprised only one grand room. If so, then this was likely used as the principal living chamber, where important guests could be received. The second floor was equally well lit, with large windows either side of the central fireplace on the south wall. A three-light window on the west wall and a two-light window on the east provided more light. Similar windows in the now-destroyed north wall probably matched these. All the windows have a lintel slab with dressed sills and jambs. In addition, the windows had wooden shutters and two of the windows have loops below sill level to provide additional protection. Joists for the successive floors were carried on the narrowing wall thickness. From this floor, a spiral stair in the thickness of the NW corner connects this floor with the one above. This floor may have provided the owner with living chambers of a more private nature.

The third floor also had a central fireplace in the middle of the south wall, with a window on either side. Additionally, there is a small fireplace in the middle of the east gable. Above this, the attic level was provided with fireplaces in the same locations. As the roof is completely gone it can only be surmised that light on this level was provided through dormer windows. Access to this level does not appear to have been via the NE tower, but the corner here is ruined and it is now difficult to confirm this. Both these floors were probably used as bedrooms for the owner's family and his household staff.

Before leaving Termon Magrath, a final circuit of the castle walls is required to appreciate the delicate stonework that survives. At roof level, a neat row of corbelled blocks carried the parapet wall. Between each pair of these corbels, channelled spouts survive which threw the roof water away from the wall tops – an important feature when using permeable limestone as a building material. Note also the superb transoms and mullions which survive on the upper windows, features which are now sadly only too rare in architecture of this period.

The overall appearance of Termon Magrath castle is more reminiscent of a late-medieval tower house with attached bawn, rather than a defended home of the plantation period. This tall tower-house building would have appeared old fashioned in the early seventeenth century, but was not unknown elsewhere. Comparison can be made to

Derryhivenny, County Galway, or the castle at Kirkistown in the Ards Peninsula, both built in the same period. Furthermore, the machicolation over the doorway of the tower house is a definite throwback to a bygone era.

However, the castle contains features that show recognition of the recent changes that had taken place during warfare, even if these are sometimes curiously applied in the design. For example, the musket loopholes are located not only in the flankers but also at numerous positions at shoulder level along the bawn walls. The number of troops required to maintain this type of defence would have been difficult to muster. However, the castle and bawn make a strong impression, with various defensive features, and would surely have impressed any visitor to the table of the owner, James Magrath.

CREVENISH
OS SHEET 17, GR 165626

In the centre of Kesh village take the Rosscolban road opposite the Lough Erne Hotel. After 1km turn right onto the Clareview road ('Enniskillen Scenic Route' sign) and proceed for a further 1.5km. The castle of Crevenish is located behind farm buildings on the right, approached down a straight lane to a modern house. The owner is currently developing the site to accommodate mobile homes and a boat jetty. Other moorings can be found at Kesh.

History

The 1,500-acre estate of Edernagh in the precinct of Lurg was originally granted to Thomas Blennerhassett in June 1610. Thomas Blennerhassett was the son of William Blennerhassett and a native of Horsford, near Norwich, in East Anglia. He was said to be rich, with an annual income of £120! Previously employed as captain of the castle of Guernsey, on arrival in Ireland he immediately set about erecting a castle for himself on the shores of Lough Erne.

In 1611, Carew's inspector reported that Thomas had arrived with six others, namely a carpenter, a joiner, three workmen and a tenant. He had already erected Castlehasset (Crevenish), described as a large house 'with windows and rooms after the English manner, wherein is a kitchen with a stove, chimney and oven'. Stones had been crushed for lime production and he had felled thirty trees, squaring and sawing some of them for later use. In addition he had built a boat, which was an essential means of transport for his loughside residence but also allowed him to take advantage of his right to free fishing in Lough Erne. Visiting the estate in 1619, Pynnar reported:

> Upon this proportion there is a Bawne of Lime and Stone; the length is 70 feet and the breadth is 47 feet, and 12 feet high, having 4 Flankers. Within this bawn there is a house of the length thereof and 20 feet broad, two stories and a half high, his Wife and Family dwelling therein. He hath begun a church. He hath also a small village consisting of six houses built of cagework, inhabited with English…

The latter part of this probably refers to the foundation of Kesh or Ederney. There were also seven English families settled on the estate capable of mustering twenty-six men, but Pynnar reported that he had not been able to confirm this, as Thomas was absent at the time. Despite these assertions, there were always a large number of Irish on the estates, in violation of the terms of the grant.

Perrott and Annesley provided further details of the castle in 1622 and reported 'a bawn of lime and stone with 4 defensible flankers, 17 feet square, 13 feet high. Within the said bawn there is already builded a house of stone and lime, slated, 3 storeys high, beside the cock-loft'.

As well as this, Thomas became a joint owner, with his brother Sir Edward Blennerhassett of Castle Caldwell, of the neighbouring 1,000-acre estate of Tollimakein. This estate had originally been granted to John Thurston but he had either failed to take up possession or he had subsequently sold it to the Blennerhassetts. Later, in 1616, Thomas bought out the remainder of this proportion from his brother, amounting to 760 acres. There is some confusion as to whether this estate was graded as a small or middle-sized proportion (both sizes are referred to in different documents), but what was not in doubt was the prominent position this family now assumed in north Fermanagh during the early plantation years.

Perhaps born around 1550, Thomas had been educated at Cambridge but by his own account had not taken a degree. Nonetheless, he was a literary man and had written several books, including *Mirror for Magistrates* (1578), which dealt with episodes in English history from Caesar to William the Conqueror, a translation of Ovid's *De Remedio Amoris*, and a poem called 'Revelation of the True Minerva' (1582), a panegyric to Queen Elizabeth. On his arrival in Fermanagh, Thomas Blennerhassett directed his writing talents to produce a guidance book for the new settlers entitled *Direction for the Plantation of Ulster*, in which he sought to encourage other settlers to consider investing in the plantation in order to secure 'that wilde countrye to the crowne of England'. Within the work he enthusiastically set out his vision:

> The county of Fermanagh, sometimes Maguire's County rejoice. Many Undertakers, all incorporated in mind as one, they, there with their followers, seek and are desirous to settle themselves. Woe to the wolf and the wood kerne [Irish outlaws]. The islands of Lough Erne shall have habitations, a fortified corporation, market towns and many new erected manors, shall now so beautify her desolation that her inaccessible woods, with spaces made tractable, shall no longer nourish devourers, but by the sweet society of a loving neighbourhood, shall entertain humanity even in the best fashion. Go on worthy gentlemen, fear not, the God of Heaven will assist and protect you.

Blennerhassett married twice, first to Frances Sampson of Harckstead, Suffolk, and then to Elizabeth Sandys of Dublin, and had several surviving children. He died on 11 March 1624/25 and was buried in the church adjacent to the castle. The estate was inherited by his eldest son, Samuel, then aged around twenty-one. Samuel had been High Sheriff in 1622 but did not long survive his father and without issue the estate passed to his brother Sir Leonard Blennerhassett.

Sir Leonard appears to have been as enterprising as his father and he established an ironworks at Clonelly on his estate. Ore rated as good as Spanish iron was worked from veins in the country rock. The huge natural forests in the area were then used to produce charcoal for the smelting of the ore at the ironworks. In addition, wood could be used for various products and as a fuel. The deforestation also ensured that there was no refuge for the outlaws and banditry, which still threatened the new settlers on a daily basis.

Like many other new landlords, Sir Leonard's enterprise resulted in a re-grant of his estates from Charles I on 27 October 1630. His estate was now known as Castlehasset and he appears to have made many profitable leases to new settlers during this period. He was married to Deborah Mervyn, daughter of Sir Henry and Lady Christian Mervyn, and they had six children: Audley, Henry, Leonard, Elizabeth, Catherine and Lucie. When Sir Leonard died on 20 May 1639 he was buried, as he had requested, at the foot of his father's grave in the little church.

By his will, witnessed by Christopher Irving (Irvine) and William Savage, Sir Leonard left one third of his lands to his wife Deborah and the remaining two thirds to his eldest son and heir Audley, when he reached the age of twenty-one. His will further provided each of his other children with specified amounts of money and a sum of £8 to be given to the poor of the parish. Lady Deborah was allowed to remain at Castlehasset as long as she desired and this act would later ensure the castle's place in history.

Lady Deborah married Rory Maguire, brother of Conor Maguire, Lord Enniskillen. Rory Maguire was a member of the native Irish aristocracy but had apparently embraced the new plantation arrangements and had clearly profited from them. Yet, presumably unbeknown to his new wife, Maguire had become deeply involved in the plot to overthrow the plantation in 1641. As the new master at Castlehasset, he planned to eliminate the senior establishment figures in the county in a single bold act by inviting them to a banquet at the castle and promptly arresting them.

This act was planned as a preliminary signal for a general outbreak of hostilities. Rory Maguire invited representatives of all the leading families to the castle. However, Sir William Cole, in his role as constable of Enniskillen, was already suspicious of the activities of Maguire and others in the county, and had been warned by Brian Maguire of Tempo to be on his guard. As he arrived at Castlehasset he was given a signal from a groom (named Coughlin in some accounts) that he was in danger and that the groom would keep his horse ready for a swift departure. We do not know exactly what happened at the banquet, but Sir William must have intimated his concerns to the other guests, who promptly made their escape with him. Another account states that they were able to make their escape quietly down the gravel lane because Cole chose to ride down the grass verge to safety.

Despite this obvious setback, Rory Maguire continued with his plans. Locally, the rebellion began on 23 October 1641 with the burning of the village of Lisnarick and capture of Necarne (modern Irvinestown). From his base at Crevenish, Maguire sent out parties to capture or destroy the property of the settlers in Fermanagh. In a matter of weeks he had cleared all of Fermanagh, with the exception of the few garrisons still held around Enniskillen by his opponent Sir William Cole. He captured Francis and Anne Blennerhassett and their children on their estate at Castle Caldwell and imprisoned them at Castle Hasset for seven weeks. The family were then sent to Ballyshannon, where Francis was executed on Christmas Eve, 1641. Anne later testified that Rory Maguire amongst others had robbed her and her family of land, livestock, buildings, crops and cash totalling £1,860. In addition, the rebels had destroyed the ironworks.

However, it was Rory Maguire's association with the incident of Christmas Day 1641 for which he is best remembered. Arriving with a large force before the walls of Tully castle situated across the lough, Rory compelled the occupant, Lady Hume, to surrender to him with assurances that no harm would come to her or the villagers who had sought refuge within the walls. When she agreed to this his troops entered the castle and commenced to murder the men, women and children gathered there. A total of seventy-five people were despatched and though Rory's presence during this episode is uncertain, his troops were acting with his authority and so responsibility for the massacre does lie with him.

Shortly after the commencement of the rebellion, Rory visited his brother-in-law Audley Mervyn at nearby Trillick castle. He intimated to Mervyn that he wished for him to act as his representative on a mission to England to explain to King Charles why the rebels has taken up arms and the conditions by which they would disarm. Mervyn declined the invitation but used the meeting to persuade Rory to slacken the pace of his actions. During the subsequent lull, Mervyn, his wife, children and two of his sisters escaped in the night. Such as remained were evidently massacred.

Rory would remain committed to the rebellion throughout the remainder of his life. He was killed leading an assault at Jamestown in County Leitrim on 13 November 1648. During the previous years, his wife Deborah produced three children for him, namely Rory, Philip and Marie. Audley Blennerhassett had been due to inherit his father's estate but died unmarried and was buried in the church with his ancestors. The estate then passed to Leonard's second son, Henry Blennerhassett.

'Henry Bleur Hassett Esq' is mentioned in the census of 1659, living at Crevenish amongst thirteen Irish residents. He was twice High Sheriff for Fermanagh, in 1658 and 1661. Following the death of William Davys, he represented the county in the Irish parliament in 1662. In 1664 he married Phoebe Hume, daughter of Sir George Hume, then of Castle Hume in Fermanagh. Phoebe produced two girls, Deborah and Mary, but there was to be no male heir. The family lived together in the castle with Henry's mother Deborah until her death around 1669.

In 1670 Henry sold his Lack estate to William Irvine of Ballindullagh. In December 1676, he died and bequeathed his estates to his wife and after her death to his two daughters in equal proportion. Interestingly, in his will Henry Blennerhassett provided for his three Maguire half-siblings as well. Rory and Philip Maguire were given all his horses to share out equally and a case of pistols each. In addition, Rory was given Henry's sword. Marie was bequeathed fourteen cows. It seems that Henry held no grudge for the behaviour of their father during the earlier rebellion.

The co-heiress Deborah Blennerhassett was to marry a total of four times. Her fourth husband was Captain John Cochrane and they had a son, Henry, who succeeded to the castle. Deborah's sister Mary married Major Charles Bingham and they had a son also named Henry, who sold his half-interest in the Crevenish estate in 1719 to Colonel Christopher Irvine of Castle Irvine, Gerard Irvine and William Humprys.

The castle did not take as prominent a role in the later revolutionary wars, though its then owners would have held it for the Williamites. Writing in 1739, Dean Henry reported, 'near to the castle stands a splendid large house belonging to Captain Cochlan [*sic*]'. It would thus appear that the castle had been abandoned for the comforts of a more modern residence. Deborah died in 1716 and her husband Captain John in 1743. Their son and heir Henry Cochrane succeeded at Crevenish. Sometime in the middle of the eighteenth century, George Vaughan of Buncrana bought up much of the remaining lands of the estate. Henry Cochrane died in May 1799 and was interred in the church along with his ancestors. By this stage, the vast estate built up by his great-great-grandfather Thomas, nearly two centuries previously, had been broken up and sold off into various other estates.

The name of Blennerhassett is now absent from Fermanagh and must be all but forgotten. Another branch of the family received lands in Kerry following the confiscation of the Earl of Desmond's lands in the reign of Elizabeth I and remain there to this day. However, the legacy of the huge Fermanagh estate built up by Thomas Blennerhassett remains in the landscape, as this area contains some of the best agricultural land in the county. In addition, the ruins of Thomas's fine castle and church, nestling against the lapping water of Kesh Bay, make this one of the most pleasant spots around the lough.

Castle Tour

Castle Hasset is now referred to as Crevenish castle and is approached from the road along a straight gravel drive into a farmyard with a modern house located beside it. One can imagine the muffled hoof beats as Sir William Cole made his escape along the grass verge on that fateful night in 1641! One's first impression is that this is the castle described by Nicholas Pynnar in 1619. The castle backs directly on to the lake and although today there is a meadow reaching down to the water's edge, the lough level in the 1600s was higher and would have lapped the rear wall in the winter.

Passing through the farm offices, the castle ruins are best approached from the east. From here, the close proximity of the lough can be appreciated, a few metres beyond the meadow. Entry to the site is made through a doorway in the wall. The cut sandstone jambs survive to a low level in the entrance. Inside, there are a number of gravestones, indicating that the site was used as a graveyard at a later date. This enclosure, measuring 22.7m by 7m (75ft by 23ft) internally, may represent the remains of the church mentioned by Pynnar. If so, its location on the bawn perimeter is highly unusual and must have compromised the defensive capabilities of the castle. The surviving gravestones will be described later.

There is a gap in the west wall of the church, which also presumably served as the east bawn wall. Passing through this modern gap, the interior of the bawn is entered. To the north are the remains of the manor house of the castle. The south wall of the bawn is now occupied by the rear wall of a set of outhouses, but they clearly follow the same line, as a portion of the SE flanker is incorporated in the wall. The bawn measures 14.8m by 22.1m (48.5ft by 72.5ft), remarkably close to the dimensions stated by Pynnar. The west bawn wall and the SW flanker have both now been completely lost but were close to the line of recently planted trees. The wall between the bawn and the church is modern, but the ragged edge of the original wall can be seen on the manor house. It was 0.9m thick, around 4m (13ft) high and tapered at the top, once again confirming Pynnar's description.

The modern farm shed building now defines the southern limit of the bawn, but incorporates about 4m of the original walls. The easternmost farm shed also incorporates the 0.8m-wide entrance to the SE flanker. Though the western side of the bawn is now completely gone, one would presume that there was a flanker on the SW corner. The original entrance to the bawn was probably in the middle of the south wall but this has been lost under the modern farm buildings. The castle was built of local undressed whinstone blocks.

Situated along the north side of the bawn are the remains of the manor house. The ruins today consist of three sides of a house at least two storeys in height, with the NE flanker surviving to its full height. Most of the east gable and some of the north and south walls (0.9m thick) remain, though the west gable has been completely removed. About 11m of the north wall survive to near full height. About 22m of the south wall survive, but only about 9m at the eastern side are to full height. It is said that a large part of the south wall fell in a storm around 1880. However, the remaining walls indicate a house that was at least 22.1m long by 6m deep (72.5ft by 19.5ft), again confirming Pynnar's description.

The manor house appears to have been of four or five bays, with large windows on the ground- and first-floor levels. Of these, one first-floor and two ground-floor windows survive more or less intact on the south wall, at the eastern end of the house. These windows are 2m by 2m with flat stone lintels. The partially preserved third bay on the ground floor may have been another window, or it may have been the entrance doorway, as it is 3m wide (although this could be the result of later removal of the rubble walls). Unfortunately the remains are too scant to substantiate this, but one would expect the original entrance to be in the middle of the south wall.

Inside the house are the remains of six fireplaces; three on the north wall and three on the east gable. These fireplaces are arranged vertically, with one on each floor level, feeding into the same flue at an upper level, indicating that there were three storeys. This is corroborated high up in the east gable by the still evident sill and lower jambs of a window. A large chimney stack, 3m long and projecting 0.7m beyond the line of the north wall, contains the largest fireplace. This fireplace has been robbed of its original stonework and the wooden hood here may represent a later replacement. The two fireplaces above are smaller and that on the second floor has a brick hood. Until recent restoration work was carried out, the flue survived more or less intact to chimney level. The three east-gable fireplaces are also smaller. Here the chimney breast projects into the internal space.

There are no windows on the ground-floor north wall, as one would expect, for this is the vulnerable rear of the castle. A small window is located on the north wall at what appears to be a half-storey level and there is another window at first-floor level. Internal partitioning must have been achieved with the use of stud walls, but no subdivision can now be seen. This makes determining the location of the stairs difficult, though the small window to the east of the large fireplace is a possible site. More likely is the area to the west of this fireplace, along a part of the north wall which is now gone, but without proper investigation, this remains only a hypothesis.

The last part of the castle to investigate is the sub-rectangular NE flanker, entered directly from the manor house along a 2m-long passageway, which is 0.9m wide. This flanker measures 5.1m by 5.1m (17ft by 17ft) and extends the full height of the house, much as the flankers at Portora. Unlike those at Portora however, this flanker is spear shaped, with its north wall angled NNW. The ground drops away towards the lough here and perhaps as a precaution against subsidence the footing below the NE corner is underlain with large flagstones to spread the weight.

A splayed loophole is located in the centre of all four walls of the flanker, providing a mixture of offensive and defensive firing options. Each loop, though, is a different size and must have additionally been expected to light the dim inner space of the flanker. Again, due to the sloping nature of the exterior, three of the loops pierce the outside wall 1.5m above the outside ground level. The flanker ceilings look lower than the main house and direct access must have included a flight of steps within.

The last items of note are the two remaining grave slabs from the church graveyard. One of these slabs has been secured against the west wall of the church, and consists of a coat of arms and dedication to the mother of William Cochrane. The other slab, 2m tall, is currently resting against a shed wall. It is covered with an elaborate coat of arms much different to the Cochrane one, but not that of the Blennerhassetts. The stone has no names carved on it and appears too large for a gateway plaque. It may have been used as the door stone for a family vault now long demolished.

Crevenish is a delightful place, nestling on the water's edge of Lough Erne. For many years the crumbling walls were in danger of suffering total collapse, but recent restoration work has ensured that future generations will be able to rest here beside the lough and ponder the events that have given it a place in history

CASTLE ARCHDALE
OS SHEET 17, GR 187599

Located 4 km (2.5 miles) south of Kesh on the B82. Turn off on to the minor road signposted for Castle Archdale Forest. At the end of the lane, the castle ruins are observed on the hill to the left. There is adequate car parking here. There are moorings at Tom's island jetty, Castle Archdale Forest, 600m from the castle.

History
The fragmentary ruins of old Castle Archdale are all that remain of the once extensive estate here, near the wooded shores of Lower Lough Erne. The surviving masonry describes the remnants of a T-shaped fortified house, with remnants of the adjacent bawn wall and entrance doorway with its surviving plaque.

John Archdale, a native of Darsham in Suffolk, obtained a grant of the small proportion of Tallanagh, Lurg precinct, in 1612 and he immediately began to carry out the terms of the grant by erecting a residence for himself here on the slope of a gently rising hill. Visiting the area in 1618, Captain Nicholas Pynnar gives the following account:

> Upon this proportion there is a bawne of lime and stone, with three flankers 15 feet high; in each corner there is a good lodging slated, with a house in the bawne, of 80 feet long, and 3 stories high, and a Battlement about it. Himself with his family are there resident. He hath also a Watermill; and in two several places of his land he hath made two Villages, consisting of 8 houses apiece...

The castle was described in a later inquisition as:

> ...one fort or bawne of lime and stone contayninge 3 score and 6 foote square, every way, and 12 foote in height with 2 flankers in 2 corners of the bawne, contayninge 15 foote square everie way, and 17 foote in height; there is likewise built upon Killenure one castle or capital messauge of lime and stone, adjoining to the foresaid bawme or forte, contayninge 3 score and 10 foote in length and 37 foote in height, and in breadth 28 foote...

John Archdale was appointed High Sheriff of Fermanagh in 1616. When Perrott and Annesley reported on the estate in 1622, Archdale had died the previous year and the castle was inhabited by his widow and their family. His son Edward succeeded him to the estate and was the landlord when the castle was attacked and captured by Rory Maguire in 1641. Tradition asserts that the castle was burnt and all nine Archdale children perished except the youngest, named William, who was in the care of a native Irish woman. This woman also had a son of her own and during the investment it is said that she supposedly threw the young heir William from an upper window in order that he would be saved. However, the child was actually her own infant boy and the Archdales are therefore allegedly descended from this exchange.

A 'William Archdall Esq' is indeed found resident at Manor Archdall in the 1659 census of Ireland. William further added to the family estates at Castle Archdale and was married with several children. His eldest child and heir, named Mervyn, was born in 1685, followed by a sister Angel and a younger brother Edward. During the troubled period of the revolution, Mervyn and his sister were sent out of Ireland for safety. The castle was again burnt to the ground in 1689 or 1690 and it was not subsequently restored. Though they returned to their estate after the war, it is uncertain where the family lived.

On his return to Castle Archdale, Mervyn received early schooling from a Mr Wade at Trillick before entering Trinity College Dublin and graduating with a BA in 1705. In 1708, he obtained a commission as a lieutenant colonel in a militia regiment of dragoons under the command of Colonel Irvine. He served a term as High Sheriff of Fermanagh in 1714 and the following November he was made a full colonel of a regiment of dragoons in Fermanagh. During his term as High Sheriff, he informed the Lord Lieutenant that he intended to call a meeting of the local magistrates to enforce the Penal Laws, as he was aware of twenty-two Roman Catholic priests illegally practising in the area. Whether or not he ever took any action is unclear.

During his lifetime he seems to have been a supporter of horseracing and in time he ran up debts which began to cripple the family estate. In 1710 or 1711, along with other gentry of the locality, he agreed to certain articles whereby horses would compete for a plate for a period of seven years at a place called Inishway, apparently near to Monea and Ely Lodge. The horses were expected to race over four heats of four miles, with the race meeting annually on the second Wednesday of May.

On the death of his father in 1722, Mervyn became the heir to the Archdale estate. Mervyn died without an heir in 1726. He was first succeeded by his brother Edward and then his sister Angel in 1728. Angel had married Nicholas Montgomery of Derrygonnelly, who adopted his wife's family name of Archdale. As the century progressed, the Archdales became one of Fermanagh's leading families, contributing at the local level to the improvement of facilities like roads, bridges and churches within the county. At the national level, the Archdales represented Fermanagh in parliament for an unbroken period of 154 years. Angel died in 1745 and Nicholas in 1761 and their son, Colonel Mervyn Archdale, succeeded to the estates.

The steady improvement of the family's fortunes allowed Colonel Mervyn to build a new, more stately pile in 1773, on an elevated site at Rossmore, 1.5km SW of the old castle. Built in the Palladian style, the three-storey mansion was improved throughout the following years with the addition of stable blocks, formal gardens and wooded paths. This building proved controversial, however, as it exposed the family to another supposed curse. According to local tradition, the stones used to build the house came from the old monastery at nearby Kiltierney, which led to the curse that no Archdale heir would be born within its walls. Thus, when Mervyn's son Edward was born in the back entrance lodge during construction, the story appeared to have come true!

Notwithstanding this impediment, the Archdale family continued to prosper. In the nineteenth century, their estates amounted to over 13,200 hectares (33,000 acres) with an annual income at the time of £17,000. However the era of the 'big house' was to pass with the Land Acts at the end of the century, allowing tenants to purchase their holdings outright. In 1906, the land at Castle Archdale was progressively sold off to tenant farmers, starting the gradual decline of the estate.

There was to be one last important episode in the story of Castle Archdale. In 1941, due to its location, Lower Lough Erne was chosen as a base for long-range flying boats of the RAF tasked with protecting the vulnerable merchant ships as they approached the U-boat infested waters of the western approaches to Britain. Castle Archdale became the Officers' Billet for the Catalina and Sunderland aircraft that set off from the lough to patrol the eastern Atlantic. Part of the top storey of the house was altered to provide a lookout over Lough Erne and the stable buildings were converted into administrative offices. At the peak of operations, 2,000 personnel were stationed on the estate.

The greatest success for the base occurred on 26 May 1941, when the crew of a Catalina spotted the German battleship *Bismarck* and radioed her position to the British fleet. *Bismarck* had already sunk the British battleship HMS *Hood* and badly damaged another, HMS *Prince of Wales*, and so it posed a huge threat to the convoys bound for Britain. The aircraft from Castle Archdale kept up a constant surveillance of *Bismarck*'s movements, thus allowing a strong surface force to intercept and destroy her the following day.

The campaign to protect British and Allied merchant ships sailing across the ocean was later dubbed the 'Battle of the Atlantic', and aircraft from Castle Archdale played their part, accounting for the sinking of ten U-boats for the loss of 233 aircrew. However, with the war over in 1945, the estate struggled to survive. Denis Archdale, the last owner of the diminished estate, was forced to sell off more land to pay for crippling death duties, and by 1959 the house was abandoned. In 1973, after extensive salvage of roof lead and timbers, the Palladian house was demolished. Denis Archdale and his family finally left for England and the following year the grounds and the remaining buildings were bought by the government. The former estate demesne land, now managed by the Environment Agency, provides forest walks, exhibition rooms and gardens, with a marina and caravan park located within the grounds.

Castle Tour

The remaining ruins of old Castle Archdale, set on the hill at Bunaninver, can be identified with the early descriptions of the castle, though it is important to be aware of the later restoration work which in places exaggerates and even distorts some of the original features. The castle and bawn, built of a hard limestone, were also subject to some restoration work in 2003. This work stabilised the structure and rebuilt part of the east window of the manor house.

From the car park, a modern gravel path passes a small, quarried area (which may be the original source of the building material) and runs up the hill along the west side of the castle. The original entrance is located in the middle of the 1m-thick south bawn wall. Before entering it is worth stopping to read the Latin inscription above the doorway which reads, '*DATA FATA SEQVVTVS. JOHANNES ARCHDALE HOC AEDIFIDIVM STRVXIT ANNO MILLESSIMO SEX CENTISSIMO DECIMO QVINTO.*' This translates loosely as, 'Following My Destiny. John Archdale built this structure in the year 1615.' ('Following My Destiny' is the Archdale family motto.) The doorway is a fine original example of its kind and similar entrances may have formerly existed at Monea, Tully, Balfour and the like. It consists of a semicircular arched entrance, 1.8m (6ft) wide and 3m (10ft) high, with finely carved mouldings around the architrave. Passing through to the inside, it will be noticed that a narrow wall walk, only 0.6m wide, extends along the full length of the wall at a height of 2.25m. Clearly this wall walk is too narrow by itself and the six corbels spaced at 1.5m intervals were there to support an additional timber platform. The narrow parapet wall, only 0.4m thick above the wall walk, is modern but is probably similar to the original construction.

The bawn today is marked out in part by later masonry walls describing a square measuring 19.5 by 19.5m (64ft by 64ft). Though one cannot rely on this too much, it bears a remarkable similarity to the bawn dimensions described by Pynnar. Standing now in the centre of the bawn, we encounter the first conundrum. The castle was described as having two flankers (by Perrott and Annesley) or even three flankers (Pynnar) yet none are visible. This is because the rebuilt east and west bawn walls we see today were added in more recent times and have not followed the original castle plan to include the two corner flankers presumed to be buried at either end of the south wall. These square flankers would have provided defensive fire along three sides of the vulnerable bawn perimeter and thus substantiate the earlier descriptions. Pynnar's description of three flankers is perhaps more difficult to explain but he may have regarded the rear stair projection in the house, with its array of loopholes, as the third one (see below).

Moving northwards now one enters what would have been the Archdale residence. This manor house, measuring 19.5m by 6m (64ft x 20ft) occupies the full width of the bawn, as at Portora, but this one also contains a square stair projection, measuring 5m by 4m (16ft by 13ft) in the middle of the north wall. The house is constructed of harled local rubble, with the walls of similar thickness to the bawn, but only fragments of these survive – along the east gable (with a square-headed two-light window at first-floor level) and south wall (with part of a similar window). Surviving quoins and window surrounds are of dressed sandstone and the internal walls were plastered. Although it is now difficult to be certain, the house was probably of two storeys in height with a further attic level above.

Also three storeys high, the rear projection rises to near its original height and, as already mentioned, contained the wooden stair which would have provided access to the rest of the house. As the two flankers previously described were unable to provide any covering fire along the north wall, the stair projection was pierced by pear-shaped musket loops along each of the exterior faces. Of these, five remain in good condition at ground level, two along the north and west faces and one on the east. These would have ensured adequate protection was provided to the rear wall of the house. This, then, may explain Pynnar's assertion of three flankers, for in effect the stair projection could fulfil this important defensive role when required.

Above the ground floor, defence could be partially relaxed and this is seen on the first and second floors of the stair projection where square-headed three-light windows in good condition are to be found, still exhibiting their original mullions, with dripstone dressings above. Although none of the other external walls of the house remain, it is probable that there would have been some similar openings on the upper floors but none at ground-floor level. However, Archdale was shrewd enough to place his house along the north side of the bawn and undoubtedly there were ample windows along the south wall facing into it.

What survives today, then, is the fragmentary remnant of Castle Archdale. Despite the austere ruin, enough endures to provide an interesting trip to this once important caput of the Archdale dynasty.

NECARNE
OS SHEET 17, GR 236573

From Main Street in Irvinestown, proceed down Castle Street for 800m, following the sign for 'Necarne Equestrian Centre'. Necarne castle is situated within extensive parkland grounds. There is a large car park here, which also serves the equestrian centre located in the buildings at the rear of the castle complex. Irvinestown is a few kilometres inland so boat users will need to use the infrequent Ulsterbus Service 194 from Enniskillen to reach the site.

History
Despite a less than promising start, Necarne castle, located close to Irvinestown, has survived in a renovated state to the present time. Although the castle is currently lying derelict, this complete Gothic-Tudor mansion survives precariously to the present century, allowing us a glimpse of its former glory. Though much remodelled in the early nineteenth century, the rear of the castle may still comprise sections of the original structure from the time of the plantation.

Edward Warde, a Suffolk gentleman who had arrived in the company of Lord Saye, was originally granted the small proportion of Nakarney (spelt variously), in Lurg precinct, on 13 May 1611. Though his declared income of £400 per annum should have allowed him to develop his newly acquired asset, he immediately sold his interest to Edmund Sutton on 7 June 1611 for a term of 1,000 years. Sutton was the heir apparent of Harrington Sutton of Kallam in Nottinghamshire, but again little interest was shown in the estate and he sold it to Thomas Barton, owner of the neighbouring small proportion of Drumynshin.

Barton, a native of Norwich, had been the original patentee of the small proportion of Drumynshin in September 1610. Despite this apparent consolidation of the two proportions, Barton began to sell off parts of the estate, finally selling out his interest in Drumynshin (presumably including the Nekarney lands as well) to Sir Gerard Lowther on 17 June 1615. Lowther received a patent on 20 February 1618 to consolidate the two manors into the Manor of Lowther.

Sir Gerard Lowther was the fourth son of Sir Richard Lowther, High Sheriff of Cumberland, who had escorted the young Mary Queen of Scots to Carlisle castle in 1568, on her arrival in England. He evidently took his obligations seriously enough to ensure the commencement of his duties and Pynnar reported in 1619, 'Sir Gerard Lowther hath upon Necarn a strong Bawne of Lime and stone, and a House in it, and near unto the Bawne there is a Village [present-day Irvinestown] consisting of 10 Houses, and a Market-House, also a Water-Mill.'

In addition, he confirmed that Lowther had tenanted his estate with sixteen families, able to muster twenty-eight men with arms. Of these tenants, two were freeholders, renting 120 and 90 acres respectively. Twelve others held leases for twelve years for plots ranging from four to seventy-three acres. Nine of these tenants had reportedly taken the oath of allegiance. On his adjacent manor of Drumynshin, Lowther had also been busy. There, Pynnar adds, 'Upon Drumynshin there is a good Bawne of Clay and Stone, rough cast over with Lime, 60 feet square, with two Flankers, but no House in it'. Here there were five freeholders and one leaseholder, of whom three had taken the oath of allegiance.

Lowther was appointed second Baron of the Exchequer in 1628. Though he married three times, he left no heir. When he died in 1629 his estate was re-granted to Sir Adam Loftus and Sir William Parsons. An inquisition of the following year described the bawn as being 324ft in circumference, with walls 17ft high. The report also mentioned 'English-like houses', presumably of wooden cage-work design, but there is no mention of any house within the bawn. Additionally, the manor was permitted to hold a market each Tuesday, three annual fairs (May Day, 15 August and 30 November) and to have free fishing in the lough. The demesne was permitted to extend to 400 acres.

Though Loftus and Parsons were the new owners, it would appear that another Gerard Lowther, nephew of Sir Gerard, remained for a time on the estate. This Gerard eventually chose to live in Dublin and the estate was leased to Christopher Irvine, a connection by marriage, who leased the land and moved his family into the castle. Christopher Irvine had previously bought land at Lettermore in August 1613 from Thomas Barton, and though of Scottish descent, he had become a naturalised Englishman in 1616.

When the 1641 rebellion broke out, Irvine fled with his family to the comparative safety of Enniskillen. The castle was burned down in their absence but was presumably repaired or rebuilt after the war by Irvine, who continued to reside at Necarne. When Gerard Lowther died in 1667, the lands were finally sold to Christopher Irvine.

Christopher Irvine was succeeded by his second son, Lieutenant Colonel Gerard Irvine. Created a baronet in 1677, this Gerard Irvine was a justice of the peace for the county. In December 1688, he opposed the measures taken by Gustavus Hamilton and others to resist the quartering of troops on the town of Enniskillen. Though he later declared allegiance to William III, he was treated with suspicion by many of the Inniskilliners. When the Williamite North-East Association of Down and Antrim proposed Gerard Irvine and James Corry to be Colonels of the Inniskilling forces, the locals politely refused.

Irvine then accepted a commission in the Earl of Granard's Jacobite regiment, but was then promptly captured at Cavan by the Inniskilliners. He protested his innocence and claimed that he had merely acted to secure arms for the Williamite defenders of the town. Though this ensured his release, many were still unwilling to give him their unreserved trust. He later raised a troop of Williamite horse and was to die in the camp of the Duke of Schomberg at Dundalk during the winter of 1689/90.

Colonel Irvine was succeeded at Necarne by his brother Dr Christopher Irvine and then by his nephew, another Dr Christopher Irvine. The latter doctor was High Sheriff of Fermanagh in 1690 and MP for the county in 1695 and 1703. He married a daughter of Sir George Hume of Castle Hume, but when he died in May 1714, he left no heir. Dr Christopher Irvine was succeeded by his cousin Colonel Christopher Irvine.

In 1788, the then owner, Major George Marcus Irvine married Elizabeth D'Arcy, daughter of Judge D'Arcy of Dunmoe, County Meath. The surname of D'Arcy was now added to the family name and the major's eldest son William assumed the name of D'Arcy-Irvine. The Ordnance Survey memoirs of the 1830s recorded that this William had employed the architect John B. Keane to renovate the house and remove much of the old structure. He maintained the old round towers at the rear but created an Elizabethan frontage of two storeys with attics, built of local freestone and red limestone. The interior was given a classical makeover, with Corinthian columns of scagliola in the hall opening to form one long chamber with rooms on either side. The estate's gate lodge on the Enniskillen Road was also restyled to reflect the design of the main house. The demesne lands were recorded as containing 433 acres, indicating that the estate had not altered significantly in the preceding 200 years. The castle that we see today is the work of this renovation.

The D'Arcy-Irvine family remained resident at Necarne until 1922 when they retired to London. The unoccupied house was then used as a barracks for troops patrolling the border of the fledging state of Northern Ireland. In 1925, the castle was bought by Captain Richard Outram Herman, who set about restoring the dilapidated castle to its former glory. Herman had the castle rewired, added five bathrooms and placed washhand basins in all the bedrooms. He had seven painters lodged in the castle while they carried out extensive redecoration. Finally, he repaired the millrace to provide electricity for the castle and established some ducks on the pond.

In the Second World War, the US army requisitioned the castle and grounds and established a hospital in the main building. The grounds were filled with temporary accommodation for soldiers. Prince Bernard of the Netherlands spent a night at the castle when his plane was unable to take off from the nearby St Angelo airfield.

Herman died in 1976, and Fermanagh District Council eventually bought the estate. The council has turned the estate into an equestrian centre that now hosts the annual 'Balcas' Three-Day Event. The main castle building, however, is currently unused and lies derelict.

Castle Tour

Necarne castle today may comprise part of the original plantation structure within the additions made during successive centuries. As a consequence, the overlaying of these alterations makes any interpretation of the site difficult. Furthermore, the building is currently boarded up, as it is in a very dilapidated state, and a full internal inspection is therefore impossible.

The current castle at Necarne consists of a five-bay, two-storey block in limestone, measuring 30m by 9m, orientated N–S, containing the centrally located entrance facing west onto an extensive lawn. The front and gable wall tops are finished off with ornate turrets and triangular gables and dripstones above the windows. A porch, ideal for carriages arriving at the entrance, is emblazoned with a coat of arms depicting a bull and shield with the words '*un dieu, un roy*' below. Long narrow windows flank the flat-arched doorway. Set behind this main block and running south for 11m is a single-storey wing, with similar architectural detailing to the windows and walls. All of the above must be regarded as the works carried out in the 1830s by D'Arcy-Irvine.

Inside the building the very poor structural state of Necarne, since it was last inhabited, can be readily appreciated. The wide entrance hall retains the stone columns which flanked the entrance to grand rooms on either side. The former raised wooden floor has now rotted away and is in a dangerous state. Ahead, through a door, are the stairs which rose up via a scale-and-platt staircase to all the floors above. This staircase has now collapsed or been removed. Indeed, throughout the building, all of the roof, floor joists and ceilings have collapsed and are in a thoroughly dangerous state. A number of rooms to the rear here probably had various domestic uses for the castle staff.

A four-storey block, perhaps 12m by 6m (40ft by 20ft) with a flanker at the NE and SE corners, rises behind the main block. These flankers, if original, have thick walls but are now topped with mock battlements. They are each five storeys high and appear to have an external diameter of around 6m. The walls of the SE flanker are 1.2m thick and are rendered on the outside. Where some of this has fallen away, the underlying stonework displays well-cut masonry. At ground-floor level though, in both turrets, there is much internal brickwork in the visible structure and it is difficult to determine if the turret was originally built this way or if it is later alteration work. The joists for the first floor fitted into sockets in the wall thickness, but those for the floor above rested on a rebate formed by a narrowing of the walls.

The rear portion of the castle and the flankers are said to represent the oldest surviving part of the building and may date back to the seventeenth century. If this is true, then it must have been altered at some time after its original erection, as it does not resemble the building described in the inquisition of 1630. Necarne was burned during the 1641 rebellion, so this structure may be the replacement. The flankers appear to be solidly constructed and certainly give the appearance of a plantation building, though more evidence would be required to substantiate this hypothesis.

Necarne, therefore, presents us with problems when we seek to interpret the remaining structure. If any part of the original castle remains, the rear turrets are the most promising area to investigate. However, the poor condition of the building makes a full survey hazardous and in any case the presence of extensive use of brickwork forming the wall and doorways of the turrets tend not to support a seventeenth-century construction date.

With its blue, boarded-up windows and neat lawns, Necarne appears today more like an abandoned nineteenth-century country seat than a true plantation castle. Only a full survey will allow a comprehensive understanding of its history, but the building is now closed for safety reasons and unfortunately one can only hope that a new use can be found for it before it falls into terminal decay.

TRILLICK (CASTLE MERVYN)
OS SHEET 18, GR 335575

From the centre of Trillick village, take the B46 Dromore road for 2.5km (1.5 miles). Turn left at the minor crossroads into Castlehill Road and proceed for another 1.3km (0.75 mile), continuing ahead through another minor crossroads. The ruins of Trillick castle are on the left in a field belonging to Castlemervyn Demesne. Once again, Trillick is far from the lough, so boat users will need to use public transport. From Enniskillen, there is a regular weekday service (No.94).

History

Although this area is located in southern Tyrone, it is within the catchment area of the River Erne and is therefore included in this guide. The history of Trillick (or Castle Mervyn) is once again bound up in the events of the seventeenth century in this part of Ulster, but its early history is tangled by the confusion of the family names associated with its existence.

Located in Omagh precinct, allotted to English undertakers, the original grant of the great proportion of Brede (which included Trillick) was made to Sir Mervyn Touchet, eldest son of George Touchet, Lord Audley, in March 1611. Lord Audley, who was created 1st Earl of Castlehaven in September 1616, had already been granted the 2,000-acre estate of Fynagh and a 1,000-acre estate at Rarone, and his second son Sir Ferdinand had been granted the 2,000-acre estate of Fentounagh, thus making the Touchets the greatest landowners in south Tyrone.

Lord Audley had been Governor of Utrecht and had been wounded at the battle of Kinsale in 1601. His wife Elizabeth was the daughter of Sir James Mervyn of Fonthill in Wiltshire. When Lord Audley died in early 1617, Sir Mervyn Touchet succeeded him as the 2nd Earl of Castlehaven. When Pynnar visited in 1619, he recorded that the new earl owned all the original Touchet family grants. At Brede he commented, 'upon this there is nothing built', and at his other estates there was also little to show. A later inquisition confirmed that lands had been let extensively to 'meere Irish, over and above the fourth parte allotted unto them'. The Touchets were themselves Catholics, so they may well have felt more comfortable amongst their co-religionists than some of the other undertakers.

The 2nd Earl married Elizabeth Barnham, daughter and heiress of the London merchant Benedict Barnham, some time previous to 1612, and had by her six children, including his heir, James Touchet, later 3rd Earl of Castlehaven, who would play a prominent role in the 'Confederation of Kilkenny'. In the meantime, the manor of Brede became the property (somewhat confusingly) of Captain James Mervyn, brother-in-law of the 2nd Earl, at some point between 1620 and 1632, and the Touchet family ended its direct interest in the area. However, the Touchets were to become involved in a scandal that badly damaged the family reputation.

Following the death of his first wife Elizabeth, Mervyn Touchet married Anne Stanley. Anne was a widow, with a daughter called Elizabeth from her previous marriage to Grey Brydges, Baron Chandos of Sudeley. Though only twelve years old, it was found advantageous that the young Elizabeth Brydges should marry the future 3rd Earl, James Touchet, himself only thirteen or fourteen years old at the time. In 1630, James Touchet brought a complaint before the Privy Council that his father had planned to disinherit him. As the trial progressed, Mervyn Touchet was accused of sodomy with two servants, one of whom he helped to cause gross indecency with the young Elizabeth. Found guilty for these offences, Mervyn Touchet was stripped of his titles and he was beheaded at Tower Hill, London on 14 May 1631. The two co-accused were also executed. Though the trial had exposed the family to public scrutiny, the actions of James Touchet were generally approved of and he was restored to some of the family titles and estates in 1633.

Meanwhile, Sir Henry Mervyn, the new owner of Brede, had married Christian Touchet, fourth daughter of the 1st Earl of Castlehaven. (This marriage made him brother-in-law to Mervyn Tuchet, the 2nd Earl.) They had seven children who survived into adulthood, two boys, James (his heir) and Audley, and five girls, Lucy, Deborah, Elizabeth, Frances and Katherine. Sir Henry Mervyn was MP in the British parliament and admiral of the narrow seas. When he died in 1626, the estate passed to his eldest son, James Mervyn. James settled in Ireland and had the estate re-granted in 1634. James married Elizabeth Philpot, but the union produced no heir, and following his death in July 1641, his estate passed to his brother Audley Mervyn.

It is therefore not possible to date the commencement of the construction of the castle at Trillick with any great certainty. Pynnar clearly indicates that there was no castle there during his visit in 1619, but it did play a definite part in the rebellion twenty-two years later. It is therefore most likely that Sir Henry Mervyn began constructing the castle sometime after he received the grant of the estate of Brede, probably in the 1620s.

Trillick's new owner, Audley Mervyn, had a chequered career and appears to have skilfully steered through the subtle political crises of the time. Elected as MP for Tyrone in February 1639, the following year he was appointed as a captain in Sir Henry Tichbourne's regiment, formed as part of a 9,000-strong army assembled at Carrickfergus, which awaited instruction to proceed to Scotland in support of King Charles against the Scots. In the event, the crisis for Charles was concluded before the army could embark.

In parliament, Mervyn was prominent in the attempt to impeach the Earl of Strafford, and initially worked closely with his brother-in-law Rory Maguire, who was MP for Fermanagh. He later deposed that Maguire had visited him at Trillick castle and warned him of the intentions of the Catholics to rebel. Maguire asked Mervyn to represent their position to the King and explain that they rebelled through fear of the English parliament, whom they believed were intent on destroying the Catholic religion. Mervyn declined, and counselled Maguire against rebellion, but pleaded restraint should it occur, to 'repress for a little with the fury of the fire and sword'.

Thus Mervyn was able to give warning to his Protestant neighbours, 'to dispose themselves towards Derry', thus, he claimed, saving many lives, and 'He himself, two sisters, and children escaped in the night, saving nothing but their lives!' Presumably his family managed to reach the safety of Londonderry, where they may have resided for most of the rebellion. He evidently returned to Tyrone soon after and was besieged in Augher castle, before being relieved by the timely arrival of Sir William and Sir Robert Stewart.

He was appointed a senior officer in Sir Ralph Gore's Regiment of Foot, one of those regiments known as the Laggan army, raised to defend Londonderry and its environs. When Gore died in early 1642, Mervyn became colonel of the regiment. In 1644, he was made Governor of Londonderry by Ormond and was considered sympathetic to the Royalist cause, although he later took the Solemn League and Covenant. In October 1648, he and Sir Robert Stewart were, by a ruse, made prisoners and taken to London to answer questions before parliament regarding their loyalty. Both later escaped and returned in May 1649 to join the Royalist army besieging Sir Charles Coote's Parliamentarian garrison in Londonderry. When the siege failed, Mervyn made his peace with parliament, recognising the inevitability of Parliamentary success in Ireland.

In 1658 Mervyn was called to the Bar in the King's Inn, Dublin. Perhaps sensing the changing mood in the country, he advocated the return of Charles II and was later rewarded by becoming the King's Prime Sergeant-in-Law and the speaker of the House of Commons. Around this time, he was knighted and received the thanks of parliament and £1,000 for nine months work on the Act of Settlement cases. He died on 24 October 1675 and was succeeded by his son Henry Mervyn. This Henry served as MP for Augher in 1666 and as High Sheriff for Tyrone in 1686. He married Hannah Knox and they had five children together: Audley, Elizabeth, Martha, Deborah and Lucia. When Hannah died, Henry married Susannah, widow of Lord Glenawley, but they had no children.

Henry Mervyn was succeeded by his son Audley Mervyn. Audley Mervyn II followed the family tradition of public service. He was High Sheriff of Tyrone in 1692 and went on to serve as MP for Strabane in 1695 and then MP for Tyrone in the Irish parliaments of 1713 and 1715. He married Olivia Coote, the daughter of Lord Coloonley, and they had several children, including yet another Audley Mervyn, who appears to have been at the Siege of Derry.

It should come as no surprise that a Mervyn should be present in Londonderry at this time. During the revolution of 1688, Trillick castle appears to have been frequently used as a base by both Jacobite and Williamite units. When, in December 1688, the citizens of Enniskillen chose not to accept the two companies of Newcomen's regiment in the town, Trillick was included in the Williamite cordon. The main road from Dublin to Londonderry passes through Omagh to the north and when the main Jacobite army passed through on its way to the siege in April 1689, the castle became a contested outpost for both sides.

In that month, a Jacobite garrison briefly occupied the castle, but retired on the approach of the Inniskilliners and a quantity of baggage was captured. Later in June, a raiding party left from Trillick and captured a number of Jacobite horses left grazing unguarded at Fireagh near Omagh. It was at Trillick castle in July that the Duke of Berwick's force, detached from the Siege of Derry, met up with those of Brigadier Sutherland's prior to their advance towards Enniskillen, where they won the battle of Kilmacormick. He returned via Trillick, burning the home of the Rector of Kilskeery, Andrew Hamilton, who was with the Williamites in Enniskillen.

Audley Mervyn II died in 1717, and his eldest son, Henry Mervyn II, succeeded him to the estate. Once again, this Henry carried out the public service roles familiar to his family over the previous century. He died in 1747 without a male heir and the remnant of the Trillick estate passed by marriage to the Archdale family. In the nineteenth century, a hunting lodge was built close to the old castle. The estate was eventually broken up later in the century under the Land Acts and came into the possession of its former tenants. By 1910, the ruins of the castle were under threat of total destruction by the landowner. According to a letter sent to the editors of the *Journal of the Royal Society of Antiquities in Ireland*, the remaining walls were being pulled down and the stones being re-used for the erection of labourers' cottages. The scale of the destruction has been huge, as only a few fragments of gable and adjoining walls remain to indicate this once important plantation residence.

Castle Tour

The castle is situated on a level platform on the eastern side of Castle Hill, which slopes down to the road. There are some fine views to the north and east, now partly obscured by the trees of the field boundary of which it forms a part. The area between the ruins and the road is now hummocky and badly overgrown and appears to have been used over the years for landfill. Consequently, the castle's ground plan is difficult to determine.

The ruins best visible today are of the west gable and parts of the adjoining north and south walls. The gable, measuring 6.8m externally, survives to full height of over 10m, including the chimney, except for part of the north side which is missing, probably due to the of collapse of an upper window lintel. The length of the castle walls cannot be determined as they are ruined to foundation level. There were probably three windows in the gable, one at first-floor level and two at second-floor level, which indicate a building of probably three storeys. Only one window at second-floor level is now complete, measuring 1.5m high by 0.9m wide, with the sill 6m from the current field level. The opposite window, now gone, would probably have been arranged symmetrically on either side of the flue, one metre from the respective wall edges. There is only one window, incomplete, on the north side of the ground floor, 3m from ground level and with dimensions similar to the others.

The north and south walls both remain to a length of about 6m, with a uniform thickness of 0.9m. The north wall remains to a height of 2.5m and contains a splayed window opening near the west end, 0.45m wide externally with the inside 0.9m wide. There is a slight inward splay at the end of the wall section, which may indicate another window. The south wall remains to a height of only 1.5m, and contains a 1m-wide gap with splayed ingoings 3.7m from the west end, which may indicate a window or perhaps the doorway. There is a ground-floor fireplace, 1.5m wide, in the gable, the flue rising up complete to chimney level. In the SW gable corner is a circular brick-lined oven, identifying this as the kitchen. It is difficult to determine the original floor level of the interior due to the rubble.

The west gable now forms the western side of the existing field boundary and the site is fenced off, enclosing a space of approximately 26m by 21m. As already stated, the interior of this area is very uneven and overgrown and may only represent the extent of earlier landfill work. A hollow just below the castle may indicate the site of a former pond, now filled in. The castle was constructed from the local purplish limestone and was squared to ashlar blocks. All of the original quoins and window dressings have been robbed from the site, perhaps at the time when the castle stone was being used to build labourers' cottages, at the beginning of the twentieth century.

The ruins of Trillick can be inspected by seeking permission from the proprietor of Castle Mervyn Demesne, one of the three farms that formerly constituted the demesne of the estate. Though there is little left of this once fine plantation residence, the remains should be protected for the enjoyment of generations to come. Perhaps a future excavation in the adjoining ground will reveal the true extent of this once important place.

8

UPPER LOUGH ERNE CIRCUIT

CASTLE BALFOUR
OS SHEET 27, GR 362337

From Enniskillen, proceed to Lisnaskea, initially along the A4 as far as Maguiresbridge and then along the A34. From the centre of Lisnaskea, continue along the main street in the direction of Newtownbutler. The ruins of the castle can be seen on a hill on the right, adjacent to Holy Trinity parish church, and there is a sign for the castle at the corner of Church Lane. Park at the church gates. Vandalism has resulted in the castle interior being locked, but access can be obtained by contacting the Environment Agency. For boat users, there are good facilities at the Share Centre at Shanaghy Bay, where transport can be arranged to travel to Lisnaskea, 5km (3 miles) distant.

History

Castle Balfour is located on the edge of today's urban centre of Lisnaskea, and close to the former inauguration site of the Maguires, chieftains of the area in medieval times. The 1,000-acre estate of Carrowshee in Knockninny precinct was granted to Michael Balfour, Lord Burleigh, in June 1610, but in addition he was lord of the 2,000-acre estate of Legan, also in Knockninny, described as being 'in an out of the way place'. Burleigh was the eldest son of Sir James and Lady Margaret Balfour of Fifeshire, Scotland, and he appears to have been quickly succeeded by his second son, James Balfour.

James Balfour set about fulfilling the terms of his grant but was clearly far from finished when Pynnar, visiting in 1619, described the castle thus:

> He hath ... laid the foundation of a Bawne of Lime and Stone, 70 feet square, of which the two sides are raised fifteen feet high. There is also a castle of the same length, of which the one half is built two stories high, and is to be three stories and a half high. There are great numbers of Men at Work, which are bound to finish it speedily, and all materials I saw in the place. This is both strong and beautiful.

In addition to the castle, Balfour was in the process of constructing a church, '75 feet long, and 24 broad, all which is now in hand, and promised to be finished this summer', and a free school built of lime and stone, '64 feet long and 24 feet broad, and two stories high'. The school roof is described 'ready framed', waiting only to be completed.

Nearby was a town of forty timber-frame houses, all inhabited by British tenants and forming the only complete thoroughfare in the county.

Clearly, Balfour was intent on creating a new order on his estate and he had the economic potential with his vast estates, given that his eldest brother Michael Balfour, Lord Mountwhaney, had been granted the proportion of Kilspinan to the south. In October 1626, James Balfour was granted the small proportions of Carrowshee, Dristernan, Laytrim and Kilspinan (sold by his brother Mountwhaney to Sir Stephen Butler a few years earlier and then restored to the Balfour family) and the great proportion of Legan. He was raised to the aristocracy when he was created Lord Glenawley. Balfour was clearly an ambitious man who was intent on advancement, and his ambition earned him many enemies, including James Spottiswood, Bishop of Clogher.

Though he was 'an ancient man of great age', he set about ensuring that there would be an heir to his domain, by pursuing Anne, the fifteen-year-old daughter of Lord Blaney. However, Blaney was privately informed that Balfour already had a wife in Scotland and he confronted his erstwhile son-in-law. Balfour denied the allegation and claimed he was properly divorced. Unsure of what to do next, Blaney sought advice from the Primate, who agreed to carry out the wedding ceremony to reassure him. However, the matter was still not fully resolved.

Anne's dowry had been agreed at £2,000. Blaney was only willing to part with £1,200 and Balfour demanded the balance, accusing Anne's cousin Robert of having interfered with his wife both before and since the wedding. Balfour managed to extract a confession from his wife, but her friends claimed that this had been done under duress. Nonetheless, Balfour had her sequestered for a period of time (i.e. he imposed a restraining order). The incident appears to have caused no long-term effects, as Anne continued as his wife.

In another incident, again involving Spottiswood, the bishop came to suspect that Balfour's friendship was influenced by his desire to obtain control of lands set aside for the aforementioned school. Furthermore, Spottiswood was opposed to his designs. Later, they were both at the home of Lady Valencia, who intimated that she perceived some grudge between them and requested an explanation. Spottiswood accused Balfour of having slandered him, but declared that the 'counyterfeit letters and lies' would fail. Balfour became incensed and began to wrestle with Spottiswood. They fell with a great commotion onto the hearth whereupon the servants entered and separated them. It is probable that this friendship was never quite the same again!

By 1641, Master Middleton was the warden for Castle Balfour. Following his capture of the nearby castles of Shannock and Waterdrum, Rory Maguire arrived before the castle on the morning of 25 October. Middleton was clearly not suspicious, as Maguire acted 'in a friendly manner' and was thus admitted. However, according later to the deposition of Sir John Dunbar:

> The first thing he did when he entered therein was to burn the records of the county, which he forced him to deliver unto him, as likewise £1,000, which he had in his hands, of Sir William Balfour's, which – as soon as he had – he compelled the said Middleton to hear Mass, swear never to alter from it, and immediately after caused himself, his wife, and children to be hanged up, and he hanged and murdered a hundred persons at least besides in that town…

The castle, together with the public records for the county, was destroyed, though the death of so many people at this time seems exaggerated. Nonetheless, the settlers of the middle Erne area were now under threat and they banded together for a time under the leadership of Cathcart the Sheriff. However, it was clear that the rebels were too strong to be resisted and Cathcart and the settlers sought shelter at Enniskillen.

According to the Archaeological Survey of 1940, the town and castle were restored by Ludlow in 1652. In the 1659 census, Sir William Balfour and Charles Balfour are named as residents at Lisnaskea, but it is uncertain if this refers to residence in the castle. At that time, the town was noted to have a total of forty-eight residents, two-thirds of whom are classified as 'English'.

Castle Balfour was again to play a prominent role during the Williamite wars. On the approach of Lord Galmoy's Jacobite army during March 1689, the Inniskilliners fell back to their main position at Enniskillen and abandoned the castle and town. A contemporary account written by William McCarmick describes the situation:

> Ere Galmoy came the length of Lisnaskey, a cursed fellow, one Kemp, with some of the rabble of the country his consorts, burnt that pretty village, to the great loss of the inhabitants and the worthy gentlemen that owned it, as also a prejudice to Inniskilling, it being capable of quartering a regiment of men … But ere the town was burnt, we had brought from there a many tuns of iron belonging to Mr Belfore, and most of the lead of his house, which proved very serviceable to us, both to horse and foot.

In July 1689, the castle was again destroyed, this time by the retreating Jacobites as part of the manoeuvres prior to the battle of Newtownbutler. Once again the castle was restored in peacetime. The Balfour family left the county around 1780 and the castle and its estate were absorbed into the Creighton estate of Crom. A fire finally destroyed the castle in 1803 and it was never again occupied. When the ruins came under state control in 1960, the place was in a dangerous state and a long programme of restoration was required to secure it.

Castle Tour

The present main street of Lisnaskea runs along a narrow valley bottom on a NW–SE axis. To the north and east the land rises steeply from this thoroughfare to the rath at Cornashee, the former inauguration site of the Maguires. On the opposite side of the road, a long narrow esker rises from the junction with the Derrylin road and trends roughly parallel towards the SW. Castle Balfour is located towards the end of this ridge, near its junction with the Derrylin road.

The information display board should be consulted before inspecting the castle. This board shows the manor-house castle as it might have been when complete and conjectures that the bawn entrance was on the north side, with flankers on the NE and SE walls.

The castle, built of dressed Carboniferous limestone rubble, is sited on the north-western edge of the esker, at a point where the limestone rock beneath outcrops through the clay covering it. On the west side, the ground begins to slope down to the valley bottom and this change in levels was used advantageously when the function of the different rooms was designated. The house is T-shaped in plan, with the main block orientated north–south and facing eastwards into the bawn, which has now disappeared amongst the graveyard burials.

Containing many Scottish features, as befitting its builder, the castle adopted some modern features as well. The main block externally measures 24m by 8.3m (79ft by 27ft) and is of three storeys, with attic rooms. The western extension is located near the northern end of the west wall and measures 8.7m by 7.6m. These dimensions closely resemble the castle described by Pynnar and so this must indeed be the original construction of Michael Balfour.

In additon to this, an accommodation wing extends eastwards from the south wall towards the bawn. Most of the walls have now disappeared, but it was contemporaneous with the main building, being accessed from there by a doorway from the ground and first floors. Finally, there is a stone-vaulted single-storey extension on the north side of the castle, 12m by 4.7m (39ft by 15.5ft), which was built later than the main block and the function of which will be discussed later.

Approaching the castle ruins through the graveyard from the east, the building can best be surveyed in mid-morning. The south extension contains a corbel in the NW corner, which may have held a spiral stair to a third level. Only the 1m-wide doorway to the main castle building survives, but this was a substantial block, with a room depth of 4.9m (16ft). The length of the room cannot now be confirmed, as only 2m of the north and south walls survive. Though there is no concrete evidence to support it, this building could be the church described in Pynnar's report, forming an arrangement similar to that at Crevenish, in the north of the county.

Before the castle proper is entered, it is worth noting the unusual squared corbelling blocks in the east wall that help carry the slightly projecting flues of the fireplaces in the upper floors. The main castle is entered via a restored doorway in a bay projection on the east wall. This bay ran the full height of the building and is a clear example of how contemporary continental architectural features could be adapted into what was an otherwise Scottish design. The bay was faced with dressed pale limestone blocks, with a large window at first-floor level and a smaller one in the floor above. The door was flanked by two delicately carved musket loopholes cut into the thickness of the bay, at a height of 1.2m, tapering to only 7.5cm (3 inches) in diameter externally. The shafts for these loops must have posed some construction problems for the builder, as they pierce a particularly thick piece of wall here, thus providing only a very limited field of fire for the defender. This predicament must have been recognised at the time, as a second shaft was added to the loophole on the south side to increase the field of fire for the defender. The northern loophole has only a single access shaft but further protection of the doorway was provided by another loophole at the bottom of the bay window above.

The entrance hallway is a grand affair, measuring 4.9 sq m (16 sq ft) and lit by windows in the north, east and west walls. This hallway must have contained the stair to the main hall on the first floor. Though nothing remains of the original stairway, the current steel stair installed during restoration gives an idea how it must have looked, though the timber original version would of course have been much more ornate. A drawbar socket for the front door survives on the south side of the entrance

In the hallway, immediately to the left, is a stone-vaulted passageway 8m (26ft) long, 2.3m (7ft) high and 1.2m (4ft) wide, lit by a single window opening into the bawn.

Directly off this passageway to the west, are two stone-vaulted rooms, each reached down a short flight of steps. The first room measures 2.7m wide by 4.1m deep, and has no natural light. The second room is a little wider, at 2.9m, but is naturally lit by a widely splayed window cut into the SW corner wall at an angle. This window measures only 0.6m by 0.2m wide externally, but internally the sill has been chamfered to leave a 1.8m-by-1.1m-wide splay, which floods the space with light. Given the fall of the ground outside, the provision of a window did not compromise the castle security.

At the end of the passageway, a rebated doorway led to a large room measuring 8.5m by 5.1m (28ft by 17ft). Only the east wall and part of the south and west walls survive in original form, 1.1m thick (3.5ft). From the centre of the east wall, a door led into the now-ruined south extension. Sockets for lintels can be discerned at 2.5m (8ft) from the ground level on the west and east walls. Small windows in the west wall probably lighted this apartment. Some stone projections on the north wall of this room suggest that the fireplace was located here.

The first-floor room directly above must have been entered by the doorway located in the north wall. The lower parts of large windows looking into the bawn still survive, as does a small window located high up in the NW corner, which appears to have been almost obscured by later restoration work.

Returning along the vaulted passageway, the visitor comes back to the entrance hallway. At the rear, another short vaulted passageway, 3.2m long and cut at an angle into the SW wall, leads down a flight of steps to the kitchen. The passageway entrance still contains rebated stonework and a drawbar socket for a door. Proceeding down the steps, the kitchen is entered, measuring 6.1m wide by 6.6m long, with a 3m-high, stone-vaulted roof. At the west end, a large, open fireplace, almost the full width of the room, contains a small semicircular, brick-lined oven in the SW corner. The kitchen is lit by two large windows on opposite walls (north and south), only 1m above the internal floor level. Once again, the falling ground level outside these windows meant that castle security was not compromised. Altogether, therefore, the stone-roofed kitchen, storerooms and passageways on the ground level provided the castle with much-needed fireproofing in the event of an attacker breaching the ground-floor entrance.

Returning to the hallway, the visitor should proceed up the metal stair. On the first landing, a doorway in the north wall now leads out onto the vaulted roof of the problematic later extension. It is not certain if the doorway is original or if a window here was later lowered to provide the access to the outside level. The extension may have been an addition to the vulnerable north side of the castle, providing the defenders with a much-needed raised, fighting platform area.

At the top of the metal stair, a narrow doorway on the west wall leads into a corbelled-out spiral staircase, which must have provided the only access to the second floor and attic level of the castle. The clockwise-spiralling stair pattern is mirrored externally in the neatly carved corbelled turret, as it rises up through the floors. A number of small apertures open into the spiral stair to provide sufficient light.

The main hall on the first floor is entered via a flat-lintelled doorway in the north wall. This large space measures 11.8m by 6.2m (39ft by 20ft) and is lit by a pair of opposing splayed windows in the north and south walls. These windows measure only 0.8m wide externally, but are chamfered internally to 1.6m. There is a well-preserved fireplace on the east gable wall, flanked by a splayed window looking into the bawn. The fireplace causes the external eastern gable wall to project slightly, as described earlier. A sixth window is located in the west gable wall, thus providing the room with a superb light quality throughout the entire day. A small, cubic wall cupboard of 0.8m dimensions was also located in the west wall.

This room would have provided the resident lord with a most comfortable apartment for both entertaining and daily living, but it may well have been partitioned, as the ceiling joist sockets, 3m above floor level, are located in the east wall and would therefore have longitudinally spanned this considerable distance. Perhaps there was a short passageway or lobby at the top of the stairs, with a stone wall (now lost) dividing the space into two rooms, with the western part, containing the pairs of windows, being the larger.

Access to the second-floor accommodation was via the spiral stair, which led up from the first-floor landing, just outside the entrance to the main hall. This stair is corbelled out over the re-entrant angle of the house and is lit by several small windows. The main sleeping quarters were at this level. There are fireplaces in both west and east gables, so there may have been a partition separating at least two bedrooms. Light to these chambers was probably provided by a window in the south wall, as there is none in the west gable.

Above this floor was a cramped attic level, reduced in width by the addition of a low parapet wall built along the top of the outer walls. A small window at the top of the east gable lit the space within and there may have been a small fireplace. It is unlikely that there would have been sufficient space to provide a wall walk between the parapet wall and the high-pitched sloping roof, but there is a small corbelled bartizan at the NW corner of the west gable, best seen from outside, which may have been loopholed to cover attack from this direction.

The last conundrum to be solved is that of the ceiling-joists level in the entrance hallway. Above the high ceiling of the hallway were two further accommodation levels, as indicated by the windows in the north gable. However, the position of the second-floor joist holes seems to suggest that the floor cut across the top of the first-floor bay window in the east wall. Indeed, there does not seem to be any direct access to these rooms, above the hallway, from the spiral stair. The restoration work that was required to stabilise the castle is much in evidence here and there may be little of the original structure left to satisfactorily interpret this problem.

Before leaving the site, it is worth walking around to the rear to observe the castle from the west. It is really only from this side that one can appreciate how the falling ground level assisted the builders, allowing the castle to incorporate domestic features at a lower level than would normally be the case without compromising security. Additionally, the excellent corbelling of the spiral stair can best be admired from here, as well as the decorative corbelled string course high up at third-floor level, which supports the parapet wall. It will be noticed that the lower western wall has been stepped out, perhaps to provide a stronger foundation. Finally, also observe the surviving rainspout, high up above the spiral stair, which allowed water to be thrown away from the castle to the outcropping rock below.

The remains at Castle Balfour are well worth a visit, particularly to admire the bay window and wooden stair which were added to this otherwise Scottish-designed castle. Sadly though, the castle suffers from proximity to a built-up area, with the accompanying threat of vandalism, and so access to the interior must be arranged via the local Environment Agency office.

DOOHAT
OS SHEET 27, GR 384252

From Newtownbutler, take the road signposted to Crom. Just before the entrance to Crom estate, take a minor road to the left, for Bun Bridge. Doohat is about 400m along this road on the right, 150m short of Bun Bridge. There is a landing place at Bun Bridge.

History

The townland of Doohat appears in the original grant of the middle proportion of Kilspinan or Crom estate, Knockninny precinct, at the time of the plantation to Michael Balfour, Lord Mountwhaney. In an inquisition regarding Crom, held at Newtownbutler in 1629, these lands had passed to Sir Stephen Butler, whose castle at Crom is mentioned along with the following, '... and upon the tate or parcel of the land in Doohat is built in like manner, one other Castle, or capital messuage, of lime and stone, containing 22 feet in each way and in height 20 feet'.

The next reference to Doohat as the site of a castle was made in the Ordnance Survey of the 1830s. The writer, Lieutenant Greatorex, states that a castle had been erected here for a family member of Chancellor Moss or Morse. It was said that this Moss erected another castle in Drumbroughas and that he had erected and resided in a third castle at Derracorby. Doohat was believed to have been situated 'at the back of John Ebbitt's house on the roadside next to Bun Bridge'. Although Greatorex stated that nothing now remained of Doohat, this description fits well into the present house here identified.

Writing in the early twentieth century, William Trimble's *History of Enniskillen* asserted that the house here was indeed partly of the seventeenth century, and that it had been the former residence of a family named Adams, though it had changed hands several times since. But he does not mention any owner named Moss. Trimble believed the house to have originally been a long, probably single-storey, stone cottage, which had been altered in the eighteenth century, when the central portion was demolished and raised to a storey and a half in height. The only remaining plantation period parts were the two single-storey extensions on the gables, used only as animal sheds. These extensions contained gun loops which faced the ford and could be used to defend the crossing here. The house was shown in an illustration to be fully thatched and containing what appeared to be the original glazing.

In the 1960s, the Queen's University archaeologist E.M. Jope visited the house. By this time, only the small extension on the north side of the house adjacent to the road remained unaltered. It still contained a series of loopholes on the north, east and west sides, with the remains of either a wall recess or window on the east wall. These appeared to be the last remnants of the original house built near the ford at Bun Bridge.

Castle Tour

Defended homes of the tenantry and freeholder classes from the plantation era are rare in Ulster, and the remains at Doohat are therefore particularly important, as this is probably the smallest example of its type. Located beside the main waterway of the Upper Erne, and close to a minor ford over the Bun River, the house would have had an important tactical role to play in the overall defence of Crom estate.

The house today consists of a two-storey central block facing east to Bun Bridge, with single-storey extensions on each gable. A farmyard and outhouses are located at the rear. Describing the house in 1920, Trimble asserted that the original seventeenth-century central core was demolished in the following century and rebuilt as we see it today, with only the wings remaining of the original premises. Certainly, the front elevation of the house here projects 1.2m beyond the line of the wings. However, the south wing is modern and the only remaining part that could be from plantation times is the north extension, with the road running by it from the ford.

This extension, measuring in plan about 6.5m by 5.5m externally and rising to approximately 4m in height at the east gable, has no direct access to the main part of the house. It is currently used as sheds, being now divided into two parts by a recent internal partition. However, the east wall, north gable, and part of the west wall facing into the yard would appear to belong to the original building. The outer walls are almost 0.9m thick and about 2m high, with a rebate on the gable wall, probably to support a ceiling. The recess or window on the east wall can still be discerned internally through later rendering. On the gable wall, the outline of two loopholes (approximately 0.5m by 0.5m internally), 0.9m above the floor level and now filled in, can just be recognised. It is likely that these two loopholes splay to narrow slits. All of the above features are only discernible from internal inspection. From the outside, none of the features are visible.

From the description of the castle in the inquisition of 1629, it is tempting to see these remains as the castle described as '22 feet in each way'. The enclosed rear yard and the unusual thickness of the stone walls in a single-storey building certainly appear odd. However, without additional documentary or archaeological evidence, any hypothesis must remain only tentative. Perhaps this building will receive some attention in the coming years and some of these questions will finally be answered.

CROM
OS SHEET 27, GR 363238

From the centre of Lisnaskea, take the A34 to Newtownbutler village. In the centre of Newtownbutler take the road signposted for Crom, and follow it past Doohat (qv.) to Crom estate. The National Trust now manages the old castle site. There is an interpretive centre and ample car parking within the grounds. A jetty is located immediately below the interpretive centre and a few minutes' walk from the castle. The path to old Crom castle is signposted.

History
Beautifully situated overlooking a broad channel of the upper lough, Crom today is yet another site that requires a great deal of caution when attempting to interpret the remains. The present ruins are known to have been enlarged in the 1830s to give the site a more pleasing, 'romantic' atmosphere, but even after stripping these additions away, we are left with a structure that does not fit the original descriptions of the place.

Crom is one of the castle sites on the Erne whose history is a microcosm of the political turmoil of the later seventeenth century in Ireland. Its strategic location at the head of Lough Erne ensured that it could not be ignored by anyone attempting to control the river valley. Thus, it became involved at two of the most critical moments in the dynastic struggle for supremacy in Ireland between forces loyal to King James II and those of his rivals, namely his daughter Mary and his son-in-law William of Orange.

Michael Balfour, Laird of Mountwhaney in Fifeshire, erected the first castle at Crom. Balfour had been granted the middle proportion of Kilspenan or Crom, in Knockninny precinct, in or around 1610. (This Michael Balfour was eldest son of the grantee of the same name who received the nearby manor of Carrowshee.) Balfour must have immediately set out to fulfil the terms of the lease, for Commissioner Carew, reporting in 1611, wrote an interesting account of how matters were progressing, 'Mr Balfour, Laird Mountwhaney, 1,500 acres. Appeared in person: brought over 8 freeholders and leaseholders, with 4 women servants. He felled 200 oaks, provided lime, and brought over a dozen horses and mares, with household stuff.'

Balfour was re-granted the estate in 1616, but immediately sold it to Sir Stephen Butler of Belturbet. Visiting the estate in 1619, Pynnar reported, 'Sir Stephen Butler hath 1,500 acres, called Kilspenan. Upon this proportion there is a Bawne of Lime and Stone, being 60 feet square, 12 feet high, with two Flankers. Within the Bawne there is a House of Lime and Stone'.

In addition, Pynnar found twelve families (mustering a total of fifteen men) on the estate, who were leasing various tracts of land totalling 1,130 acres. He noted that none of these tenants were freeholders, and as the terms of the grant instructed that 450 acres were to be reserved as demesne, it was clear that Butler was not intending to create any. Pynnar also noted that the tenants were dispersed, and that 'many Irish' inhabited the estate too.

Perrott and Annesley visited the estate in 1622, and recorded the bawn dimensions as being 61ft by 56ft, and 11ft high with two flankers. Curiously, one of the flankers was 20 sq ft, three storeys high, and slated, while the other was round and infilled with 'wild sods'. Also contained within the bawn was a small two-storey house.

A third description of the castle exists from an inquisition held at Newtownbutler in 1629:

> Within the aforesaid proportion, upon the tate or proportion of land called Crum, was built by the aforesaid Stephen Butler, assignee of aforesaid Michael Balfour, one bawne of stone and lime, containing 61 feet everyway, and 15 feet in height; and within the same is one Castle, or capital messuage, built in like manner of lime and stone, containing 22 feet each way…

Thus, in the first twenty years of the grant, a castle and bawn had been erected, probably started by Balfour but completed by Butler. However, Butler appears never to have occupied the castle himself. In 1624, he leased the castle and adjoining lands to Dr James Spottiswood, who had been consecrated Bishop of Clogher in 1621. Spottiswood lived in Portora castle and at Clogher, so the arrangement must have been to provide for family members. When he died in 1644, he bequeathed the Crom lease to his family.

In 1655, Spottiswood's third daughter Mary married Abraham Creighton of Dromboory and settled on the Crom estate. Creighton's father, also called Abraham, lived on land leased from the elder Creighton's nephew, Thomas Creighton of Aghalane. When the father died in 1631, the younger Abraham, being an only son, inherited the family estate. In the 1659 census, Abraham Creighton is noted as the occupier at Crom.

In November 1655, Abraham Creighton bought out the Crom lease from Francis Butler of Belturbet, but continued to pay a small annual head rent of £15 twice a year. (This rent was eventually bought out in 1810.) His marriage produced five sons, James, Abraham, John, Charles and David, and two daughters, Jane and Marianna. For many years the family continued to inhabit this idyllic landscape, but political storm clouds were gathering which would catapult this sleepy backwater to the front line of a dynastic conflict. The strategic importance of the castle, located at the head of Upper Lough Erne, had been recognised many years earlier by Sir William Cole of Enniskillen, who had successfully petitioned to have it retained under British control when it had briefly been in the possession of the Irish McManus family.

Some time around 21 March 1689, Creighton found himself and his young family besieged within the castle by the Jacobite army of 2,000 foot and horse led by Lord Galmoy. Galmoy arrived before Crom, having chased the British settlers of Cavan, loyal to William of Orange, northwards out of the county to seek refuge in Enniskillen or Londonderry. However, Creighton had fortified the castle, garrisoning it with his own tenants, and he was in no mood to surrender.

As he had travelled fast through Cavan, Galmoy was without the artillery necessary to reduce the castle's walls. Undeterred, he decided to try and capture the castle by deception. From tin, he manufactured a pair of mock cannon, a metre long, bound by cord, and he covered the whole with 'a kind of buckram' to represent the colour of gunmetal. He then proceeded to have the mock cannon hauled into place by sixteen horses, with a pretend show of difficulty, and demanded the castle's immediate surrender. Creighton refused, and to continue the deception, Galmoy ordered a wooden bullet to be fired from one of the cannon. However, the mock cannon burst, almost killing the gunner, and Galmoy's bluff was well and truly called. He then settled down to a regular siege at Crom and sent a letter to Enniskillen, informing him of the recent arrival of King James into Ireland and demanding the immediate surrender of the town to himself, under terms.

Although its walls were considered strong, Crom castle had no earthworks or ditches in front of it and it was clear that it could not withstand a long siege. Of more immediate concern was the fact that, 'it was commanded by hills within musket shot'. Clearly, Creighton could not withstand a determined enemy who could entrench right up to the castle walls without hindrance.

Governor Hamilton at Enniskillen then intervened to ensure that Crom did not fall. On 23 March, he despatched 200 men by night (another account states 300) to Crom, some by land and some by water. The waterborne troops arrived at Crom in daylight hours and Galmoy's soldiers fired numerous volleys, hoping to prevent the landing and managing to kill one of the boatmen. Those in the boats replied in kind and forced their way ashore to join the garrison in the castle. Wasting no time, the combined Inniskilliners and garrison immediately sallied forth. The besiegers were driven from their trenches, with the loss of thirty or forty men, and the garrison captured, amongst other things, the two mock cannon and two sets of armour. Creighton's fifth son, David Creighton, then only eighteen years of age, is recorded as having greatly distinguished himself during the conflict. For his part, Galmoy realised he could not now easily capture Crom and so retired to Belturbet.

Two stories regarding Lord Galmoy's conduct at this time were later recorded for posterity. The garrison of Crom lacked proper artillery, but this was in some measure offset by long fowling pieces they had in their possession. These firelocks were fitted with double rests and were normally used to kill wildfowl around the lough, but were employed in a more deadly fashion against the besiegers. On one occasion, Galmoy was spotted with a party reconnoitring the castle from a hill nearly a mile away, with a glass of wine in his hand. An expert fowler was summoned from amongst the garrison, who ascended the castle battlements and fired at the distant crowd. Galmoy's glass was hit and the man standing next to him killed by the shot. Galmoy was forced to beat a hasty retreat and in future made the besiegers wary of exposing themselves too near the castle. The distance is undoubtedly exaggerated, but a shot across to persons standing on neighbouring Inishfendra was certainly possible.

The second story concerns the perfidious nature of the lord in his dealings with the Williamites. During his lightning strike into Cavan, Galmoy had managed to capture Captain Woolstan Dixey (eldest son of the Dean of Kilmore), Cornet Edward Charlton and some eight or ten troopers from the recently raised Inniskilling cavalry. At the same time, Bryan MacConagher MacGuire, a captain in the Irish army, was being held a prisoner in Crom. On the retreat of Galmoy's army to Belturbet, Creighton proposed to him an exchange of prisoners, MacGuire for Dixie and Charlton. Galmoy acceded and Creighton released MacGuire, awaiting the imminent release of the two Inniskilling officers.

But instead, Galmoy held a court martial for the two officers and charged them with possessing on their persons a commission from King William to levy troops for him. Both prisoners were found guilty and sentenced to death the following day. In the meantime, promises were made to them of life and preferment if they became Catholics and took service under King James. Neither was willing to become a recusant, and the offers were flatly refused. Captain MacGuire then spoke up and reminded Galmoy of his arrangement with the Williamites, and that failure to keep his part of it would cause a stain on his character. But his lordship was in no mood to overrule the earlier decision and both prisoners were hanged from a signpost in Belturbet, their heads struck off and given to the soldiers for footballs. Later, the heads were hung up on the market house.

Galmoy's action only served to strengthen the resolve of the Inniskilliners to resist. But the story is not complete without recounting the effect this had on MacGuire. Disgusted by his lord's breach of faith, MacGuire returned to Crom, resigned his commission and refused to further serve his king, James II.

Crom was besieged a second time at the end of July 1689. This time, Lieutenant General Justin MacCarthy, Lord Mountcashel, led the Jacobite army, and this time he had brought artillery with him. Creighton sent word to Enniskillen to warn them of his plight. The following day, Mountcashel began to batter Crom. Creighton sent a second plea for assistance and this time Governor Hamilton promised relief in two days' time. This would ordinarily have been enough time for Mountcashel to reduce the castle, but his efforts must have been half-hearted, as the castle walls survived the bombardment. Perhaps his real purpose in besieging Crom was to draw the Inniskilliners out onto ground of his own choosing. Whatever the reason, the Inniskilling army, now led by General Wolesley, marched south to give battle and as they approached Mountcashel withdrew his army to Newtownbutler. The following day, 31 July 1689, was fought the Battle of Newtownbutler, where the Williamites were victorious against the Jacobite army and the threat to Crom was finally lifted for good.

Both Abraham Creighton, as Colonel of an Innisikilling Regiment of Foot, and his eldest son James were present at the great Williamite victory at Aughrim in July 1691, which finally settled the matter of the dynastic succession in Britain. James had married Hester Hume, eldest daughter of Sir John Hume of Castlehume, in October 1686 and they were to have a son named John and two daughters, Sidney and Mary. Abraham Creighton died in March 1706 and the estate should have passed to James but he had died four years before, so the estate passed to Abraham's grandson John.

John's details are sparse. He continued to live at Crom, becoming High Sheriff of Fermanagh in 1715. But he died the same year without an heir and, under the conditions of inheritance, the estate passed to his uncle David Creighton. This was the same person who had so distinguished himself during the sieges of Crom in 1689. David had married Katherine Southwell some time before 1697 and together they had at least six children, of whom two died in childhood.

David, the hero of two sieges at Crom, became a Major General, commanding Lord Charlement's regiment in Spain during the War of Spanish Succession. He had married Katherine Southwell before 1695. They had several children but only one son, Abraham, survived to adulthood. David was later made Master of the Royal Hospital at Kilmainham in Dublin and died on 1 June 1728, being succeeded by his eldest surviving son Abraham Creighton. Dean Henry visited the still-famous castle in 1739 and described it as having 'no outer wall'. This suggests that the castle that had withstood the two sieges had been altered or rebuilt, either by Spottiswood after the 1629 inquisition, or by the elder Abraham Creighton following the siege.

David Creighton's son and heir, Abraham, was born in 1703. In 1729, he married Elizabeth Rogerson, eldest daughter of Right Honourable John Rogerson, Lord Chief Justice of the King's Bench. Elizabeth died in August 1761, and Abraham remarried, this time to Jane King of Charlestown, in September 1763. He was created Baron Erne of Crom castle in June 1768 and died in June 1772.

Crom castle was accidentally burned down in 1764. Tradition has it that Abraham Creighton and his family were attending the house-warming party of the newly finished Florencecourt House, home of the Cole family, when they became aware of a glow in the sky to the south. A letter from Lord Shannon to the family written on 1 September 1764 condoles with the loss of their home, and acknowledges the part it had played in the previous century, 'unhappy indeed to be consumed by a few accidental sparks of fire when it had so bravely withstood the firing of 6,000 men so many years ago, directly levelled at it; but our Castles, as well as our persons, must submit to the chances of time and accident'.

Abraham Creighton was succeeded in 1772 by his son John. Born in 1731, John became 2nd Baron Erne but was to see rapid advancement in the status of the family at this time. He was made a viscount in 1781 and became the First Earl Erne in 1789. Following the 1801 Act of Union between Britain and Ireland, he sat as an Irish representative peer in the British House of Lords. When John died in 1828, his eldest son, another Abraham, succeeded to become the 2nd Earl. Abraham died in 1842, and as he had no heir, the title passed to his nephew John Creighton, 3rd Earl Erne.

In the years following the fire at Crom in 1764, the family lived mainly in Dublin, but sometimes stayed at Knockballymore. They also built a lodge on Inisherk Island, but they did not take up permanent residence in the locality until the present Crom castle was completed in 1838. Neo-Gothic in style, as designed by the eminent Irish architect Edward Blore, it was commissioned by the 3rd Earl of Erne on land near the original castle site. But the new castle itself suffered an accidental fire in 1841, which gutted the building and caused it to be rebuilt again.

The old castle site at Crom was visited by the officers of the Ordnance Survey in October 1835. They commented on the new castle built by the 3rd Earl and noted that the old castle ruin had been made into a 'folly' with the addition of walls and towers built against the old structure. These changes, costing £190, had been wrought to enhance the formal garden and avenues which led to the ancient yew tree. More folly towers were added to the scene, together with a new entrance, steps and flags, in 1858.

Born in 1802, John Creighton, the 3rd Earl, was a representative Irish peer in the British House of Lords from 1845 until his death in 1885. He served as Lord Lieutenant of Fermanagh for the same period and was created a baron in the United Kingdom peerage in 1876, allowing him to sit in the House of Lords as of right. In 1878, the family estate was over 40,000 acres, with land in Fermanagh, Donegal, Sligo and Mayo, making Creighton one of the largest landowners in Ulster. He was also responsible for changing the spelling of the family surname to Crichton. On his death he was succeeded by his son John Henry Crichton.

John Henry Crichton, the 4th Earl, was born in 1839. Politically Conservative, he served at the Treasury in Disraeli's second administration. Like his father, he was Lord Lieutenant of Fermanagh. He was also heavily involved in the Orange Order, succeeding the Earl of Enniskillen in 1886 as Grand Master. He was later elected Imperial Grand Master by a unanimous vote, a post he held until his death, over a quarter of a century later.

Many writers from the mid-eighteenth century onwards visited the castle during their grand tours of Ireland, and saw fit to pass comment. In his book *The Tourists' Picturesque Guide to Ireland*, written early in last century, the author W.F. Wakeman described the remnants of Crom:

> … [this] picturesque and venerable ruin, now, as if in irony, clothed from turret to foundation stone in a uniform of 'ivy green', successfully resisted two sieges. It was the frontier garrison of the northern Protestants during the trying times of the great revolution, and though unprovided with artillery, was at all times enabled to hold its own.

In the late nineteenth century, Upper Lough Erne became the focus of great socialising, which involved the various upper-class families living around the shore, including the Crichtons, Saundersons, Massy-Beresfords, Gartside-Tippings and Butlers. The waters off Crom are ideal for sailing, and a friendly rivalry grew up between the families as they competed and entertained on the lough. This era came to an end with the First World War. Viscount Henry William Crichton, heir to the estate, was killed in October 1914, while serving with the Royal Horse Guards in Belgium. Other prominent loughshore families suffered similar losses and with the passing of the older generation, the activities of the previous era were not repeated.

The 4th Earl died in December 1914, and was succeeded as 5th Earl by his grandson John Henry George Crichton, a boy of only seven years of age. Like his father, he was to choose a military career, and he entered the same regiment as his father. At the outbreak of the Second World War, he immediately raised the North Irish Militia as a much-needed defence force for the country. He was killed when serving with the British Expeditionary Force in France in May 1940. He left a three-year-old son, Henry George Victor John Crichton, who is the current and 6th Earl Erne. Despite the tragic losses on behalf of their country in two World Wars, the Crichton family continue in residence at Crom to the present day.

The National Trust now own and manage part of the estate, including the old Crom castle site, and they have constructed a visitor and interpretative centre nearby. Uniquely, amongst the plantation families of the Erne, after almost three and a half centuries, the Crichton family continues to reside in the estate first occupied by their ancestor, Abraham Creighton, all those years ago.

Castle Tour

With the water of Lough Erne lapping gently close by, the visitor can be forgiven for first indulging in the glorious location of the castle. Crom has perhaps the most illustrious history of any of the surviving castles of the Erne basin, but today its story appears to have fallen into the backwaters of history. The story of the castle and the Crichton family are amply retold at the National Trust Visitor Centre, which is well worth a visit before going to examine the ruins. From the visitor centre, Crom is approached along a raised grass track. A copse of oak trees to the right of the path is pointed out as the burying place of the Jacobites killed during the sieges of the castle in 1689.

The first thing one must do when assessing Crom is ignore much of the later building work on the site. The site of the original castle at Crom was enhanced in the early years of the nineteenth century by the addition of walls and towers for dramatic effect, and the unwary visitor can obtain a false impression of the extent of the original building. In truth, any interpretation of the ruins is speculative and open to debate. Nonetheless, some attempt must be made to assess the evidence and untangle the site in order to gain an appreciation of the castle remains. In fact, the first stone tower and the wall containing the arched, gated entrance to the ruin are part of the later works and so it is perhaps best to initially view the ruins from the grass area on the north side. Here, the extent of the original castle can be determined as consisting of the central section, containing the tall circular flanker, and the ends of two gable walls. On each side of this, all the walls are part of the nineteenth-century building work.

Moving into the site through the modern gateway, the castle ruins can now be inspected. The castle plan consists of a two-and-a-half-storey double pile (i.e. two gable-ended buildings joined by the walls of their long axes). These buildings were aligned in a north–south direction. Two circular flankers are located on the NE and SE corners of the eastern building. The easterly building measures 5.8m by 11.7m (19ft by 39ft) and was separated from the western building by a stone partition wall, 0.75m thick. Part of this dividing wall remains at its north and south ends.

The rear or western building is slightly larger, measuring 3.8m by 13.6m (12.5ft by 45ft) and thus extends 1.8m northwards beyond the line of the eastern building. In total, this gives us a ruin of approximately 15m by 12m (50ft by 40ft), which is a long way from the dimensions given by Pynnar, Perrot and Annesley, or the 1629 inquisition. The original castle must have been become unfit for purpose, and we are therefore looking at the structure that was rebuilt later in the seventeenth century. If so, then the most likely builder was Abraham Creighton, who became the owner in the 1650s. Creighton must have torn down the original structure or partly adapted it to create his own design for Crom. Alternatively, the blackened ruins from the 1764 fire may have been further altered during the 1830s, thereby confusing the site even more.

Apart from these ruins, which lie in the centre of the site, it is probably correct to state that the other walls round about here are parts of the later folly. Though that is not to say that all of the walls and masonry work in the defined area of the castle are original, as closer examination will confirm that even here, rebuilding and modifications have been made to beautify the ruins. As already stated, it is always prudent to be careful in interpreting this site!

It is best to begin with an examination of the east wall of the castle. The wall is almost a metre thick, with a 3m (10ft) section on the north end surviving to over 2m in height. The opening between the NE tower and the wall here may indicate the site of the entrance, and this theory is supported by what appears to be a socket for a drawbar. It must be said that the drawbar would no longer line up with the socket in the opposite lintel, but time and subsidence may have created this anomaly. If this was the doorway, and hence a vulnerable point in the castle defence, it was amply protected by a loophole in each of the two adjacent flankers.

Further south along this wall there is what appears to be the splayed ingoing for a window. The east wall then continues as foundations, or a low wall, to the SE tower. This window, if indeed it is one, presents a problem, as it would have created an obvious weak point in the castle's defences. One is, however, reminded of the other Crichton castle at Aghalane, where windows similarly placed in the outer wall are to be found, so this is not unprecedented.

Passing through the supposed doorway described above, one enters the eastern part of the castle. The north gable wall is almost complete to roof level, but the west and south walls are ruined to a low level, with only a short section of the west wall (0.75m thick) projecting from the north gable. This wall lines up with a short section projecting from the south wall, of a similar thickness, so one can postulate that the intervening wall has been removed at some earlier date. At the SW corner, the 1m-thick wall narrows in a gentle curve to 0.6m, but the purpose of this is unclear.

There are some sockets in the west wall for joists at ceiling level to support the floor above. However, there is a small window at ground-floor level in the north gable that cuts across this floor level, so these features were not contemporaneous. Above, in the first floor of the north gable, there is another window, partly rebuilt or strengthened using brick, and approximately 1.2m high by 0.90m wide (4ft by 3ft). The second-floor level has no window, but there are the remains of three fireplaces at three different levels, each with a flue that must have passed up through the thickness of the gable wall.

Viewed outside from the north, the upper two floors of the north gable wall overstep the wall beneath. They were supported on a wooden beam, a stump of which remains in view on the eastern side. This wall was repaired at some time in the more recent past, and again, it is difficult to be certain if this is an original feature or part of the shoring process of later masons.

Beyond the eastern building, and separated from it by a stone partition wall, is the rear extension, measuring internally 3.8m by 13.6m (12.5ft by 45ft). Once again these dimensions are tentative, as the wall arrangements may have been altered at a later date, so it's good to be cautious. As in the adjacent building, only the north gable wall stands to its original height of two and a half storeys, projecting 1.8m northwards beyond the line of the east building. There are two small windows with flat stone lintels in the gable, which are now blocked up. Both are only visible from the outside. Above this, there appears to have been a narrow window on both the first and second floors but each has since collapsed or been robbed for building stone, and they are therefore difficult to size. Brickwork has been used to shore up the weakening caused by the removal of the stone.

High up on the remnant of the west wall, facing west, there is a small window. What appear to be six sockets for floor joists are located in the north gable wall about 0.9m above the current ground level. Once again, interpretation is difficult as some of these features cut across each other to create a fairly confused picture. At roof level, a carved stone on either side of the pitched roofline finishes off the gutter.

Moving next to the SE flanker, it is entered from the eastern building. Ruined to a low height of only 0.6m or so, it is oval in plan, with an internal diameter measuring between 2.2m and 2.7m. It contains a loophole facing north, now partially blocked up, which covered any approach to the east wall. Measuring 0.6m wide by 0.4m high internally, on the external face the loop splays to 0.2m high by 0.05m wide (8 by 2 inches).

The NE flanker is better preserved. Entered via a lintelled passageway from the castle, it measures 2.8m internally and contains four loopholes. One loophole, on the north wall, is larger than the others and located higher up the wall, and so it may have functioned primarily as a window to provide light to the interior space. The other three loopholes are all similar, located 1m above the present floor level and providing a mixture of offensive and defensive fire options for the garrison. One loophole faces south and protected the east wall, but is now partially blocked up. Internally it measures 0.6m wide by 0.65m high (24 by 26 inches), splaying down to only 0.25m high by 0.08m (10 by 3 inches) on the outer face. A second loophole provides flanking fire along the north gable, while a third faces north to the meadow.

Part of the ground-floor flanker wall has been repaired at some later date, possibly during the 1830s alterations. Unusually, the first and second floors are vaulted in brick, though only part of each floor now remains. There is other brickwork in the flanker, which appears to have been used to repair weak parts of the structure, so these floors are not likely to be original. There is no access to either floor, so close inspection is not possible, but each contains a loophole of exceptional quality. On the first floor, facing south and protecting the east wall, a limestone block has been carefully loopholed in the shape of a Roman arched window with a gable surround. Directly above it on the second floor is another loophole, this time diamond shaped with a stone flourish surround. Both are highly unusual in their exuberant design and represent the best in defensive plantation architectural features.

This, then, is the famous old castle of Crom that withstood two famous sieges all those years ago. Yet it must be said that the ruins, as they are, fail to yield that historical place with any great certainty. Where are the marks of the cannon fired at her? Where were the siege lines and entrenchments? How did two companies of Williamite soldiers fit into so small a space? It is now difficult to be certain, but it is probable that the Creightons refurbished or rebuilt the structure originally described by Pynnar and others, some years before the famous sieges took place. The subsequent damage and later the fire here must have robbed the building of its features, and finally, the creation of pleasure gardens and the Victorian folly works combined to obscure the true identity of the castle beneath the additional veneer. Only a full archaeological survey would allow us to interpret the site with any conviction. In the meantime, we must be content with the scant remains and the wonderful lakeside scenery.

AGHALANE
OS SHEET 27, GR 341200

Crossing over to the west side of Upper Lough Erne on the B127, the village of Derrylin is reached. Turn south along the A509 to Belturbet. Just before crossing the border into the Republic of Ireland, at the Senator George Mitchell Peace Bridge, there is a minor road junction to the left for Aghalane moorings on the Erne–Shannon Waterway. The castle ruins are 200m on the left, on the summit of a drumlin.

History
These lands, in Knockninny precinct, were originally granted in October 1610 to Thomas Moneypenny, Laird of Kinkell in modern Fifeshire. The estate consisted of the small proportion of 1,000 acres, 300 of which was to be held in demesne and a further 60 acres were excepted for glebe (i.e. for the living of a clergyman). A perpetual rent of £5 6s 8d was to be paid.

However Moneypenny had no intention of developing the estate and swiftly sold it on to Captain Thomas Creighton of Brunston in July 1613. Creighton immediately set about building for himself the castle which we see today and placing his family within. In 1619 Pynnar reported the following account:

> Upon this there is a bawne of Clay and Stone, rough cast over with Lime, 50 feet square and 12 feet high, with two Flankers. It hath a poor thatched House within. I find planted upon this proportion, of British tenants, ten, but I saw no estates more than by promise, which are here named. Freeholders, 6 – *viz*, 1 having 180 acres, 1 having 60 acres, 4 having 120 acres jointly. Lessees 4 – *viz*, 2 having 60 acres le piece, 1 having 30 acres, 1 having 40 acres. These ten Families are all that I can hear of: the rest are Irish.

The perennial problem of securing sufficient subtenants to take land is again evident. Pynnar also disclosed that Creighton had recently died (in 1618) and the estate was now in the possession of Mr Adwick, second husband of Creighton's widow Katherine and guardian of his adoptive children, including the young heir, David, and his brother James.

Adwick was thus the castle's custodian when he was visited by rebels during the evening of Saturday 23 October 1641. They forced him to vacate his property, but unlike many others at the time, Adwick was permitted to escape unmolested which he did in the company of Revd Dr Teate of nearby Dresternan. They fled to Virginia, County

Cavan, to the home of Revd George Creighton, brother of the deceased Captain Thomas, informing him of the uprising that had broken out across the country. The family were thus absent from their estate for a number of years and it is unclear exactly when they returned. During this period, David died in 1644 without issue and the estate passed to his uncle Revd George Creighton. Why David's younger brother James was not the inheritor is unknown; he was provided with a house and lands at Gortgorgan, where he was still living with his mother in 1668.

Revd George Creighton resided at Aghalane for the rest of his life, dying in 1676. He was succeeded by his daughter Jane and her husband John, coincidentally also named Creighton. This John Creighton was a member of the Dumfries branch of the family and no relation of his wife. They had two sons, Robert and John. When Jane died, John Creighton married Jane Saunderson and they had four children together: Catherine, Jane, Penelope and William. As the threat of war loomed again at the end of 1688, this was the family group in residence at Aghalane castle. Curiously, there is no separate mention of the castle or its inhabitants during this time, though it must be inferred that it endured the same experiences as its close neighbour Crom, situated on the opposite side of Upper Lough Erne, only 5km (3 miles) away.

When John Creighton died in 1693, his son Robert inherited the estate. However, Robert immediately sold the estate on to his younger brother John, who then quickly abandoned the castle around 1700 for a newly built modern residence in nearby Killynick with his new bride, Henrietta Townley. The castle must then have rapidly fallen into disrepair and indeed may have been partially dismantled (to the condition we see it today) to provide the new house with a ready source of building material.

John was the last Creighton at Aghalane. He died in 1738 and the estate, including the castle, was sold off equally between his six daughters. In the early nineteenth century, it all became part of the lands of the Earls of Erne, living at Crom.

Castle Tour

The remains of Aghalane castle present problems of interpretation for the visitor. The site was much overgrown in the past, but the landowner has recently cleared away much of the undergrowth, so that an investigation of Aghalane is now possible for the first time in years. However, there are still rubble mounds at the rear and a full understanding of the castle will only be possible when it has been fully surveyed and its crumbling walls restored for future generations. But this should not deter the visitor from exploring these picturesque ruins.

The castle is approached up the hill, from the road from the SW. The site is entered through a modern farm gate in the south wall, between two circular flankers. The line of wall is broken by a central gap, 3.2m in width, which may represent the remains of the original entrance doorway. There is what appears to be a socket, 0.8m deep, on the west side of the gap, which could represent a drawbar socket for a gate. If this is an entrance, it is much wider than one would expect for a castle of this time. However, the gap may be caused by later removal of dressed stones from around the entrance.

Before entering the site we are confronted with the first conundrum. The south bawn wall is pierced by two windows, symmetrically located each side of the entrance gap. The western window measures 0.9m high by 0.7m wide internally, rebated for a wooden window frame, with its sill about a metre above the current ground level. Externally, the window was probably smaller but has been robbed of its sill, lintel and jambs. The eastern window is slightly larger, at 1m high by 0.55m wide internally and is about 1.2m above the current ground level. Again, the stonework is rebated for a wooden frame, though the sill and some jamb stones are missing. Both windows have sockets in their masonry frame to contain iron bars. This would have prevented any trespassers' immediate entrance to the interior, but it is a strange feature, and their location at ground-floor level in a bawn wall must surely have compromised the castle's defences.

Passing through this gap in the south wall, one enters the enclosure of the castle. The bawn measures approximately 15.1m west to east by about 18m north to south, and is constructed of unusually large random blocks of rubble fieldstones. The south bawn wall is 2.7m high and measures 1.2m in thickness; the west and east bawn walls are thinner (only 0.9m thick) but survive to a height of approximately 3.2m for a distance of about 9m from the two flankers. Piercing the west bawn wall are two windows of similar size. Each measures externally 0.44m wide by 0.6m, and they retain their plain-dressed stone sills, lintels and jambs. Once again, each has a pair of sockets in the sill and lintel to allow iron bars to cover the glazing on the external side. As with the windows in the south bawn wall described above, these windows at ground-floor level, a mere 0.9m above the ground outside, would have seriously compromised the castle's defences. One can only assume that Creighton believed that other defensive measures around the structure were sufficient.

As previously described, the south bawn wall contains two circular flankers. The SW flanker is entered from the interior of the bawn, via a narrow doorway. Part of the jamb of this doorway can just be detected at ground level. The flanker, constructed of undressed local stone, is 3m in diameter with walls 1.2m thick and surviving to 3.2m in height. It was only one storey tall. Four well-preserved apertures at ground-floor level pierce these walls, of which two are loopholes and two are windows. The loopholes are positioned to allow flanking fire along the west and south bawn walls. Internally they measure 0.6m by 0.6m, at a height of 0.9m from the floor, tapering down to an external measurement of 0.1m or so. The loophole protecting the west wall has the external appearance of an inverted pear, but the other loop is a more conventional circle, created by the neat joining together of two stones which have had semicircular slots cut along an edge. The two windows in the flanker face SW and SE respectively. Each window measures 0.5m high by 0.6m internally, splaying to external dimensions of only 0.36m high by 0.15m, with the sill of each approximately 0.9m from the floor level.

Similarly, the SE flanker is entered directly from the bawn through a narrow doorway. It measures 3m in diameter, with walls 3m high, and has four apertures, two conventional windows and two loopholes. The two loopholes protect the south and east bawn walls, and they taper externally to a small, 0.1m circle. Again, the two windows are similar in scale to those in the SW flanker and face SE and SW. Near wall-top level there are a number of sockets around the circumference, which must have contained wooden ceiling joists to support a conical roof.

The recent clearance has allowed the rear of the site to be partially visible once more. It is now possible to determine that a flanker was constructed at each end along the north bawn wall. Unusually, these flankers were not circular like the two on the south side, but sub-rectangular. Of the two, the NW flanker is better preserved, with walls almost a metre in height. Internally, it measures about 3.3m square, but the flanker's north wall is angled towards the north bawn wall. There was presumably an identical flanker on the NE corner, but today only about 0.5m of the wall stands, with the remainder lying within the rubble.

Between these two flankers, and lying beyond the line of the north bawn wall, is a rectangular room. It measures 2.7m by 2.3m internally. Its exact purpose can only be guessed at, as it seems too small for a stair projection. The house mentioned by Pynnar is no longer visible at all, but may be represented by the rubble along the north side of the enclosure. This is the conventional site for a manor house within a bawn, but Aghalane is an unusual site. In the 1830s, the castle was visited by Ordnance Survey staff who drew up a plan of the castle ruins, showing it to have been in much the same condition as it appears today. This plan shows the spear-shaped flankers at both corners of the north wall but does not postulate that the house was also in this location. The position of the bawn entrance and the manor house thus still need to be located.

A sketch of the south elevation of Aghalane made by the same Ordnance Survey staff appears to show that the bawn wall here was continuous at that time. However, writing in the *Ulster Journal of Archaeology* in 1896, the Earl of Erne included a sketch of the castle that clearly shows the gap in the south wall. It is possible that between both sketches the wall was robbed of masonry to provide building material for some other project. However, except for part of the north wall hidden under rubble, the bawn perimeter has no other gap to fit the role of an entrance. Conventional wisdom would strongly suggest that the entrance was on the south side here, with the manor house located along the north wall, facing south into the bawn.

This hypothesis adequately accounts for the entrance to Aghalane, but there is still the matter of the windows in the south and west walls, which need to be explained. It is worth looking again at the surviving structures, to see if there are clues which we can use to interpret the site. Beginning with the west bawn wall, it will be noted that there are four large sockets for ceiling joists in the masonry at a height of about 2.5m. The uniform wall height here also suggests that this is the original height of the wall, albeit that dressed stones have been removed from the internal framework of both windows.

It is therefore suggested here, as a hypothesis, that the manor house described by Pynnar was, in fact, located along the west bawn wall. This explains the need faced by the builder to include windows in the external bawn walls. This would obviously weaken the defensive capability of the castle, but Creighton must have believed that the integral flanker with loopholes could adequately provide protection from attack. Assisted by the barred windows, the combination would adequately prevent ingress to the house. If true, then one would expect to find some evidence of other walls within the bawn. Sadly, the nature of the uneven ground means that these cannot be confirmed. Likewise, there is no indication of a hearth here, though again this may have been lost by later demolition.

Similarly, there are large sockets about 2.4m above ground level on the inside of the east bawn wall, which could carry ceiling joists. Near the north end of this high part of the wall there is a large stone protruding, which could be interpreted as the remnants of a hearth and flue. There is an irregular recess in the wall here too, which could indicate a useful dry cupboard. Although there are no windows in the east wall, the window on the south wall could be incorporated in this building, together with the SE flanker. Again, no evidence of other walls is forthcoming but they may exist beneath the soil.

The remains of Aghalane today consist of a bawn with four flankers, unusually combining two circular and two spear-shaped flankers. The rear part of the bawn enclosure has been demolished to a low level at some point in the past, probably robbed as a source of building material, making it difficult to interpret. But if the above hypothesis is correct, the entrance was in the south bawn wall. Once inside, the manor house was sited, unusually, at right angles to the entrance, and faced other buildings across the yard. This castle is therefore something of a riddle and is well worth the walk to the top of the hill, with the spire of Belturbet parish church clear in the distance to the south.

CORRATRASNA
OS SHEET 27, GR 279300

Take the A509 road from Enniskillen to Derrylin. Passing through Bellanaleck, after 10km (6 miles) take a road to the left signposted for Knockninny Quay. Proceed for a further 1.6km (1 mile), passing a small Methodist church on the left. The ruins of Corratrasna can be seen in a field on the hillside, behind a modern farmhouse. There is a pier at Knockninny Quay for pleasure boats.

History
Traditionally associated with Brian Maguire, this house may have instead been built by a member of the Balfour family, on whose Legan estate it was located. Brian Maguire was granted land in Clanawley, but there is no conclusive proof that it included Corratrasna. However, he may have acquired it from the Balfour family at a later date and was thus resident here at the time of the 1641 rebellion. The subsequent history of the house is unclear, though it was, at a later stage, a great source of building material.

The 1659 census return for Fermanagh notes a total of sixteen Irish tenants and no British on the land at 'Cortrasna' but does not shed any light regarding the occupier of the fortified house. Similarly, in the 1830s, the Ordnance Survey staff noted then that the history of the place was vague and uncertain. They did record a tradition that the house was built by Bishop Bedell, who was forced to vacate the building on account of his involvement in the execution of some robbers who ransacked the place.

Another account states that the castle was later occupied by a Captain Maguire, who was present as a prisoner at the first siege of Crom castle in 1689. This may refer to a Maguire who resided in the adjoining townland of Farquagh and whose son, Captain Terence Maguire, erected a memorial to his father at Callowhill graveyard, near Derrylin, which can still be seen.

Castle Tour
The ruins of Corratrasna are approached up a lane beside a farmhouse and across a muddy field. The house is sited at the rear of the field. It would appear that the exterior ground level around the rear of the house has risen by up to 0.6m. The house is strongly built and rectangular in plan, and resembles some other fortified homes without bawns around the

Erne. However, there are traces of a rampart in front of the house, which, together with anecdotal evidence by the landowner of underlying structures in the ground, may indicate the former existence of a sod or stone bawn here. If so, then the house sat at the rear of the bawn, with superb views east and south towards the Upper Erne.

Externally, the house measures 12.8m by 6.5m (42ft by 21ft) and was originally two storeys high, with a third, attic level located in the steep roof pitch. Today, the north and south gables are near complete, but the west wall survives to only around 2.5m internally. The east wall has been almost completely removed, except for short sections near each gable end that survive to roof level. The house was constructed of random field rubble, with the edges squared off with larger stones. Most of these quoins have been robbed out for other uses. Some of the upper windows retain their original cut stonework, as they were probably too high up to be worth the bother of removing.

The front and rear walls are only 0.75m (30 inches) thick, with the north and south gable walls being 0.9m (3 feet) thick. The entrance was probably in the centre of the east wall, though this cannot now be exactly determined. The west wall contains the sills and part of the jambs for two widely splayed windows measuring 1.4m externally. There is a walled-up opening on the south end of the wall, which may indicate a third window, altered later, perhaps to a doorway. One might presume that the window arrangements were repeated along the missing east wall. It seems odd that windows should be located so low to the ground, as they would have compromised the building's defence. The ground level at the rear of the house is now much higher than the interior, but this infill is likely to have occurred at a much later date. Nonetheless, it shows the preoccupation of the builder with finding a suitable compromise between comfort and defence.

Inside the house, there are the remains of substantial fireplaces in each gable. The well-cut stone fireplace in the south gable is the larger, measuring 3.3m (11ft) in width and to a depth of 1.2m. Directly above this, there is a fireplace at first-floor level. Both fireplaces have separate flues, still complete to chimney level. In the attic level above this, a small fireplace was constructed at a right angle to the main chimneybreast, thus allowing all levels of the house to be heated. The gable also contains two narrow loopholes at first-floor level, arranged either side of the chimneybreast. They are widely splayed, each measuring 0.4m (15 inches) high internally but only 0.1m (4 inches) externally. Both retain the original lintels and sills. Above them, on the second floor, are two larger windows, of which only the east window is now complete. These measure 0.6m by 0.45m (24 inches by 18 inches) and may have provided the only natural light for the attic storey accommodation, as they are contained in the steep pitch of the roof. The gable tapers up to a fairly complete chimney stack, which retains its capping.

In the north gable, the ground-floor fireplace is 2.7m (9ft) wide, with a complete flue. Once again, there is a fireplace on the first floor also, with a separate flue complete to chimney level. There is no visible internal division of the ground floor and the room partitions may have originally been of stud-wall construction, but it can be determined that there were at least two rooms on each floor, well provided with fires. The gable also contains two narrow splayed loops at first-floor level, on either side of the chimney, and these measure 0.6m high (24 inches) but only 0.1m wide (4 inches). The one on the west is incomplete, but that on the east retains the original squared stonework. On the second floor, there is a larger window in the steep roof pitch, without its lintel, and there was probably a similar one on the west side. Removal or collapse of this part of the gable means that this feature can only be surmised. Once again, the chimney stack survives nearly complete, to a height of 12m (40ft).

There are sockets for joists on either side of both ground-floor fireplaces, at a height of 2.2m (7ft), but in addition the east wall is rebated by up to 0.15m (6 inches) along its remaining parts. Additionally, there are sockets in both gables to carry the floor at second-floor level. Given that there appears to be no masonry subdivision within the house, one must conclude that the rooms had timber partitions and that the joists ran longitudinally to meet these walls.

The location of the stairs is also difficult to determine, but was presumably in the centre of the house, opposite the entrance. The location of the windows along the west wall makes this somewhat problematic, but presumably the house was divided longitudinally into three rooms comprising the central hallway with the stairs, flanked on either side by a room with a large fireplace. This arrangement was most probably repeated on the floors above. Given the number of windows and the numerous fireplaces, this must have provided a comfortable home for its owner.

Despite the removal of stones from the castle over the years, the remaining walls are remarkably well bonded. There is a tradition that during the castle's construction, the mortar was mixed with ox blood, making it more adhesive. This practice is not unknown elsewhere in Ireland and, if true, represents a continuity of building skills from the distant past.

Roughly speaking, this relatively small manor house provided the owner with around 250 sq m (2650 sq ft) of living space. As with many other buildings erected during this period, the owner at Corratrasna was trying to meet the needs of security and those of comfortable living. Situated on a hillside, providing long views across the countryside, and constructed of stout walls containing loopholes for the use of pistol or musket, this fortified house was nevertheless compromised by the insertion of wide windows. But as always the owner sought to find a compromise to satisfy the needs of both competing requirements.

Today, Corratrasna presents a pleasant and tranquil location. With superb views of Lough Erne below and with the lofty wooded slopes of Knockninny mountain behind, it is obvious why the owner chose this beautiful location for his home.

GARDENHILL
OS SHEET 17, GR 099403

Proceed along the A4 to Belcoo. At the quarry just before the village turn right along a minor road signposted to Boho. About 1km along this road, there is a white bungalow, with cowsheds on the opposite side of the road. At the side of the bungalow is a long gated laneway. Seek permission to proceed. Gardenhill is 500m along this lane. For boat users, Belcoo is best reached by bus from Enniskillen (Service No.66).

History
In the Ulster Plantation, the precinct of Clanawley was reserved for both servitors and native Irish, though this area around modern-day Belcoo was only awarded to the latter.

Gardenhill is not specifically mentioned in any grant, but the neighbouring townlands of Drumman and Mullylusty were granted to Shane McHugh, Connor McTirlagh, Shane McDonnell, Brian and Ballagh O'Skanlan in several plots. As these small estates were not subject to castle-building obligations, Pynnar's 1618 survey remains silent on any progress or changes in estate ownership.

The Hassard family first appear as soldiers employed by Captain William Cole of Enniskillen during the 1641 rebellion. There were at least three brothers living in the area at the time – Robert, William and Jason Hassard. Cole used them to police the country during the unsettled times and they were described as, 'forward men of sound judgement and good confidence', clearly the type of reliable people needed during this period. The 1659 census return for Fermanagh noted a 'Jason Hassert, gent' resident in Enniskillen, at that time a town with a population of 210 persons.

At the conclusion of the rebellion, the most noted member of the family was Jason Hassard (probably the Enniskillen gentleman noted above), who took advantage of his improved fortune by purchasing an estate in Clanawley barony at Mullymesker, near Arney. Jason was appointed High Sheriff of Fermanagh in 1676 and is described as a Crown tenant in 1678. In 1689, 'Jason Hassart, sen, of Mullyvesker, gent', was attainted, like many of his settler neighbours, by the Irish parliament in Dublin for his support of William of Orange. Following the Inniskilliners' victory at Newtownbutler, he signed the loyal address from the garrison sent to the joint sovereigns. Jason died the following year and was succeeded by two sons, Robert (the elder) and Richard, neither of whom had reached maturity. The administration of his estate and all personal effects were left in the care of Jason Hassard junior, nephew of Jason senior and son of William, mentioned previously. This appears to have been expected, as Jason junior had managed his uncle's affairs in a prudent manner for a number of years before his death.

Jason Hassard junior continued to manage this estate and he was made a JP, public treasurer for the county and held a captain's commission in the militia. Later, Jason bought an estate at Menterfodaghan and some other freeholds in Fermanagh, keeping good livestock and a well-run tanyard. In 1702, he was one of the eight members of Enniskillen corporation who supported a claim for compensation by James Corry of Castlecoole. Corry's house had been deliberately fired on, on the orders of Governor Hamilton, in July 1689, to prevent it falling into the hands of the Duke of Berwick.

Jason junior had several children: Robert, William, Jason III and Rose. Jason III succeeded his father at Skea (near Arney) and was county treasurer. He married Ann, daughter of Colonel Johnston, and they had four children: Anne, Rose, Nicholine and Robert. Jason junior's son Robert was also successful, becoming High Sheriff in 1719, a town burgess, and a captain in the militia.

Jason Hassard senior had bequeathed his own estate between his two sons, Robert and Richard, and to Jason junior. Robert appears to have died young (perhaps without issue) and Richard Hassard inherited the estate. He appears to be the ancestor of the Hassards of Gardenhill and of Bawnboy in County Cavan. In the 1830s, the Ordnance Surveyors noted the single-storey cottage at Gardenhill, belonging to W. Hassard Esq. The description provided must refer to the long, single-storey cottage, still in existence on this site. As late as 1876, a landowners' list named Alex Hassard as the incumbent at Gardenhill, described as an estate of some 461 acres and valued at £204.

Castle Tour

Gardenhill is approached along a partially rock-hewn lane, 600m long, and is not visible until the last bend in the road is reached. The estate sits in parkland on the side of a hill, with excellent panoramic views to Cuilcagh and Lough Macnean, with the Cavan hills in the distance. The site today consists of a long, low cottage, elongated east–west, with outhouses and buildings arranged around the rear, creating a triangular-shaped yard. All of the buildings have been constructed using well-dressed blocks of local sandstone and limestone.

The yard is entered through a gateway, with outbuildings forming the perimeter on the north and east sides. These offices, with distinctive crow-stepped gables and small windows on the outward facing walls, give this yard the impression of being an enclosed bawn. Subsequent rendering and partial dismantling of some of the buildings, though, make it impossible to identify any defensive features to substantiate this claim.

The long, single-storey cottage on the south side, noted by the Ordnance Surveyors in the 1830s, has eight bays, and is 95ft long by 24ft broad, with the entrance via a porch on the south side that led into a flagged hall. Rooms on either side of the hall contained a fireplace and a wooden floor, and each retain some cornicing. The portrait-shaped windows, 2.2m x 0.9m (7ft by 3ft), are spaced along the south elevation, but there is only one window on the north wall at the east end of the cottage. There are four complete chimneys spaced along the roofline. The roof is pitched at 45 degrees and still covered in Bangor Blue slate.

Due to the falling land surface on the west, the cottage has a lower ground-floor level at this gable end, entered via an arched doorway with a fanlight above. The doorway led to a flagged passageway, with two rooms off to the right. A wide stone stair then led up to a flagged rear hallway, which gave access via an archway to either a wooden stair to the attic level or through a door on the right to the main flagged hall of the house described earlier. This lower ground-floor level, therefore, ran for approximately half the length of the cottage.

However, the real curiosity on the site is the two-storey house located against the rear of the cottage, at its lower west end. Built of well-squared stone blocks, each up to 0.75m long, the house measures 10.5m by 6.6m externally, with a huge flue located in the centre of each gable wall. Due to an abundance of undergrowth, the exterior of the east gable cannot be inspected. However, the west gable is outshot by a further 1.1m to accommodate the chimney flue inside, and on the side adjacent to the cottage's lower entrance, is rendered over and harled in the Scottish fashion. The walls and flues of the house survive to full height. The flue is harled to around 6m above ground level and a flat coping edges the chimney top.

The two-storey house is of three bays on the ground floor, with walls 0.65m thick. The house was entered via a centrally sited door, now blocked up, on the north wall. This was flanked on either side by a symmetrical window with lintels and sills of stone. The wooden frame of one window still retains its glazing bars. Internally, brick walls subdivide the ground floor into three different-sized rooms, but these may not be original. The most westerly room measures 6m by 5.5m internally and contains a large fireplace on the west gable, 2.7m wide and 0.6m deep. There is a small cupboard recess on the north wall at the west end.

The other two rooms at the east end are separated from the main room, and from each other, by brick partition walls. The large flue evident by external examination must have been blocked at a later date, because the brick partition wall cuts across it. The walls were plastered, but the floor is littered with the debris of the collapsed roof and floor. A single beam still spans the width of the building and a portion of the plaster ceiling survives beneath. Originally, there were openings on the south wall, but when the adjoining cottage was completed, these were blocked up.

The first-floor elevation has four evenly spaced windows, again placed symmetrically along the north wall. On the south wall, the window openings were later adapted to provide access from the rooms at the west end of the cottage. Indeed, there is no longer any evidence of a stair connecting the two storeys of the house and it is unclear how the first floor accommodation was accessed.

Gardenhill today is an interesting and attractive set of buildings, and has fine views across the Fermanagh countryside towards Cuilcagh and Lough Macnean. Further excavation will someday undoubtedly shed more light on these clustered buildings, but in the meantime it is worth the time to visit this pretty, out-of-the-way place.

9

COUNTY CAVAN CIRCUIT

FARNHAM
OS SHEET 34, GR 394059

From the centre of Cavan town, take the R198 (signposted to Killeshandra) and proceed along Railway Road, passing the hospital on the way. After 3km (2 miles), the entrance to the Radisson Hotel is on the right. Drive carefully through the golf course to the hotel and conference centre beyond. The bus to Killeshandra passes this entrance to the Farnham estate.

History

In the division of land in Loughtee barony, the proportions of Dromehill and Drommellan, both estates of 1,000 acres, were granted to the English undertaker Sir Richard Waldron in July 1610. A native of Leicestershire, Richard Waldron was the son of John Waldron, one of the three infamous 'discoverers' who became rich during the reign of Elizabeth I by exploiting loopholes in the land deeds of Irish lords. Waldron was initially unable to cross to Ireland, as he was involved in a lawsuit in England, so he sent his agent Clement Cotterel and twenty tenants to begin the work of plantation.

At the outset, Sir John Davies, who had already been granted substantial holdings in Fermanagh and Tyrone, also claimed these lands, but he eventually gave up his claim. Carew, writing in 1611, claimed that Davies had actually sold the estates to Richard Waldron, who then sold them to Rignold Horne, who in turn sold them to Nicholas Lusher. Whether this is true or not, in 1618 Pynnar confirmed Thomas Waldron to be in possession of these estates, as heir to his father Richard Waldron, who had died in 1617. Pynnar described the estates thus:

> Upon this Proportion there is a Bawne of Sodds of 200 feet square, and four Flankers; but much of it is fallen down. The castle or Stone House is now finished, and himself, with his Mother, the Lady Waldron, with all their Family, are dwelling in it. There is built a Town consisting of 31 Houses, all inhabited with English. There is also a Wind-mill. There is a Thoroughfare and common Passage into the Country, and here is a little Tillage.

Settled on the land were a total of fifty-three families, who could muster eighty-two men.

Thomas died in February 1627 and was succeeded by his son, also Thomas, who was a minor of only two years. Despite these changes of ownership, the estates were not forfeited under the surrender and re-grant of Charles I, so the articles of plantation must have been more or less faithfully carried out.

The 1630 muster roll for Cavan shows that the estate was still in the possession of Lady Waldron, widow of Thomas. The estate could at this stage only muster a total of fifty-four men, who together could produce just five swords, four pikes, and a single pistol. Likewise, around 1640, the above castle, situated at Farnham, was described as being unfinished and in need of repair. It was sold at this time to a Richard Castledyne, originally the carpenter to Sir Richard Waldron. Castledyne had only daughters, and one of these married Waldron's youngest son, who was then to re-inherit the estate on the death of Castledyne.

In his book *The Irish Rebellion of 1641* (1920) Lord Ernest Hamilton states that on the morning of 23 October 1641, the castle at Farnham was visited by Mulmore O'Reilly, the High Sheriff of the county, who stripped it of all its arms and ammunition and used it to equip his own troops. The owner was absent at the time and therefore unable to prevent O'Reilly from helping himself to this considerable arsenal, described as being sufficient to arm forty men. It would appear, however, that Castledyne was apprehended on or about this time, as he next appears as a prisoner at Clough Oughter castle in December.

The fate of the castle during the remainder of the rebellion of 1641 is unknown, but presumably afterwards the estate was restored to Castledyne. In 1664, the estate was sold to a Robert Maxwell, Bishop of Kilmore. This Robert Maxwell was the son of Robert Maxwell of East Kilbride, who had come to Ireland at the end of the reign of Queen Elizabeth. Robert senior was described as 'one of 4 lowland Scots of any consequence who lived in the English Pale' and his son succeeded Bishop Bedell as Bishop of Kilmore in 1643, later becoming Bishop of Ardagh in 1661. It was Maxwell who renamed the estate 'Farnham', apparently in honour of the wife of Sir Richard Waldron, the first owner. Robert Maxwell died in 1672 but the estate continued to thrive.

Similarly, the effect of the upheavals of the revolution of 1688 and the consequent years of war are not known, but appear to have had little lasting effect, for Maxwell's descendants continued to absorb neighbouring estates. Lisnamaine (originally granted to John Fishe), with an annual rental of £258, was bought in 1715. Over 7,000 statute acres, providing a rental of £766, was acquired from Viscount Masserene in 1718, and the 6,500-acre estate of Castle Craig in the 1730s. These purchases, together with urban land acquisitions in Cavan town, made the family the largest landowners in the county, a position they held until the Land Purchase Acts at the end of the 1800s.

Titles followed the accumulation of wealth. John Maxwell, MP for the county from 1727 to 1756 and descendant of Bishop Robert, was created 1st Baron Farnham in 1756. He was created a viscount in 1760 and an earl in 1763. When he died in November 1779, his titles became extinct, as he had no living heir. His brother Barry Maxwell succeeded to the estate and was in turn recreated Viscount and Earl Farnham. This succession became extinct again when his son John Maxwell failed to produce an heir and the barony passed to John's cousin John Maxwell-Barry.

Visiting the estate in 1739, Dean Henry acknowledged John Maxwell's estate of Farnham, but made no mention of a house, so presumably it was a modest affair. One hundred years later, Samuel Lewis remarked:

> Farnham, the seat of lord Farnham, is one of the noblest ornaments of the county, for though the house does not possess much exterior magnificence, it is surrounded by a demesne of nearly 3000 acres, comprising the richest pastures and the greatest variety of scenery adorned with wood and water, and everywhere improved by art...

The first modern house to supersede the castle was probably built around 1700 by John Maxwell. Presumably it contained stone from Waldron's old castle of Farnham. In 1780, Barry Maxwell commissioned the eminent architect James Wyatt to build a library, and fifteen years later to draw designs for three ceilings in the house. It is not certain if these were ever installed, but Wyatt did design the library case, now in the stair landing alcove. In 1802, Francis Johnston carried out a rebuild and extension at Farnham to provide a three-storey house consisting of two ranges at right angles, thus providing an edifice to the gardens on the SW side. In 1839, the 7th Lord Farnham further enlarged the house, by building new offices in the re-entrant between the two ranges.

Farnham estate continued to grow throughout the nineteenth century and by 1879 stood at 29,455 acres, giving it a value of over £20,000. The Maxwells continued to reside at Farnham throughout the nineteenth century and into the twentieth. Lieutenant Colonel Somerset Arthur Maxwell, son and heir of Arthur Maxwell, the 11th Baron Farnham, died in December 1942 following wounds received at the Battle of El Alamein. When Arthur Maxwell died in 1957, his grandson Barry Maxwell succeeded. Around 1960, an inspection of the house discovered extensive dry rot, and the new lord dismantled many of the additions of the previous century and a half, including the 1839 wing. The house was reduced to the existing pedimented, nine-bay, three-storey Johnston range.

Barry Maxwell was the last Maxwell to reside at Farnham. During the 1990s, he gave up farming and leased out the agricultural land to local farmers. When he died in 2001, the remaining 1,300 acres were bought by a local businessman and the house became a 158-bed Radisson hotel complex with golf course. Thus, the Maxwell connection with Farnham has been severed after 330 years, but the estate continues to function in its new role and has found a sustainable future for the twenty-first century.

Castle Tour

This extensive site, incorporating the Georgian house together with modern conference and hotel facilities, has now generally obscured the original landscape, and only a full excavation of the site could reveal anything of the original structure. Working in the 1940s, the archaeologist Oliver Davies visited the site and claimed to have found two of the bawn walls and a two-storey building, which he believed was the SE flanker. In 2004, some further excavation was carried out at the dismantled wing of Farnham, prior to the hotel construction, but this did not throw any light on the original castle site.

Do the remains described by Davies in the 1940s still survive? There is a curious building, now sandwiched between the conference suite and the hotel kitchens. This two-storey house with basement presents many difficulties, particularly as it can no longer be viewed in its entirety from a single point. The building is 11m by 5.7m (36ft by 19ft) in plan, with the ground falling away on two sides to allow the insertion of a basement storey. Although the surrounding area has been altered and raised here, it is clear that the basement level was always below ground level on two sides, as there are no windows on the opposite walls.

The basement can be entered by a door in the gable and, curiously, by a second door on the adjacent wall, both now leading to a small lobby. Masonry teething on the outside wall may indicate the location of a lean-to structure since removed, which would explain the arrangement of the doors. The walls are of random rubble construction, 0.9m thick and covered for the most part in rough cement render.

From the entrance lobby, a door leads to a large room, approximately 4m by 4m, lit by a single window and containing a fireplace with alcove wall cupboards. The window is not splayed and contains what appears to be the original glazing. Also off the lobby was a long narrow store area, lit by a single small window in the gable. There is no access from this level to the upper storeys.

At the east end of the building, four steps led up into an entrance lobby and stairwell for the upper storeys. Wooden stairs rise up in stages to access above. Directly off the first-floor landing was a square room, 4.3m by 4.3m, lit by opposing sash windows and containing a vaulted plaster ceiling, rising from four corner corbels. The room was heated by a fireplace on the wall adjacent to the stairwell, and a door led off opposite into a narrow room measuring 4.3m by 1.8m, lit by a single window and thus reflecting the compartment arrangement in the basement below. The floor above is similar in layout and presumably contained the sleeping quarters. The whole is finished off with a slated hipped roof.

What, then, is to be made of this curious building? With its thick walls and modest un-splayed windows it is something of a conundrum, trapped as it is between more modern constructions. It is tempting to see it as the successor of Waldron's castle, though it is somewhat modest in size. Was the basement a separate servants' apartment, with the master living in the two-storey house above?

This building seems to reflect Davies's observations, but it is difficult to interpret it as the remnants of a flanker. It is possible that the building was drastically modified at a later date, but the plan is somewhat large for a flanker. Moreover, both the basement and two-storey house would be accessed from outside the bawn. A proper examination of the house will reveal its true age and purpose.

Before leaving, it is well worth inspecting the wonderful parklands that comprise the surviving estate at Farnham. Part of the demesne has now been converted to a golf course and there are many long walks through the mature grounds to be enjoyed.

BELLANACARGY
OS SHEET 27, GR 478110

From the centre of Cavan, head north along Farnham Street, taking the R212 Ballyhaise Road for about 7km (4 miles). From Ballyhaise, take the minor road east towards Tullyvin. Approximately 3.5km (2 miles) beyond Ballyhaise, turn left along a minor road and proceed for

400m to the concrete causeway bridge across the Annalee River. The site of Bellanacargy castle is 200m downstream on the southern side of the river. Boat users should berth at Belturbet, the highest navigable point on the River Erne. There is an infrequent daily weekday service from Cavan to Cootehill (No. 166 or 175), which passes close to Bellanacargy. Other, more convenient travel options to the site should also be considered.

History

Bellanacargy (or Ballincarrig) is situated close to an important ford over the River Annalee, and a castle, known as Castle Carrick, existed on this site in the sixteenth century. In 1608, the castle was garrisoned with Crown forces consisting of Archibald Moore, the constable, and six warders. At the time of the Ulster Plantation, Lord Deputy Chichester planned to reserve it for the Crown, but the garrison was dismissed in 1610.

Tullygarvey barony was assigned to servitors and deserving natives, but the castle and adjacent lands were assigned in March 1610 to Mulmory Oge McMulmory McShane O'Reilly, grandson of Sir John O'Reilly and son of Mulmory O'Reilly, who had been killed at the Battle of Yellow Ford in 1598, while fighting on the side of the Crown. O'Reilly received a grant totalling 3,000 acres, which he held at a rent of £21. At this time he was still only a boy, living at Bellanacargy with his widowed mother, Lady Katherine, niece of the Earl of Ormonde.

Archibald Moore, the former constable, was compensated with a pension and an estate around nearby Tullyvin. The castle at Bellanacargy is shown on contemporary maps as a square tower close to the river and surrounded by a rectangular bawn, with two projecting towers on the landward side. Nearby were located a church, a mill, a hurdle bridge and another building. In 1619, Nicholas Pynnar described the estate thus, 'Mulmorie Oge O'Reilie hath 3,000 acres. Upon this there is a Bawne of Sodds, and in it an old Castle, which is now built up, in which himself and Family Dwelleth. He hath made no Estates to any of his Tenants, and they do plough by the Tail'.

Though only a boy at the time he took possession, an inquisition at Belturbet in 1622 confirmed that Mulmory had actually died on 27 February 1617. The castle came into the possession of a kinsman, Philip McHugh O'Reilly, who was MP for the county in 1641. Despite being part of the establishment, O'Reilly was heavily involved in the plan to expel the settlers from the county. On the morning of 23 October 1641, he rode into the centre of Belturbet, reckoned to be the largest British settlement in Cavan, and demanded the immediate withdrawal of the settlers from Ireland or to suffer death.

Throughout the rest of the day, this extraordinary proclamation was recounted around the countryside, as stories of murder and robbery being carried out in neighbouring Fermanagh began to filter in. By the end of the day, the colonists at Belturbet recovered their nerve and were for resisting any attempt to make them give up their homes and possessions. O'Reilly returned to the town that evening and was confronted by this determination. Unperturbed, he addressed the crowd and assured them that the murders in Fermanagh were exceptional and that the leaders of the rebellion had pledged themselves to a peaceful removal of the colonists. He then promised that if they gave up their arms he would personally ensure their protection.

This assurance convinced most settlers, though some still voiced reservations. Reluctantly, they agreed to give up their arms. However, no sooner had they disarmed than the native Irish fell amongst them and robbed and stripped them of their personal possessions. The colonists condemned O'Reilly for his evident breach of faith, but he replied that the mob was out of hand and the colonists should therefore not delay and set out immediately for Dublin. Again, the colonists gathered some possessions for this journey, but a second time they were robbed and stripped as they prepared to leave, and this time there was bloodshed as well. Around 30 persons were killed and another 150 injured by the looters before the column of refugees set off for Dublin. They arrived in the capital a few days later.

Philip McHugh O'Reilly returned to Belturbet a few months later, in similar circumstances. For several months the rebel army had been besieging Keelagh and Croaghan castles at Killeshandra, defended by Sir Francis Hamilton and Sir James Craig. Following another bloody repulse at the walls of Keelagh, a section of the defeated rebels, led by two Mulpatricks and a man named Philip O'Togher, entered Belturbet and carried out a series of murders amongst the remaining settlers in the town. They began by hanging two men, but finding this too lengthy a process, they herded the remainder of their victims to the bridge across the River Erne. With the aid of pikes and swords the luckless victims, mainly women and children, were forced off the bridge into the river below. A total thirty-five persons were drowned in this way.

Philip McHugh O'Reilly entered the town later that evening and condemned the Mulpatricks for the atrocity. But they haughtily replied that they had acted in accordance with the wishes of his family, in particular his wife, Rose Ny Neil O'Reilly. It would appear that Rose was not well disposed to the British and sought their complete expulsion from the county by whatever means. This difference of opinion in the O'Reilly household appears to have caused much domestic friction, and Philip is said to have threatened his wife with confinement for her extreme views on several occasions. However, it was his wife who later confined her husband's nephew Philip McMulmory O'Reilly at Bellanacargy for a month, because of his friendly relations with the British.

Bellanacargy was clearly an important castle, described in contemporary government letters as, 'O'Reilly's castle – the strong fort of the enemy in Cavan', and its relative remoteness within the bogs and forests of the Erne basin ensured that it remained a difficult place to subdue. It was not until September 1651 that the Parliamentarians, under Colonel Robert Venables, gathered a large force of 1,500 foot and 500 horse and marched from Dundalk into Cavan with the intention of taking the castle and placing garrisons in Belturbet and other places capable of defence. Venables arrived before the castle and proceeded to batter it with cannon for two days without success. The castle garrison had been strengthened to 400 men, and a large force of 3,000 rebels were situated only 2 miles (3km) away, which posed a constant threat to the Parliamentarian army. When requests for more provisions, powder and ammunition were not forthcoming, Venables decide to raise the siege and returned to Dundalk.

The exact damage caused by Venables' cannon is unknown, but it was clear that such a strong place could not be allowed to remain in native hands. Although the fate of the castle during the following thirty years is uncertain, Bellanacargy did feature prominently on two occasions during the Williamite wars of 1688 to 1691. This part of Cavan was quickly overrun by Lord Galmoy's troops in March 1689, and the castle was repaired and fortified with a Jacobite garrison.

Following the success of the Inniskilliners at Belleek in May 1689, their victorious commander Thomas Lloyd led them on a raid into County Cavan via Wattle Bridge. The Jacobites were known to hold two strongpoints at that time – Redhills and Bellanacargy. The garrison at Redhills surrendered without a shot being fired and the next morning Bellanacargy was invested. Once again the garrison sought terms, which were accepted. The Jacobites were set free, but the Williamites procured a store of arms, ammunition and provisions. Afterwards, the castle wall was undermined and the building set on fire, causing it to fall to the ground, as it was deemed to be too remote from the main base at Enniskillen to install a permanent Williamite garrison. Lloyd then swept south as far as Finnea and Kells, only 50km (30 miles) from Dublin. A large quantity of cattle, sheep and horses were captured during the raid and driven back to Enniskillen in triumph. North Cavan became a frontier area between the opposing armies.

A year later, the Williamites returned. In April 1690, Colonel Wolseley was ordered to clear Cavan of its remaining Jacobite garrisons. Accompanying him were a contingent of Danes, hired by King William from the Danish King Christian V. This force first assaulted the Jacobite stronghold at Killeshandra and then turned east to invest the castle at Bellanacargy. The garrison consisted of a force of 200 men, and the castle was described as being surrounded by water. Wolseley decided to attack with a force of 1,200 Williamite troops, including the Danes, who had to wade through the waist-high water of the castle ditches. A sharp exchange of fire ensued; seventeen Williamites were killed and Wolseley was wounded. However, the defenders realised their predicament and requested terms for surrender. Wolseley agreed, and the garrison were allowed to march out without their firearms. Thus, the county was secured for King William and the land south of Cavan town became the frontier zone between the two opposing sides.

Presumably the destruction wreaked by Lloyd and Wolseley rendered the castle uninhabitable, and it was evidently abandoned for good after the war. The castle site was quickly robbed of its stonework for other building projects around the district, and in the passage of time the memory of this castle was soon lost. It is therefore timely that the site of Bellanacargy is now returned to the common memory, so that it can be appreciated again for its contribution to history in the Erne valley.

Castle Tour

Bellanacargy castle exists today only as a memory. A concrete bridge across the minor road represents the ford that was once here, 200m upstream from the castle site, located on the south side of the river. It is possible to park at the bridge and visit Bellanacargy, first passing behind some derelict two-storey farm buildings. (The land belongs to Mr John Brady, a farmer who lives in a two-storey house on the roadside about 1km south, and before proceeding permission should first be sought.) About 100m eastwards from the derelict farm buildings, a 2m-deep drainage channel is crossed near the riverside by a wooden bridge. Beyond, about 30m south of the river, is a rubble-filled knoll covered by hawthorn bushes. This marks all that remains of this once-vital castle and fortress.

The land here has undoubtedly been levelled and drained in the time since the castle was erected. The site now appears as a level field, with so sign of the moat that once surrounded the castle. Unless properly surveyed, the story of this site will remain a well-kept secret, tucked away in this picturesque, out-of-the-way location in the Cavan countryside.

LISNAMAINE
OS SHEET 27, GR 340154

Retrace your steps to Ballyhaise and proceed along the R212 to Cavan for 4km (2.5 miles), before turning onto the N3 signposted for Belturbet. From the town of Belturbet, take the N3/N87 west for Ballyconnell, then turn off left on to the R201 for Killeshandra. After only 200m, there is a minor crossroads. Turn right here and proceed up a steep convex hill. At the summit there is an area of gravelled access to a coarse field on the left. Lisnamaine is reached across this field. Once again, boat users will need to avail of the moorings at Belturbet and follow the above directions.

History

The barony of Loughtee, next to Fermanagh, was assigned to English undertakers in the plantation. Lisnamaine formed part of the 2,000-acre large proportion of Drumany, granted to John Fishe, a native of Bedford, in 1610. Fishe arrived in Ireland in September, taking the Oath of Supremacy at Dungannon and he appointed Robert Burowe of Drumlane as his agent before returning to England. According to Sir George Carew in 1611, Fishe returned the following May with his wife and family, and:

> Brought with him four freeholders, two whereof returned for their families, none of them yet settled. Brought with him artificers and servants of all sorts, 33 or thereabouts. Two English teams of horses with English carts continually employed in drawing materials; oakes felled, and carpenters employed in the woods of Fermanagh, felling more. Arms of all sorts for 35 men, or thereabout; a barrel of powder with match and lock proportionate.

He chose a former hilltop rath at Lisnamaine as the site for his castle, as it had extensive views across his estate, above the former Belturbet to Kildallen road. By July 1611, he had assembled 140,000 locally made bricks at the site and was operating two boats of ten and six tonnes respectively on the River Erne to transport timber. In that year also, he was involved in an ownership dispute with Captain Hugh Culme over the poll of Inishmuck, which both claimed as part of their plantation grant. Inishmuck lay in the midst of Dromany and the commissioners of plantation ruled in favour of Fishe, 'believing that … the grant to Captain Culm [sic] is expressly contrary to the Articles of plantation'.

In April 1613, Sir Josias Bodley reported the manor house at Lisnamaine to be complete, but the bawn still unfinished:

> Mr Fisher hath built a brick house on his proportion of Drumany which is thoroughly finished, being 36 feet square and with defence from spikes and battlements at the top. His house is situated in a rath or Danish fort, on the circumference of which he intendeth to raise a stone wall with six flanks to scour the same.

Nicholas Pynnar visited the estate in 1618/19 and found the following:

> Upon this Proportion the Bawne and castle is long since finished, being very strong, and
> himself with his wife and Family dwelling therein. He hath also built two villages, consist-
> ing of 10 Houses the piece, which are built of Lyme and Stone, and two good Innholders;
> for they stand upon a Road Way.

Twenty-two families were planted, as well as cottagers, and they were able to muster
sixty men. Thus, both bawn and manor house were complete when the Commissioners
Perrott and Annesley reported in their survey of 1622:

> Sir John Fishe, Baronet, hath 2,000 acres, called Drumany. Upon this there is a strong
> bawne of lyme and stone, 8 feet high and 415 feet compasse built upon a rath with a cham-
> ber and drawbridge. Within the bawn there is a strong and handsome house of brick and
> lime, 34 feet square and four stories high.

Fishe had just recently become a baronet, when, as required, he made a generous donation of £1,000 to the Crown in exchange for his title. Previously, he had represented
the county in the parliament of 1613 and was clearly an important player in the early
years of plantation development in Cavan. Sir John died on 25 March 1624, and was
buried in the old churchyard at Drumlane. He was survived by his wife, Lady Mary, his
son, Edward, and two daughters, Mary and Anne. However, the estate was then disputed
between Edward and his sister Mary. Edward resided in England at that time, with his
wife Elizabeth Heton, daughter of the Bishop of Ely, but in 1625 he arrived at Drumany
to take up his entitlement. He was eventually successful in his dispute with his sister, and
received the patent to all his father's lands in February 1629.

But Edward's delight was short-lived, for an inquisition held at Cavan on 30 October
1630 declared all his lands forfeit to the Crown because farms had been leased to tenants who had not taken the Oath of Supremacy. This offence would normally have led
to a large fine and re-granting of the estate under stricter terms, but Edward appears
to have lost total control. Edward may have continued to reside at Lisnamaine, but by
January 1638, the estate had been broken up into smaller parcels and granted to some
of the principal tenants. Thomas Burowes, son of Robert, the original agent to Sir John
in 1610, received land in the Stradone area. The remainder of the estate was divided
between Sir Arthur Culme of Clough Oughter and his uncle, the Revd Benjamin
Culme, Dean of St Patrick's Cathedral, Dublin.

Arthur Culme was one of the largest landowners in the county. On the death of his
father, Captain Hugh Culme in June 1630, he inherited the castle and lands at Clough
Oughter, fourteen townlands at Tullyvin, and the former Waldron estate (later known as
Farnham). The purchase of part of Drumany, therefore, increased his already substantial
portfolio. But later, his lack of preparation for defence at Clough Oughter and the
sudden loss of the castle at the outbreak of the 1641 rebellion damaged his reputation.

After the departure of Edward Fishe in 1638, Lisnamaine was leased to Richard Ashe
Esq. Ashe had previously been employed by Sir Stephen Butler in Belturbet and was
MP for the same borough in 1639. In the rebellion that broke out in October 1641,

Ashe strongly sympathised with the rebels, which led his landlord Sir Arthur Culme to testify that:

> I have been credibly informed that Richard Ashe of Lisnamaine goes to Mass and was at the siege of Drogheda and at most of the rebels' meetings within the county, and at sessions which the rebels kept in the first week of lent he with several others bound himself publically by oath to maintain the cause they had in hand for the freedom of their religion and the liberty of the kingdom they desired.

Ashe was mentioned in other depositions and described as one of the leaders attacking Sir James Craige's garrison at Croaghan castle, near Killeshandra. For this act of rebellion he was expelled as MP from the Irish House of Commons on 26 June 1642. Ashe appears to have remained at Lisnamaine for the remainder of the rebellion and is likely the person who entertained Owen Roe O'Neill, when his army quartered in the area during the winter of 1649. His fate at the end of hostilities in 1653 is unrecorded, but he was probably forced to flee his home.

In the meantime, Sir Arthur Culme had recovered from the loss of Clough Oughter castle on the first day of the rebellion of 1641 and had served as an officer in the army of the Duke of Ormonde. However, in 1649, he changed his allegiance to parliament and achieved the rank of colonel in the New Model army. He was killed at the Siege of Clonmel in May 1650. His widow, Lady Mary, was left without any independent means, as the estates were still in rebel-held areas. Her entitlement, therefore, was, 'the moiety of what rents should be received from his [Sir Arthur's] estates in County Cavan, when again it should please God they should be enjoyed'.

The family estates passed to Sir Arthur's eldest son, Hugh. Two other sons, Philip and Arthur, were both bequeathed £100 each on reaching their twentieth birthdays. A daughter, Elizabeth, was to receive £200 on reaching eighteen, and a daughter Anne was given £115. Lady Culme was also bequeathed 40s to pay for a mourning ring. It would appear, then, that Sir Arthur had left behind a very young family.

Hugh Culme, the heir, returned to his Cavan estates after the war. Clough Oughter castle had been destroyed by the retiring Parliamentarian army in 1653 and it is likely that the house on the mainland opposite had also sustained substantial abuse after twelve years of military occupation by the rebels. He therefore returned to the house at Lisnamaine. In 1662, Hugh married Margaret Parsons, second daughter of Sir William Parsons of Birr, County Offaly. Margaret produced four children: Arthur, Mary, Dorothy and Margaret. Arthur was provost of Belturbet Corporation in 1668 and High Sheriff of Cavan in 1670. When he died in June 1684 at Lisnamaine he was only forty-seven. His mother was still alive and had been living with the family in the house.

Hugh's only son Arthur succeeded him at Lisnamaine. This Arthur married Nicola Cecil Hamilton, who produced a child called Francelina, who died in infancy. Like many of his neighbours, in 1689, Arthur was attainted by the Irish parliament. His wife Nicola died in 1691 and Arthur later married Elizabeth Smyth of Dublin. They had two children, Jane and Hugh. Hugh died young and when his father Arthur died sometime before 1715, the estate passed to Jane Culme, described as, 'the only daughter and heir of the late Arthur Culme of Lisnamaine'.

Jane soon left Lisnamaine to live in England and the estate was sold, together with the castle at Lisnamaine, to the Revd Robert Maxwell of Farnham. Maxwell handed the estate management to his cousin John Maxwell of College Hall, Monaghan. John lived at Lisnamaine for a time, at least until 1719, but when the Revd Robert died, John was bequeathed the Lisnamaine and Farnham estates and chose to live in the latter. He married Judith Barry of Newtownbarry, became Lord Farnham in 1756, and died at his home there in 1759.

Lisnamaine was allowed to quietly decay. A map of 1721 by John Norris shows the house with orchards and gardens. To this day, a field on the side of the hill below the site is known as 'The Castle Park'. In 1819, the castle grounds were leased to a Major Bailie of Carrig Hill. Bailie died in 1852 and the grounds came into the possession of Patrick McGearty, whose Fitzpatrick descendants still own it. What became of Lisnamaine castle, which formerly stood here, has unfortunately been lost in the passage of time.

Castle Tour

Lisnamaine is included here as an example of the difficulty in identifying sparse plantation remains in Cavan. Given the well-documented occupation of the castle in the seventeenth century, it is remarkable that the demise of the castle building is unrecorded. The site today is approached across damp pasture, and all that remains is a rath-shaped earthwork, more resembling of an Iron Age rath. Entrance to the interior is through the bank at the northern perimeter.

The banks and interior of the site are much overgrown, with no masonry evident. The rath bank slopes steeply on all sides but particularly on the east side above the main road, where the bottom of the ditch is 5m below the level of the bank. In the centre of the rath is a long, rectangular, water-filled hollow that has been conjecturally interpreted as the former cellars of a house. If true, then this is the site of Fishe's house, making use of a defensive feature (the rath) of the previous millennium. Only substantial archaeological excavation though would confirm that a brick building once stood here, surrounded by a masonry bawn wall. Today, however, there are no visible remains of brick or masonry to suggest that this was ever a castle.

From the bank of the rath, there are excellent views over the Milltown road below and this would have been a desirable place for a residence. The land hereabouts consists of small, thickly wooded drumlins, containing only small fields of poor grazing. Of the gardens and orchards once shown on John Norris's map, there is no trace.

It is disappointing that so little remains of this historically important castle, and today there is nothing to indicate the contribution of Fishe, Culme and Ashe to the unfolding events that once occurred in this now sleepy backwater of Cavan.

BAWNBOY

OS SHEET 27, GR 213196

From the centre of Bawnboy, take the R200 NW to Swanlinbar for a few hundred metres. Opposite a minor road marked for 'Corlough' is the entrance to 'Bawn Lodge self-catering cottage', on the right through a pair of whitewashed pillars. Pass the entrance cottage and proceed for another

500m along a tree-lined avenue. The overgrown ruins are at the roadside on the left, at the fork of two lanes. Ballyconnell is on the Erne–Shannon Waterway and has moorings. There is a single, daily bus sevice (No.296), which stops at Bawnboy, 7km (4 miles) west on N87.

History

The barony of Tullyhaw, in NW Cavan, was allocated to servitors and deserving Irish at the plantation. During the O'Neill wars, two brothers, Sir Richard and George Grimes (or Graham), each commanded troops of horse under Sir George Carew, President of Munster. Sons of Sir George Graham, a respected servitor from the Reiver country of the Scottish borders, both were highly regarded for their courage in battle and were ideal candidates to receive lands as servitors in the less favourable marchlands of Cavan. Thus, in June 1615, they each received an equal share of the 2,000-acre estate of Corrasmongan in Tullyhaw, which consisted of two proportions each of 1,000 acres.

Describing the estate and presumably the castle at Bawnboy, in 1618, Pynnar noted the following, 'Sir Richard and Sir George Grimes have 2,000 acres. Upon this there is built a Bawn of Stone and Lyme, 60 feet square, and 10 feet high, with a little House in it.' Sir Richard, who was the elder, was styled of 'Corismongan', though he often lived at Ballylynan in Leix, probably the estate of his wife, Elisabeth Hetherington. The Hetheringtons were one of the original seven English families who had settled in the plantation of Leix and Offaly, created by Queen Elizabeth in the 1560s. Sir Richard and Elisabeth had ten children and when he died in November 1625, Sir Richard was succeeded by his son Thomas, then forty years old and already married.

George Grimes had no separate residence and so must have lived at Bawnboy. He was married to Jane Huntingfield and had six children. In 1624, his son William, who was married to Jane Browne of Mulrankan, succeeded him. Davies (1948) states that by 1641, William appears to have owned the whole estate, minus three townlands. The fate of the castle and estate are unknown after this date.

Castle Tour

The ruins of Bawnboy are located in a field at the side of the road, but are difficult to decipher as the interior has become so overgrown. The castle can be inspected by viewing from the roadside here on the Bawn Lodge lane or proceeding further up the lane to the old Templeport GAC grounds and then taking a lane on the left. Neither viewpoint casts a great deal of clarity in deciding which parts, if any, are of the seventeenth century and which are later additions.

The visible ruins here consist of a stone wall facing north across a rough field, 40m in length, with a window in the centre, dressed with sandstone jambs, measuring 0.9m tall by 0.1m wide (36 inches by 4 inches). The window is splayed internally. The full height of the wall is difficult to determine due to overgrowth and collapse.

At the west end of the wall is an extension which projects north, measuring 7.3m by 7.3m (24ft by 24 feet) with walls 0.6m (2ft) thick and up to 4m (13ft) tall. A small splayed loop is located in the middle of the north wall, 1.1m above external ground level, but only 0.45m (18 inches) above the present interior floor level. Internally, this window measures 0.37m high by 0.3m wide (15 inches by 12 inches), narrowing to just 0.1m (4 inches) width on the external face. Curiously, two corbels, 0.3m (12 inches) apart, are located 1.5m above ground level on the east wall.

The west wall of the projection continues south for 25m, but is pierced in the centre by a circular open-backed tower, approximately 8m in diameter externally, which appears to contain a filled-in window on the SW face. Immediately to the north of the tower is a ruined doorway or window. The tower is built of uncoursed rubble masonry. *The Archaeological Inventory of County Cavan* surveyed the site in 1995 and determined that this tower might be a remaining part of the original castle structure. Further internal inspection of the site is difficult, as it is very overgrown, but judging by the unjointed nature of the 8m wall to the south of the tower, this must represent a later addition.

And so it is difficult to determine whether these ruins contain parts of the original structure described by Pynnar, or are part of a later rebuilding scheme by the owners. Perhaps in the future the site will be cleared, and additional archaeological or documentary evidence will become available.

BALLYMAGAURAN
OS SHEET 27, GR 211133

The hamlet of Ballymagauran lies midway between Ballyconnell and Ballinamore, on the R205, close to the Leitrim border. In the hamlet, turn off on to the minor road signposted for Sruhagh Amenity Site. A new brown information sign also directs the traveller to 'Tullyhaw Heritage Trail – Ballymagovern Castle'. The ruins of the castle are situated 100m along this road, in a field on the left, overlooking Ballymagauran Lough. The lough is on the Erne–Shannon Waterway, with the nearest mooring at Sruhagh, about 800m SE of the castle.

History

This territory belonged to the Magauran sept long before the plantation. A rare, fourteenth-century vellum manuscript called the *Book of Magauran*, still in existence, was written as a family book of poetry and indicates the importance of this family here during the latter part of the Middle Ages. At the commencement of the Ulster Plantation, the family received several grants in Tullyhaw, the precinct which had been allotted to both servitors and deserving native families. Phelim Magauran received a 1,000-acre grant in the vicinity of the lough now known as Ballymagauran Lough, on the border with Leitrim. There already was a castle on the lough shore here from the previous century, together with another, now lost, at Lissanover, so this grant was merely a confirmation of the existing status quo. Pynnar described the place in 1618, 'Magauran, a Native, hath 1,000 acres. And upon this he hath built a strong house of Lime and Stone, with a Ditch cut about it.'

Four other grants in Tullyhaw were made to other Magauran family members, totalling 600 acres. Phelim Magauran died in January 1622/3 and was succeeded by his thirty-year-old son Brian, who was married to Mary O'Brien. However, Brian did not enjoy his estate long, dying in 1631, and his son Edward, then only fifteen, succeeded. The family continued to hold the land until at least the end of the 1641 rebellion, when it was likely forfeited by the Cromwellian re-grants.

Though Edward's participation in the rebellion is unknown, the Magauran sept was definitely involved with the rebel cause at the siege of Keelagh castle, during the 1641 rebellion. Following a sortie by the British garrison on 22 April 1642, sixty cows were captured and brought into Keelagh. The raiders suffered no loss, but the Irish later admitted losing forty-five men, of whom fourteen belonged to the Magauran sept. In a deposition by Anne Reid of Drumrelighe, Leitrim, in February 1642, she names Phelim, Daniel and Charles Magauran as persons who 'are and have been in actual rebellion, and have borne arms … robbed, stripped, and received the Protestant's goods when they were taken from them, and have committed other outrages'.

Perhaps less convincingly, Ambrose Bedell, son of the Bishop of Kilmore, deposed that he had been informed by Philip Magauran that his brother Shane Magauran, 'did stab and run through with a skean one Peter Crosse, after another rebel had made him confess his money, and gave it to them, he being a very old man'. Shane is also alleged to have cut off the arm of Crosse's very elderly wife, and supposedly 'he then threw her on the body of her murdered husband, and cast a bank of earth over them both, so that she was thereby smothered or buried alive'.

Such exaggerated tales, related to the demoralised and terrified settlers, were certain to rebound should the rebellion not succeed, and the subsequent confiscation of Magauran land during the Cromwellian period was the inevitable outcome.

Castle Tour

The ruins on this site at Ballymagauran lie beside a minor road, a few metres away from the lough, at the base of a gently rising spur of land. The remnants of the ditch described by Pynnar can be discerned between the south wall and the road, but elsewhere appear to have been filled in. The castle walls are much overgrown, but there are some interesting features to identify in the surviving structure.

The manor house was rectangular in shape, probably a storey and a half high, constructed of rough limestone masonry. Only the west gable and part of the south wall remain to any significant degree. The walls are 0.9m thick, rising to a maximum height of 5m, and the castle plan measured approximately 15.9m by 7.8m (52ft by 25ft) externally. A partition wall, 6m (20ft) long, which appears to be of a later date, runs north from the centre of the south wall to create a room approximately 6 sq m (20 sq ft) internally on the west side.

The SW corner of the gable has been robbed of its cornerstones, but on the NW, the finely hewn quoins remain. There is also apparently a much-ruined stone head on the NW corner, but the upper walls are covered in growth and it can no longer be seen. There is a square recess in the thickness of the wall at the north end, 0.8m by 0.8m (32 inches by 32 inches), with a plain stone lintel, which would have functioned as a cupboard.

The south wall contains a splayed window on the ground floor at the west end, measuring 0.9m by 0.9m (3ft by 3ft) internally, narrowing to 0.45m (18 inches) wide on the outside. The window, only 0.9m (3ft) above the present internal floor level, has lost all of its detailing. Further along the wall, a blocked recess with a flat stone arch can be discerned in the masonry. Eastwards from the partition wall, the south wall projects outwards to accommodate the flue for a hearth. Part of the flue can still be seen, but the external wall has been robbed of its masonry to create a hole at a low level. At the east end of the wall there are traces of a doorjamb. The last 5m (16ft) of visible walling here can only be traced as foundations in the earth, and a proper survey in the future may find that the wall extended beyond this estimate.

First-floor features in the building are even more difficult to determine. The west gable is fairly intact and rises to a peak of 6m (20ft). It contains a window measuring approximately 1.5m by 0.9m (5ft by 3ft), the sill of which is 3.8m (12.5ft) above the current ground level. Once again, a dense ivy covering prevents a closer inspection of the gable. Thus, the scant remains give no real indication of room layout or the possible location of the stairs.

The remains here today appear to describe a long dwelling house rather than a castle-type building. Indeed, the building shows no features of defence whatsoever and if they are indeed the remnants of a castle, it more resembles the defended house-type dwelling as found at Doohat or at Corratrasna. It therefore remains to be proven that these walls are the house described by Pynnar or a later replacement on the same site.

Although there are only meagre remains of this once-important castle, the site chosen by Magauran for his caput, on the shore of this peaceful lough, can be readily appreciated. The lough has a wide variety of wildlife and the visitor will not be disappointed by the beautiful views out across the water to the distant hills of Leitrim.

CROAGHAN
OS SHEET 34, GR 301085

From the centre of Killeshandra, take the R199 for Newtowngore for 1km. Crossing over a bridge, turn immediately right up a steep hill, past Croaghan Presbyterian church, for 300m. The scant remnants of the castle are in the field near the top, on the right. Boat users should again berth at Ballyconnell. There is a Tuesday-only bus service to Killeshandra (No.465) so other private-transport options need to be considered.

History

This castle, together with its neighbour at Keelagh, 2km (1.25 miles) away, played an important part in the 1641 rebellion and the subsequent fate of the British settlers in this area of Cavan, withstanding a seven-month siege and only capitulating when the garrison and refugees were facing starvation.

The precinct of Tullyhoncho, in western Cavan, was originally assigned to Scottish undertakers in the plantation, and the 1,000-acre manor of Drumheada was granted to Alexander Achmootie in June 1610. At the same time, his brother John received the neighbouring small proportion of Keylagh (not to be confused with Keelagh, below), also of 1,000 acres. From this time, the two estates were considered as one. In 1611, Carew reported that the two brothers had not yet appeared on their lands but they had appointed a steward:

> James Craigie [Craig] is their deputy for five years, who has brought four artificers of divers sorts with their wives and families and two servants. Stone raised for building a mill; and trees felled; a walled house with a smith's forge built; four horses and mares upon the land; with competent arms.

However, it is clear that the Achmootie brothers had each already sold their estate to Sir James Craig (or Craige) in August 1610, only two months after receiving the patents for them! In addition to these lands, in 1615 Sir James purchased the 400-acre estate of Dronge from a native, Brian McKernan, who had originally been allotted this land in Tullyhaw precinct by the Crown. Craig was evidently an energetic and resourceful landlord, who was intent on creating a colony of settlers in this part of Cavan. In 1619, Pynnar described the castle Sir James had erected on the estate, now known as the manor of Drumheda and Keylagh:

> Upon this Proportion there is built a strong Bawne of Lime and Stone, 75 feet square, 16 feet high, and four round Towers to flank the wall. He hath also a strong and large Castle of the length of the Bawne, 20 feet broad within the walls, and five stories high. There is another House in building within the Bawne, which is now built to the Top of the wall, and shall be a Platform for two small Pieces [of cannon].

This was a description of the castle at Croaghan. Pynnar also noted that Sir James Craig had settled a total of thirty-three families on his lands, able to muster one hundred men, of which five were freeholders, seven were lessees, and the remainder were cottagers, each with a house and garden and rights to graze their cattle on common land. The nearby town of Killeshandra was clearly part of the colony, providing a site for tradesmen to live and service the estate. However, it is clear that numerous natives still remained resident on the land.

In the 1631 re-grant of the estate to himself and his wife Jane, these lands were described as the manor of 'Castlecraige', containing 2,400 acres with Craig's principal residence at Croaghan. For a period, Sir James was involved in a complex issue regarding 'mearing' (fixing of boundaries) with his neighbour Sir Francis Hamilton of Keelagh, but the matter appears to have been resolved to their mutual satisfaction.

Croaghan was described in 1629 as being 35ft high and within an enclosure perimeter measuring 240ft. If these, and the descriptions of the castle mentioned above, are to be taken at face value, they represent spacious living quarters in the centre of a flourishing colony. In the 1630 muster roll, the estate was able to call up a total of fifty-four men (only half the figure recorded by Pynnar), who could present a total of sixteen swords, fifteen pikes, six muskets and a halberd. However, thirty of these men possessed no weapons at all.

Sir James Craig was also granted an estate of 1,000 acres in the neighbouring Leitrim plantation in Connacht, a scheme which commenced in 1618. The Leitrim plantation was less structured that the Ulster one, and there were fewer conditions with regards to encouraging settlers to the land, but there was an expectation that each grantee

> ...shall within three yeares builde a castle of 30 foote in length 20 foote in breath and 25 foote in height, The castle to be built of stone or bricke with lyme and compassed with a bawne of 300 foote, and 14 foote high of stone or bricke with lime.

This manor was known as Craigstown and stretched west from the border with Cavan at Killegar, thereby marching on the estate at Croaghan. A castle was apparently constructed in the townland of Longfield, just across the border in Leitrim, but has since been removed. This estate was apparently re-granted to Sir James in 1640, which, together with the Castlecraige estate, made him one of the major landholders in this part of the country.

The sustained development at Castlecraige would, however, prove crucial in the survival of the new colonists during the troubled times of the following decade. It is probable that Sir James received a warning about the imminent outbreak of rebellion on 23 October 1641, for the speed at which the surrounding colonists descended on his castle at Croaghan for protection suggests that he had been able to signal his intent to resist the aims of the rebels. In a short space of time the castle was thronged with refugees, 120 men and 340 women, children and old men. They were not long left unhindered.

An Irish army estimated as 2,000 strong, under the command of Edmund O'Reilly, descended on the castle and the neighbouring castle of Keelagh and invested both of them. Judging Croaghan to be the weaker, O'Reilly attacked it first, but was driven off, with the loss of fourteen men. Encouraged by this, Sir James managed to send a message to Sir Francis Hamilton in Keelagh requesting a joint punitive action. As neither castle had sufficient powder for their firearms, scythes were tied onto long poles to create a fearsome pike. At the appointed time, both garrisons sallied forth and assaulted the rebel camp, causing them to scatter and leaving behind thirty-seven dead and several prisoners, including three prominent O'Rourkes and Philip O'Reilly, uncle of Philip McHugh. These four were later exchanged for Bishop Bedell of Kilmore, his two sons, and Thomas Price, Archdeacon of Kilmore, who had been detained at Clough Oughter by the rebels.

As a result of this failure, leadership of the rebels passed to Edward O'Reilly's son Mulmore, who collected together a larger force and invested the two castles in January 1642. Deterred by the size of this force, both Sir James and Sir Francis declined to attack in open combat. Mulmore next assaulted Keelagh, but was again repulsed with huge loss. This defeat is said to have caused the retaliatory massacre of settlers in Belturbet (see Keelagh), which in turn led the two garrisons to raid the surrounding countryside. The Croaghan garrison reported killing fourteen persons, some of whom may have been civilians. Ethnic atrocities were now part of warfare in Cavan.

Mulmore O'Reilly decided to lay siege to both castles, posting strong forces at Brady's Bridge and Ballyhillian Bridge. This soon achieved results, and the castles' inhabitants were reduced to starvation. On 8 April, Sir James died, probably weakened by the awful conditions prevailing at Croaghan, and his wife died a few weeks later. Sir James was buried in Killeshandra churchyard, but his body was later dug up by the besiegers and mutilated. Thomas Price and Ambrose Bedell, son of the bishop, then assumed joint command at Croaghan, but their position was increasingly precarious. At least 160 of the refugees had died, mostly through unclean water and malnutrition. Water had originally been taken from springs outside the castle, but the rebels had poisoned these by throwing dead dogs into them. Sir James had ordered wells to be sunk inside the castle walls, but these had only yielded muddy water, and it is likely that the unsatisfactory sanitation arrangements were also responsible for the high death toll.

With the raising of the siege of Drogheda in the late spring of 1642, more rebel troops were available for a closer investment of the two castles and their fate was sealed. Following joint negotiations, a formal surrender of both castles took place on 15 June.

The two garrisons were permitted to march out with their arms and colours, and were to be escorted to safety, by troops commanded by O'Reilly, to the royal garrison at Drogheda. Over 1,100 colonists then set off on a seven-day journey to safety.

The conditions of surrender allowed the Craig family safe conduct back to Scotland. The fate of the castle at Croaghan after its surrender is not recorded, though undoubtedly the rebels garrisoned it. It must, however, have fallen to the Parliamentarian forces prior to the surrender of Philip O'Reilly in April 1653 at Clough Oughter. One of the articles of capitulation states that, 'Colonel O'Reilly with the party now with him on the west side of Loughern lay down their arms and deliver such forts in the islands, with all the ammunition and provision therein that is in his power, at or before 18 of May at Croghan'.

With Cromwell's victory in Ireland, the Craigs were able to return to Croaghan and reclaim their estates. Hearth Money Rolls (tax levied on the number of hearths in a house) of 1666 record that a Dame Mary Craig had a house with two hearths at Croaghan, so we can surmise that the castle survived the rebellion or was repaired soon afterwards. But war was never very far away in seventeenth-century Ireland.

During the Williamite wars, the importance of the Killeshandra area was again recognised. In April 1690, Colonel Wolseley was ordered to capture the fortress here. Wolseley left Belturbet during the evening with a strong force of Enniskilleners, supported by a regiment of Danish troops under their colonel, Hans Hartman von Erffa. They arrived before the castle at daybreak the following day and surrounded it.

Wolseley had brought scaling ladders and he ordered his engineer Nolibois to reconnoitre the Jacobite position. Colonel Erffa described the castle as having an outer court containing four bastions. Within this was an inner courtyard, 'enclosed by the house and the walls of the old castle. It is flanked by three very high towers, one of which commands the gate of the small court, while the others are in front.' The Jacobites abandoned the outer courtyard (perhaps deeming that they had not enough men to hold it) and withdrew into the house and the old castle. Mining operations to breach the inner courtyard were begun by Nolibois and completed by eleven o'clock. Realising their predicament, the Jacobites sought terms for surrender. They requested to be allowed to march out with arms and baggage, but Wolseley initially answered that they would be treated as prisoners of war. However, as the time to set off the charge drew near, Wolseley relented, and the garrison of 100 marched out. With the loss of only a handful of casualties, the Williamites captured the castle of Croaghan.

What then of the Craig family who had originally settled at Croaghan? A list containing a Robert Craige's County Cavan tenants in 1703/4 is still in existence, so the family may have survived into the following century. However, as the century progressed, the family seem to have hit difficult times. This circumstance may in part be due to internal family squabbling, but whatever the reason the estate was eventually declared bankrupt. The 6,500-acre estate of Castle Craig was finally sold off to the Maxwells of Farnham in the 1730s to pay for accumulated debts. Similarly, the Leitrim lands were sold off at this time, eventually falling into the hands of the Godley family, later Lords Kilbracken, who still reside at Killegar.

The Croaghan estate has since changed hands several times and the name of Craig is now locally quite unknown. The Craig family would appear to have vanished from Cavan, and thus the part played by their former home has almost vanished from memory.

Castle Tour

Considering Croaghan's central role in the events of 1641, the remains of the castle are rather disappointing. All that remains of the castle is a much-ruined circular turret, probably a flanker, which was used in the past as a burying vault for a Presbyterian minister. However, the site will reward the visitor with excellent views towards Killeshandra and will help explain how the proximity of this castle to its equally defiant neighbour at nearby Keelagh was crucial to the settlers' long resistance in 1641/42.

The castle site is on the edge of flat ground at the top of a hill, and 100m south of the present eighteenth-century residence. Today, one approaches the site past mature parkland trees across a somewhat boggy field. To the south and east of this platform, the land falls steeply away in the direction of Killeshandra, but the north and west sides are at the same level as the castle interior. There is no indication of a ditch having separated the castle from the level area to the north, but the passage of time may account for this.

The archaeologist Oliver Davies, who inspected the site in 1950, believed the castle was approximately 50 sq m (165 sq ft), with the surviving turret representing the SW flanker of the original bawn perimeter. However, the recently published *Archaeological Inventory of County Cavan* believes that the turret may be merely a later mausoleum for the minister mentioned earlier, which has reused stone already available on site in the construction. The turret is in a weak condition, with much collapsed stonework lying around.

So, before coming to any workable hypothesis here, the remains of the site need to be closely inspected. This task must begin with the remaining turret. This turret sits on the edge of the field boundary at the SW corner of the flat field described above. To the south, the adjacent field level is up to 1.5m lower and falls away steeply downhill. The circular turret is entered on its north side and has a diameter of 3.2m (10.5ft). The walls are constructed of well-dressed local limestone blocks, presenting a smooth appearance internally. The walls are 0.7m thick and rubble filled, but the southern face of the outer wall has either subsided or, more likely, been robbed of its stone to create two irregular holes. Internally, the walls are up to 3.4m (11ft) high, but are obscured by growth, particularly ivy, which is gradually causing collapse of the structure.

The entrance on the north side is about a metre wide and appears to contain the east jamb of the doorway. But the stonework for the complete circumference of the turret can still be traced in the grass, and it is unclear if the jamb is a later alteration of the site for the burial previously described. The interior level of the turret appears to be much the same as for the ground outside, and a cement render is still extant on the exterior face on the SE.

There is a well-cut loophole facing west, 0.8m above the current internal level. It measures 0.4m high by 0.3m wide (15 inches by 12 inches) internally, narrowing to 0.4m by 0.1m wide (15 inches by 4 inches) externally. The lintel, jambs and roof of the loop are constructed of the same well-cut sandstone as elsewhere. Above this, at a height of about 2m, are three windows which face NW, south and east. Once again, all are well constructed, and internally measure 0.5m by 0.3m wide (18 inches by 12 inches), narrowing to only 0.1m wide (4 inches) externally. The south-facing window has been damaged, possibly by the falling away of the outer wall, but the other two are still in good condition. The NW facing window retains its stone rebate for a window frame.

Externally, the turret wall rebates about 0.15m to form an irregular ledge, which corresponds to the sill of the three windows described above. Although the walls are partly obscured, there is no indication of the turret being connected to any adjoining walling. Again, this could be due to its later remodelling as a mausoleum.

Returning to the site outside again, there are few indications of habitation. About 30m north of the turret there is a mature sycamore tree. To the east of this are some small saplings growing over a low bank. On inspection, the bank contains a lot of rubble, and taken with the two descriptions of the castle in the seventeenth century, may describe the north bawn wall. Of the other features mentioned during the siege (the well containing only fouled water, burial pits of numerous dead, the artillery platform) nothing can be seen.

Finally, mention must be made of the adjacent house, which has the appearance of an eighteenth-century mansion, together with a modern porch and a south wing extension. Stones from the original castle must surely have been quarried to construct this new residence, and this may explain the paucity of remains of the once potent castle of Croaghan.

A square stone plaque leaning against a wall of the adjacent house corroborates the idea that the turret was transformed for use as a mausoleum. Taken from the turret at some time in the distant past, the plaque records that the Revd George Carson and his wife Mary were buried inside the structure. Presbyterian records for the Killeshandra congregation confirm that Carson took up post in May 1735 and served for forty-five years, before illness forced his resignation. He died in January 1782.

What, then, of the theory of the remaining circular turret here? The remains are indeed difficult to determine and a fuller inspection of the site would be beneficial. Much evidence would suggest that the turret is contemporary with the burial. The cut stone in the windows and walls is well constructed and there is no sign of other walls abutting the turret. If the site was robbed for later buildings, why would this one turret survive? Then again, a round mausoleum is unusual and the site, on a hillside field boundary, seems strange, unless the turret was already in existence.

It may well be that part of the old SW flanker survived into the late eighteenth century and that the aging minister favoured this tranquil spot overlooking the town lough as the place of his final repose. The works required to make it suitable may have obscured much of the original structure, so an easy interpretation is no longer possible. However, the site remains to lure the visitor to inspect this peaceful landscape that once witnessed such tragic events, over three centuries ago.

KEELAGH (CASTLE HAMILTON)
OS SHEET 34, GR 318072

From the centre of Killeshandra village, take the left fork for Belturbet on the R201. After 200m, the road bends left but take the lane straight ahead, leading between stone pillars, into the former estate. The old castle site is now indicated by a later walled enclosure with date stones in the entrance arch. The site has now been converted to holiday accommodation. Boat users should see entry for Croaghan.

History

The history of Keelagh castle is bound up with its near neighbour of Croaghan, 2km away to the NW, on the far side of Killeshandra. The part both castles played in a seven-month siege, which began in 1641, was pivotal in the prolonged resistance of the Ulster Plantation settlement in this area of Cavan.

The barony of Tullyhoncho was assigned to Scottish undertakers. The small proportions of Clonkine and Carrotubber were originally granted in July 1610 to Sir Alexander Hamilton of Enderwicke in Scotland. Each grant was of 1,000 acres, but it was hereafter always treated as a single estate. Sir Alexander also received the 'advowson, donation and right of patronage of and in the rectory or church of Killeshandragh', allowing him the right to receive any inherent benefit and to choose its incumbent. However, some ninety acres were exempted from the estate for unspecified reasons.

In addition to these lands, Sir Alexander's second son, Sir Claude Hamilton, was granted the neighbouring small proportion of Clonyn (Clooneen) at the same time. Carew reported in 1611 that Sir Alexander had not appeared on his estates, and that Claude had taken possession of them, supplying the estates with colonists and under-taking various building works, described as follows:

> …two tenants, three servants, and six artificers: is in hand with building a mill, trees felled; hath a minister, but not yet allowed by the Bishop; has raised stones, and hath competent arms in readiness. Besides, there are arrived upon that proportion since our return [to Dublin] from the journey, twelve tenants and artificers who intend to reside there, and to build upon the same.

However, Sir Claude appears to have almost immediately lost interest in his own estate of Clonyn and disposed of it to John Hamilton of Corronery, Cavan, in October 1611. Hamilton sold it to William Lawder of Belhaven in Scotland in December 1614. However, Lawder died on 30 March 1618, and two days later his son Alexander sold it back to Sir Alexander Hamilton, thus returning this estate to the family to whom it had originally been granted. The exact reasons for these convoluted transactions are not clear, but the sale of one of the estates may have been to alleviate cash-flow problems. Given the evident commitment to the development of the estates, however, the frequent sales should not be seen as necessarily a cynical 'fast buck' exercise. George Lawder later appears as a freeholder of two polls on this estate and of course Sir Claude's wife was from the house of Lauder.

Sir Claude was not to enjoy his possessions for long, for he died soon after. Visiting in 1618, Pynnar reported the estate to be in the possession of Sir Claude's widow, Lady Jane, and he described the castle at Keelagh, 'Upon this Proportion there is a strong Castle, and a Bawne of Lime and Stone thoroughly finished, herself with her Family dwelling therein'.

In addition to this, Pynnar reported a total of six freeholders and twenty-five leaseholders, making a total of thirty-one families, together with their undertenants, mustering fifty-two men. Of the neighbouring estate of Clonyn, the picture was less satisfactory, as the early death of Sir Claude had prevented its full development. No castle had been erected on the estate, but a town of twenty-two houses had been built.

However, tenants had not yet been issued with their estates, as Lady Jane held the estates in trust for her son and heir, Sir Francis, who was still a minor.

A later inquisition recorded that in July 1621, Sir Alexander had granted the estates of Carrotubber and Clonkine to his grandson Sir Francis, probably on his coming of age. Lady Jane, Francis's mother, had, in the interim, married Sir Arthur Forbes of Granard (later Earl of Granard), a knight and baronet in his own right. This inquisition also recommended that the weekly Monday market at Killeshandra should be moved to a Wednesday and that the two fairs currently held on St Simon's and St Jude's Days should be augmented with a third on St Barnaby's Day. These changes were not deemed detrimental to any fairs or markets, 'there not being anie town or place within 8 myles distant of the said towne of Killeshandra'.

The castle at Keelagh built on the Clonkine proportion is described a few years later as:

> ...one bawne of lyme and stone 60 foote square and 12 foote in height; and within the same is built a fayre and sufficient castle or capitall mansion house of lyme and stone, four storyes in height, with flankers and turretts for the better defence thereof, and two turrets of lyme and stone upon the wall, for defence thereof.

At this time the town of Killeshandra had grown to thirty-four English-style wood-framed houses.

The three proportions of Carrotubber, Clonkine and Clonyn were re-granted to Sir Francis in June 1631, and were henceforth to be known as the manor of Castlekaylaghe, consisting of 3,000 acres. Under the original terms of his plantation grant, a bawn was to be built on the Clonyn proportion and this was duly completed at Derendreheid (now Bawn townland overlooking a lough of the same name). All trace of this residence, described as a two-storey house within a rectangular bawn, has since disappeared.

In the 1630 muster roll for the county, it is recorded that Sir Francis Hamilton owned an estate consisting of 3,000 acres, and that from his tenantry he could muster a total of 114 men. These were in possession of a number of weapon types: swords, pikes, muskets, calivers and snaphaunces (a type of pistol). However, seventy-four men were recorded as having no arms.

Sir Francis had been created 1st Baronet of Killaugh, Cavan, on 29 September 1628, with a grant of 16,000 acres in Nova Scotia. He was invested as a Privy Counsellor and was the MP for Jamestown from 1639 to 1648. Sir Francis married Laeticia Coote, daughter of Sir Charles Coote of Castle Coote, Roscommon, the Marshall of Connacht, and they had a son called Charles. Hamilton was thus in a position to exploit his Cavan lands, but the progressive development of the estate was soon to be to be rudely shattered.

Though there is no conclusive proof, Sir Francis appears to have been warned by Sir William Cole of the imminent outbreak of the rebellion of 23 October 1641, for he sent word of it to the inhabitants of Belturbet that evening and was able to hastily gather in all the outlying settlers and bring them under the protection of his castle at Keelagh. He was not of a mind to give up his hard work so easily, and together with Sir James Craig, his countryman at nearby Croaghan castle, he resolved to resist the rebels' demands to leave the country. A total of 286 able-bodied men and 700 women, children and old men (those deemed too old to take up arms) now sought his protection, with a further 460 persons sheltering within the walls of neighbouring Croaghan. The part played by the third castle at Bawn, a little to the south of Croaghan, is today unclear, though it would have been foolish to simply abandon it and allow it to be occupied by the rebels. Furthermore, Killeshandra lies between two loughs, and garrisons placed in Croaghan, Bawn and Keelagh would undoubtedly have protected the town from any assault on the open flanks.

On 23 October 1641, the citizens of Belturbet and the surrounding district accepted the terms presented by Philip O'Reilly and began to evacuate on that first day of the rebellion. In the town of Cavan, John Bayley commanded a force of fifty soldiers, but lack of supplies prevented him withstanding a siege and he surrendered to the O'Reillys on 29 October. The ordinary soldiers were disarmed but Bayley and the officers were allowed to retain their weapons for self-defence and to live in a thatched house in the town. In a foray from Keelagh led by Sir Francis's son Malcolm, together with David Creighton and James Somerville, Bayley and his companions were brought into the castle. This move was probably unopposed by the rebels, who would have been relieved to dispense with the obligation to feed these extra mouths.

The lull in hostilities was soon to be broken. An Irish army allegedly numbering 2,000, composed of equal numbers of men from Cavan and Leitrim under the command of Edmund O'Reilly (father of Mulmore, or Myles), approached the settler enclave at the end of October, and, judging Croaghan to be the weakest point, began an assault. However, they were beaten off, leaving behind fourteen killed. The commander at Croaghan, Sir James Craig, now sent word across to Sir Francis Hamilton at Keelagh, arguing for a simultaneous assault the following evening, to which Sir Francis agreed. Due to the lack of gunpowder for their firearms, the defenders attached their scythes to long poles, creating a ferocious weapon. The next evening, being frosty, they sallied out of their respective castles and attacked the rebel camp, causing it to scatter, killing thirty-seven and capturing three prominent O'Rourke family members and Philip O'Reilly, the uncle of the rebel leader Philip McHugh.

These prisoners proved valuable. They were exchanged on 7 January for the Bishop of Kilmore, William Bedell, his two sons and Mr Thomas Price, Archdeacon of Kilmore, all of whom had been held prisoner at the insurgent camp of Clough Oughter castle since December. But Keelagh was soon to be threatened again. During January 1642, another Irish army was assembled, this time numbering 3,000 strong under the command of Mulmore O'Reilly, son of Edmund, who had previously led the rebel army before the walls at Croaghan.

Sir Francis went out from Keelagh to meet this threat on open ground but was evidently deterred by the numbers of his opponents and retired to the safety of the castle. The following morning, Colonel Mulmore O'Reilly gathered an assault team of selected men, reportedly fortified by whiskey, and threw them into a desperate attack on Keelagh. But again they were repulsed, with the reported loss of 167 men, although the rebels did succeed in driving away all the garrison's cattle. Such an act was fatal to the garrison's survival and placed the defenders in a precarious situation. However, a raid into Leitrim brought back 40 cows and 200 sheep, which helped to relieve the dwindling food situation.

The failure of the insurgents before the walls of Keelagh was to have more tragic consequences. Angered at their stinging defeat, a party of armed insurgents entered the town of Belturbet at the end of January. Despite the earlier exodus of settlers, some British families had remained. The insurgents, led by two Mulpatricks and a man named Philip O'Togher, began to round them up and murder them. Two settlers were hanged and a further thirty-five persons, mainly women and children, were forced into the icy waters of the River Erne and drowned. Many of these victims were related to the defenders at Keelagh and Croaghan, so it was inevitable that a revenge attack would be undertaken. Vowing to give no quarter, parties from both Keelagh and Croaghan simultaneously raided out into the adjoining countryside, bent on revenge. The Keelagh party are reported to have killed thirty-nine and the Croaghan party fourteen. Undoubtedly some of those killed were civilians.

Following the second reversal, Mulmore decided that the best tactic would be to starve out the garrisons, rather than attempt to capture them by direct assault without artillery. He thus posted large pickets at Brady's Bridge and Ballyhillian Bridge, which also ensured easy communications were no longer possible between the two castles. These tactics soon began to take effect. The defenders were increasingly forced to expose themselves in foraging raids into the countryside with diminishing returns. By April, Sir James Craig and his wife at Croaghan had died, along with 160 refugees.

Likewise at Keelagh, conditions deteriorated to famine conditions, with the inhabitants forced to eat horse and dog meat. Sir Francis and his wife also fell ill, and in desperation, his son Malcolm and the seventeen-year-old Sir Archibald Forbes took charge. On 22 April they sallied out, accompanied by the more robust women and children, on their desperate mission. Sixty cows were seized and with the men protecting their flanks, the women and children successfully drove them into the much-relieved camp. The insurgents were reported to have lost forty-five men, fourteen of whom were of the Magauran clan. There is no record of the settler casualties, but such a mixed group must surely have suffered some losses.

This raid brought momentary relief, but such acts were becoming increasingly difficult to carry out, as the noose around the enclave tightened. When the Siege of Drogheda by the investing Irish army was lifted, extra troops became available to press the desperate defenders at Keelagh and Croaghan. By the end of May, the siege was so complete that no supplies could be brought into the castles and the end of the road was in sight. Having withstood seven months of privation, Sir Francis offered to surrender and requested that he be permitted to meet with the garrison at Croaghan to discuss its terms. This was granted, and he crossed to Croaghan to confer with Ambrose Bedell and Thomas Price, the leaders there since the demise of Sir James Craig. After a lengthy debate, Mulmore O'Reilly was recalled and surrender terms were agreed between both parties.

The garrisons and the civilians were permitted to march out of their castles with all their guns and colours and, under the personal protection of Mulmore O'Reilly, were escorted to the Crown garrison at Drogheda. Thus, on the 15 June, 800 survivors from Keelagh and 300 from Croaghan abandoned their refuge of seven months. After a march of seven days the weary and starving refugees reached the protection of Drogheda, where the garrison, under the command of Sir Henry Tichbourne, came out to meet them. So ended one of the longest and costliest sieges of the entire 1641 rebellion in Ulster. The fall of both castles had effectively cleared Cavan of settlers, and it became a stronghold of the insurgent army for the remainder of the war.

The war ended in 1653 and Sir Francis Hamilton returned to Cavan. We do not know in what state he found Keelagh, but he quickly set about restoring his home. During the restoration of Charles II, he acted as a commissioner for the Act of Settlement and represented Cavan County as MP from 1661 to 1666. During this time, his title was adapted to 1ˢᵗ Baronet Hamilton of Castle Hamilton, County Cavan, thus recognising his efforts to sustain the plantation at Killeshandra during the late rebellion. Following the death of Laeticia Hamilton, he married Elizabeth Barlow, daughter of Randall Barlow.

Sir Francis Hamilton died in 1673 and was succeeded by his son Sir Charles, born sometime before 1641, who became the 2ⁿᵈ Baronet. Charles was MP for County Donegal from 1661 to 1666 and held the office of *Custos Rotulorum* in February 1674. He married Francelina (or Catherine) Sempill (or Semple) of Letterkenny, and they had a son, Francis and two daughters, Nicola and Dorothy. Francelina evidently died, for Charles married Penelope Haward sometime after December 1685. His wedded bliss was cut unexpectedly short, as he died before May 1689, without having written a will.

Francis, born in 1656 or 1657, succeeded his father and became the 3ʳᵈ Baronet. Like his father, he would be twice married, first to Catherine Montgomery, daughter of the Earl of Mount Alexander (who died when only twenty-nine), and later to his cousin Anne Hamilton, daughter of Claud and Anne Hamilton, on 26 March 1695. However, neither marriage produced surviving children, although he had an illegitimate daughter named Frances Tweedy. Francis was evidently an active politician and was attainted by the 1689 parliament of James II, although he returned safely to his inheritance following the cessation of hostilities. His political career was likewise unharmed, for he served as MP for County Cavan on three separate occasions – 1693, 1695 to 1699, and 1703 to 1713 – with a spell as MP for Donegal in 1694.

When he died, aged fifty-eight on 4 February 1714, he had no son to succeed him and the baronetcy thus became dormant. His two sisters, Nicola and Dorothy, both of whom had married, became co-heiresses. A large memorial was placed in the old parish church in Church Street, Killeshandra by his widow Anne, commemorating the achievements of the Hamilton family of Castle Hamilton. It was later removed to the present church when it replaced the older building in 1841.

Nicola Hamilton married Philip Cecil and had a son, Arthur Cecil Hamilton, who became heir to his maternal uncle's estate at Castle Hamilton. Part of the arrangement for inheritance must have required Arthur to take the surname of Hamilton. In 1720, Arthur Cecil Hamilton married Anne Connor, heiress of Thomas Connor of Dublin. They had two daughters, Margaret Cecil Hamilton and Nicola Cecil Hamilton.

Writing in 1739, Dean Henry, in his diary *Upper Lough Erne*, is clearly referring to this family in his account of Castle Hamilton. The estate mansion is described as standing 'on an eminence, to which there is on every side an ascent … The imagination cannot easily conceive the various agreeable prospects of wood, water hills, lawns and plantations which on every side encompass this sea.'

The description of the building also throws some light on the changes that had been made since the previous century:

It has two fronts: the western, which is the principal front, is extended about 200 feet …
The entrance into this front is by a spacious stucco'd hall, properly adorned with Cornish
pilasters and niches; this is reputed the largest hall in the kingdom, being forty-four feet in
length, and in breadth thirty-four; the height is equal to the breadth.

In 1744, Margaret Cecil Hamilton married Sir Thomas George Southwell, 1st Viscount
Southwell. Their second son, Lieutenant Colonel Robert Henry Southwell, Lieutenant
Colonel of the 8th Dragoons, bought the estate at Castle Hamilton for himself and
his family. In the Statistical Survey of County Cavan (1801), the owner is cited as a
Colonel Southwell, who was living in a newly built mansion, presumably a successor
to the Georgian period building. *Slater's Directory of 1846* records that Robert Henry
Southwell, MP for Cavan (son of the above), was the current owner. However *Burke's
Peerage* (1879) states that this Southwell had sold the estate to James Hamilton, a wine
merchant from Dublin, in 1844. Hamilton was a far-out descendant of the original
occupier, Sir Alexander Hamilton, and thus the estate returned to the family after a long
period of absence. In June 1843, James married his cousin Mary Matilda Dickson, and
they had three sons and four daughters. In 1878, the estate consisted of 1,949 acres and
was valued at £1,875. A fire in 1911, started accidentally when a heater was overturned
in a chicken outhouse, damaged the remnants of Castle Hamilton and the mansion. A
new house was subsequently built nearby.

The last Hamilton at Castle Hamilton was Major William J. Hamilton, who lived there
with his wife, Florence Frances. William died in 1931, aged eighty-one years, and when his
widow died in 1952, the estate was sold to a family named Fletcher. Since that time, the
remnant of the estate has been further fragmented, with the site of the original castle now
surrounded by later buildings, and some converted to holiday accommodation.

Castle Tour

As with its neighbour on the other side of Killeshandra, the castle of Keelagh has not
survived to the present day. The site is approached along a modern road beside well-
tended parkland and borders, and the stable enclosure to the right represents the site of
the former castle of Keelagh, which once stood here, although the exact position is now
a mystery. The Georgian mansion described by Henry in 1739 must have incorporated
or superseded the original castle. Burned in 1911, this house once stood in the parkland
here, between mature oaks.

The restored stable enclosure has two datestones of 1610 and 1789, placed either side
of the main entrance. The 1610 stone refers to the original grant, but the reason for the
1789 date is unclear, though it may refer to the erection of the stable blocks and yard in
that year. This stable-yard area, which has been refurbished to provide holiday accommodation, is accessed through a stone archway, and it has a modern appearance and
has been pleasantly conserved. The modern, well-cut blocks of the walls, however, do
contain a few courses of older rubble masonry in places near ground level, which may
indicate the original castle site, but it is impossible to be more certain.

Visiting the site in the 1940s, the archaeologist Oliver Davies believed that part of the
original might still exist. He described a rectangular tower, 7 sq m with walls 0.7m thick,
which he believed to be part of the bawn. Three first-floor windows did not look original,

but a smaller, blocked one on the north side may have been a loophole. Davies was unable to ascertain the exact location of the rest of the bawn, though he noted that the stable yard was said locally to be on the site of the old castle. Tantalising as this description is, the tower described by Davies can no longer be identified. There are large foundations just west of the stable yard, where other sheds were demolished quite recently, but only a full excavation on the site will allow definite conclusions to be drawn.

There is an interesting small stone plaque now placed in the wall of the stable yard. It appears to show a coat of arms depicting an animal, possibly a gryphon, standing on its rear legs, flanked by a trio of roses above a rectangular chequerboard. Beneath the chequerboard is another rose motif. It is tempting to believe that it once looked down across the original castle of Keelagh, erected by the Hamiltons all those years ago.

So as with its neighbour, the remains at Keelagh are elusive and now very difficult to determine with any certainty. Given the importance of the site in the town's history, it is a pity that no permanent reminder is visible in the landscape today.

CLOUGH OUGHTER
OS SHEET 34, GR 358078

From the centre of Cavan, take the Crossdoney road (R198) for about 5km (3 miles) and then take the road on the right signposted for Killykeen Forest Park. Follow these signs as far as the park. Once at the entrance, continue right, now following the signs to 'L Oughter'. The lake is visible on the left of the road. After about 3km (2 miles), the road ends in a small car park. The castle is just out of sight, around the shore to the right, on an island in the centre of the lake. Walk along the shore to view it.

Lough Oughter is navigable but unfortunately there is no access to it from other waterways. The castle is not on a public transport route. Boat users will need to consider other transport options.

History

Clough Oughter is not, strictly speaking, a plantation castle, though the ruins we see today represent the last modifications carried out on the structure at the commencement of the Ulster Plantation. However, as with other medieval castles in use during the seventeenth century, such as Enniskillen, its importance in the subsequent course of history in the Erne valley ensure that it is here included.

Situated on a rocky island, 120m from the shore of Lough Oughter, the early history of Clough Oughter castle is shrouded by uncertainty, with its construction date a matter of some debate. Most sources attribute the erection of the castle to William Gorm de Lacy in the 1220s, when the Normans were attempting to penetrate this area of south Ulster. At the same time, an earthen motte-and-bailey castle was constructed beside the river at Belturbet and at Kilmore and it is unclear if the first castle was similarly constructed.

But the de Lacys then fell out with the Crown regarding their attempt to control the earldom of Ulster, and in 1224, the Irish, led by an O'Reilly, laid siege to the castle. The Irish managed to capture the castle, together with William's mother (a daughter of Rory O'Connor), William's wife, and his sister-in-law. When finally the differences with the king were resolved, the Crown permitted the return of other captured castles to de Lacy, but not Clough Oughter. It thus fell under the control of the O'Reillys, who emerged as the prominent family in East Breifne (later Cavan county) during the later medieval period. In any case, the presence of a stone castle at Clough Oughter is first mentioned in 1327. The O'Reillys remained in control of the castle until the end of the sixteenth century, though it was not their principal seat.

The O'Reilly chieftain, Hugh Conallagh O'Reilly. died in 1583 and was succeeded by his son John, who visited the court of Elizabeth I. Here he was knighted and placed in possession of most of Cavan, including Clough Oughter. But John later sided with Hugh O'Neill against the Crown and was killed in rebellion in 1596. His eldest son, Maol Mordha O'Reilly, an ally of the Crown, succeeded him, but was killed at Yellow Ford in August 1598, fighting Hugh O'Neill, and the O'Reilly succession was left undecided. Maol's widow, Katherine Butler, was described as the warden of Clough Oughter in 1601 and 1602.

The castle appears to have already fallen into disrepair by the end of the sixteenth century. But Lord Deputy Chichester was aware of its strong position and ensured that the castle was included in the plantation as one of the proposed royal arsenals. He described its attributes:

> … an old castle without roof, standing in a lough in the county of Cavan which he [Chichester] meant to take into the King's hands and make fit to contain a store of munition and victuals to supply that county upon occasion it being passable by boat, with a little help over a ford or two, almost to Balashanan.

Thus, from the outset, Clough Oughter was destined to play an important role in the development of the Ulster Plantation in the Upper Erne area. But before Chichester could put his plans into action, Richard Nugent, Baron Delvin, escaped from imprisonment in Dublin in late 1607 and made his way to Clough Oughter, described as 'a strong castle … which standeth in the middle of a great lough'. Nugent wrote to the Lord Deputy, Sir Arthur Chichester, pleading for mercy, but he received no reply. The Marshall of Ireland, Sir Richard Wingfield, arrived before the castle's walls at the head of 200 foot and a troop of horse and promptly captured it, finding the young son of Delvin inside. The baron himself had already fled, making his escape in disguise, dressed as a 'woodkerne in mantle and trouses'.

In November 1610, the castle, fishing rights in the lough, and five polls of adjacent land were finally granted for a period of twenty-one years to the servitor Captain Hugh Culme, also a grantee of lands in Ballyconnell and Virginia. Culme was responsible to the government for the repair and provisioning of the castle, as well as providing it with a garrison. Estimates for such costs were submitted in 1608 and 1610, but the government were keen to reduce military expenditure and so the garrison was later discharged. Culme's lease was renewed in 1620 for a further twenty-one years and he remained in the role of constable as before, being expected to carry out repairs from the revenue raised from the grant of the attached lands.

Culme also built himself a fortified house on the mainland, directly opposite the castle. Known as the 'castle offices', this appears to have been an L-shaped building, the long axis aligned NE–SW. In 1620, a bill was submitted for £200 for repairs at Clough Oughter, but three years later the castle was described as needing repairs, so this bill may refer to the building of Culme's house on the mainland. No trace of this house is visible today.

Culme was elected MP for the borough of Cavan in 1613, but the election was later declared void due to irregularities in the process. Instead, in 1619, Culme turned his attention to the establishment of the plantation borough of Virginia. He was knighted in 1623 and reportedly died at Clough Oughter (probably the house on the mainland) in 1630. On his death, the castle and its lands passed to his son Sir Arthur Culme. Arthur also lived in the mainland house and was later to be accused of failing to meet his obligations with respect to the proper repair and provisioning of the island stronghold, including the neglect of doors, windows and floors, circumstances that would later have tragic consequences. Of Arthur Culme's neglect, the following contemporary account bears witness:

> …though he had in his house ten pounds worth of sugar and plums, yet he had not one pound of powder, nor one fixed musket for the defence of it; and therefore it was the first place they [the rebels] seized upon; and he the first that was clapped in it…

Thus, it was on 23 October 1641, at the commencement of the rebellion, that the castle fell to the rebel Irish, with Owen McTurlough O'Reilly becoming the constable. Culme, his wife and family were kept prisoners in their own home. Richard Castledyne, the owner of Farnham castle, also appears to have been apprehended by rebels around this time, and he too ended up as a prisoner at Clough Oughter.

In his defence, Arthur Culme later stated that he had only become aware of the situation around 7p.m. on 23 October, when a report reached him that stated Clones had fallen to a group of the rebels supported by some 'Scotch forces' and that the Sheriff, Mulmore O'Reilly, was raising forces to restore order. Soon after, O'Reilly called at his home and asked to speak to him. Not suspecting foul play, Culme opened the door, and 'there rushed in divers men with skeans, swords, pistols and pikes, and seized his house, demanding the key of Clough Oughter castle'. It would therefore appear that Culme was apprehended in his house on the mainland. Such a circumstance greatly contributed to the ease with which one of the main arsenals in Cavan fell so conveniently into the hands of the conspirators.

On 18 December, the prisoners were joined by William Bedell, the Bishop of Kilmore, together with his two sons William and Ambrose, his step-son-in-law Alexander Clogy, and Edward Parker the rector of Belturbet, in retaliation for the capture of four O'Rourkes by the Keelagh and Croaghan garrisons. These persons were transferred to Clough Oughter from Bedell's home at Kilmore, where the bishop had established a refuge for fleeing British settlers from the surrounding countryside. Curiously, Bedell had not been disturbed in this activity, despite the tumultuous events occurring around him. The reason may have been his usefulness as an intermediary in negotiations with the Lord Justices in Dublin. In any case, the Irish treated him with great respect and had allowed him to continue his pastoral care at Kilmore unhindered, until now. The men named were thus taken to Clough Oughter, while the wives of the two Bedell brothers were transferred to the home of Dennis Sheridan, a native Protestant clergyman, who lived nearby.

Clogy described this new prison in unflattering terms when he stated, 'there was of old a little island about it, but it worn all away to the bare stone walls, and not one foot of ground was to be seen only a tall, round tower, like a pidgeon house, standing in the midst of the waters'.

O'Reilly treated all his captives with some humanity and allowed the bishop to continue his worship in the castle. Mr Clogy, a prisoner and eyewitness had this to say of the gaolers, 'They often told the bishop, that they had no personal quarrel with him; and no other cause to be so severe with him, but because he was an Englishman.'

The prisoners were kept in an upper room of the castle, with the garrison occupying rooms below. There could have been little communication with the outside world, but Bedell could speak Gaelic and we are told that by means of placing an ear over a chink in the floor, they overheard the soldiers discussing the siege at Drogheda. Sir Arthur Culme's earlier neglect, particularly the lack of window glazing, meant that the conditions during a cold winter were grim indeed, despite the efforts of Castledyne to make good with his skills as a carpenter. The bishop's health quickly deteriorated, and on 7 January 1642 he was transferred, along with his two sons and Mr Clogy, to the mainland, to the house of Dennis Sheridan, where they were reunited with the wives. Sheridan, a former Catholic priest who Bedell had earlier converted to Anglicanism, had also taken an English wife, but this transformation had not brought down the wrath of the rebels and he had been left undisturbed at his home near Kilmore.

Despite the move to better accommodation, Bedell's condition never improved and he died around midnight on 7 February. His funeral in Kilmore graveyard two days later was treated as a semi-military affair and attended by many prominent native families involved in the on-going rebellion. Philip O'Reilly had the army form a guard of honour, from Sheridan's house to the graveyard at Kilmore. At the graveside, a volley of shots was fired and the troops cried out in Latin, 'may the last of the English rest in peace'.

On 23 April, Sir Arthur Culme, his wife and eldest son, were exchanged for rebel prisoners and transferred to the Crown garrison at Drogheda. William and Ambrose Bedell remained at Sheridan's under a form of open arrest until the castles at Keelagh and Croaghan surrendered on terms, during June 1642. They were then permitted to leave with their wives (who had been detained at Sheridans since December). At the same time, Richard Castledyne and his family were also freed and permitted to accompany the exodus of over 1,200 British refugees to Dublin. Culme then joined the service of the Duke of Ormond, becoming an officer in the army. He later transferred his loyalty to the cause of Cromwell and died at the Siege of Clonmel in 1650.

The inaccessible nature of Clough Oughter meant that it continued to be used by the rebels as a prison and a headquarters throughout the uprising. In June 1646, it was used to incarcerate Viscount Montgomery and other officers captured following the defeat of Robert Monro's Scottish army at the battle of Benburb. In late June 1646, Owen Roe O'Neill brought the Irish army of Ulster to the area and encamped at Crossdoney, near to the castle of Lismore, which belonged to Philip 'The Black' O'Reilly.

O'Neill was later joined here by Monsignor Massari of Fermo in Italy. Massari had accompanied Papal Nuncio Rinuccini to talks with the Confederation and arrived at Crossdoney to present some gifts to O'Neill and his officers to celebrate their victory. Massari then accompanied O'Neill to Clough Oughter, which he described as, 'an impregnable fortress in the middle of a large lake', surrounded by a thick wall and capable of holding a garrison of 100 men. Massari then met the captive Lord Montgomery and two of his senior officers in a room near the top of the castle, striking up a conversation with him in Italian. As the Monsignor left, Montgomery presented him with an elaborate watch, which was capable of indicating the hours, days and months of the year including the phases of the moon. The following day, Montgomery wrote to Massari to ask if an exchange of prisoners could be made. But the Monsignor explained in his reply that the matter was not in his hands, although he would use his influence with O'Neill to affect that outcome. However, the value of the captured lord was, at this time, too great to bring about the exchange, and he remained incarcerated. Following requests made by both the English and Scottish parliaments in December 1647, Lord Montgomery and Colonel Theophilus Jones were finally released in a prisoner exchange.

In the summer of 1649, Owen Roe O'Neill's army somewhat surprisingly assisted the Parliamentarian garrison of Londonderry in raising the Royalist siege, and then returned to Clough Oughter. By now, O'Neill's health was failing and he is reported to have died at Clough Oughter castle on 6 November 1649. As the castle was probably in a poor state, as previously described, it is likely that O'Neill had been confined to Culme's house on the shore. He was buried in the Franciscan monastery of St Mary in Cavan town.

By early 1653, nearby Trinity island was seized by the Parliamentarian army, leaving Clough Oughter the only stronghold left in rebel hands in Ulster. It finally succumbed to the Parliamentarian army on 27 April, when Philip MacHugh O'Reilly signed the Articles of Clough Oughter, and handed it over to Colonel Theophilus Jones, its former prisoner. O'Reilly and his garrison were permitted to join the army of Spain. The castle was then slighted on the south side, facing the land, by the removal of approximately one third of the tower walls using a large amount of gunpowder. As a consequence of the damage caused by the explosion, the castle has remained abandoned ever since. So ended over 400 years of history at Clough Oughter.

Castle Tour

The remains of Clough Oughter castle are located on a small island in the middle of the passage between Inishconnell and Rinn, 130m from the former. The island today measures 60m by 35m, but the historical lake level was at least 2m higher, reducing its size to a little more than 25m. The lough would have been even higher in winter, and water must have lapped the castle walls. Following its inclusion in a list of 'National Monuments' by the Republic of Ireland government, the castle was excavated over a six-week period in 1987 as part of an extensive conservation programme.

The remains today consist of a cylindrical tower of four storeys, 18.35m (61 feet) tall and with an external diameter of 15.5m (52ft). The massive walls, 2.5m (8ft) thick, are constructed of random rubble blocks. As a result of the 1653 explosion, about one third of the perimeter wall on the south side has been destroyed down almost to ground level. The tower was filled with this debris for over 300 years, until the site was fully excavated in 1987, leading to extensive conservation work.

Removal of the debris uncovered four bodies. Three skeletons were found in a shallow grave outside the SW perimeter. One of these was a woman and she had been buried with most of her skull missing. These bodies are likely to have belonged to some of the garrison killed in the siege of 1653. The fourth body was found directly under the debris. It was that of a contorted male, who appears to have been killed by the explosion that destroyed the south side of the tower.

Remains of an L-shaped, clay-bonded wall, perhaps constructed to protect the present doorway, can still be seen just in front. Today, the ground floor is entered through the remains of a splayed doorway in the south wall. This doorway was not the original entrance and was only later cut through the ground floor perimeter wall. The explosion destroyed the east jamb of this doorway, but part of the lower west jamb survives, containing a portcullis slot and rebate for a door behind. An iron grill also protected the doorway. The floor was mortared, overlying a 2m fill of loose stones.

Remnants of a cross-wall, 1.8m thick and running east–west, can be seen, which would have divided the tower's interior into two equal spaces. This wall rested on huge timbers, long rotted away. In the southern part, near the middle of the wall, there was a fireplace. West of this was a doorway, which allowed access to the northern part of the ground floor. This wall is not bonded into the perimeter wall and so must be part of a later remodelling.

Two large embrasures, roofed by flat stone arches, survive on the perimeter, facing east and NW respectively. The east embrasure measures 1.6m wide by 1.5m high. The NW embrasure is 2m wide and 1.4m high. Both embrasures penetrate the wall for most of its thickness, before splaying to narrow vertical lights on the external face. Both are 1m above the current interior level and display marks of wicker centring in their roof construction. There is a possibility that a third such embrasure was located in the south wall, but the explosion has destroyed any trace of it. The design and construction of both surviving embrasures suggests they were part of the original medieval castle.

Eleven large sockets, 0.3m deep, to carry the first-floor joists, can be seen along the internal north perimeter wall. A single socket also survives on the south wall near the doorway. These joists ran at right angles to the cross-wall, which may have partially supported the floor. In addition, there is a groove in the east and west walls, which must indicate the marks of the floorboards which ran across the joists. The boards were between 0.05m and 0.07m thick. Castles constructed in the medieval period were generally entered via a stone or wooden stairway at first-floor level and this was also the case at Clough Oughter. Part of the original doorway arch with drawbar slot can still be seen on the SW perimeter. Two other doors, one on the north and one on the SE, once led out to a curtain wall. This wall was removed at some time in the past and the doors partly walled up to act as windows. There were three windows on this floor as well. The one beside the north door was later closed up and a new loop cut through the wall to the left to form a smaller loop.

Above this level, there is a distinct change in the masonry. The bottom two storeys were constructed of quarried limestone, but the upper two storeys are different, constructed from a more weathered grey limestone that contrasts with the stonework below. The upper two storeys must therefore be later work. This view is supported by the different design used in the construction of the upper windows. Two splayed window embrasures survive at second-floor level, facing north and east. Above this, a single window of two lights, facing north, still exists at third-floor level. Above this level, part of the parapet wall remains. Nine merlons remain, up to 2.5m high, with the intervening embrasures measuring 0.9m in height. The roof appears to have been slated, as excavation of the site discovered red roof tiles in the rubble of the explosion.

And so, the castle shows at least four phases of construction over its 400-year period of occupation. The original structure, perhaps of 1220, comprised a two-storey round tower with a curtain wall, which ran from the north doorway around to the west to join up with the doorway on the SE, enclosing a narrow yard about 6m wide. Entrance to the castle was via a wooden stair to the door at the SE on the first floor. At some later time in the medieval period, the tower was raised by a further two floors and the curtain wall removed to make space for a stair tower of similar height on the north side. This stair tower meant that the first-floor window to the left of the north doorway had to be blocked up and the new loophole cut through to the east of the original window.

A third remodelling saw the removal of the turret on the north side and the cutting of the entrance at ground-floor level on the south. To protect this doorway, a portcullis and iron grill were added to this now-vulnerable doorway for further protection. These works may have formed part of the claim for £200 for alterations carried out before 1620 to incarcerate priests. This view is supported by the contemporary descriptions of the castle by Bishop Bedell and Richard Castledine, which mention Clough Oughter resembling a circular pigeon house with internal wooden stairs. At this time too, the ground-floor fireplace was likely inserted in the cross-wall, allowing a degree of modern convenience, at least on this level of the castle.

Finally the L-shaped wall outside the ground-floor entrance was constructed during the period of occupation following the commencement of hostilities in 1641. The three shallow graves were also dug at this time. During excavation and conservation, a number of military items were discovered in the debris, including fragments of cannonballs (presumably from the siege of 1653), musket balls and a decorated spur. In addition, a number of domestic items were retrieved, including a cast-iron fireback, a metal skillet, candlesticks and knives. The castle ruins viewed today, therefore, represent the final, seventeenth-century phase of modifications carried out on the castle over the course of its history. It is the castle which Bedell and Castledine would have recognised from their incarceration in 1641/2 and Lord Montgomery following his capture at Benburb in 1646. Similarly, the present structure is the castle to which the ailing Owen Roe O'Neill and his army returned in the winter of 1649, just prior to his death. So in one sense, the castle *is* of the plantation era and is a must on any itinerary of the Upper Erne. The only shame is that due to its island location, it cannot be viewed up close.

10

OTHER PLANTATION SITES ALONG THE ERNE

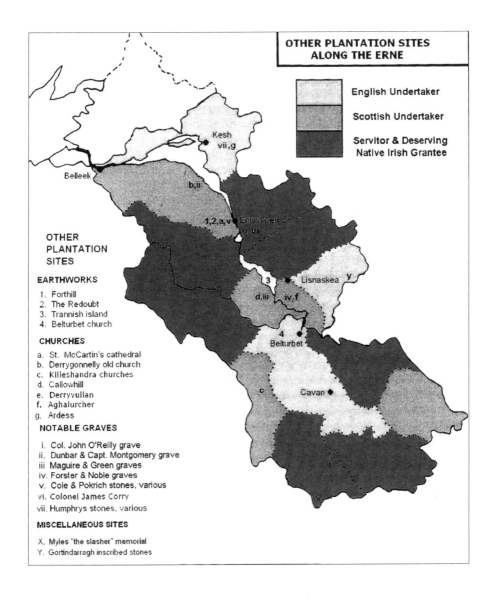

OTHER PLANTATION SITES ALONG THE ERNE

- English Undertaker
- Scottish Undertaker
- Servitor & Deserving Native Irish Grantee

Kesh
vii,g

Belleek

b,ii

1,2,a,v Enniskillen
e, vi

3 Lisnaskea y

d,iii iv,f

4 Belturbet

c Cavan

X

OTHER PLANTATION SITES

EARTHWORKS

1. Forthill
2. The Redoubt
3. Trannish island
4. Belturbet church

CHURCHES

a. St. McCartin's cathedral
b. Derrygonnelly old church
c. Killeshandra churches
d. Callowhill
e. Derryvullan
f. Aghalurcher
g. Ardess

NOTABLE GRAVES

i. Col. John O'Reilly grave
ii. Dunbar & Capt. Montgomery grave
iii Maguire & Green graves
iv. Forster & Noble graves
v. Cole & Pokrich stones, various
vi. Colonel James Corry
vii. Humphrys stones, various

MISCELLANEOUS SITES

X. Myles "the slasher" memorial
Y. Gortindarragh inscribed stones

EARTHEN FORTIFICATIONS, PLANTATION CHURCHES, GRAVES & MEMORIALS

The Articles of the Ulster Plantation scheme laid out a number of conditions that resulted in the construction of more than just castles and bawns. Undertakers were expected to build a church, construct watermills and generally improve the land. Although many of these duties were performed, the constant warfare during the seventeenth century, and the passage of time since, has reduced the number of surviving examples to a mere handful. However, a number of churches (albeit modernised over the years), together with memorials of the personalities from that era, still exist and so their inclusion is worthwhile here.

In addition, defensive campaigning at that time recognised the need for earthworks at key points in the rural and urban landscape, and several excellent examples survive and can be inspected. Finally, there are a small number of miscellaneous features and later commemorative memorials that are worth including, in order that the reader can gain a broader knowledge of the time and gain insight into our inherited memory of these events.

EARTHEN FORTIFICATIONS

FORTHILL PARK (EASY BATTERY), ENNISKILLEN
OS SHEET 17 OR 18, GR 239441

From the centre of Enniskillen, proceed eastwards across the river to Belmore Street. Directly ahead is a steep set of steps that leads up to Forthill Park. On the summit of the hill, the park contains the earthworks, together with a tall memorial column to General Sir Galbraith Lowry-Cole.

The earthworks at Forthill crown this steep drumlin, which rises above the eastern side of the town beyond the island. Although Enniskillen was an island town, by the end of the seventeenth century it was clear that an enemy force equipped with artillery, entrenched on either of the hills at both ends of the town, could easily overawe the town's defences. It was therefore imperative that the Inniskilliners fortify the hills at each end of the town to protect themselves from long-range cannon fire.

Fortification of the Forthill, formerly known as Commons Hill, began in early 1689. Two soldiers, Majors Hart and Rider, 'good mathematicians', created a star-shaped earthwork with spear-shaped corner bastions at the crest of the hill, using captured prisoners. The importance of the fort was underlined in July 1689, when the Jacobite Duke of Berwick defeated a body of Inniskilliners at Kilmacormick, just north of Enniskillen. This force had ventured beyond the safety of the guns at Forthill to engage with the Duke, who completely overwhelmed them. A total disaster was only avoided by the fact that Berwick did not possess his own artillery and therefore declined to make a direct assault on the fort.

It would appear that four small brass cannon were taken from Enniskillen castle to be used at Forthill. A contemporary account states that Sir Michael Cole's servant at the castle had previously refused to deliver the cannon, and Malcolm Cathcart and Henry Smith had then seized them and brought them up to the fort. Over succeeding years, cannonballs weighing two or three pounds (0.9 to 1.5kg) have been retrieved in the area about 400m north of the fort, which suggests that the battle took place there and that the fort provided supporting artillery fire.

The fort was presumably abandoned after the end of hostilities, though the town did not forget its importance. In the 1840s, a suitable memorial to the memory of the Peninsular War hero General Galbraith Lowry-Cole was proposed. Cole had been one of the Duke of Wellington's generals during the long Peninsular War in Spain against Napoleon. It ended in 1814 with the final expulsion of the French from Portugal and Spain. The fluted column, commonly known as 'Cole's Monument', was erected in 1857 and is topped with a statue of the general. The names of the Peninsular War battles are listed around the four faces at the base. An internal spiral stair allows access to the summit, and a climb of 108 steps is rewarded with superb views across Enniskillen, to Cuilcagh and beyond.

The fort we see today is square in plan with four angled corner bastions. The four sides are raised about 3m above the external ground level, with the spear-shaped bastions raised a further metre higher. The faces of each bastion are 10m long with the re-entrants measuring 4m. The steep sides are sloped at 50 degrees and each bastion would have held artillery. There does not appear to have been a ditch. At 30 sq m (100 sq ft) the fort is large enough to contain a force sufficient to protect the artillery and repel any but the most determined of attackers. On a map of Enniskillen drawn in the 1690, the fort was marked as the 'East Battery'.

There is some rock outcropping around the edges of the fort and the remains of the stone revetment can still be seen in places. Much of this was removed in 1825 to provide road stone. A sunken and covered path led from the fort down to the bridge, allowing the fort to be reinforced in safety. Today, the steep steps down to the bridge follow this line.

Before returning to the centre of Enniskillen it is worth inspecting the old bridge leading across to East Bridge Street. The first bridge, 3.3m (11ft) wide, was built at this location around 1614, and had a drawbridge that could be drawn up in the evening to safeguard against raids. This bridge was replaced in 1688 by one 4.5m (15ft) wide, which also had a drawbridge and which was 53m (174ft) long. The central core of the present bridge is said to contain the earlier structure. Today, only three arches are visible, but it is believed that two more were infilled on the Belmore Street side.

THE REDOUBT (WEST BATTERY), ENNISKILLEN
OS SHEET 17 OR 18, GR 229443

From the west end of Enniskillen, proceed across the Erne Bridge. A steep laneway, 4m wide and flanked by stone walls 1.5m high, rises at the junction of Henry Street and Brook Street. Proceed to the top of the lane, where there is some parking. The Redoubt is located at the top of the hill. The building inside is private.

The Redoubt is the descendant of the earthen fort thrown up in 1689 by the Inniskilliners, to defend the vulnerable western approach to the town, given that, until the defeat of Mountcashel's army at Newtownbutler on 31 July 1689, Sarsfield's Jacobite army, based at Ballyshannon and Sligo, was always within striking distance of

Enniskillen. Possession of this hill would have allowed an attacker with cannon to over-awe the castle and island of Enniskillen. Therefore, it was important that earthworks were constructed here, contemporaneous to those on Forthill at the opposite end of the town, to fully protect the Inniskilliners from an assault. This was a 'sod' or earthen fort, and in a map of Enniskillen in the 1690s, it is shown as a square with four bastions. As it was named as a battery, these bastions were clearly for use with artillery.

The seventeenth-century defences at the Redoubt were not tested, but at the end of the following century, a stone fort was constructed on the hill when the threat of a French invasion loomed large. The resulting stone fort, built around 1798, measures 45 sq m (50 yards²), with the walls 6m (20ft) thick, to withstand Napoleonic artillery. The 5m-high walls are constructed of smooth stone blocks. A wide ditch, which is 5m wide with steep sides and best seen on the east and south, surrounds the site.

Entrance was via a passageway in the middle of the SE wall, facing the town. A 2m-high parapet wall, with gun emplacements located at each of the four corners, pro-tected the fort's interior. In the centre of the fort, a hospital was built, measuring 25m by 9m. It is a seven-bay, two-storey harled block, aligned NE–SW, with the entrance in the centre of the NW wall.

The site here commands the castle of Enniskillen, just visible to the SW, and there are great views west and south towards Belmore Mountain, the expected approach route of a hostile army. Though the structure here today is of the late eighteenth century, we can imagine its seventeenth-century earthen predecessor and appreciate the significance of the hill at the west end of town and the importance of the Williamite garrison in ensuring that it was properly fortified to withstand an assault from an enemy lurking somewhere beyond.

TRANNISH ISLAND, UPPER LOUGH ERNE
OS SHEET 27, GR 328297

Trannish Island is 1.3km west of the 'Share Centre' in Upper Lough Erne. Access to the island can only be achieved by boat, though there is no proper landing stage. The island is roughly trian-gular in shape, with the artillery fort located at the northern end. The island is private property and any planned visit will require permission.

The earthworks on Trannish Island were only discovered in the 1970s. Strangely, there are no definite contemporary references to the site, so its construction date is uncertain, though it is shown on a map of 1700 as a 'redoubt'. Situated in the middle of the chan-nel, its location would have allowed the defenders to challenge hostile craft hoping to pass this way through the lough. Curiously though, a fort located at the southern end of the island would have effectively overawed all lough traffic, and so it is strange that the builders chose to the place the fort where they did.

The fort is square in plan, measuring 30m by 30m (100ft by 100ft), with four demi-bastions at each corner. The embankment of the fort was formed from the material excavated to form a ditch around the site. A narrow entrance was located in the middle of the west bank. The interior is generally level.

The demi-bastion was a common feature in seventeenth-century fortification. Unlike the fully developed spear-shaped bastion, the demi-bastion consisted of one face at 90 degrees and the other at 45 degrees to the flanking ditch and bank. It therefore allowed both offensive fire from the angled face and defensive fire along the line of the ditch.

Control of the Erne waterways was critical to the survival of the colonists in both the 1641 rebellion and during the revolution. The location of the fort's entrance would suggest that the settlers constructed it in one or other of the conflicts. Given the paucity of artillery in the 1640s, a date in 1689 or 1690 seems more likely. Perhaps it was constructed as a precautionary measure during either winter when the Upper Erne still formed the boundary between the opposing sides. Given that the Jacobites did not launch any significant raids before the war ended, the fort remained untested and therefore fails to be mentioned in contemporary accounts. Perhaps some future research will throw up more information on this enigmatic find.

PARISH CHURCHYARD FORT AND 'DEANERY BANKS', BELTURBET
OS SHEET 27, GR 363168

From Main Street in the centre of the town, proceed up the rising hill of Church Street. The Church of Ireland church and graveyard are 100m directly ahead. There is parking in the street. The River Erne can be navigated to Belturbet, where there is a marina.

The parish church of Annagh was founded in the seventeenth century and, despite being re-built in 1829, may contain parts of the original structure in its fabric. Cruciform in shape, it has a square tower surmounted by a slender spire. The pointed east window, with simple gothic tracery of intersecting arcs, may be from the earlier building, as may grouped, round-headed windows and the plain round-headed door to the transept.

The fortifications in the churchyard are best seen at the rear. The first reference to the earthworks occurs in the 1660s. Roving bands of dispossessed Irish, named as 'divers rebels', caused the citizens of the town to have a fort constructed overlooking the River Erne. These faced the medieval earthworks on Turbet Island in the middle of the river, but it is unclear if they were ever connected in any way.

In the 1689 and 1690 campaigns, the Jacobite and Williamite troops undoubtedly reactivated the fort. The Williamite Colonel Wolseley is credited with the works we see today, though the Jacobite Brigadier Sutherland had fortified the churchyard in June 1689 in anticipation of an attack. Presumably, therefore, Wolseley added substantially to earthworks that had already been established at this site.

The earthworks visible today consist of the complete south rampart, together with the SE and SW corner bastions and substantial lengths of the east and west ramparts. A fosse, or ditch, surrounded the site on the north (later filled in due to the adjacent road), south and east, but was probably unnecessary on the west side, where the ground slopes steeply to the River Erne. The south rampart, measuring 30m between the bastions, is about 2.5-3m above the field outside. The ditch on the south side is about 2m wide and located a little forward of the rampart face.

The SE bastion is raised another metre or so higher than the south rampart, and was spear-shaped, with the angles 22m long. Clearly this feature was created to hold artillery. Today, this area holds a number of military graves from the last two centuries, clearly set aside to continue the military origins of this part of the graveyard. A section of the east rampart runs north here for at least 15m, but becomes obscured by later burials and family vaults. Likewise, the SW bastion has similar dimensions to its neighbour, though the west face has been destroyed. A long section of 40m can be traced along the west side, with a low stone revetment visible, though this feature may be later.

There are no visible remains of the northward extent of the fort, though one supposes the road outside the graveyard to mark the furthest possible limits. The graveyard has, inevitably, become filled up with burials, which have partially obscured the form of the earthworks. Thus, the exact size of the fort cannot be exactly determined, but it appears larger than Forthill in Enniskillen.

Wolseley also erected an associated earthwork in 1689, known as the 'Deanery Banks', on the approach to Belturbet from the direction of Cavan. Situated near the side of the road (Deanery Street) at the top of a drumlin with good fields of view east and south over the Cavan road, these works provided additional early warning and protection to the main fort described above. It was believed to be a square fort with triangular bastions set inside each of the corners.

Today, though, the works consist of two, small, steep-sided platform areas separated by a gap. Both of these platforms are surrounded by a partially filled ditch. The distance from the bottom of the ditch to the platform top is about 4m. The remains are therefore much altered and reduced, making proper identification of the defensive nature of the earthworks difficult.

NOTABLE SEVENTEENTH-CENTURY GRAVES

DERRYVULLAN GRAVEYARD, TAMLAGHT, COUNTY FERMANAGH

Colonel James Corry, Williamite soldier
OS SHEET 18, GR 274404

Take the A4 Enniskillen to Belfast road for 6km (4 miles), turning right at Tamlaght and immediately right again after a petrol filling station, on to the Derryvullan road. Proceed a distance of 500m, before turning right up a steep hill. The road stops at a dead end, in front of the old walled churchyard of Derryvullan. About 3m west of the ruined west gable is the raised vault of the Corry family.

There are few memorials around the Erne to the major personalities who strutted the seventeenth-century stage, but a vault at the old church here contains the bones of the Corry family of Castlecoole. The horizontal slab on top of the vault begins thus:

This stone was erected by Somerset Richard Lowry Corry EARL OF BELMORE, to the memory of the following members of his family who were interred in the vault beneath or in the Church Yard JOHN CORRY formerly of Belfast settled at Castle Coole 1655 Died 16[??] Colonel JAMES CORRY formerly MP for this County Died 1718 Colonel JOHN CORRY formerly MP for Enniskillen and this County Died 1726 Aged 60 and Sarah his wife and daughter of William Leslie...

John Corry, a Belfast merchant, bought the plantation manor of Coole from Roger Atrkinson in 1656. He served as a Justice of the Peace for Fermanagh and Cavan in 1662 and was High Sheriff of Fermanagh in 1666. When he died soon after 1683, his eldest son James succeeded.

Born in 1633 or 1634, James Corry had been handed control of the estate at Coole in 1679. He was married to Sarah Ankitell of Monaghan and they had four children who survived to adulthood. In 1666, he was appointed a Captain of Foot by the Duke of Ormonde, and he served as High Sheriff in 1671. After the death of Sarah, he married Lucy Mervyn of Trillick in 1683, and was to marry a third time in 1692. He was a Justice of the Peace at the time of the constitutional crisis in 1688. His initial instinct was to maintain the status quo by objecting to the plans of William MacCarmick and others to resist the quartering of Colonel Newcomen's soldiers in the town. When the armed townspeople caused the troops to retire, Corry (who had been entertaining their officers at his home) attempted to have the perpetrators arrested. He was warned in no uncertain terms that such an act would jeopardise his own safety, and he retired to his estate.

The resistance party were slow to forgive Corry, and a later request for him to be appointed colonel one of the raised foot regiments was flatly refused. Instead, Gustavus Hamilton was appointed colonel, with Thomas Lloyd as lieutenant colonel. A contemporary quote reflects the suspicion that was felt at the time, 'the man in the world we most doubt, we having had several admonishments from very good hands that our fears are not groundless'.

However, he later came across to the Williamite cause and is listed amongst the attainted, along with his son John. In July 1689, his home at Castlecoole was razed by Governor Hamilton to prevent it falling into the hands of the Duke of Berwick, who had just won a victory at nearby Kilmacormick. Corry was for years to pursue his claim for compensation from the government, apparently to little effect. Despite this flawed reputation, he maintained a body of 60 horse and 100 foot for the Williamites, which he armed and supplied from his own estate. Opinion, therefore, remains divided on this historical figure, but these events surrounding his life merely reflect the complexity of the political situation unfolding in Ireland at the time.

James Corry died in May 1718. His son John Corry, born in 1667, succeeded him. This John entered Trinity College in 1686, but there is no record of his graduation, perhaps due to the deteriorating political situation, which caused him to return home. His brother Robert was killed at Newtownbutler on 31 July 1689. John served as a captain in King William's army in Ireland and Flanders. He was MP for Enniskillen in 1703. His only surviving son Leslie died in 1740, aged only twenty-eight years and without an heir. The Corry family thus died out in the male line.

The east gable of old Derryvullan church is still intact and contains a fine, semicircular arched east window, with a carved stone head above. Perched on the top of a hill, with the waters of Tamlaght Bay and Ballycullion Lough lapping around three sides, the church and its graveyard make a charming, tranquil spot in a hidden corner of Lough Erne.

KILL GRAVEYARD, KILNALECK, COUNTY CAVAN

Colonel John O'Reilly, Jacobite soldier
OS SHEET 34, GR 433908

Kilnaleck village is on the R154 Bellananagh to Oldcastle road. From Kilnaleck village, proceed along the R514 towards Bellananagh for 800m, turning left on to a minor road. After 1,000m, Kill graveyard will be seen on the right. Pass through the white gates, and turning right, proceed for 30m. Colonel John O'Reilly's raised box tomb is now visible near some trees.

Two adjacent raised tombs in the graveyard record the death of Colonel John O'Reilly, and, in truth, either may be the final resting place of this old soldier. The larger of the two measures 2.5m by 1.5m and reads, 'Here lieth intombed the body of Collonell John O'Reilly who was elected knight of the shier for the county of Cavan in the year 1689 and departed this life 17th day of Feby 1717 and left 5 sons and 2 daughters'.

The graves of seventeenth-century Jacobites are as rare as hens' teeth in Ulster, and perhaps the relative isolation of this graveyard has allowed this one to survive. John O'Reilly was the son of the famous Myles 'the Slasher' O'Reilly, who had been a cavalry officer and notable figure in the 1641 rebellion.

John O'Reilly lived at Baltrasna castle in County Westmeath and was elected Knight of the Shire of Cavan at the parliament called by James II at Dublin in May 1689. He raised a regiment of Dragoons to fight for King James during the Williamite wars, and fought at the famous Siege of Derry, and at the battles of the Boyne and Aughrim. He was one of only three individuals specifically named in the articles of the Treaty of Limerick in 1691, and as a result, was able to maintain his estates after the war. He died in February 1717, aged seventy years, and is buried here in Kill graveyard.

One final puzzle that needs solving is the age of the colonel on his death. If only seventy years at his death, his birth post-dates the traditional demise of his father, Myles, in 1644. Recent research has supported a rival tradition that Myles was not killed at Finnea and was thus able to raise a family in later years. Colonel John was thus the eldest of five children of Myles and Catherine O'Reilly.

DERRYGONNELLY OLD CHURCH, DERRYGONNELLY, COUNTY FERMANAGH

Richard Dunbar, Planter

Captain Hugh Montgomery, Williamite soldier
OS SHEET 17, GR 120534

Entering Derrygonnelly village from Enniskillen, turn immediately right at a petrol station and proceed for about 200m. The churchyard is on the left, just after a primary school. The gravestone of Dunbar and Montgomery lies below the east window, inside the walls of the old church. The recumbent slab, 1.76m by 0.7m, depicts the normal symbols of death: a sand-timer, bell, skull and crossbones. The weathered stone reads, 'Virtus Movet Rex Fovet. Here lieth the bodies of Richard Dunbar and Hugh Montgomery Esq. Richard died Nov 6th 1666. Hugh died Sept 26th 1722 aged 71 years.'

The church ruins here are the finest example of plantation works anywhere along the Erne. A wall constructed of well-cut limestone blocks surrounds the church and grave-yard. The church is approached from the road up a flight of steps through this wall. It measures 17.m by 7.5m externally, with large masonry foundation blocks at the gable corners, presumably to spread the load. The walls and gables are nearly complete to full height, with the gables 0.9m thick, and the sidewalls 0.6m. The structure still contains its well-cut quoins, and the walls are of generally dressed blocks.

The church is entered from the west, through an arched doorway, 1.5m wide, surmounted by a plaque containing Dunbar's coat of arms, together with that of his wife Catherina and the construction date of 1627. The doorway is decorated with an arris roll carried continuously around the head and jambs, and with a row of raised, pointed blocks forming a pattern around the outside. This type of ornament is often seen in contemporary Scottish architecture, which should be no surprise, as Dunbar was a Scottish settler. There is a bell cote on the gable, also in the vernacular Scottish style.

Two large splayed windows on the south wall, and a small pointed arch window in the centre of the north wall, originally lighted the interior. There is a large arched recess near the centre of the north wall, which is flanked to the east by a small, square recess, presumably to hold sacred vessels. Another similar-sized recess is built into the east gable. The large east window remains almost complete, consisting of three Gothic-arched lights. The Dunbar gravestone lies just below the window.

Sir John Dunbar, the original grantee of the 1,000-acre estate of Drumcro, had four children: James, John, William and Ann. He built the church in 1627 and the castle, now vanished, in the field behind the churchyard. When he died in 1657 his eldest son, James, succeeded him. James died in 1666 and was succeeded by his son Richard, described as a 'captain in the army' and here remembered. His military experience was presumably acquired during the 1641 rebellion.

Richard had married Anna Catherina, the Swedish widow of Ludovick Hamilton, and their one child and heiress, Catherine, born in 1666, later married Hugh Montgomery, son of the Revd Nicholas Montgomery, Rector of Derrybrusk. This Hugh Montgomery, born in 1651, therefore acquired the Dunbar estate by marriage. He was attainted by the parliament called by James II in 1689 and was present during the Williamite defence of Enniskillen, when he served as a captain of horse. He later served at the Boyne.

Montgomery bought half of the estate of Monea from William Hamilton (son and heir of Gustavus Hamilton, the late Governor of Enniskillen in 1689) in November 1701 and became one of the county's wealthiest men. He was High Sheriff of Fermanagh in 1713 and a JP. He had eight children, and died in 1722.

The gravestone at Derrygonnelly is dedicated to both Richard Dunbar and Hugh Montgomery, although they died over half a century apart. Though there is no direct evidence, it is tempting to postulate that the widow Catherine Montgomery (who was still alive in 1722) erected this memorial, to remember her departed father and husband.

AGHALURCHER GRAVEYARD, AGHAMORE, LISNASKEA, FERMAMAGH

Major Arthur Noble, Williamite soldier

James Forster, Williamite soldier
OS SHEET 27, GR 365314

From the centre of Lisnaskea, take the A34, SE towards Newtownbutler. Almost immediately on leaving the town, take the road to the right signposted for Aghalurcher. The old graveyard is 2km along this minor road on the left, entered through an iron gate.

Aghalurcher is first mentioned in 1447, when Thomas Maguire junior was recorded as having put a 'French roof' onto the church and repaired the east gable. In 1484, a Maguire slew a kinsman at the altar, which may have led to the abandonment of the site. Today, only a small vaulted area remains, but the extensive foundations of the church can be traced through the graveyard beyond. The planters reused the site in the seventeenth century and there are a number of Balfour and Galbraith gravestones stored in the vault (usually locked). Some ancient plaques have been placed into the vault's external wall.

Grave of Major Arthur Noble
From the entrance gateway proceed about 25m along the path, to the point where it turns left towards the church. The Noble family graves are located about 3m on the right. The stone bearing the following inscription appears to have been inverted, though the other Noble graves can be inspected. If overturned, the stone would read:

> Here lyeth the body of Mag. Arthur Noble who departed this life the 29 day of August 1731 aged 77. It is remarkable he was loyal active and corragious in the late revolution defending Londonderry in 1689 and in storming the fort of the mouth at Limerick wich restored ye Protestant cause uner the glorious KW of happy memory.

Arthur Noble was a Protestant landowner from Derryree, Lisnaskea, who won acclaim during the Siege of Derry in 1689. He hailed from a Cornish family who had settled in Fermanagh some time during the early years of the century. Noble was mentioned by all the contemporary accounts written by the besieged within the city

On 18 May 1689, Noble and a Captain Cunningham led a body of the defenders out across to Pennyburn, where they fought and defeated a large force of Jacobite troops under the command of Lord Galmoy. Galmoy was reported wounded and the Jacobites retreated to their siege lines. Later, on 18 June, he was entrusted with a message to the

Enniskillen garrison, and he boarded a boat, which sailed up the river. His party was attacked by two boats, which closed with him, and fierce hand-to-hand fighting ensued, during which four of the enemy were killed, thirteen taken prisoner, and their store of arms captured.

Noble was also involved in the successful defence at Butcher's Gate on 28 June and in the trench lines beyond the Gallows on 17 July, the Jacobites being repulsed on both occasions. He appears to have been used for difficult operations throughout the siege, and his exploits came to the attention of Governor Walker, who paid tribute to his energy and courage.

Grave of James Forster

Forster's grave is about 13m from the entrance to the Balfour vault, just beyond the corner foundations of the old church. It lies flat on the ground alongside more recent Forster family members. The stone, measuring 1.9m by nearly 1m wide, has the family coat of arms, under which the faint lettering reads, 'By John Forster of Rathmoran in memory of his honoured father James Forster who was killed in His Majesty's service King Willian III 1689. Also the body of Rob Forster grandson of above James Forster.'

In view of the information that is known about Arthur Noble, it is curious that no mention of the career of John Forster can be found. He is neither mentioned in the lists of contributors at Londonderry nor Enniskillen. Nor does he feature in any account of the period for these places. Perhaps his contribution is of a less sanguinary, or more humble, nature, and research in the future will throw some light on the claim of his final testimonial.

Before leaving the graveyard, it is worth spending a little time admiring the superb entrance archway, flanked by two stone crucifixes and with a much-weathered gargoyle head above. Other eroded masonry carvings can also be seen on the outer face.

CALLOWHILL OLD CHURCHYARD, KINAWLEY

Knogher Maguire, son of Brian, Native inhabitant

Henry Green, son of Marmeduke, Planter
OS SHEET 27, GR 279263

From Derrylin, take the A509 Belturbet road to the mini-roundabout and then turn right along the road for Ballyconnell. Callowhill graveyard is 1km on the left, on a bend, behind a wall. This is a busy road and caution is required if parking and crossing to the ruins.

Callowhill church and graveyard are on the site of a fourteenth-century chapel. However, the present ruins are of the seventeenth-century church built by a Maguire and dedicated to St Ronan. Built of local rubble masonry, it measured 12.5m by 5.5m (41ft by 18ft) internally, with the walls 0.75m thick and the gables 0.7m.

In 1967, due to the unstable nature of the building, the local council removed the gables and lowered the walls to 2m. At that time, all the remaining quoins and dressings of Carboniferous limestone were removed. The site has become overgrown.

Grave of Knogher Maguire

Just through the graveyard gate, and situated to the left of the ruined entrance to Callowhill church, is the slab dedicated to Knogher Maguire. The very faint inscription is flanked by pillars carved onto the surface, with an elaborate coat of arms covering the top half of the slab. Contained between the pillars is the inscription, which is now very faint, but the word 'Knogher' can just be discerned near the top. A Brian Maguire raised a monument to his father, Knogher Maguire in 1682, with a Latin inscription. The word 'Knogher' means big, fat or 'well-looking'.

Grave of Henry Green

This memorial is situated on the rear, exterior wall of the church. It consists of a large slab flanked by columns with a coat of arms on the top half, an inscription below, and a skull and crossbones at the bottom. The slab reads, 'Here layeth the body of Henry Green son to Marmeduke Green of Drumininskein, Gent, who departed the 24th day of August anno dom 1675 being of age 20 years'.

Marmeduke Greene of Druminiskin was the son of William Greene, who came to Ireland at the commencement of the Ulster Plantation with his relation Lord Burleigh. This William purchased an estate in this part of Fermanagh and married into the family of Spenser. He had at least one known offspring, his son Marmeduke. This Marmeduke Greene married Jane Creighton, sister of Colonel Abraham Creighton of Crom, the defender of that place in two sieges during 1689. They had at least three sons, Henry, William and Abraham. Marmeduke died on 24 June 1681. His will still exists in the Public Record Office in Belfast.

Of these three sons, Henry died young and is commemorated on this gravestone. Abraham later became a captain and served the Williamite faction during the revolution, before settling at Ballymacreese, County Limerick. In 1694, he married Annabella Blennerhassett, but died without surviving issue in 1724.

His brother William later became Rector of Killesher, succeeding Dennis Sheridan, the native Irishman who had comforted Bishop Bedell following his release from imprisonment in Clough Oughter castle in 1642. Revd William married a sister of Colonel Brock Newborough of Cavan, and they had two sons and two daughters. He purchased an estate from Sir James Caldwell and built for himself a house and chapel-of-ease as a burying place for his family. He was attainted by James II but remained Rector at Killesher until succeeded by Revd William Henry after 1719. Of his children, Henry Greene of Dresternan and Ballymacreese was later High Sheriff for County Fermanagh, Brockill Greene married Sarah, daughter of Hugh Montgomery of Derrygonnelly, Mary Greene married the Revd James Cottingham, MA, and Jane Greene married Major Christopher Carleton of Cooles, Fermanagh.

The family coat of arms, three running stags in a green field, can be seen at the top of the stone. Druminiskill is 3km SE of Derrylin, along the A509 Belturbet road.

ST MARY'S CHURCH, MAGHERACULMONEY PARISH, ARDESS, COUNTY FERMANAGH

Gravestones of Humphrys family, McMulchon and Muldoon

The 'Hanging Tree' memorial
OS SHEET 18, GR 209630

From the centre of Kesh village, take the main Ederny road for about 2.5km (1.5 miles) to the signpost for Ardess. Turn right and proceed for another 1km (0.75 mile) before reaching a signpost for Ardess. Turn left and proceed to the church car park.

Humphrys Family Graves

The present towered church is on the site of a previous one and has an extensive grave-yard to the rear. Now propped against the bank of the path outside the east gable of the church, are four ornately engraved pink limestone slabs, presumably moved from their original site elsewhere in the graveyard. The first stone is rectangular, with a pointed top. The second and larger is about 1.2m high, with the top half taken up with a coat of arms. It reads, 'Heare lyeth the bodyes of Thomas and Elizabeth Humphrys decesed 88 and 1703'. Below the inscription is a skull-and-crossbones carving with the words '*memento mori*' inscribed above. Directly beside this stone are two more sandstone head-stones, one situated above the other. The lower stone has a curved top and is decorated with a shield motif and carved face. The upper one is similarly inscribed with a shield and decorative symbols, though it may have been inverted incorrectly when re-erected. The Humphrys family have long been associated with this part of Fermanagh.

McMulchon Grave

Return to the west door again and proceed into the graveyard. The oldest graves are situated near the western boundary. Walk southwards for about 30m and then turn east (left) along the path for another 10m. Two stones together here, at the corner of the path, were erected to the McMulchon family. The one nearer the church, 0.5m high, is carved at the top with a Celtic cross. The raised lettering reads, 'Here lyeth the body of John McMilchon who died the year 1679'.

This is the oldest legible gravestone in the churchyard. Glancing around, there are a dozen graves of similar design. It is believed that these stones indicate that one sculptor, or perhaps a school, was responsible for their creation over a number of years from the late seventeenth century. Other examples near the west boundary were carved for Maguire.

Muldoon Grave

A few metres behind the McMulchon grave and near to the path, is another headstone in the same Celtic-cross style. It reads, 'Here lys the body of Edmond O Muldoon who dyed the 17 of April 1689'.

Another Muldoon buried in the graveyard (though not found during a site inspec-tion) is said to have fought at the Battle of the Boyne on the Jacobite side, and his gravestone records that he fought for King James.

The 'Hanging Tree' Memorial

Further down the rear gravel path is a blackened tree stump, less than half a metre high. Attached to the surface of the stump is a plaque, which reads, 'The Hanging Tree. According to folklore this is the exact site of the Hanging Tree. Local Protestants were hanged here during the Maguire rebellion of 1641'.

The graveyard here contains some of the finest seventeenth- and eighteenth-century gravestones in the country, with many elaborately decorated with coats of arms and the symbols of death – coffin, timer, skull and crossbones. Others have Masonic motifs of suns and moons and compasses. Many also have smiling winged angels carved at the top of the stone.

At the rear of the site, there is a memorial plaque placed on a large vault, to the victims of the 1845 famine in the district. Recently, a storyboard has been placed nearby to explain the significance of this and neighbouring locations.

However, the most unusual feature of the graveyard is the interdenominational nature of the burials. There are many graveyards in Ulster which have both Catholic and Protestant burials, but uniquely at Ardess, the graves are all mixed in together without any form of segregation. A walk through the graveyard is rewarded with the rich mixture of Irish, English and Scots surnames, reflecting the cultural harmony later experienced across this community in north Fermanagh.

ST MCCARTIN'S CATHEDRAL, ENNISKILLEN

Cole family crypt, various settler graves

This church owes its origins to the plantation period, but the one seen here today has been restored and altered on several occasions. Captain William Cole was granted one third of the island of Enniskillen in 1611 and part of the conditions of this grant obliged him to build a town, school, market house and church. He chose the higher of the two hills on the island for the erection of the parish church, which was completed by 1627. Almost nothing remains of this earliest church, except part of the tower, which contains a small three-light lattice window unit and an Agnus Dei date stone of 1637 above, containing a lamb and flag motif.

In the 1840s, the old parish church was rebuilt, and this is essentially the building that is seen today. In 1921, the parish church was raised to the status of a cathedral and dedicated to St McCartin.

Inside can be seen the carved sandstone font presented by the then rector of the parish, William Vincent, in 1666, which has been in continuous use since that date. The church has some interesting communion silver, the Davis chalice of 1638 and the Cathcart flagon of 1707, which are not on display due to their value. The Cole family vault is located under the floor of the church, and entrance to this is along a sunken way outside the north wall. A grave slab is attached to the wall here. The lower part contains the usual funerary symbols, with the upper part bearing the Cole family arms of a bull passant, armed and unglued. A list of those Cole family members buried within is given on the wall beneath the statue of General Cole, inside the church.

In addition, the church contains several seventeenth-century memorials, including the Pokrich stone of 1628 and one to Elizabeth Vincent and Margaret Ryno, of 1673. The Pokrich stone has an inscription written around the edges which reads:

> Grant me, merciful Saviour, that when Death hath shut up the eyes of my body, yet the eyes of my soul may still behold and look upon Thee; and when Death hath taken away the use of my tongue, yet my heart may cry and say – Unto Thee, Lord, unto Thy hands I commend my soul; Lord Jesus receive my spirit.

This inscription is slightly altered from the last words of Thomas Cromwell, Earl of Essex, who was beheaded by King Henry VIII in 1540.

KILLESHANDRA OLD CHURCH, CHURCH STREET, KILLESHANDRA
OS SHEET 34, GR 307076

From the junction of Main Street and Castle Lane in the centre of Killeshandra, proceed along Church Street. The old church and graveyard are on the right behind a high wall.

The church ruins seen today represent the last reconstruction on this site. Located inside a semicircular rath, there was probably an older building here when the first Anglican Rector was appointed in 1619. It was from this graveyard that the body of Sir James Craig, of nearby Croaghan, was dug up by rebels in 1642.

The church was remodelled in 1688 and remained in use as the parish church until 1842. Today, the graveyard is entered between two stone pillars decorated with motifs. A handsome Jacobean doorway can be seen, together with round-headed windows, in the nave. The graveyard contains a large number of surnames that must reflect the influx of Scots and English settlers since the time of the plantation. The church is currently undergoing a long-overdue programme of restoration.

KILLESHANDRA PARISH CHURCH, MAIN STREET, KILLESHANDRA

Planter memorial to Hamilton family
OS SHEET 34, GR 310071

From the centre of the village, take the R199 for Crossdoney, along Main Street. The church, with tower, is on the right-hand side of the street, as one leaves the built-up area. The marble memorial is located on the north wall inside the church.

The large Hamilton memorial, measuring over 3m by 2m, was probably removed from the older church in Church Street and brought to the new church erected here in 1841. The plaque contains the arms of the Hamilton family. The lengthy inscription on the memorial is in Latin but an interpretation has been provided in a frame below it and reads:

Sacred to the memory of a most distinguished man, Francis Hamilton of Castlehamilton in the county of Cavan, Baronet, sprung from the ancient and numerous nobility of the House of Hamilton of Lunerwick in Scotland, related by the closest ties of blood and marriage to the Earls of Angus, Mar and Douglas; of whom Claude was the first settler to make his home in Ireland, whose son Francis, the first of that name, left as heir his eldest son Charles who married Francelina, the only daughter and heiress of William Semple of Letterkenny in the county of Donegal, Knight. The son born to these parents was Francis, the second of the name, and unhappily the last male of this great line. An ornament to his country and Church he departed to the grief of both, an example of integrity in evil times, shining as a steady light, the strenuous opponent of heretics and schismatics; he was a kind and liberal patron of the clergy and the Church. He enjoyed very great wealth upon his father's ancestral estates; he gave constantly and without display in charity and he distributed gifts to the poor generously and secretly. His heart was sincere and without taint or guile, his conscience clear; his tongue had no bitterness and proved his sincerity; he never failed to fulfil his pledged word even as he would an oath.

His devotion to God was humble and unfeigned. His loyalty towards the throne, the Royal Family and the rights of the Crown never faltered, true to the tradition of his family. He was friendly to all whom he encountered; he never injured even the most humble, he showed kindness also to the highest. He was universally and deservedly beloved but he thought little of himself, being most humble, in spite of his great position; he was always determined to be just and upright. He performed his public duties equally worthily. He won praise as a commander of a troop of horses. He was a justice of the peace for the country, unequalled as a soldier and for years a most respected magistrate.

He married twice; first the honourable Lady Catherine Montgomery, daughter of the Right Honourable Earl Mountalexander who bore one daughter, Catherine, buried here, and died 6th January 1692 aged 29.

He married a second time on March 26th 1695, his bride being the honourable Lady Anna Hamilton his cousin, a devoted, most loving and beloved wife. They lived in great affection and devotion but his health failed and he succumbed to a long illness (which brought less pain to him than to his neighbours) and amidst the deep sorrow of all he laid mortality aside and passed to heaven on the 4th February 1713, aged 58.

To his dearest and most loving memory his sorrowful wife, surviving her husband, has placed this memorial of grief and honour.

The Hamiltons mentioned above were original settler stock who came to live at Killeshandra in 1610, following their award of the plantation estates of Clonkine, Carrotubber and Clonyn. The reader of this memorial is reminded of the eulogy on the Hansard memorial in Clonleigh church, Lifford, County Donegal. However, the sentiment here is much more personal, and reflects the bitter loss of the passing of Francis Hamilton felt by his widow Anne, made more poignant by the fact that the line of Hamilton at Killeshandra had now come to a close.

But his passing must have been widely regretted across the community for the decision to be made, a century and a quarter after his passing, to transfer the memorial in its entirety to the new church. This memorial is now flanked by the Hamiltons, distant relatives of Sir Francis, who replaced the original family in the nineteenth century, before themselves dying out in the 1950s.

MISCELLANEOUS ITEMS

MAIN STREET, FINNEA, COUNTY WESTMEATH

Myles 'The Slasher' Memorial Cross
OS SHEET 34, GR 403813

From Cavan, take the N55 south towards Granard. After about 20km (12 miles), take the R394 to Finnea, which is reached after a further 8km (5 miles). The memorial cross is conspicuous in the main street of the village. The memorial takes the form of a Celtic cross within an iron-railed enclosure, with the arms of O'Reilly, 'Fortitudine et Prudentia', and inscriptions below.

Although a little beyond our area, this memorial is too important to ignore. The panel at the base reads:

> In Memory of
> Myles O'Reilly
> (The Slasher)
> Who fell on the 5ᵗʰ August 1646
> While defending the bridge of Finea
> against the English–Scottish Forces under General Monro. He fought till the red lines
> before him,
> Heaped high as the battlement lay,
> He fell but the foot of a foeman
> Proceed not on the bridge of Finea.

> The Slasher had with him 100 horse while the enemy were 1,000 strong. He fought them the whole day long till his followers were nearly all slain. Finally he was encountered by a gigantic Scotchman who thrust the point of his sword through the Slasher's cheek. The latter closed his jamws on the blade and held it as if in an iron vice, while he slew his antagonist cutting him through steel helmet, down to his chin with one blow both falling together. At that moment reinforcements arrived from Granard and the bridge was saved.

An Irish gentleman and cavalry officer in the rebellion of 1641, Myles 'the Slasher' O'Reilly's fierce-sounding name belies the general respect held for him by his British opponents. In recent years, research has thrown some new light on this enigmatic figure and allowed a revision of the traditional view of his fame. Although believed to be accurate at the time of its erection in 1913, the date recorded on the memorial must refer to the battle fought with Monro's Ulster army during its excursion into Cavan and Westmeath in June 1644.

Lord Castlehaven's Confederate army was still preparing for the campaigning season ahead, and so he chose not to confront Monro in the field at this time. Instead, hoping to delay Monro's advance into Leinster, he placed a detachment of troops at Finnea, where the Ulster army might be expected to cross. Myles was thus present at the bridge and supposedly died there in its defence. However, an alternative tradition asserts that

Myles was not killed but escaped the battle and fled to France, where he died later. Clearly both traditions are at variance, but can the matter be resolved with any certainty?

Some recent research work has stated that Myles later married Catherine, daughter of Charles O'Reilly of Leitrim, and that they had five children: John, Edmund, Philip, Honora and Rose. The eldest was John, who later became a celebrated Jacobite colonel and lies buried in Kill graveyard near Bellananagh. John was seventy years old when he died, so must have been born, along with his other siblings, after the battle at Finnea.

Therefore, the tradition of an escape to France must be wrong. It would appear that Myles 'the Slasher' has been confused with his cousin Colonel Myles O'Reilly of Denn, who was High Sheriff of Cavan in 1641. This Colonel Myles appears to have gone to Spain and later France, and died at the Irish monastery at Charleville in 1670. Hence the confusion between the two similarly named family members.

One final word on Myles 'the Slasher' O'Reilly. On the evening before the battle at Finnea, Myles stayed at Ross castle, on the southern shore of Lough Sheelin. A plaque in the restored hall of the castle commemorates this brief stay. Anna Marie O'Reilly, a direct descendant of Myles, restored Ross castle in 1864.

INSCRIBED STONES, GORTINDARRAGH, ROSSLEA
OS SHEET 27, GR 503314

From the centre of Rosslea take the B36 to Lisnaskea for 4km (2.5 miles). Turn left at Dernawilt junction and proceed for 500m to a minor crossroads. The farmhouse is down a long lane on the left.

The carved stones are located at the rear of a farmhouse in Gortindarragh townland. This substantial farmhouse, approximately 15m by 7.5m (50ft by 24ft), has the appearance of being from at least the eighteenth century, and consists of a central hallway with rooms either side, at front and rear. Part of the original oak staircase still remains to first-floor landing level but dating the building is difficult, as it was extensively modernised in the early 1970s, when the original fireplaces, doors and architraves were removed. At the same time, the house was reduced from three to two storeys.

The two inscribed stones in question are located either side of the rear door, about 2.5m above ground level. Both stones read, in raised relief, 'IA MM, 1626', though on one stone the initials are written one set above the other. They resemble marriage stones – a tradition for carving initials of a betrothed couple and the date of their union. The concave stone faces on which the initials have been carved were clearly meant to be read from below, but whether they are contemporary with this house, or have been removed from another to this location, is uncertain.

Two valuation books from the early nineteenth century show that a family called Mitchell occupied the farm here, and the stones may refer to them. Likewise, in Griffith's Valuation of 1862, an Ebeneezer Mitchel is recorded as living in Gortindarragh. The townland of 'Gortnedrragh', rated at two thirds of a tate, was part of the small proportion of Lyreske, in Clankelly, and was allocated to the English undertaker Thomas Flowerdew, Esq. in June 1610. Around 1630, the estate was sold to Arthur Champion, who built a castle at nearby Shannock. Champion's wife Alice later deposed that on 23 October 1641, her husband and six other men were killed at the gate of the castle by a band of rebels numbering over 100. In the 1659 census for Fermanagh, a 'James Arnot, Esq.' was living in the townland, though it is uncertain if it was at this precise location. There were a total of seven persons living in Gortindarragh, but all were classed as Irish.

11

FINAL THOUGHTS

The events of the seventeenth century in Ireland are crucial to any understanding about the current political situation that exists here today. It is rather puzzling, therefore, to note that the two wars of that century are nowhere commemorated as one might expect, with the usual obelisk, statue or tower. In fact, it would appear that the events have been lost from the public consciousness. This might be understandable within the polity of the Republic of Ireland, where the connection with Britain has been so violently contested over centuries. But it is also equally true in Northern Ireland, the state created by the descendants of the Ulster Plantation's British settlers.

There is not, at the time of writing, any signpost to the battlefield of Newtownbutler, surely the glowing example of settler self-sufficiency and survival, despite the odds. There is no stone to acknowledge the solemn avowal by the five Protestants in Enniskillen to resist the entry into the town of the Jacobite troops in December 1688, thus precipitating a three-year civil war in Ireland. Nor can we, on any brass plaque, read the famous words of the then newly appointed governor, Gustavus Hamilton, who rousingly declared, 'We do stand upon our guard and do resolve by the blessing of God rather to meet our danger than expect it.'

The divisive nature of the events in Ireland in the seventeenth century have understandably been a sensitive issue for each community to grasp, and a collective unconscious will to prevent further ill feeling has led, in many cases, to the troubles of the past being ignored or even actively suppressed. This pragmatic reality is not necessarily the case everywhere. The massacres at Tully in 1641, or Belturbet in 1642, have their equivalent event in every county in Ulster. Yet the resonance of the massacre at Portadown Bridge in the same rebellion remains much more poignant for the communities in Armagh than the largely forgotten ones at Tully or Belturbet for the people in Fermanagh or Cavan.

Perhaps the nature of the ongoing development of relationships within Ireland and the British Isles will allow each community to reconsider the past, and to learn lessons, however difficult to digest, so that a fuller mutual understanding can be reached. Only time will tell if this can be achieved.

APPENDIX A

GLOSSARY OF ARCHITECTURAL TERMS USED IN THE GUIDE

ASHLAR Masonry constructed of square, hewn stones as opposed to rubblework. The blocks are therefore shaped or 'dressed' by the mason.

BAROQUE A seventeenth-century (and in some places eighteenth-century) style of ornament and architecture characterised by exuberant decoration and frequently by extreme, often pompous, grandeur.

BARTIZAN A turret, square or round in plan, corbelled out from a wall or tower of a castle or fortified house, often at a corner, hence 'corner bartizan'.

BASTLE Supposedly from the French *bastille*, meaning 'stronghold'. A fortified house built by farmers and country families in the English and Scottish borders after 1500. It generally consisted of a two-storey house with thick walls and small windows. The ground storey was used to stable farm animals at night. Access to the living quarters on the upper storey was usually via an internal ladder from the stable, pulled up at night. To reduce the risk of deliberate arson, the ground storey was stone vaulted and the roof steeply pitched, usually with shingle or slate.

BATTERED The inward-sloping stone courses at the base of a castle, used to provide a more substantial foundation.

BAWN From the Gaelic *bó dhrain* meaning 'cattle enclosure', as it provided a secure place for livestock if attacked. A walled courtyard of a tower house, castle or fortified house, often provided with corner towers (flankers) for improved defence. The term was specifically applied as a condition laid down in the scheme of the Plantation of Ulster.

BAY WINDOW A window of one or more storey, projecting from the line of the building at ground level. Rectangular or polygonal in plan.

CAPITAL MESSAUGE The principal dwelling house of an estate, together with its outbuildings.

CASTLE A large building, or buildings, fortified to provide defence against an enemy. By the seventeenth century this was usually constructed of stone, or less commonly, brick. Strictly speaking, the buildings erected in Ireland throughout the time of the plantation were fortified homes occupied by the owner and his family, not by military personnel.

CENTRING Wooden framework used in arch and vault construction. It is removed when the mortar has set and the structure has become self-supporting. In Irish construction, the centring is often faced with wickerwork matting (*see* Wickerwork) and the impression of the rods is to be seen in the mortar of their vaults.

CHAMFER The cutting of a right-angle edge at forty-five degrees.

CORBEL A stone block projecting from a wall, used to support a beam on its upper surface.

CORBELLING The process of building out a turret by the progressive projection of masonry. Corbelling was widely used in Scottish castle building and is virtually diagnostic when deciphering the provenance of an owner. Often ashlar blocks were used, but not exclusively so.

CROW-STEPPED Squared stones set like steps on a gable end. Characteristic of Irish architecture.

FLANKER A turret projecting from the line of a wall, usually at a corner, so as to flank, or defend, the adjacent walls. Flankers were often loopholed to provide defensive fire along the base of adjoining walls.

GARDEROBE The privy, or latrine, of a castle. Usually a small chamber from which a shaft leads downwards, through the wall, to the outside.

HARL A roughcast external weatherproofing finish to walls, composed of lime, gravel or sand. The term is peculiar to Scotland and Northern England.

JAMB The side of a doorway, window or other opening.

LIGHT A window opening. A window divided by one mullion (*see* Mullion) has two lights, etc.

LOOPHOLE A narrow, vertical opening (often unglazed), usually widening inwards, cut into a wall or other defence, to allow for the discharging of a musket or pistol.

MACHICOLATION A small gallery projecting on brackets from the outside of a castle wall, with apertures in the floor through which objects may be dropped on attackers. Often used to protect a vulnerable doorway.

MULLION A vertical post or stone dividing a window into two or more lights.

MURDER HOLE Small rectangular trap in the entrance ceiling of passageway in a castle, used to shoot or drop objects on unwelcome visitors. (*See also* Machicolation.)

OUTWORK Any detached or advanced structure, forming part of a castle's defences.

PALLISADE A fence of stakes, especially a feature of defensive works.

PARAPET The upper part of a wall, behind which the defender can shelter from attack.

QUOIN A dressed stone, often using better material, used at a corner of a building.

REVETMENT A retaining wall or facing used to support earthworks.

RUBBLE Stones of any size used in the construction of a wall, giving an uneven appearance.

SCALE-AND-PLATT STAIR A staircase with short straight flights and right-angled turns at each landing.

SCARCEMENT The vertical thinning of a wall, which creates a ledge upon which joists can be placed to support a floor.

SPLAY Chamfered opening of window or loophole, creating a wider internal opening.

SQUINCH Arch thrown across an angle between two walls to support a wall above.

STOCKADE A defensive enclosure made of closely set stakes.

STRING COURSE A stone course of distinctive moulding or colour on a wall surface.

TRANSOM A horizontal bar of wood or stone across a window, dividing it into separate lights.

WALL WALK A walkway near the top of a wall, protected by a parapet.

WATTLE Flexible sticks used for interlacing with others to form walls, screens, etc.

WICKERWORK The weaving together of pliable twigs or sticks, especially of willow, to form baskets, mats, fencing, etc.

APPENDIX B

GLOSSARY OF OTHER TERMS

ACRE In tilled or arable land, this was originally measured as thirty-two furrows of the plough, each a furlong in length. It was later standardised to 4,840 square yards (4,125 sq m approx.). 'A Scotch [*sic*] acre was 6,084 square yards [5180 sq m].'

BARONY An Irish administrative subdivision of a county. Often it comprised territory representing an older Gaelic boundary.

DEMESNE Manorial land directly controlled by the lord and not held by a subordinate tenant, often used as a park, home farm, etc.

ERENAGH In Ireland, land in the personal possession of clergy, usually in a hereditary arrangement. *See also* TERMON.

GLEBE A portion of land assigned to a church as part of the clergyman's benefice.

INNISKILLINER Term used to identify the Williamite garrison that was based on the town of Enniskillen, but included inhabitants from Cavan, Sligo, Leitrim, Tyrone and south Donegal. Initially, the garrison controlled a large swathe of the Erne basin, but under pressure from the Jacobite advance from March 1689, the area became concentrated along a line of strongpoints from Ballyshannon to Crom. The term 'Inniskillen' is derived from one of the contemporary names for Enniskillen.

JACOBITE A supporter of the Stuart king James II and his descendants in the late seventeenth century and the eighteenth century. Until the birth of his son in 1688, James had no heir and so his eldest daughter Mary, married to William, Prince of Orange, was expected to succeed him. James was supported mainly by Catholics, especially in Ireland, but also by some Protestants who were prepared to accept him as the rightful monarch.

MANOR The demesne lands of a lord, together with any other land over which he has rights. It can also refer to the landlord's house.

PLANTATION The settlement of persons into a locality, especially the planting of a settlement or colony. The Ulster and Virginia Plantations were early-seventeenth-century examples.

PLANTATION ACRE The unit of measurement used for the distribution of land in the plantation. A 'plantation acre' was the geographic area required to provide an arable acre of land and hence townland size was proportional to its rated arable content. The measurement was therefore a useful comparator for assessing land potential.

PLANTER One of the persons who 'plant', or found, a colony. In Ireland, these were English or Scots pioneers who settled on forfeited land in the sixteenth and seventeenth centuries. Planters were obliged to settle British tenants on their estates.

POLL The land division in Cavan, generally reckoned to contain fifty acres of arable land. Townlands in Cavan were rated as polls or as a proportion of one. *See also* TATE.

PRECINCT The subdivision of a county, generally equivalent to a barony, used to designate an area for a particular beneficiary.

PRIMOGENITURE The right of succession of the first born. By this principle, introduced to Britain by the Normans at the Conquest, property or title descends to the eldest son.

PROPORTION The term used to indicate the estate of the beneficiary. It could be defined as a small, middle or large proportion, depending on the amount of land allocated.

SERVITOR These were 'deserving' civil and military servants of the Crown in Ireland who were given grants in the Ulster Plantation. Unlike the planters, they were free to settle their estates with native tenants, though encouraged by the reward of lower state rents if they settled British ones.

TATE A land division in Fermanagh equivalent to sixty acres of arable land. Most townlands were rated as a tate or as a proportion of one. Sixteen tates equalled a Ballybetagh, four tates a Quarter. *See also* POLL.

TANISTRY A system of life tenure among the ancient Irish and Gaels, whereby the succession to an estate was conferred, by election, upon the worthiest of the surviving kinsmen.

TERMON In Ireland, land belonging to, or forming the precinct or liberties of a religious house, which was free or exempt from all secular charges.

UNDERTAKER The principal English or lowland Scottish settlers granted land in Ulster on condition that that they would 'undertake' to carry out the provisions of the settlement scheme.

WILLIAMITE A supporter of the Dutch prince William of Orange, husband of Princess Mary, the daughter of James II. The accession of William and Mary to the British throne ensured a Protestant succession. English, Scottish and Irish Protestants mostly favoured this option.

APPENDIX C

SOME CASTLE PLAN SKETCHES TO ASSIST IN
INTERPRETATION OF THE SITES

1. AGHALANE

Aghalane, near Belturbet

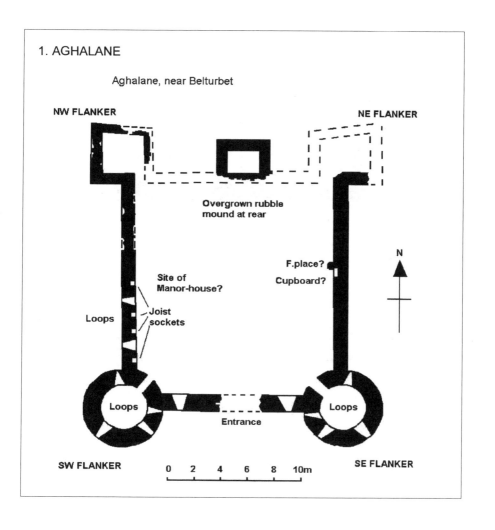

2. BALLYMAGAURAN

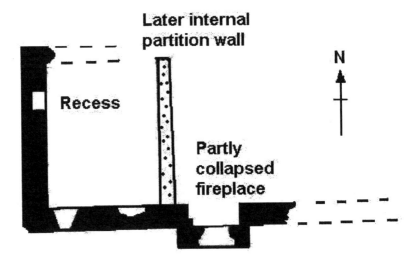

Ballymagauran

Later internal
partition wall

Recess

Partly
collapsed
fireplace

N

0   2   5   10 m

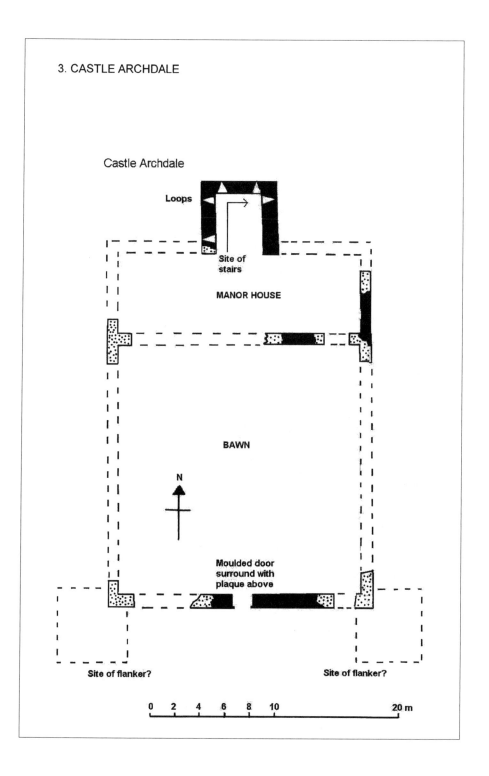

3. CASTLE ARCHDALE

Castle Archdale

Loops

Site of stairs

MANOR HOUSE

BAWN

N

Moulded door surround with plaque above

Site of flanker?

Site of flanker?

0 2 4 6 8 10   20 m

4. CASTLE BALFOUR

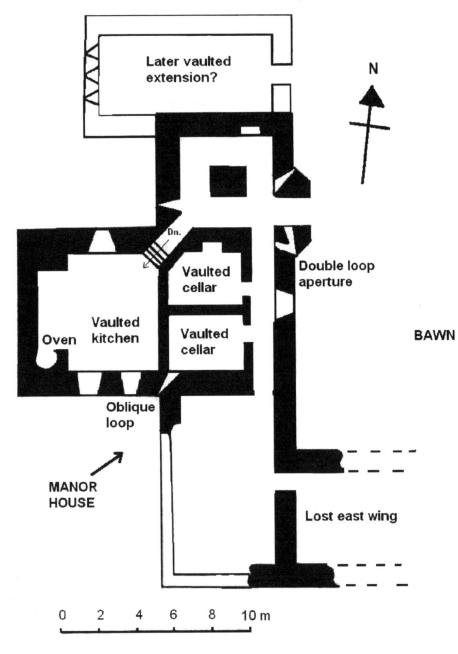

Castle Balfour, Lisnaskea

Later vaulted extension?

N

Dn.

Vaulted cellar

Double loop aperture

Oven Vaulted kitchen

Vaulted cellar

BAWN

Oblique loop

MANOR HOUSE

Lost east wing

0   2   4   6   8   10 m

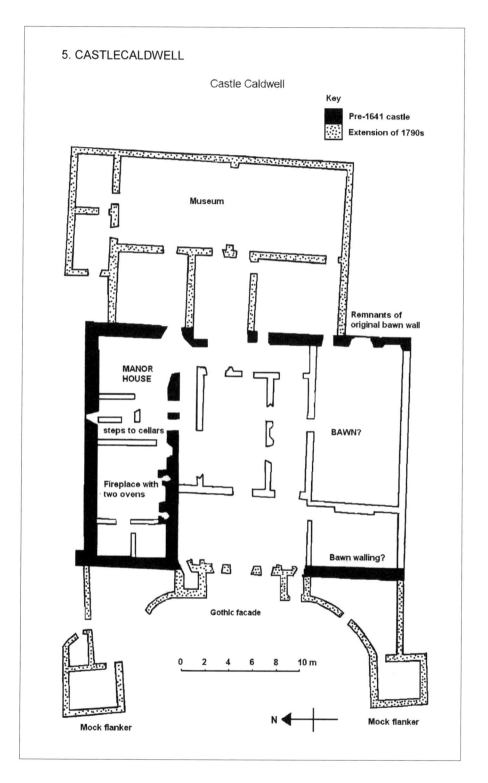

5. CASTLECALDWELL

Castle Caldwell

Key

◼ Pre-1641 castle

▒ Extension of 1790s

Museum

Remnants of
original bawn wall

**MANOR
HOUSE**

steps to cellars

BAWN?

**Fireplace with
two ovens**

Bawn walling?

Gothic facade

0 2 4 6 8 10 m

N

Mock flanker

Mock flanker

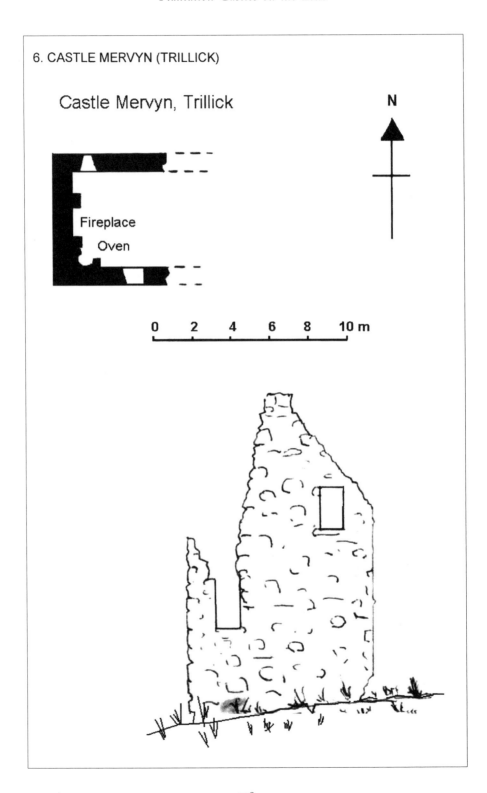

6. CASTLE MERVYN (TRILLICK)

Castle Mervyn, Trillick

N

Fireplace

Oven

0   2   4   6   8   10 m

7. CLOUGH OUGHTER

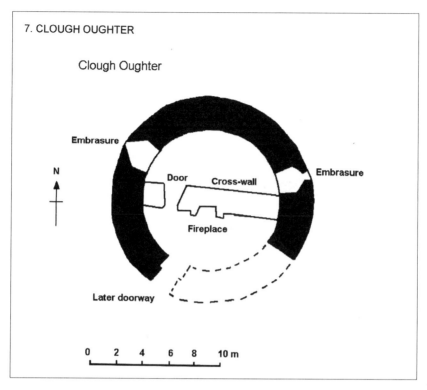

Clough Oughter

8. CORRATRASNA

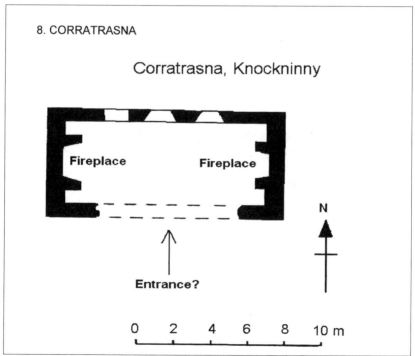

Corratrasna, Knockninny

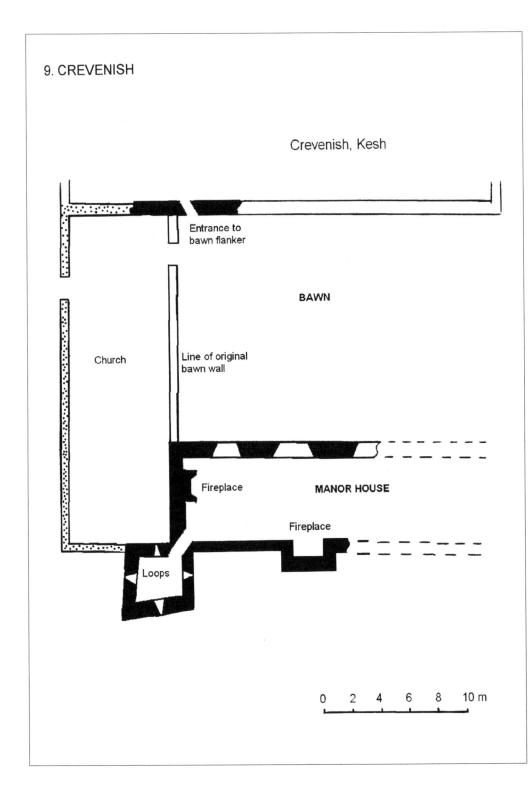

9. CREVENISH

Crevenish, Kesh

Entrance to
bawn flanker

BAWN

Church

Line of original
bawn wall

Fireplace

MANOR HOUSE

Fireplace

Loops

0 2 4 6 8 10 m

10. CROAGHAN

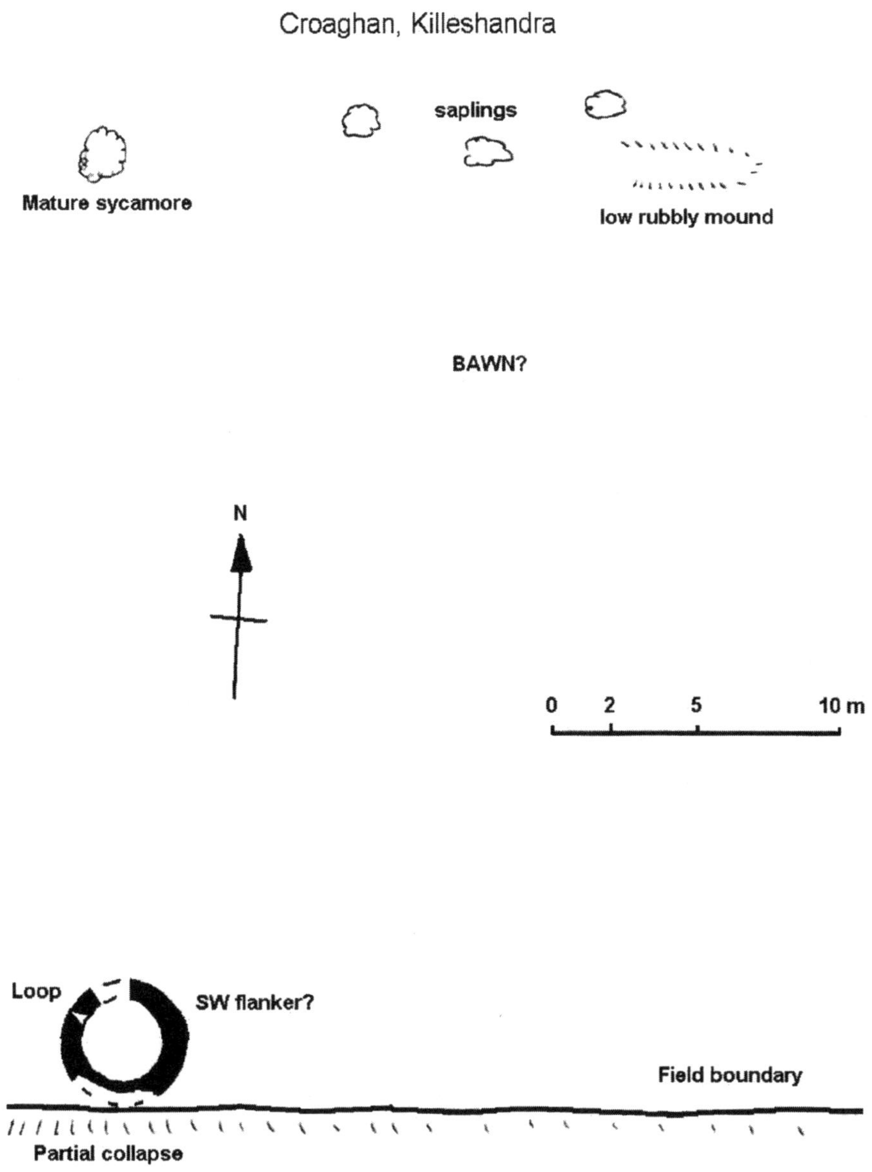

Croaghan, Killeshandra

saplings

Mature sycamore

low rubbly mound

BAWN?

N

0   2   5   10 m

Loop   **SW flanker?**

Field boundary

Partial collapse

1.5m drop to next field

11. CROM

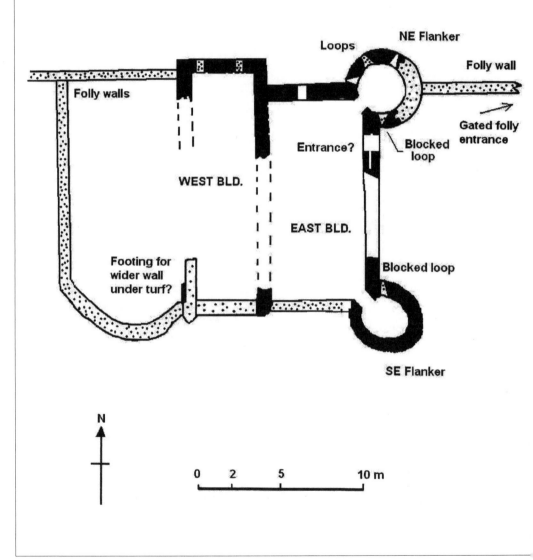

12. DOOHAT

Doohat, Bun Bridge, Crom

Blocked loop

Blocked loop

N

0   2   4   6   8   10 m

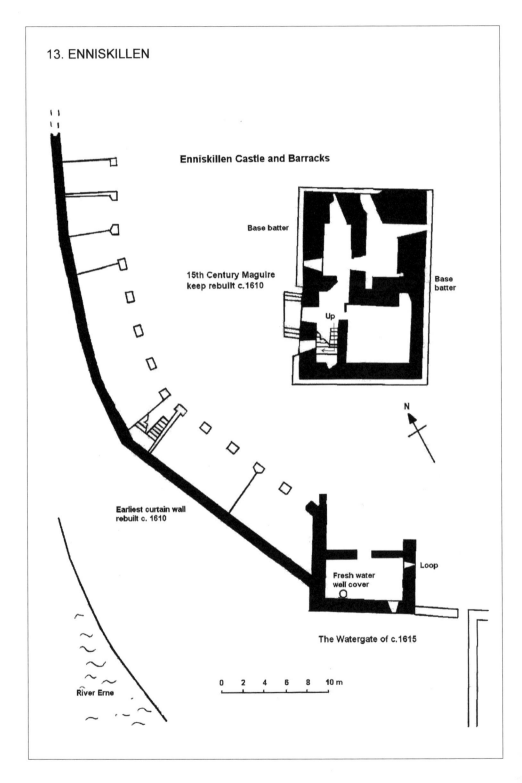

13. ENNISKILLEN

Enniskillen Castle and Barracks

Base batter

15th Century Maguire
keep rebuilt c.1610

Base
batter

Up

N

Earliest curtain wall
rebuilt c. 1610

Loop

Fresh water
well cover

The Watergate of c.1615

River Erne

0   2   4   6   8   10 m

14. GARDENHILL

Gardenhill, near Belcoo

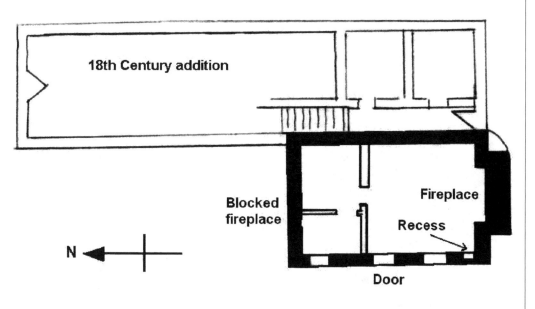

18th Century addition

Blocked fireplace

Fireplace

Recess

N

Door

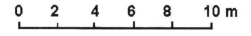

0 2 4 6 8 10 m

15. MONEA

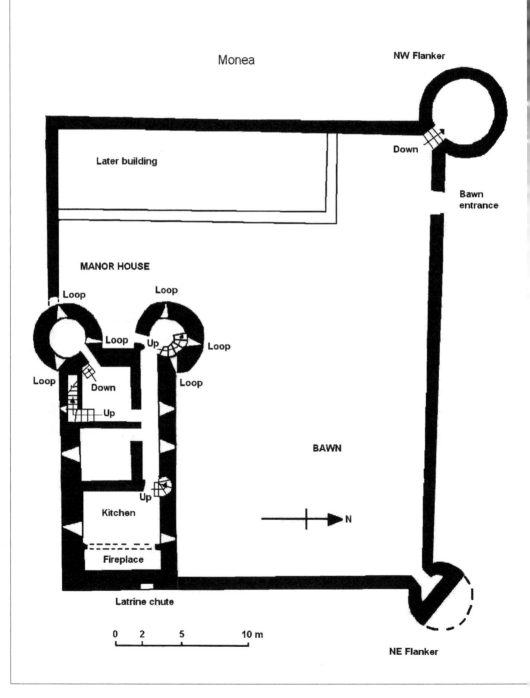

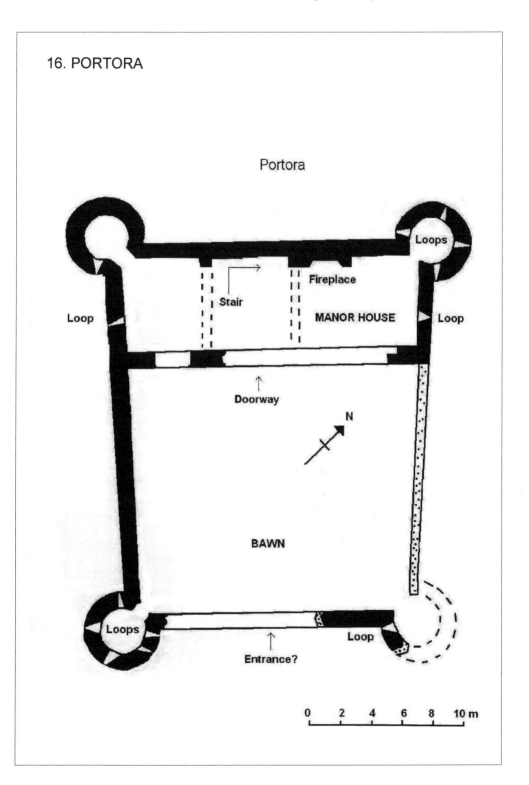

16. PORTORA

Portora

Loops

Loop

Stair

Fireplace

MANOR HOUSE

Loop

Doorway

N

BAWN

Loops

Entrance?

Loop

0   2   4   6   8   10 m

17. TERMON MAGRATH

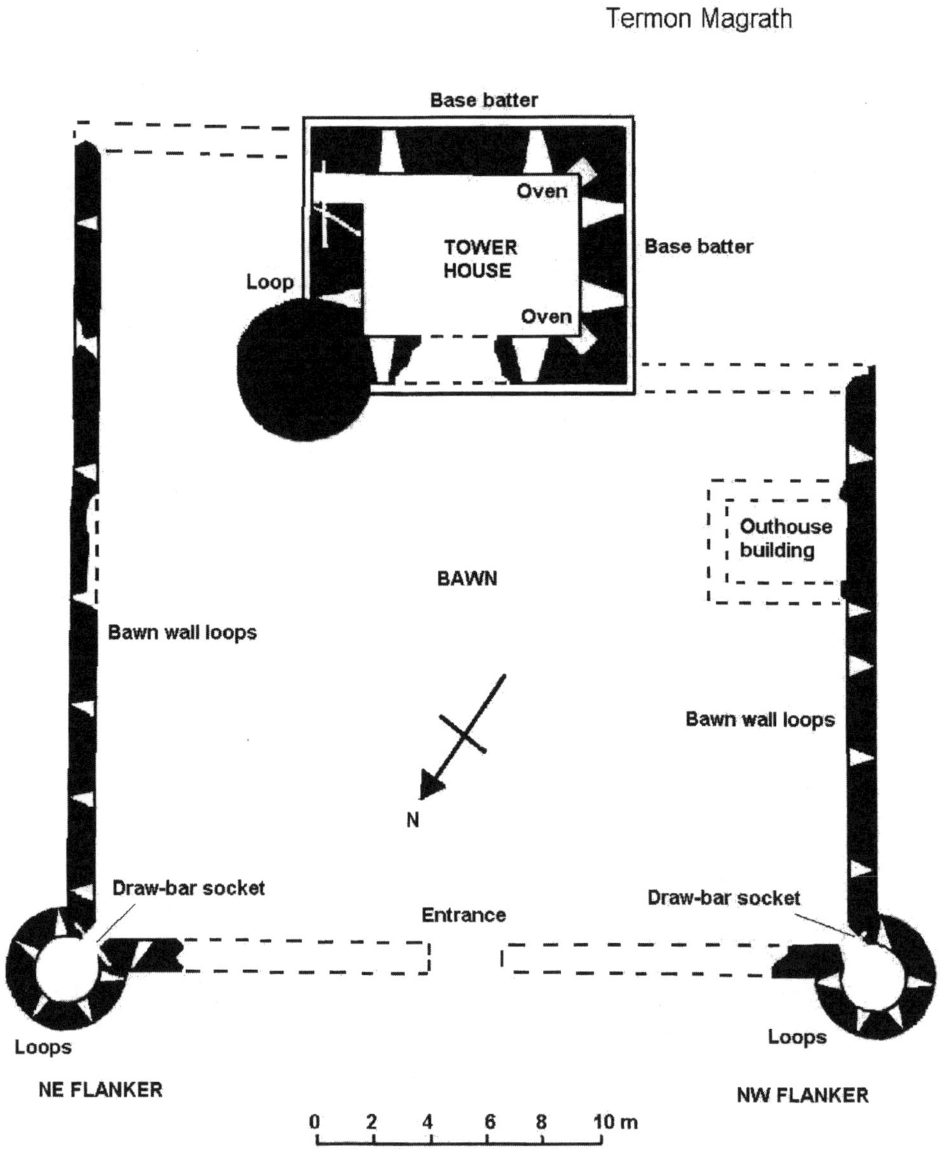

Termon Magrath

Base batter

Oven

TOWER
HOUSE

Base batter

Loop

Oven

Outhouse
building

BAWN

Bawn wall loops

Bawn wall loops

N

Draw-bar socket

Draw-bar socket

Entrance

Loops

Loops

NE FLANKER

NW FLANKER

0   2   4   6   8   10 m

18. TULLY

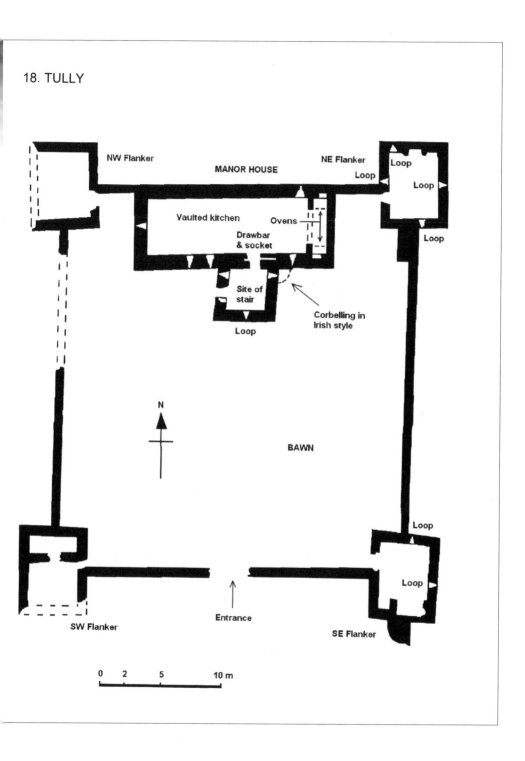

19. TULLYKELTER

Tullykelter, near Monea

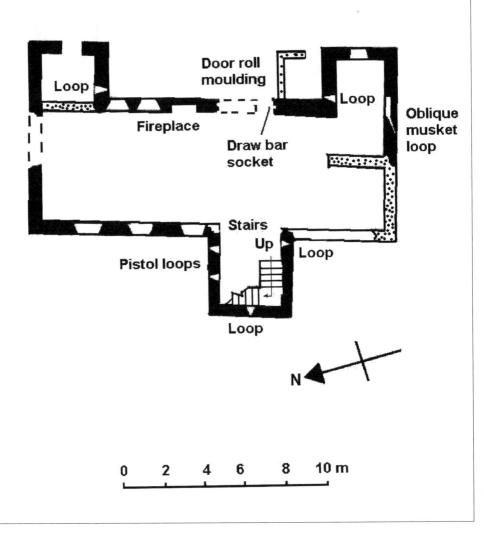

SELECT BIBLIOGRAPHY

There are numerous scholarly reference books which deal in great detail with seventeenth-century Irish history and the Ulster Plantation in particular. In compiling this guide I found the following books to be of great use.

SEVENTEENTH-CENTURY IRISH HISTORY – GENERAL BACKGROUND

Bartlett, T. & Jeffery, K. (eds), *A Military History of Ireland* (Cambridge, 1996).
Brady, C., O'Dowd, M. & Walker, B., *Ulster: An Illustrated History* (London, 1989).
Falls, C., *The Birth of Ulster* (London, 1936).
Foster, R.F., *Modern Ireland 1600-1972* (London, 1988).
Moody, T., Martin, F. & Byrne, F, *III: Early Modern Ireland, 1534-1691* (Clarendon, 1976).

THE PLANTATION OF ULSTER (AND OTHER IRISH PLANTATIONS)

Hill, Revd G., *An Historical Account of the Plantation in Ulster at the commencement of the Seventeenth Century, 1608-1620* (1877 & reprint).
Perceval-Maxwell, M., *Scottish Migration to Ulster in the Reign of James I* (London, 1973).
Robinson, P., *The Plantation of Ulster, British Settlement in An Irish Landscape, 1600-1670* (Dublin, 1984).
Scott, B., *Cavan, 1609-53: Plantation, war and religion* (Dublin, 2007).
Trimble, W., *History of Enniskillen* (Enniskillen, 1919-21).

CASTLES AND ASSOCIATED ARCHITECTURE

Bence-Jones, M., *A Guide to Irish Country Houses* (London, 1988).
Craig, M., *The Architecture of Ireland – From the Earliest Times to 1880* (London, 1982).
Davies, O., 'Castles of County Cavan' in *UJA*, 3rd Series, 1947, pp73-100, & 1948, pp81-126.
Kerrigan, P., *Castles and Fortifications 1485-1945* (London, 1995).
Mallory, J.P. & McNeill, T.E., *The Archaeology of Ulster* (Belfast, 1991).
Rowan, A., *NW Ulster – Buildings of Ireland* (London, 1979).
Salter, M., *Castles and Stronghouses of Ireland* (England, 1993).

THE 1641 REBELLION

Hamilton, Lord E., *The Irish Rebellion of 1641* (London, 1920).

Hickson, M., *Ireland in the Seventeenth Century* (London, 1884).

O'Gallochair, P., 'The 1641 War in Clogher' in *Clogher Record* (1962), p.135.

McKenny, K., *The Laggan Army in Ireland, 1640-1685* (Dublin, 2005).

Perceval-Maxwell, M., *Outbreak of the Irish Rebellion of 1641* (Dublin, 1994).

Stevenson, D., *Scottish Covenanters and Irish Confederates* (Belfast, 1981).

Wheeler, J.S., *Cromwell in Ireland* (London, 1999).

THE WILLIAMITE WARS

D'Alton, J., *King James's Irish Army List 1689* (Dublin, 1855).

Doherty, R., *The Williamite War in Ireland, 1688-1691* (Dublin, 1998).

Regimental Historical Records Committee, *The Royal Inniskilling Fusiliers from Dec. 1688 to July 1914* (London, 1928).

Simms, J., 'The Williamite War in South Ulster' in *Clogher Record* (1979), pp153.

Wauchope, P., *Patrick Sarsfield and the Williamite wars* (Dublin, 1992).

Witherow, T., *Derry and Enniskillen in the Year 1689* (Belfast, 1913).